The Consumer Credit and Sales Legal Practice Series

CONS[...]

CONSUMER LAW PLEADINGS ON CD-ROM

Pleadings from All NCLC Manuals Including Consumer Law Pleadings Number Ten (2004)

2004 Cumulative CD-Rom and Index Guide

Robert J. Hobbs, Editor

National Consumer Law Center
77 Summer Street, 10th Floor   Boston, MA 02110   www.consumerlaw.org

About NCLC	The National Consumer Law Center, a nonprofit corporation founded in 1969, assists consumers, advocates, and public policy makers nationwide who use the powerful and complex tools of consumer law to ensure justice and fair treatment for all, particularly those whose poverty renders them powerless to demand accountability from the economic marketplace. For more information, go to www.consumerlaw.org.
Ordering NCLC Publications	Order securely online at www.consumerlaw.org, or contact Publications Department, National Consumer Law Center, 77 Summer Street, Boston, MA 02110, (617) 542-9595, FAX: (617) 542-8028, e-mail: publications@nclc.org.
Training and Conferences	NCLC participates in numerous national, regional, and local consumer law trainings. Its annual fall conference is a forum for consumer rights attorneys from legal services programs, private practice, government, and nonprofit organizations to share insights into common problems and explore novel and tested approaches that promote consumer justice in the marketplace. Contact NCLC for more information or see our web site.
Case Consulting	Case analysis, consulting and co-counseling for lawyers representing vulnerable consumers are among NCLC's important activities. Administration on Aging funds allow us to provide free consulting to legal services advocates representing elderly consumers on many types of cases. Massachusetts Legal Assistance Corporation funds permit case assistance to advocates representing low-income Massachusetts consumers. Other funding may allow NCLC to provide very brief consultations to other advocates without charge. More comprehensive case analysis and research is available for a reasonable fee. See our web site for more information at www.consumerlaw.org.
Charitable Donations and Cy Pres *Awards*	NCLC's work depends in part on the support of private donors. Tax-deductible donations should be made payable to National Consumer Law Center, Inc. For more information, contact Suzanne Cutler of NCLC's Development Office at (617) 542-8010 or scutler@nclc.org. NCLC has also received generous court-approved *cy pres* awards arising from consumer class actions to advance the interests of class members. For more information, contact Robert Hobbs (rhobbs@nclc.org) or Rich Dubois (rdubois@nclc.org) at (617) 542-8010.
Comments and Corrections	Write to the above address to the attention of the Editorial Department or e-mail consumerlaw@nclc.org.
About This Volume	*Consumer Law Pleadings on CD-Rom, 2004 Cumulative CD-Rom and Index Guide*, supersedes all prior editions of *Consumer Law Pleadings with Disk* and *Consumer Law Pleadings on CD-Rom*. Discard all prior editions, CD-Roms, and disks. Readers can retain the print versions of *Consumer Law Pleadings* Numbers One through Five (1994-1999) for a hard copy of the pleadings contained herein. There is no reason to retain the accompanying disks.
Cite This Volume As	National Consumer Law Center, Consumer Law Pleadings on CD-Rom (2004 Cumulative CD-Rom and Index Guide).
Attention	*This publication is designed to provide authoritative information concerning the subject matter covered. Always use the most current edition and supplement, and use other sources for more recent developments or for special rules for individual jurisdictions. This publication cannot substitute for the independent judgment and skills of an attorney or other professional. Non-attorneys are cautioned against using these materials to conduct a lawsuit without advice from an attorney and are cautioned against engaging in the unauthorized practice of law.*

Copyright

© 2004 by National Consumer Law Center, Inc.
All Rights Reserved

ISBN 1-931697-64-7 (this volume)
ISBN 0-943116-10-4 (Series)

Library of Congress Control Number 2004114726

About the Editor

Robert J. Hobbs is an NCLC staff attorney and its Deputy Director. He has been writing and consulting since 1972 on fair debt collection and other consumer credit issues. Prior to that, he was a staff attorney with New Orleans Legal Assistance. He is the author of *Fair Debt Collection* (1988, 1992, 1996, 2000, 2004); NCLC REPORTS, *Repossessions and Debt Collection Edition*; co-author of *Practice of Consumer Law* (2003); and editor of a number of prior editions of *Consumer Law Pleadings*. He advises attorneys on their clients' fair debt collection claims, was counsel to amicus curiae in *Heintz v. Jenkins*, 514 U.S. 291 (1995), has served on the FRB's Consumer Advisory Council, and is a founder, board member, and treasurer of the National Association of Consumer Advocates.

Acknowledgments: We are especially grateful to Shannon Halbrook, who is in editorial charge of both the Guide and the CD-Rom, Xylutions for typesetting services, and Neil Fogarty of Law Disks for developing the CD-Rom and for assisting with the listings in this volume. We also want to especially thank John Rao and Carolyn Carter, who edited prior editions of Consumer Law Pleadings. Of course, this volume is primarily the work of approximately one hundred attorneys specializing in consumer law all over the country who have contributed pleadings, and we are greatly indebted to them. A list of these attorneys with brief biographies is found later in this volume at "Pleadings by Contributor." This volume's "Contributors by State" also provides a graphic demonstration that these attorneys practice in thirty-four different states.

What Your Library Should Contain

The Consumer Credit and Sales Legal Practice Series contains 16 titles, updated annually, arranged into four libraries, and designed to be an attorney's primary practice guide and legal resource in all 50 states. Each manual includes a CD-Rom allowing pinpoint searches and the pasting of text into a word processor.

Debtor Rights Library

2004 Seventh Edition with CD-Rom, Including Law Disks' Bankruptcy Forms

Consumer Bankruptcy Law and Practice: the definitive personal bankruptcy manual, with step-by-step instructions from initial interview to final discharge, and including consumers' rights as creditors when a merchant or landlord files for bankruptcy. Appendices and CD-Rom contain over 130 annotated pleadings, bankruptcy statutes, rules and fee schedules, an interview questionnaire, a client handout, and software to complete the latest versions of petitions and schedules.

2004 Fifth Edition with CD-Rom

Fair Debt Collection: the basic reference in the field, covering the Fair Debt Collection Practices Act and common law, state statutory and other federal debt collection protections. Appendices and companion CD-Rom contain sample pleadings and discovery, the FTC's Official Staff Commentary, *all* FTC staff opinion letters, and summaries of reported and unreported cases.

2002 Fifth Edition, 2004 Supplement, and 2004 CD-Rom

Repossessions and Foreclosures: unique guide to VA, FHA and other types of home foreclosures, servicer obligations, motor vehicle and mobile home repossessions, threatened seizures of household goods, tax and other statutory liens, and automobile lease and rent-to-own default remedies. The CD-Rom reprints relevant UCC provisions and numerous key federal statutes, regulations, and agency letters, summarizes hundreds of state laws, and includes over 150 pleadings covering a wide variety of cases.

2002 Second Edition, 2004 Supplement, and 2004 CD-Rom

Student Loan Law: student loan debt collection and collection fees; discharges based on closed school, false certification, failure to refund, disability, and bankruptcy; tax intercepts, wage garnishment, and offset of social security benefits; repayment plans, consolidation loans, deferments, and non-payment of loan based on school fraud. CD-Rom and appendices contain numerous forms, pleadings, interpretation letters and regulations.

2004 Third Edition with CD-Rom

Access to Utility Service: the only examination of consumer rights when dealing with regulated, de-regulated, and unregulated utilities, including telecommunications, terminations, billing errors, low-income payment plans, utility allowances in subsidized housing, LIHEAP, and weatherization. Includes summaries of state utility regulations.

Credit and Banking Library

2003 Fifth Edition, 2004 Supplement, and 2004 CD-Rom

Truth in Lending: detailed analysis of *all* aspects of TILA, the Consumer Leasing Act, and the Home Ownership and Equity Protection Act (HOEPA). Appendices and the CD-Rom contain the Acts, Reg. Z, Reg. M, and their Official Staff Commentaries, numerous sample pleadings, rescission notices, and two programs to compute APRs.

National Consumer Law Center ■ **77 Summer Street** ■ **10th Floor** ■ **Boston MA** ■ **02110**
(617) 542-9595 ■ **FAX (617) 542-8028** ■ **publications@nclc.org**
Order securely online at www.consumerlaw.org

2002 Fifth Edition, 2004 Supplement, and 2004 CD-Rom	**Fair Credit Reporting:** the key resource for handling any type of credit reporting issue, from cleaning up blemished credit records to suing reporting agencies and creditors for inaccurate reports. Covers credit scoring, privacy issues, identity theft, the FCRA, the new FACT Act, the Credit Repair Organizations Act, state credit reporting and repair statutes, and common law claims.
2002 Second Edition, 2004 Supplement, and 2004 CD-Rom	**Consumer Banking and Payments Law:** unique analysis of consumer law (and NACHA rules) as to checks, money orders, credit, debit, and stored value cards, and banker's right of setoff. Also extensive treatment of electronic records and signatures, electronic transfer of food stamps, and direct deposits of federal payments. The CD-Rom and appendices reprint relevant agency interpretations and pleadings.
2000 Second Edition, 2004 Supplement, and 2004 CD-Rom	**The Cost of Credit: Regulation and Legal Challenges:** a one-of-a-kind resource detailing state and federal regulation of consumer credit in all fifty states, federal usury preemption, explaining credit math, and how to challenge excessive credit charges and credit insurance. The CD-Rom includes a credit math program and hard-to-find agency interpretations.
2002 Third Edition, 2004 Supplement, and 2004 CD-Rom	**Credit Discrimination:** analysis of the Equal Credit Opportunity Act, Fair Housing Act, Civil Rights Acts, and state credit discrimination statutes, including reprints of all relevant federal interpretations, government enforcement actions, and numerous sample pleadings.

Consumer Litigation Library

2004 Fourth Edition with CD-Rom	**Consumer Arbitration Agreements:** numerous successful approaches to challenge the enforceability of a binding arbitration agreement, the interrelation of the Federal Arbitration Act and state law, class actions in arbitration, collections via arbitration, the right to discovery, and other topics. Appendices and CD-Rom include sample discovery, numerous briefs, arbitration service provider rules and affidavits as to arbitrator costs.
2002 Fifth Edition, 2004 Supplement, and 2004 CD-Rom	**Consumer Class Actions: A Practical Litigation Guide:** makes class action litigation manageable even for small offices, including numerous sample pleadings, class certification memoranda, discovery, class notices, settlement materials, and much more. Includes contributions from seven of the most experienced consumer class action litigators around the country.
2004 CD-Rom with Index Guide: ALL pleadings from ALL NCLC Manuals, including Consumer Law Pleadings Numbers One through Ten	**Consumer Law Pleadings on CD-Rom:** Over 1000 notable recent pleadings from all types of consumer cases, including predatory lending, foreclosures, automobile fraud, lemon laws, debt collection, fair credit reporting, home improvement fraud, rent to own, student loans, and lender liability. Finding aids pinpoint the desired pleading in seconds, ready to paste into a word processing program.

Deception and Warranties Library

2004 Sixth Edition with CD-Rom	**Unfair and Deceptive Acts and Practices:** the only practice manual covering all aspects of a deceptive practices case in every state. Special sections on automobile sales, the federal racketeering (RICO) statute, unfair insurance practices, and the FTC Holder Rule.
2003 Second Edition, 2004 Supplement, and 2004 CD-Rom	**Automobile Fraud:** examination of title law, odometer tampering, lemon laundering, sale of salvage and wrecked cars, undisclosed prior use, prior damage to new cars, numerous sample pleadings, and title search techniques.
2001 Second Edition, 2004 Supplement, and 2004 CD-Rom	**Consumer Warranty Law:** comprehensive treatment of new and used car lemon laws, the Magnuson-Moss Warranty Act, UCC Articles 2 and 2A, mobile home, new home, and assistive device warranty laws, FTC Used Car Rule, tort theories, car repair and home improvement statutes, service contract and lease laws, with numerous sample pleadings.

National Consumer Law Center ■ **77 Summer Street** ■ **10th Floor** ■ **Boston MA** ■ **02110**
(617) 542-9595 ■ **FAX (617) 542-8028** ■ **publications@nclc.org**
Order securely online at www.consumerlaw.org

NCLC's CD-Roms

Every NCLC manual comes with a companion CD-Rom featuring pop-up menus, PDF format, Internet-style navigation of appendices, indices, and bonus pleadings, hard-to-find agency interpretations and other practice aids. Documents can be copied into a word processing program. Of special note is *Consumer Law in a Box*:

December 2004 CD-Rom

Consumer Law in a Box: a CD-Rom combining *all* documents and software from 16 other NCLC CD-Roms. Quickly pinpoint a document from thousands found on the CD through keyword searches and Internet-style navigation, links, bookmarks, and other finding aids.

Other NCLC Publications for Lawyers

issued 24 times a year

NCLC REPORTS covers the latest developments and ideas in the practice of consumer law.

2003 First Edition with CD-Rom

The Practice of Consumer Law: Seeking Economic Justice: contains an essential overview to consumer law and explains how to get started in a private or legal services consumer practice. Packed with invaluable sample pleadings and practice pointers for even experienced consumer attorneys.

2002 First Edition with CD-Rom

STOP Predatory Lending: A Guide for Legal Advocates: provides a roadmap and practical legal strategy for litigating predatory lending abuses, from small loans to mortgage loans. The CD-Rom contains a credit math program, pleadings, legislative and administrative materials, and underwriting guidelines.

National Consumer Law Center Guide Series are books designed for consumers, counselors, and attorneys new to consumer law:

2002 Edition

NCLC Guide to Surviving Debt: a great overview of consumer law. Everything a paralegal, new attorney, or client needs to know about debt collectors, managing credit card debt, whether to refinance, credit card problems, home foreclosures, evictions, repossessions, credit reporting, utility terminations, student loans, budgeting, and bankruptcy.

2002 Edition

NCLC Guide to Mobile Homes: what consumers and their advocates need to know about mobile home dealer sales practices and an in-depth look at mobile home quality and defects, with 35 photographs and construction details.

2002 Edition

NCLC Guide to Consumer Rights for Immigrants: an introduction to many of the most critical consumer issues faced by immigrants, including international wires, check cashing and banking, *notario* and immigration consultant fraud, affidavits of support, telephones, utilities, credit history discrimination, high-cost credit, used car fraud, student loans and more.

2000 Edition

Return to Sender: Getting a Refund or Replacement for Your Lemon Car: Find how lemon laws work, what consumers and their lawyers should know to evaluate each other, investigative techniques and discovery tips, how to handle both informal dispute resolution and trials, and more.

> Visit **www.consumerlaw.org** to order securely online or for more information on all NCLC manuals and CD-Roms, including the full tables of contents, indices, listings of CD-Rom contents, and **web-based searches of the manuals' full text.**

National Consumer Law Center ▪ **77 Summer Street** ▪ **10th Floor** ▪ **Boston MA** ▪ **02110**
(617) 542-9595 ▪ **FAX (617) 542-8028** ▪ **publications@nclc.org**
Order securely online at www.consumerlaw.org

Finding Aids and Search Tips

The Consumer Credit and Sales Legal Practice Series presently contains sixteen volumes, ten supplements, and sixteen companion CD-Roms—all constantly being updated. The Series includes over 10,000 pages, 100 chapters, 100 appendices, and over 1000 pleadings, as well as hundreds of documents found on the CD-Roms, but not found in the books. Here are a number of ways to pinpoint in seconds what you need from this array of materials.

Internet-Based Searches

www.consumerlaw.org

Electronically search every chapter and appendix of all sixteen manuals and their supplements: go to www.consumerlaw.org/keyword and enter a case name, regulation cite, or other search term. You are instantly given the book names and page numbers of any of the NCLC manuals containing that term.

www.consumerlaw.org

Current indexes, tables of contents, and CD-Rom contents for all sixteen volumes are found at www.consumerlaw.org. Just click on *The Consumer Credit and Sales Legal Practice Series* and scroll down to the book you want. Then click on that volume's index, contents, or CD-Rom contents.

Finding Material on NCLC's CD-Roms

Consumer Law in a Box CD-Rom

Electronically search all sixteen NCLC CD-Roms, including thousands of agency interpretations, all NCLC appendices and almost 1000 pleadings: use Acrobat's search button* in NCLC's *Consumer Law in a Box CD-Rom* (this CD-Rom is free to set subscribers) to find every instance that a keyword appears on any of our sixteen CD-Roms. Then, with one click, go to that location to see the full text of the document.

CD-Rom accompanying this volume

Electronically search the CD-Rom accompanying this volume, including pleadings, agency interpretations, and regulations. Use Acrobat's search button* to find every instance that a keyword appears on the CD-Rom, and then, with one click, go to that location on the CD-Rom. Or just click on subject buttons until you navigate to the document you need.

Finding Pleadings

Consumer Law Pleadings on CD-Rom and Index Guide

Search five different ways for the right pleading from over 1000 choices: use the *Index Guide* accompanying *Consumer Law Pleadings on CD-Rom* to search for pleadings by type, subject, publication title, name of contributor, or contributor's jurisdiction. The guide also provides a summary of the pleading once the right pleading is located. *Consumer Law Pleadings on CD-Rom* and the *Consumer Law in a Box CD-Rom* also let you search for all pleadings electronically by subject, type of pleading, and by publication title, giving you instant access to the full pleading in Word and/or PDF format once you find the pleading you need.

Using This Volume to Find Material in All Sixteen Volumes

This volume

The Quick Reference at the back of this volume lets you pinpoint manual sections or appendices where over 1000 different subject areas are covered.

---

* Users of NCLC CD-Roms should become familiar with "search," a powerful Acrobat tool, distinguished from "find,"another Acrobat feature that is far slower and less powerful than "search." The Acrobat 5 "search" icon is a pair of binoculars with paper in the background, while the "find" icon is a pair of binoculars without the paper. Acrobat 6 uses one icon, a pair of binoculars, that brings you to a menu with several search options.

Contents

How to Use This Manual

Overview

The Companion CD-Rom contains over 1000 pleadings, comprised of *all* pleadings found in *all* NCLC manuals, and includes:

- *Consumer Law Pleadings*, Number Ten (2004) (first released as part of this volume);
- *Consumer Law Pleadings*, Numbers One through Nine (1994–2003);
- Numerous class action pleadings found in the appendices and on the 2004 CD-Rom accompanying NCLC's *Consumer Class Actions* (5th ed. 2002 and Supp.);
- Over 150 bankruptcy pleadings found in the appendices and on the CD-Rom accompanying NCLC's *Consumer Bankruptcy Law and Practice* (7th ed. 2004);
- All the model and sample pleadings found in all other NCLC individual manuals;
- Additional pleadings found on the CD-Rom accompanying all other individual NCLC manuals.

The CD-Rom contains numerous types of consumer law pleadings, including:

- Demand Letters, notices, retainers, and forms;
- Complaints, answers, counterclaims;
- Interrogatories and document requests, requests for admissions, deposition preparation, and discovery motions;
- Numerous types of pre-trial and trial motions;
- Briefs, memoranda;
- Post-trial motions and orders;
- Attorney fee documents;
- Numerous class action pleadings, including authorization to represent, complaints, discovery, protective orders, certification pleadings, class notices, briefs, memoranda, pre-trial motions, trial practice, attorney fee documents, settlements, objections to settlement, and cy pres awards; and
- Over 150 bankruptcy pleadings, including initial forms, automatic stay, turnover of property, utilities, steps after filing, claims, exemptions and lien avoidance, litigation generally, discharge and reaffirmation, plan conversion, modification, dismissal, farm reorganization, and consumers as creditors.

This manual contains numerous aids to help the user quickly locate the desired pleadings on the CD-Rom. Once the pleadings are identified, they may be found in PDF (Acrobat) format on the companion CD-Rom, read on screen, printed out, and pasted into a word processing document for editing. Virtually all the pleadings are available on CD-Rom in word processing format, allowing the user to copy pleadings that retain their original formatting.

Using the Book to Search for Pleadings

Many users will find that using this book is their preferred method of searching for pleadings. The book contains seven different listings that will facilitate the user's search:

- "Pleadings by Type" is organized first by the type of pleading (for example, complaint, interrogatory, or jury instruction) and then, within a given type of pleading, by the subject area of the pleading (for example, automobile fraud or insurance). This listing is particularly useful for those interested in a specific type of pleading, irrespective of the subject area.
- "Pleadings by Subject" is organized first by the subject area of the pleading (for example, arbitration or Truth in Lending) and then, within a given subject area, by the type of pleading (for example, demand letters or pre-trial motions). This listing is particularly useful for those interested in various types of pleadings within a subject area.
- "Pleadings by Title" specifies all pleadings found in all NCLC manuals. This listing is organized by manual title and then by chapter or appendix of each title.
- "Description of Pleadings" provides a description of each pleading found in the nine *Consumer Law Pleadings* volumes. The listing is organized by volume and chapter order and provides a brief overview of each pleading, its context, and related information. Use *alternative* listings to locate a specific pleading and then use the "Description of Pleadings" to obtain information about the pleading selected.
- "Pleadings by Contributor" provides biographical information on the authors who have contributed to the nine *Consumer Law Pleadings* volumes. (This listing does *not* include those who have contributed pleadings

to other manuals.) This listing is recommended for readers who want the background of an attorney drafting a specific pleading or who wish to contact that attorney.

- "Contributors by State" facilitates the search for pleadings and/or consumer law experts from a particular state. The listing is organized by the state that the contributor is from (not the state in which the pleading was created) and indicates the name of the contributor and the pleadings which the contributor has submitted to NCLC's ten *Consumer Law Pleadings* volumes.
- "Contributors by Title" identifies by chapter each of NCLC's ten *Consumer Law Pleadings* volumes, the contributors of specific pleadings, and the state in which they practice law.

Using the CD-Rom to Search for Pleadings

The CD-Rom offers many of the same categories and powerful search capabilities as the book:

- Pleadings by Type;
- Pleadings by Subject; and
- Pleadings by Title.

While many users will search for pleadings using the seven listings in the book (preferring paper to computer screens), using the CD-Rom as a search tool has certain advantages:

- *Key word searches* allow the user, with one key word submission, to search every sentence in every pleading on the CD-Rom. For example, the user can quickly identify all pleadings in which the acronym "HOEPA" appears near the word "trigger" or the phrase "nursing home."
- *The full text instantaneously appears* when the user clicks on the name of a pleading found on the CD's "Pleadings by Type," "Pleadings by Subject," or "Pleadings by Title" listings. Clicking on the back arrow will move the user from the text of the pleading back to the listing to search for other pleadings.
- *Bookmarks and links.* When the user calls up a particular pleading on the CD-Rom, the bookmarks on the left will identify related links. Clicking on a bookmark will bring the user to a related pleading. Clicking on the back arrow will return the user to the original pleading.

Installing and Using the CD-Rom

A pop-up menu makes installation and use of the CD-Rom extremely easy. The first button allows the user to load Acrobat 5 or 6.0.1 on a computer if the computer does not already have Acrobat 5 or 6.0.1 (one-time installation). The second button allows the user to install a desk-top icon (one-time installation and not strictly necessary). The third button runs the CD-Rom from the pop-up menu. More details on the contents of the CD-Rom, installation, and use are found on the last two pages of this volume.

Tips on Finding Pleadings

Here are pointers on finding desired pleadings:

- A key word search on the CD-Rom is always a powerful search technique, particularly when the user wants to locate unusual subject areas or unusual types of pleadings.
- Searching by pleading *type* is best when the user is less interested in a subject area than in finding a type of pleading, irrespective of the subject area. For example, use pleading type to search for voir dire questions.
- Searching by pleadings *subject* is best when the user is interested in a particular subject area (and is more interested in any type of pleading in that area) than in pleadings of a similar type in other subject areas.
- In general, pleadings found in individual subject manuals (for example, *Truth in Lending* or *Fair Debt Collection*) are most representative of pleadings within those subject areas and have been more carefully selected. Pleadings appearing in *Consumer Law Pleadings* are more likely to relate to current litigation in narrowly-focused areas. The use of "Pleadings by Title" will help the user to differentiate between these two types of pleadings.
- An indirect method of finding pleadings from your state is to use the "Contributors by State" listing. Identify attorneys from your state on that listing, then review the pleadings they have contributed. (Some pleadings are also identified by state. The state's abbreviation is in parentheses at the end of the name of the pleading. A key word search for the name of a state or the state's abbreviation in parentheses—for example, "(CA)"—may also produce results.)
- When a pleading of interest is found, consider reading a description of that pleading contained in "Description of Pleadings" and information about the attorney who contributed the pleading in "Pleadings by Contributor."
- Regular subscribers to *Consumer law Pleadings* will want to go to "Pleadings by Title" and peruse *Consumer Law Pleadings*, Number Ten (2004), a large number of pleadings appearing for the first time in this volume.

Pleadings by Type

The following listing is organized first by the type of pleading and then, within a given type of pleading, by the subject area of the pleading. This listing is particularly useful for those interested in a specific type of pleading, irrespective of the subject area. Those needing a specific subject area, irrespective of the type of pleading, will find more useful the listing found at Pleadings by Subject, *infra*.

Important Note:

- Class action pleadings are separated from pleadings in individual cases. When looking at a specific type of pleading, also refer to the comparable class action pleading found later in the listing.
- Bankruptcy pleadings are at the end.
- Discovery that covers interrogatories and document requests are listed first, followed by discovery that covers only interrogatories, and then by a listing of document requests only.

The type of pleadings are listed in this order:

- Demand Letters, Notices, Retainers
- Complaints, Answers, Counterclaims
- Discovery, Interrogatories and Document Requests
- Discovery, Interrogatories
- Discovery, Document Requests
- Discovery, Requests for Admissions
- Discovery, Depositions
- Discovery Motions
- Pre-Trial Motions, Trial Practice
- Briefs, Memoranda
- Post-Trial Motions, Orders, Attorney Fee Documents
- Class Actions, Articles
- Class Actions, Authorization to Represent
- Class Actions, Complaints
- Class Actions, Discovery
- Class Actions, Protective Orders
- Class Actions, Certification Pleadings
- Class Actions, Class Notices
- Class Actions, Briefs, Memoranda
- Class Actions, Pre-Trial Motions, Trial Practice
- Class Actions, Settlements
- Class Actions, Objections to Settlement
- Class Actions, Cy Pres
- Class Actions, Attorney Fees
- Bankruptcy, Petitions, Schedules, Official Forms
- Bankruptcy, Initial Forms
- Bankruptcy, Automatic Stay

- Bankruptcy, Turnover of Property
- Bankruptcy, Utilities
- Bankruptcy, Steps After Filing
- Bankruptcy, Claims
- Bankruptcy, Exemptions and Lien Avoidance
- Bankruptcy, Litigation Generally
- Bankruptcy, Discharge and Reaffirmation
- Bankruptcy, Plan Conversion, Modification, Dismissal
- Bankruptcy, Farm Reorganization
- Bankruptcy, Consumers as Creditors

The cross-references are:

Arbit = Consumer Arbitration Agreements
Auto = Auto Fraud
Bankr = Consumer Bankruptcy Law and Practice
CBPL = Consumer Banking and Payments Law
CCA = Consumer Class Actions
CD = Credit Discrimination
CLP = Consumer Law Pleadings (Numbers One through Ten)
COC = Cost of Credit
FCRA = Fair Credit Reporting Act
FDC = Fair Debt Collection
Repo = Repossessions and Foreclosures
Stud = Student Loan
TIL = Truth in Lending
UDAP = Unfair and Deceptive Acts and Practices
Warr = Consumer Warranty Law

Demand Letters, Notices, Retainers, Forms		Retainer Agreement with Contingent Fee in a Consumer Case	CLP10 Ch. 16
	Auto Fraud	Client Letter—Settlement: Undisclosed Sale of Lemon Buy-Back RV (OH)	CLP10 Ch. 2.1.7
		Settlement Letter: Undisclosed Sale of Lemon Buy-Back RV (OH)	CLP10 Ch. 2.1.8
	Auto Warranties, Lemon Law, Auto Repair	Letter to National Highway Traffic Safety Administration for Preliminary Evaluation File	CLP4 Ch. 15.13
		Notice of Rejection or Revocation of Acceptance	Warr App. J.1
		Notice That Consumer Is Deducting Damages From the Outstanding Balance	Warr App. J.2
	Bankruptcy	Notice of TILA Rescission	CLP9 Ch. 19.1
	Credit Reporting	Client Retainer Forms	CLP4 Ch. 8.1
		Repeatedly Obtaining Credit Reports Without an Authorized Purpose	CLP9 Ch. 17.2.1
		Sample Letter Explaining Damages and Legal Theories to Opposing Counsel	FCR CD Extra
		Sample Request for Consumer's Credit Report	FCR CD Extra

		Student Loans Request for Reasonable and Affordable Repayment Agreement	CLP2 Ch. 13.1
		Teacher Loan Forgiveness Application	Stud CD Extra
		Temporary Total Disability Deferment Request	Stud CD Extra
		Unemployment Deferment Request	Stud CD Extra
		Unpaid Refund Affidavit, Student Loans	Stud App. D.1.6
	Deceptive Practices, Fraud, RICO	Car Rental Company Including Illegal Limitations on its Insurance Coverage	CLP9 Ch. 17.1.1
	Mortgages, Predatory Loans, Foreclosures	Notice of TILA Rescission	CLP9 Ch. 19.1
		Qualified Written Request Under RESPA to Obtain Mortgage Loan Information	Bankr App. G #69
		Rescission Notice Truth in Lending Act	TIL App. D
		Sample Qualified Written Request Under RESPA After Bankruptcy Filing	Repo Supp. O.5.2
		Sample Qualified Written Request Under RESPA	Repo Supp. O.5.1
		Veteran's Letter to VA Concerning Mortgage Foreclosure	CLP2 Ch. 3.1
	Truth in Lending	HOEPA Points and Fees Worksheet	TIL App. H
		Notice of TILA Rescission	CLP9 Ch. 19.1
		Rescission Letter TILA Bankruptcy Court	CLP1 Ch. 8.1
		Rescission Notice Truth in Lending Act	TIL App. D
	Utilities, Energy	Letter to Utility Company Giving Notice of Stay and Requirements of 11 U.S.C. § 366	Bankr App. G #39
Complaints, Answers, Counterclaims	*Arbitration*	Arbitration Issues: *Ting v. AT&T*, Violation of the Consumer Legal Remedies Act, Unfair Business Practices Act (CA)	Arbit App. C
		Compulsory Arbitration Denied in Class Action Alleging Home Repair Fraud, RICO and Unauthorized Insurance Practices; Discovery	CLP4 Ch. 1.1
		Corbett v National Arbitration Forum, Alleging NAF Violates CA Disclosure Law	Arbit CD Extra
		Long Distance Telephone Company's Arbitration Clause is Unconscionable	CLP8 Ch. 1.1
		Truth in Lending Rescission for HOEPA Violations Argued to be Not Subject to Arbitration	CLP8 Ch. 11.1
	Auto Credit, Leases, Repos, Deficiencies	Against Auto Dealership Alleging Hidden Credit Charges by Its Alter Ego Finance Company	CLP3 Ch. 9.1.2
		Answer Counterclaim Discovery Usury Retail Installment Sales Act, Car Credit Sale	COC App. E.1
		Answer Repossession Delay Discharges Obligation of Cosigner on Car Sale UCC	CLP6 Ch. 13.1

	Auto Sale, Lender Liability Where FTC Holder Notice Improperly Omitted	CLP1 Ch. 4.2
	Auto Spot Delivery, Repossession, Conversion, Fraud, Violation of UCC 9-504	CLP7 Ch. 5.2
	Commercially Unreasonable Sale as Defense to Automobile Creditor's Deficiency Action	CLP2 Ch. 12.3
	Complaint, Failure to Disclose that a Trade-in was Given in a Car Lease	CLP8 Ch. 5.1
	Counterclaims and Defenses Based on UCC § 9-615(f)	Repo App. D.2
	Failure to Honor Credit Life Insurance after Debtor Died, Repossession, UCC	CLP7 Ch. 16.1
	Injunction against Boat's Repossession Sale and Claim for Damages Relating to Sale Abuses	CLP2 Ch. 12.2
	Misrepresenting APR in Car Financing; Yield Spread Premium: TILA, UDAP, RISA, Car Titling Statute, (MI)	CLP9 Ch. 2.1
	Repossession Deficiency Action	Repo App. D.1
	Repossession, Enjoin Sale	Repo App. D.3
	Repossession, Violation of 42 U.S.C. § 1983, Conversion, Breach of Peace	Repo App. D.4
	Sample Consumer Leasing Act Complaint	TIL Supp. E.7
Auto Fraud	Auto Dealer and Financer, Undisclosed Wreck History	Auto App. G.5
	Auto Dealer and Lender—Odometer Misrepresentations, Lender's Information Sent to Credit Reporting Agency	Auto App. G.3
	Auto Dealer for Concealment of Salvage Branded Title (*Summers*) (Unabridged)	Auto CD Extra
	Auto Dealer for Concealment of Car's Prior Use	Auto App. G.7
	Auto Dealer for Concealment of Salvage Branded Title	Auto App. G.4
	Auto Dealers for Tampering, False Statements, and False Disclosures	Auto App. G.2
	Auto Fraud Sales Practices	CLP6 Ch. 9.1
	Auto Spot Delivery, Odometer Act, TILA, conversion, UDAP	CLP7 Ch. 5.1
	Auto Spot Delivery, Repossession, Conversion, Fraud, Violation of UCC 9-504	CLP7 Ch. 5.2
	Automobile Odometer Fraud and Threat of Violent Repossession	CLP5 Ch. 3.1
	Complaint, Failure to Disclose that a Trade-in was Given in a Car Lease	CLP8 Ch. 5.1
	Concealed Wreck (*Petrie*)	Auto CD Extra
	Concealment of Car's Prior Use by Car Rental Agency	CLP9 Ch. 5.3

	FDCPA Against Attorney for Seizing Exempt Bank Account Funds	CLP2 Ch. 12.1
	West Virginia v. TeleCheck	CBPL CD Extra
Bankruptcy	Mortgage Adversary Complaint: TIL Rescission in Bankruptcy, RESPA, UDAP, Yield Spread Premium	CLP9 Ch. 19.2
	Mortgage Servicer for Disregarding Chapter 13 Plan Provisions	CLP3 Ch. 7.1
Credit Cards, Open-End Credit	Credit Cards Failure to Recognize Defense also Discovery	CLP2 Ch. 9.1
	Fair Credit Billing Act	TIL App. E.5
Credit Discrimination	Action Against Subprime Lender, Discriminatory Overcharges by Affiliated Mortgage Brokers (*U. S. v. Long Beach Mortgage Co.*)	CD CD Extra
	Action Alleging Discrimination in Use of Credit Score Overrides (*U. S. v. Deposit Guaranty National Bank*)	CD CD Extra
	Action Alleging Discriminatory Credit Score Thresholds (*U. S. v. Associates National Bank*)	CD CD Extra
	Action Alleging Redlining and Marketing Discrimination (*U.S. v. Decatur FSLA*)	CD CD Extra
	Action Alleging Redlining and Marketing Discrimination (*U. S. v. Chevy Chase Federal Savings Bank*)	CD CD Extra
	Action Alleging Redlining By Use of Correspondent Lenders (*U. S. v. Albank, FSB*)	CD CD Extra
	Auto Dealerships Alleging Race Discrimination and Rebate Theft	CLP3 Ch. 9.2.1
	Car Dealer Discrimination Against Mandarin Speakers (state law claims) (*A. v. Wondries Associates, Inc.*)	CD CD Extra
	Denial of Home Mortgage and Discriminatory Appraisal Practices as ECOA, Fair Housing and Civil Rights Violations	CD App. F.1
	Discrimination in Collection of Subprime Credit Card Accounts (*U.S. v. Fidelity Federal Bank*), also Settlement Agreement	CD CD Extra
	Discrimination in Mobile home Purchase Loans (*U.S. v. First National Bank of Dona Ana County*), also Settlement Agreement	CD CD Extra
	ECOA and FHA Case Alleging Bank Refused to Lend to Native Americans (*United States v. Blackpipe State Bank*)	CD CD Extra
	ECOA and Regulation B Violations (*Franklin Acceptance*)	CD CD Extra
	ECOA Cosigner Violation	CD App. F.2
	ECOA Notice Provisions, also TILA, FCRA	CD Supp. App. F.6
	ECOA Notice Violations (*Lane v. Southside Bank*)	CD CD Extra

	ECOA Notice Violations and Violations of the Federal Fair Credit Reporting Act (*Cleaver v. Greater Mid-Atlantic Finance Co., Inc.*)	CD CD Extra
	Fair Housing Act Violation, Segregation, Dual Housing Market (*Honorable v. The Easy Life Real Estate Systems*)	CD CD Extra
	Insurance Redlining (*United States v. Nationwide Mutual Insurance Company*)	CD CD Extra
	Lending Discrimination Against Native Americans (*U.S. v. First National Bank of Gordon*), also Consent Order	CD CD Extra
	Redlining and Adverse Impact of Mortgage Lender's Business Practices (*United States v. Chevy Chase Federal Savings Bank*)	CD CD Extra
	Reverse Redlining, Gender (*Eva v. MidwestNational Mortgage Banc*)	CD CD Extra
	Subprime Lender Violation of FHA, ECOA, RESPA, TILA (*United States v. Delta Funding Corp. and Delta Financial Corp.*)	CD CD Extra
	Violations of the FHA and ECOA in Marketing of Lending Products and Services (*U.S. v. Mid America Bank*), also Consent Order	CD CD Extra
Credit Reporting	Continuously Reporting Inaccurate Information to a Credit Reporting Agency after Notice	CLP9 Ch. 9.3.1, 9.3.2.1
	Credit Repair Organization Statute against Car Dealer	CLP6 Ch. 2.2
	Failure to Correct Inaccurate Credit Reports that Result from Mixed Credit Data	CLP9 Ch. 9.1.1, 9.1.2, 9.1.3
	Failure to Correct Inaccurate Credit Reports After Learning of an Identity Theft	CLP9 Ch. 9.2
	Fair Credit Reporting Act, Impermissible Purposes	FCR App. I.1.2
	Fair Credit Reporting Act, Accuracy	FCR App. I.1.3
	Fair Credit Reporting Act, Investigative Report	FCR App. I.1.4
	Fair Credit Reporting Act, Failure to Reinvestigate	FCR App. I.1.1
	FCRA, Against Credit Reporting Agency, Furnisher for Failure to Have Reasonable Procedures to Ensure Accuracy and Failure to Reinvestigate Accuracy of Information	FCR CD Extra
	FCRA, Against Credit Reporting Agency—Failure to Have Reasonable Procedures to Ensure Accuracy and Failure to Reinvestigate Disputed Accuracy of Information	FCR CD Extra
	FCRA, Against Credit Reporting Agency and Furnisher of Information for Failure to Ensure Accuracy and Investigate Disputed Information	FCR CD Extra
	FCRA, Against Credit Reporting Agencies, Creditors and Furnishers of Information: Theft of Identity, Failure to Use Reasonable Procedures, Failure to Reinvestigate	FCR CD Extra

	Credit Union Wrongfully Setoff a Customer's Exempt Social Security Funds	CLP7 Ch. 13.1
	Fair Debt Collection Including Both Federal and State Causes of Action	FDC App. H.1
	Fair Debt Collection Practices Act	FDC App. H.2
	FDCPA: Collector Pretending to be Creditor, state debt collection statutes	CLP9 Ch. 3.1
	FDCPA Suit in Federal Court vs. Attorneys Who Sued Consumer a Second Time after First Suit Settled	CLP8 Ch. 12.2
	Harassment; Unauthorized Practice of Law by Debt Collector, FDCPA	CLP7 Ch. 3.1
	Invasion of Privacy, Intentional Infliction, Severe Distress, Amended Complaint Adding Party (AL)	CLP10 Ch. 5.2
	Invasion of Privacy, Intentional Infliction, Severe Distress, Complaint (AL)	CLP10 Ch. 5.1
	Tort Suit for Outrageous Debt Collection Practices	CLP8 Ch. 20.1
Debt Collection, Hospital	Answer, Counterclaims, Hospital Collection Suit	CLP8 Ch. 4, VI
	Article: "Defending Hospital Collection Cases, 2001"	FDC CD Extra
	State Public Assistance Agency Payment of Hospital Bill	CLP8 Ch. 4, X
	Third-Party Complaint Against Health Insurer	CLP8 Ch. 4, IX
Debt Collection, Student Loans	(Individual Student) Against School	CLP2 Ch. 13.3
	Action Challenging Private Student Lender Practices	Stud CD Extra
	Challenge to Disability Discharge Denial	Stud App. E.2.4
	Challenge to Student Loan Collection Letters	Stud App. E.3.1
	Challenging Denial of False Certification Discharge	Stud CD Extra
	Challenging Federal Benefit Offsets to Collect Old Student Loans	Stud App. E.4.2
	Complaint to Determine Dischargeability of Student Loan	Bankr App. G #106
	Complaint to Enjoin Discriminatory Denial of Guaranteed Student Loan	Bankr App. G #121
	Complaints: *Article*: "Primer on Bankruptcy and the Sovereign Immunity of States: When You Can't Sue State Agencies, When You Can Sue State Officials"	CLP6 Ch. 7.1.2
	Dischargeability Complaint Raising School's Fraud	Stud App. E.6.2
	Dischargeability of Student Loan	Stud App. E.6.1
	For Declaratory Relief that School's Fraud Is Defense on the Student Loan	Stud 2001 E.5.3
	Individual Case Challenging Denial of Disability Discharge	Stud CD Extra
	School's Fraud in Bankruptcy Proceedings	CLP2 Ch. 13.6

	Seeking Declaratory Relief That School's Fraud is Defense on the Student Loan	CLP2 Ch. 13.5
	State Court Complaint Against Trade School	Stud CD Extra
	To Enjoin Discriminatory Denial of Guaranteed Student Loan	Stud App. E.6.3
	Trade School Abuse, Complaint and Demand for Jury Trial	Stud Supp. App. E.5.2.3
	Trade School Abuse, State Court Complaint Against School	Stud App. E.5.1
Deceptive Practices, Fraud, RICO	Auto Finance Upcharge Cases GMAC Links:	UDAP CD Extra
	Auto Finance Upcharge Cases: NMAC Links	UDAP CD Extra
	Auto Lease Early Termination UDAP	CLP1 Ch. 9.1
	Befriending Scam, also Discovery	CLP3 Ch. 1.2
	Credit Repair Organization Statute Fraud Claims against Car Dealer	CLP6 Ch. 2.2
	False Threat of Foreclosure, FDCPA, UDAP	CLP6 Ch. 3.1
	Furniture Non-Delivery	CLP2 Ch. 7.1
	Home Construction Claims, Discovery	CLP5 Ch. 7.1
	Home Improvement Fraud, Agency $28 Million Punitive Damages Award for Bank's Involvement	CLP1 Ch. 5.1
	Home Repair Contractor Assignee, Fair Credit Reporting Act, Truth in Lending Act, UDAP	CLP6 Ch. 17.1
	Infertility Program, Unfair and Deceptive Practices	CLP4 Ch. 13.1
	Predatory Mortgage Lending Involving Multiple Parties RICO TILA	CLP1 Ch. 7.1
	Rescission of Deed in Sale Leaseback Scheme	CLP3 Ch. 1.3
	Scheme to Defraud Elderly Homeowner	CLP3 Ch. 1.1
	Storage of Consumer's Possessions	CLP2 Ch. 7.2
	Theft of Identity by Unknown Person; Discovery	CLP3 Ch. 5.2
	Theft of Identity by Salesman at Auto Dealership	CLP3 Ch. 5.1
	TIL Rescission and Deceptive Practices Case—Home Improvement Contract (*Mount*)(Class Action)	CCA99 D.2
	Travel Agency Who Recommended Insolvent Tour Operator	CLP4 Ch. 5.1
	Travel Agent Alleging Failure to Investigate Reliability of Tour Operator	CLP4 Ch. 5.2
	Travel Club and Tour Operator Alleging that Tour Operator Was Insolvent	CLP4 Ch. 5.3
Fringe Lenders: Pay Day Loans, Auto Pawn, Rent to Own, Refund Anticipation Loans	Auto Pawn Business Subject to Regulation under State Credit Statutes	CLP3 Ch. 4.2
	Complaint Against Payday Lender for Disguising its Loans as Sales of Internet Access (FL)	CLP10 Ch. 9

	Pay Day Loan—Check Advance Transaction Is Loan Under State Finance Act	CLP3 Ch. 4.1
	Payday Loan also Opposition to Motion to Dismiss, Discovery, Usury, Small Loan Act, RICO, Truth In Lending, and UDAP	COC App. F.1
	Payday Loans, Ace Cash Express, MD	COC Supp. App. F.6
	Rent to Own	CLP2 Ch. 8.1
	Rent-to-Own Company—Usurious Interest, Discovery, Briefs	CLP4 Ch. 11.1
Installment Loans, Closed-End Credit, Usury	Answer Counterclaim Discovery Usury Retail Installment Sales Act, Car Credit Sale	COC App. E.1
	Answer Repossession Delay Discharges Obligation of Cosigner on Car Sale UCC	CLP6 Ch. 13.1
	Auto Sale Lender Liability Where FTC Holder Notice Improperly Omitted	CLP1 Ch. 4.2
	Loan Flipping	CLP3 Ch. 2.6
	Payday Loan Opposition to Motion to Dismiss, and Discovery, also Usury, Small Loan Act, RICO, Truth in Lending, and UDAP	COC App. F.1
	Payday Loans, Ace Cash Express, MD	COC Supp. App. F.6
	Refund Anticipation Loan Debt Collection Case	COC Supp. App. G.1
	Rent-to-Own Company—Usurious Interest, Discovery, Briefs	CLP4 Ch. 11.1
	Small Loan Usury	COC App. E.3
Insurance	Failure to Honor Credit Life Insurance after Debtor Died, Repossession, Constructive Fraud	CLP7 Ch. 16.1
	HMO Health Maintenance Organizations for Delay in Authorizing and Paying for Cancer Treatment	CLP6 Ch. 5.1
	Home Repair Fraud, RICO and Unauthorized Insurance Practices	CLP4 Ch. 1.1
	Third-Party Complaint Against Health Insurer, in Hospital Collection Suit	CLP8 Ch. 4, IX
Mobile Homes, Landlord-Tenant	Answer to Motion of Landlord for Relief from Automatic Stay	Bankr App. G #30
	Complaint to Determine Dischargeability of Tenant's Claims Against Landlord	Bankr App. G #148
	Complaint to Prohibit Eviction from Public Housing Based upon Dischargeable Debt for Rent	Bankr App. G #84
	Damages for Breach of Implied Warranty of Merchantability	Warr App. K.2.2
	Dealer and Financer for Improper Setup of Mobile Home	Warr App. K.7
	Landlord-Tenant Challenging Lease Provisions	CLP2 Ch. 1.1

	Mobile Home Constructive Eviction Through Utility Shut Off	CLP2 Ch. 1.3
	Mobile Home Conversion of Mobile Home Park; Retaliatory Eviction; Tie-In of Home Purchase to Park Space, also Discovery & Briefs	CLP2 Ch. 2.2
	Mobile Home Dealer and Manufacturer	CLP5 Ch. 4.2.1
	Mobile Home Sale Complaint for Damages and Cancellation	CLP2 Ch. 4.1
	Mobile Home Uninhabitable Park Conditions, also Discovery & Briefs	CLP2 Ch. 2.1
	Nursing Home—Quality of Care, Discovery	CLP4 Ch. 3.1.1
	Nursing Home—Unlawful Business Practices, Memorandum	CLP4 Ch. 3.2.1
	Real Estate Broker Fraud, also Motion for Class Certification (Class Action)	CLP2 Ch. 4.2
	Uninhabitability Defense to Eviction	CLP2 Ch. 1.2
Mortgages, Predatory Loans, Foreclosures	Action to Enjoin Foreclosure and Bring Affirmative Causes of Action	Repo Supp. O.3.1
	Answer to FHA Foreclosure Complaint, also Discovery, Brief	CLP2 Ch. 3.2.1
	Chapter 13 Plan Providing for Filing of Adversary Proceeding Involving Predatory Mortgage Lending Claims	Bankr App. G #13
	Complaint Against Lender for Fraud Against Non-English Speakers and Truth in Lending Violations (OR)	CLP10 Ch. 14.1
	Complaint for Responding to Residential Mortgage Billing Errors with Foreclosure	CLP10 Ch. 7
	Complaint Objecting to Mortgage Servicer's Claim Based on RESPA and FDCPA Violations	Bankr App. G #72
	Complaint Objecting to Secured Claim in Bankruptcy, also Discovery, Memorandum, Chapter 13 Plan, Attorney Fee Request	CLP2 Ch. 3.3
	Complaint Objecting to Secured Claim on the Basis of Usury and Warranty Defenses	Bankr App. G #67
	Credit Overcharges Usury UDAP Mortgage Refinancing	CLP6 Ch. 6.2
	Foreclosure Answer with TILA and RESPA Affirmative Defenses	Repo Supp. O.2.1
	Foreclosure Defense: Answer, Counterclaim, Third Party Complaint	CLP8 Ch. 22.1
	HOEPA Rescission and Damages	TIL App. E.4
	Home Improvement Case	Warr App. K.4
	Home Improvement Contractor, Fraud	Repo Supp. O.4
	Home Improvement Fraud, Agency, $28 Million Punitive Damages Award for Bank's Involvement	CLP1 Ch. 5.1

		HOEPA Rescission and Damages	TIL App. E.4
		Home Repair Contractor Assignee, Fair Credit Reporting Act, Truth in Lending Act, UDAP	CLP6 Ch. 17.1
		In Bankruptcy Court Objecting to Secured Claim, TILA Rescission	CLP1 Ch. 8.2
		Mortgage Adversary Complaint: TIL Rescission in Bankruptcy, RESPA, UDAP, Yield Spread Premium	CLP9 Ch. 19.2
		Truth in Lending Act Damages	TIL App. E.2
		Truth in Lending Rescission	TIL App. E.3
		Truth in Lending Rescission for HOEPA Violations Argued to Be Not Subject to Arbitration	CLP8 Ch. 11.1
	Utilities, Energy	Complaint Against Municipal Water Utility Shutting off Water of Tenants Without Notice (OH)	CLP10 Ch. 17.1
		Complaint Seeking Reconnection of Utility Service and Damages After Bankruptcy	Bankr App. G #42
		Complaint to Enjoin Termination of Utility Service for Nonpayment of Deposit by Bankrupt Current on Her Utility Payments	Bankr App. G #41
		Complaint—Inadequacy of Utility Allowance	AUS CD Extra
		Long Distance Company Rates NARUC, NCLC and Others' Petition to FCC to Impose Notice Requirement	AUS CD Extra
		Long Distance Phone Overcharges	CLP7 Ch.2.1
		Long Distance Telephone Company's Arbitration Clause Is Unconscionable	CLP8 Ch. 1.1
Discovery, Interrogatories and Document Requests	*Arbitration*	Arbitration, Auto Financer	Arbit App. D.3
		Arbitration, Credit Card Issuer, AL Suit	Arbit App. D.2
		Arbitration, Credit Card Issuer, Interrogatories and Document Requests	Arbit App. D.1
		Arbitration, Discovery Directed to Pay Day Loan Company	Arbit App. D.5
	Auto Credit, Leases, Repos, Deficiencies	Auto Fraud Alleging Hidden Credit Charges by Dealer's Alter Ego Finance Company	CLP3 Ch. 9.1.3
		Auto Repossession	CLP4 Ch. 4.1
		Auto Sale Lender Liability Where FTC Holder Notice Improperly Omitted	CLP1 Ch. 4.5
		Automobile Repossession Deficiency Suit	Repo App. E.1
		Failure to Honor Credit Life Insurance after Debtor Died, Repossession, UCC	CLP7 Ch. 16.2
		Misrepresenting APR in Car Financing; Yield Spread Premium: TILA, UDAP, RISA, Car Titling Statute (MI)	CLP9 Ch. 2.2–2.7

Pleadings by Type

Credit Cards, Open-End Credit	Defendant's Interrogatories in Dischargeability Case Based on Credit Card Fraud	Bankr App. G #110
	Fair Credit Billing Act	TIL App. F.4
Credit Discrimination	ECOA Adverse Action Notice Violation	CD App. G.1
	ECOA Cosigner Violation	CD App. G.2
	ECOA Zip Code Redlining	CD App. G.3
	Reverse Redlining Case, Gender, Defendant Midwest National, Document Requests*(Eva v. Midwest National Mortgage Banc)*	CD CD Extra
	Reverse Redlining, Gender, Defendant Thomas Butzer, Document Requests *(Eva v. Midwest National Mortgage Banc)*	CD CD Extra
	Reverse Redlining, Gender, Defendant USMR, Document Requests *(Eva v. Midwest National Mortgage Banc)*	CD CD Extra
Credit Reporting	Credit Reporting Agency	CLP9 Ch. 9.5.3
	Fair Credit Reporting Act, Reinvestigation, To Furnisher	FCR Supp. App. I.2.4
	Fair Credit Reporting Act, Accuracy	FCR App. I.2.1
	Fair Credit Reporting Act, Permissible Purpose	FCR App. I.2.3
	Fair Credit Reporting Act, Metro 2 Format	FCR App. I.2.2
	FCRA, Directed to Creditor	FCR CD Extra
	FCRA, Interrogatories to Reporting Agency, Permissible Purposes	FCR CD Extra
	FCRA, Interrogatories to User, Permissible Purposes	FCR CD Extra
Debt Collection, General	Invasion of Privacy, Intentional Infliction, Severe Distress, Interrogatories (AL)	CLP10 Ch. 5.4
Installment Loans, Closed-End Credit, Usury	Refund Anticipation Loan Debt Collection Case, to bank	COC Supp. App. G.2
	Refund Anticipation Loan Debt Collection Case, to Tax Preparation Firm	COC Supp. App. G.4
Truth in Lending	Fair Credit Billing Act	TIL App. F.4
	Truth in Lending	TIL App. F.2
Discovery, Document Requests *Arbitration*	American Arbitration Association Documents—Relationship of AAA and AT&T	Arbit CD Extra
	Arbitration, Auto Title Pawn Company	Arbit App. D.6
Auto Credit, Leases, Repos, Deficiencies	Sample Consumer Leasing Act Request for Production of Documents	TIL Supp. App. F.7
Auto Fraud	Dealer—Undisclosed Wreck History	Auto 1998 Appx F.2.2
	Floor Plan Financier, Document Requests	Auto Supp. App. H.6

	Initial Document Requests—Concealed Wreck	Auto CD Extra
	Lemon Laundering, Document Request to Dealer	Auto App. H.3.3
	Lemon Laundering, Document Request to Manufacturer	Auto App. H.3.5
	Odometer Fraud	Auto App. H.1.3
	Undisclosed Auto Repair History, Dealer	Auto 1998 Appx F.4.2
	Undisclosed Auto Repair History, Lender	Auto 1998 Appx F.4.4
	Undisclosed Auto Repair History, Manufacturer	Auto 1998 Appx F.4.3
	Undisclosed Damage History	Auto App. H.2.3
	Undisclosed Sale of Lemon Buy-Back RV, Second Document Request to Dealer (OH)	CLP10 Ch. 2.1.5
Auto Warranties, Lemon Law, Auto Repair	Lemon Law Case (TN)	Warr CD Extra
	New Car Lemon Suit (TN)	CLP8 Ch. 7.2
	To Mobile Home Manufacturer	Warr App. L.7
	Warranty Document Requests	Warr App. L.3
Credit Cards, Open-End Credit	Defendant's Requests for Production of Documents in Dischargeability Case Based on Credit Card Fraud	Bankr App. G #109
Credit Discrimination	Fair Credit Reporting Act, to Furnisher	FCR Supp. App. I.3.3
	Fair Housing Case, Segregation, Dual Market	CD App. G.4
Credit Reporting	Credit Reporting Agency	CLP9 Ch. 9.5.7
	Creditor, in Credit Report Case	CLP9 Ch. 9.5.5, 9.5.6
	Failure to Correct Credit Report Error	CLP9 Ch. 9.3.2.4
	Fair Credit Reporting Act, Users	FCR App. I.3.1
	Fair Credit Reporting Act, Subpoena Custodian of Records	FCR App. I.4.1
	Fair Credit Reporting Act, Metro 2	FCR App. I.3.2
	FCRA, Document Request, Permissible Purpose	FCR CD Extra
	Subpoenas for Production of Documents	CLP9 Ch. 9.5.8, 9.5.9, 9.5.10
Debt Collection, General	Invasion of Privacy, Intentional Infliction, Severe Distress, Second Request for Production of Documents (AL)	CLP10 Ch. 5.8
	Invasion of Privacy, Intentional Infliction, Severe Distress, Third Request for Production of Documents (AL)	CLP10 Ch. 5.9
	Invasion of Privacy, Intentional Infliction, Severe Distress, Request for Production of Documents (AL)	CLP10 Ch. 5.6

		Invasion of Privacy, Intentional Infliction, Severe Distress, Fourth Request for Production of Documents (AL)	CLP10 Ch. 5.1
	Installment Loans, Closed-End Credit, Usury	Refund Anticipation Loan Debt Collection Case, to Tax Preparation Firm	COC Supp. App. G.5
		Refund Anticipation Loan Debt Collection Case, to Bank	COC Supp. App. G.3
	Mortgages, Predatory Loans, Foreclosures	Request for Production of Predatory Lender's Loan Documents and Policies (OR)	CLP10 Ch. 14.2
	Truth in Lending	Fair Credit Billing Act	TIL App. F.5
		Truth in Lending	TIL App. F.3
Discovery, Requests for Admissions	*Auto Credit, Leases, Repos, Deficiencies*	Repossession Vehicle Valuation after Repossession	Repo App. E.5
	Auto Fraud	Odometer Fraud	Auto App. H.1.4
		Undisclosed Damage History	Auto App. H.2.4
	Auto Warranties, Lemon Law, Auto Repair	To Manufacturer New Car Lemon Case	Warr App. L.5.2
	Credit Cards, Open-End Credit	Defendant's Requests for Admissions in Dischargeability Case Based on Credit Card Fraud	Bankr App. G #111
	Credit Reporting	FCRA, Requests for Admissions	FCR CD Extra
	Debt Collection, General	Invasion of Privacy, Intentional Infliction, Severe Distress, Admissions (AL)	CLP10 Ch. 5.5
	Installment Loans, Closed-End Credit, Usury	Small Loan Usury	COC App. E.3
Discovery, Depositions	*Arbitration*	Affidavits Indicating Hours and Hourly Rates in AAA and NAF Arbitrations	Arbit CD Extra
		Affidavits—AAA Conflict of Interest	Arbit CD Extra
		American Arbitration Association, Employee Depositions, Affidavits—AAA Procedures, Costs	Arbit CD Extra
		Deposition Notice, Bank's Relationship to National Arbitration Forum	Arbit App. D.2.4
		Deposition of Edward Anderson, National Arbitration Forum (Sept. 29, 2003)	Arbit CD Extra
		Subpoena for Document Production to National Arbitration Forum	Arbit App. D.2.5
	Auto Credit, Leases, Repos, Deficiencies	Deposition of Automobile Dealer F & I Director about Closing Deals and Yo-yo Sales (FL)	CLP10 Ch. 15.1
		Deposition of Automobile Dealer Sales Manager about Closing Deals and Yo-yo Sales (FL)	CLP10 Ch. 15.2

	Auto Fraud	Deposition (With Comments) of Business Manager Regarding Sale of a Rebuilt Wreck (MO)	CLP10 Ch. 18.3
		Deposition of Former Used Car Manager about the Resale of a Wrecked Car (MO)	CLP10 Ch. 18.2
		Deposition of Used Car Manager Regarding Resale of Wrecked Car (MO)	CLP10 Ch. 18.1
		Deposition Outline: Immediate, Remote Sellers, Undisclosed Wrecked Cars	Auto CD Extra
		Outline for Deposition of Car Dealer in Concealed Wreck Damage Case	Auto App. H.2.5
	Credit Reporting	Deposition of Consumer Reporting Agency Employee about Correcting Errors in a Credit File	CLP10 Ch. 11
		Deposition of Credit Reporting Agency Employee Regarding Changes in Information in the Credit File	CLP10 Ch. 10
		Deposition of Trans Union Employee—Reinvestigation Process and Procedures 2/25/03	FCR CD Extra
		Deposition of Trans Union Employee— Reinvestigation Process and Procedures 10/9/01	FCR CD Extra
		Deposition of Trans Union Employee—Reinvestigation Process, Procedures, Including Use of Quotas for Reinvestigating Disputes 1/9/03	FCR CD Extra
		Fair Credit Reporting Act, Sample Notice of Deposition	FCR App. I.4.2
	Debt Collection, General	Deposition of Collection Lawyer/Owner (CT)	CLP10 Ch. 3.2
		Deposition of Collection Lawyer (CT)	CLP10 Ch. 3.1
		Deposition of Debt Collection Employee Representing the Debt Collection Agency (TX)	CLP10 Ch. 8.2
		Deposition of FDCPA Class Representative	CLP10 Ch. 4.5
		Invasion of Privacy, Intentional Infliction, Severe Distress, Notice of Taking Deposition	CLP10 Ch. 5.7
		Invasion of Privacy, Intentional Infliction, Severe Distress, Deposition of Collection Agency Owner (AL)	CLP10 Ch. 5.12
		Invasion of Privacy, Intentional Infliction, Severe Distress, Deposition of Collection Agency Employee (AL)	CLP10 Ch. 5.11
	Debt Collection, Hospital	Deposition Outline, Hospital Employee Witness	CLP8 Ch. 4, XI
Discovery Motions	*Auto Fraud*	Consumer's Access to Other Cars Sold by Dealer	Auto App. H.5
	Credit Reporting	Compel Discovery with Supporting Memorandum	CLP9 Ch. 9.5.12, 9.5.13
		Discovery Briefs—Case Involving Settlement Issues Credit Reporting Agencies Identity Theft	CLP5 Ch. 1.2.3
		FCRA, Decision in *Zahran v. Trans Union*—Denial of Protective Order for Discovery Material	FCR CD Extra

		FCRA, Discovery Order	FCR CD Extra
	Debt Collection, General	To Compel Discovery, Fair Debt Collection Practices Act	CLP4 Ch. 4.2
	Mortgages, Predatory Loans, Foreclosures	Motion to Compel Discovery, Extend Time, and for Sanctions, Misrepresentation that Refinancing Would Lower Payments	CLP9 Ch. 7.1.2– 7.1.4
Pre-Trial Motions, Trial Practice	*Arbitration*	Affidavit of Edward F. Sherman — Importance of Class Action Remedy, *Sullivan v. QC Financial Servicers, Inc.*	Arbit CD Extra
		Opposition to Demurrer—Unconscionable Mandatory Arbitration Clauses in Consumer Credit Contracts	CLP5 Ch. 12.1.1
		Plaintiffs' Memoranda in Support of Motion for Preliminary Injunction, Long Distance Telephone Company's Arbitration Clause is Unconscionable	CLP8 Ch. 1.2
		Trial Briefs, Long Distance Telephone Company's Arbitration Clause is Unconscionable	CLP8 Ch. 1.3
	Auto Credit, Leases, Repos, Deficiencies	Expert Analysis, Car Dealer and Bank Incentives to Inflate Interest Rate on Non-Recourse Credit Sale	CLP10 Ch. 12.3
		Motion for Summary Judgment, Material Facts, Memorandum, Failure to Disclose that a Trade-in was Given in a Car Lease	CLP8 Ch. 5.2
	Auto Fraud	Auto Fraud, Sample Motions and Briefs (List)	Auto App. J
		Closing Argument to Jury, Federal Odometer Act	Auto App. I.5
		Expert Report of Professor Ian Ayres, Disparate Racial Impacts in Finance Charge Markups, NMAC	CD CD Extra
		Expert Report on Racial Impact of NMAC's Finance Charge Markup Policy by Mark Cohen, PhD.	CD CD Extra
		Jury Instruction Regarding Missing Evidence	Auto App. I.10
		Jury Instructions Automobile Odometer Fraud and Threat of Violent Repossession	CLP5 Ch. 3.4
		Jury Instructions in Odometer Case	Auto App. I.8
		Jury Instructions in Wrecked Car Case	Auto App. I.9
		Jury Instructions, Misrepresentation of Vehicle Characteristics (*MacArthur*)	Auto CD Extra
		Jury Instructions Undisclosed Sale of Salvaged vehicle	CLP2 Ch. 6.2.7
		Mediation Presentation: Undisclosed Sale of Lemon Buy-Back RV (OH)	CLP10 Ch. 2.1.9
		Motion for Preliminary Injunction (NMAC)	CD CD Extra
		Motion for Summary Judgment, Material Facts, Memorandum, Failure to Disclose that a Trade-in was Given in a Car Lease	CLP8 Ch. 5.2
		Motion in Limine and for Bifurcation	Auto App. I.7
		Opening Statement to Jury, Federal Odometer Act	Auto App. I.4

	Opening Statement to Jury Rebuilt Car Litigation (*Sloan*)	Auto CD Extra
	Outline for Questioning of Expert Witness on Condition of Vehicle	Auto App. I.6
	Plaintiff's Motion for Summary Judgment in "Spot Delivery" Case	FCR CD Extra
	Response to Motion to Dismiss and Plaintiffs' Motion for Partial Summary Judgment, FTC Holder Rule (*Potter*)	Auto CD Extra
	Special Verdict Form in Wrecked Car Case	Auto App. I.11
	Undisclosed Sale of Lemon Buy-Back RV Repair History, Trial Parts and Labor Comparison Chart (OH)	CLP10 Ch. 2.1.10
	Verdict Form, Misrepresentation of Vehicle Characteristics (*MacArthur*)	Auto CD Extra
	Voir Dire Outline, Rebuilt Wreck	Auto App. I.3
	Voir Dire, Wreck Damage Case	Auto App. I.2
Auto Warranties, Lemon Law, Auto Repair	Closing Argument Before a Jury and Excerpt of Rebuttal	Warr App. M.7
	Direct Examination of Consumer's Expert	Warr App. M.6
	Direct Examination Outline: Buyer in Case Involving Breach of Warranty, Fraud	Warr Supp. App. M.6a
	Jury Instructions: Express Warranty, Merchantability, Revocation and Magnuson-Moss Warranty Act	Warr App. M.8.1
	Jury Instructions for Magnuson-Moss Warranty Act Claims	CLP5 Ch. 6.3
	Jury Instructions, Lemon Law	Warr App. M.8.4
	Jury Instructions: Rejection, Revocation, Merchantability, Fitness for a Particular Purpose and Disclaimer	Warr App. M.8.2
	Jury Instructions: Substantial Impairment and Shaken Faith Doctrine	Warr App. M.8.3
	Jury Instructions: Title, Vehicle Defects (OH)	Warr CD Extra
	Jury Instructions: Warranty	Warr App. M.8
	Jury Verdict Form, Automobile Lemon case: UCC, Magnuson-Moss Warranty Act, Michigan Lemon Law, Motor Vehicle Service and Repair Act, Misrepresentation, UDAP	CLP9 Ch. 8
	Motion to Enjoin Repossession (OH)	Warr CD Extra
	Motion to Exclude Discussion of Attorney Fees (CA)	Warr CD Extra
	Motion to Exclude Disparagement of Attorney (OH)	Warr CD Extra
	Opening Statement Before Jury	Warr App. M.5
	Pre-Trial Statement—New Car Case	Warr App. M.2
	Trial Brief, New Car Case	Warr App. M.3
	Verdict Form, Auto Lease (MI)	Warr CD Extra

	Verdict Form New Car Case	Warr App. M.9.2
	Verdict Form Used Car Case	Warr App. M.9.1
	Voir Dire, Car Warranty case	Warr App. M.4
Banking, Electronic Fund Transfers	Credit Union Wrongfully Setoff a Customer's Exempt Social Security Funds, Motion for Summary Judgment (D.N.M.)	CLP7 C.13.2
Credit Cards, Open-End Credit	Expert Analysis, Illusory Benefit of Secured Credit Card	CLP10 Ch. 12.2
	Opposition to Demurrer—Unconscionable Mandatory Arbitration Clauses in Consumer Credit Contracts	CLP5 Ch. 12.1.1
Credit Discrimination	Pre-Trial Order Including Jury Instructions in ECOA Notice Case (*Cleaver v. Greater Mid-Atlantic Finance Co., Inc.*)	CD CD Extra
	Reverse Redlining, Gender, Opposition to Defendant's Motions for Judgment on the Pleadings (*Eva v. Midwest National Mortgage Banc*)	CD CD Extra
	Reverse Redlining, Gender, Surreply in Opposition to 12(b)(6) Motions (*Eva v. Midwest National Mortgage Banc*)	CD CD Extra
	Segregation, Dual Housing Market, Fair Housing Act Violation, Opposing Motion for Summary Judgment (*Honorable v. The Easy Life Real Estate Systems*)	CD CD Extra
Credit Reporting	Closing Argument, Case Involving Accuracy and Reinvestigation	FCR CD Extra
	Confidentiality Order, FCRA	FCR App. I.6
	Cross-Examination of Trans Union Employee in Case Involving Accuracy and Reinvestigation, Pt. 2	FCR CD Extra
	Cross-Examination of Trans Union Employee in Case Involving Accuracy and Reinvestigation, Pt. 1	FCR CD Extra
	Expert Witness Report Regarding Mixed Credit Files	CLP10 Ch. 13.1
	FCRA, Jury Instructions—Maximum Possible Accuracy, Defamation	FCR CD Extra
	FCRA, Jury Instruction—Obtaining Credit Report Without Permissible Purpose (False Pretenses)	FCR CD Extra
	Joint Pretrial Order Proposal	CLP9 Ch. 9.6.11
	Jury Instructions, *Bryant* case: FCRA	FCR App. I.5.3
	Jury Instructions FCRA, Furnisher Reinvestigation, Impermissible Purpose	FCR App. I.5.5
	Jury Instructions, *Jones* case	FCR App. I.5.4
	Jury Instructions Punitive Damage Claims Against Credit Reporting Agencies and Creditors for Identity Theft	CLP5 Ch. 1.1.11
	Jury Instructions—Accuracy	FCR CD Extra
	Jury Instructions—Furnisher Reinvestigation	FCR CD Extra
	Memorandum Attacking Credit Reporter's Affidavit	CLP9 Ch. 9.6.10

	Motion for Summary Judgment in a Merged Report Case	CLP9 Ch. 9.6.9
	Motion to Strike Answer, Memo—Preemption	CLP9 Ch. 9.6.1
	Opposition to Motion to Join Identity Thief, Memo	CLP9 Ch. 9.6.2
	Opposition to Motion to Compel Arbitration in Credit Reporting Case: No Privity	CLP9 Ch. 9.3.2.3
	Opposition to Summary Judgment: Disputed Facts, Statute of Limitations	CLP9 Ch. 9.6.7
	Plaintiff's Closing Arguments to the Jury: FCRA	FCR App. I.5.2
	Plaintiff's Direct Testimony Relating to Damages FCRA suit	FCR App. I.5.1
	Plaintiff's Motion for Summary Judgment in "Spot Delivery" Case	FCR CD Extra
	Statement of Material Facts Opposing Summary Judgment	CLP9 Ch. 9.6.8
	Transcript of Jury Instructions, FCRA	FCR Supp. App. I.5.6
	Trial Transcript—Furnisher Reinvestigation	FCR CD Extra
Debt Collection, General	Confusing Debt Validation Notice, FDCPA, Motions for Partial Summary Judgment	CLP7 Ch. 7.6
	Credit Union Wrongfully Setoff a Customer's Exempt Social Security Funds, Motion for Summary Judgment	CLP7 C.13.2
	Jury Instructions in an Abusive Debt Collection and Repossessions Case	CLP10 Ch. 19
	Jury Voir Dire Questions, Jury Instructions, and Proposed Verdict Sheet—Fair Debt Collections Practices Act	FDC App. J.2
	Motion for Partial Summary Judgment, Memorandum, Seizure of Exempt Funds in Bank Account	CLP8 Ch. 2.3
	Motion in Limine, Memorandum, to Preclude Discussion of Attorney Fees, Fair Debt Collection	FDC App. J.5.2
	Motion in Limine, Memorandum, to Preclude Attacks on Plaintiff's Character, Fair Debt Collection	FDC App. J.5.1
	Motion to Strike Affirmative Defenses, Fair Debt Collection Practices Act	CLP7 Ch. 4.2
	Pretrial Order, Fair Debt Collection Practices Act	FDC App. J.3
Debt Collection, Hospital	Jury Instructions, Closing Argument, Hospital Suit	CLP8 Ch. 4, XIII
	Medicaid Patient, Illegal Collection, FDCPA, Motion for Summary Judgment	CLP7 Ch. 8.1
	Motion for Summary Judgment, Hospital Suit	CLP8 Ch. 4, XII
	Motion to Dismiss Hospital Collection Suit	CLP8 Ch. 4, IV
	Trial Memorandum, Hospital Collection Suit	CLP8 Ch. 4, XIII
	Voir Dire Questions, Hospital Collection Suit	CLP8 Ch. 4, XIII

Debt Collection, Student Loans	Motion for Preliminary Injunction in Case Challenging Denial of Disability Discharge	Stud CD Extra
	Motion for Preliminary Relief in Complaint to Enjoin Discriminatory Denial of Guaranteed Student Loan	Bankr App. G #122
	Proposed Order for Preliminary Relief in Complaint to Enjoin Discriminatory Denial of Guaranteed Student Loan	Bankr App. G #123
Deceptive Practices, Fraud, RICO	Application for Temporary Restraining Order, Befriending Scam	CLP3 Ch. 1.2.2
	Closing Argument in Fraudulent Door to Door Sale of Satellite Dishes	CLP9 Ch. 18
	Expert Witness Affidavit, Corporate Identity Home Improvement Fraud, Agency $28 Million Punitive Damages Award for Bank's Involvement	CLP1 Ch. 5.6
Installment Loans, Closed-End Credit, Usury	Affidavit: Broker's Fee as a Hidden Finance Charge	COC App. E.5
	Affidavit: Interest Calculation Broker Fee Usury	COC App. E.5
	Expert Report on the Economic Cost of Debt Consolidation	COC App. E.6.2
	Expert Report on the Spiraling Costs and Profits to Lenders Due to Multiple Refinancings	COC App. E.6.3
	Expert Testimony in *Besta v. Beneficial Finance*—Insurance Packing	COC App. E.6.1
	Jury Instructions in Case Alleging Fraud by Mortgage Lender and by Investment Banker Who Securitized the Paper	COC CD Extra
	Motion for Summary Judgment: RESPA, Unearned Referral Fee, Delta Funding, PA	COC Supp. App. H.1
	Verdict Form, *Austin v Chisick, Lehman Brothers, MBIA*	COC CD Extra
Mobile Homes, Landlord-Tenant	Motion for Relief from Stay by Tenant to Raise Counterclaims to Eviction	Bankr App. G #146
Mortgages, Predatory Loans, Foreclosures	Action Challenging MERS as Plaintiff	Repo Supp. App. O.6
	Affidavit of Homeowner	TIL Supp. App. E.6.3
	Expert Analysis, Direct Damages to Consumer Caused by Recording of Foreclosure	CLP10 Ch. 12.1
	Expert Report— HOEPA Predatory Mortgage Lending Abuses, by Gary Klein	CLP6 Ch. 1.5
	Expert Witness Affidavit Corporate Identity Home Improvement Fraud, Agency $28 Million Punitive Damages Award for Bank's Involvement	CLP1 Ch. 5.6
	Expert's Exhibits—Interest Rates, Home's Loss of Value, by Mark Leymaster	CLP9 Ch. 1.2

		Proposed Findings of Fact, TILA Rescission, Fraud Claims in Bankruptcy Court	CLP4 Ch. 14.16
		Summary Judgment Memoranda and Draft Order, Mortgage Loan Claims for TIL Rescission and for Illegal Yield Spread Premium	CLP9 Ch. 19.4.2, 19.5
		Truth in Lending Jury Instructions, TIL Disclosures	TIL App. G.3
		Truth in Lending Jury Instructions, Finance Charge	TIL App. G.4
		Truth in Lending Jury Instructions, General	TIL App. G.2
	Utilities, Energy	Long Distance Phone Overcharges, Opposition to Motion to Dismiss	CLP7 Ch.2.2
		Motion for Modification of Security Deposit for Utility Service in Bankruptcy	Bankr App. G #43
Briefs, Memoranda	*Arbitration*	Arbitration Costs, Damage Limitations, and Unconscionability, Reply Brief	Arbit App. E.2
		Arbitration Costs, Damage Limitations, and Unconscionability, Opening Brief	Arbit App. E.1
		Arbitration, Employment Contract, Forum in Philippines is Unconscionable, *Bautisa v. Star Cruises and Norwegian Cruise Line, Ltd.* Amicus brief, Eleventh Circuit	Arbit CD Extra
		Arbitration, Unconscionable High Costs; Waiver By: Company's Breach of Agreement, *Sanderson Farms, Inc. v. Gatlin*, Miss. Sup. Ct.	Arbit CD Extra
		BDO Seidman LLP v. Hottle, Amicus Brief, CT Sup. Ct., Arbitration Clause Is Unenforceable If Three Accounting Partners Resolve All Disputes Between Firm and Employees	Arbit CD Extra
		Boghos v. Certain Underwriters at Lloyds, Brief Cal App. Ct, Disability Insurer's Arbitration Clause Foreclosed Suit on Failure to Pay Claims; Unconscionable Based on Non-mutuality and Cost Requirements.	Arbit CD Extra
		Boghos v. Certain Underwriters at Lloyd's of London, Appellee Answer Brief, Insurer's Arbitration Clause Unconscionable, Excessive Costs to Disability Claimant, Insurer Consented to Court Jurisdiction over Coverage Claims, CA Sup. Ct.	Arbit CD Extra
		Car Lease Arbitration Clause Attacked as Not Binding or Unconscionable	CLP7 Ch. 12.1
		Cardegna v. Buckeye Check Cashing, Inc.—Reply Brief Fla Sup Ct since Payday Lending Contract Is Criminal under State Law and Void *Ab Initio*, an Arbitration Clause Embedded in the Contract May Not Be Enforced	Arbit CD Extra
		Cardegna v. Buckeye Check Cashing, Inc. Opening Brief Fla Sup Ct. Since Payday Lending Contract Is Criminal under State Law and Void *Ab Initio*, an Arbitration Clause Embedded in the Contract May Not Be Enforced	Arbit CD Extra

McDougle v. Silvernell, (Ala. Sup.Ct.), Brief of Appellees: Arbitration Clause Unilaterally Added to Agreement after Consummation	Arbit CD Extra
Mintze v. American General Finance, Inc.—(3d Cir.) Brief: Bankruptcy Code Supercedes FAA	Arbit CD Extra
Nagrampa v. MailCoups, Inc.—(9th Cir.) Reply Brief: Requiring Arbitration in Boston, Excessive Costs, and Appear Before the American Arbitration Association is Unconscionable under California Law.	Arbit CD Extra
Nagrampa v. MailCoups, Inc.—(9th Cir.). Brief: Requiring Arbitration in Boston, Excessive Costs, and Appear Before the American Arbitration Association Is Unconscionable under California Law	Arbit CD Extra
Objections to Magistrate's Recommendations, Truth in Lending Rescission for HOEPA Violations Argued to be Not Subject to Arbitration	CLP8 Ch. 11.2
Opposing Compulsory Arbitration, Home Repair Fraud	CLP4 Ch. 1.4
Raymond James Financial Services, Inc. v. Saldukas (FL Sup Ct), Brief, Party Need Not Prove Prejudice Before it Can Establish Waiver of Other Party's Right to Compel Arbitration	Arbit CD Extra
Sanderson Farms, Inc. v. Gatlin, Miss. Sup. Ct. Supplemental Authority: High Arbitration Costs as Grounds to Void Arbitration Agreement	Arbit CD Extra
Trial Brief, Class Action, Arbitration Issues Unconscionabity in Formation and Terms of Arbitration Agreement, *Ting v. AT&T*, (N.D.Ca)	Arbit CD Extra
Unconscionability Based on Bias of National Arbitration Forum, *Toppings v. Meritech Mortgage Services, Inc.*, W. Va. Sup. Ct.	Arbit App. H
Unconscionability Based on Bias of National Arbitration Forum, *Toppings v. Meritech Mortgage Services, Inc.*, W.Va. Sup. Ct., Reply Brief	Arbit CD Extra
Unconscionability of Arbitration Clause, Brief Opposing Petition for Writ of Certiorari *American General Finance, Inc. v. Branch*, Ala. Sup Ct.	Arbit CD Extra
Unconscionability of Arbitration Clauses Restricting Class Actions, Amicus Brief: *Hayes v. County Bank* (NY)	Arbit App. F.3
Unconscionability of Arbitration Clauses Restricting Class Actions, Reply Brief (CA)	Arbit App. F.2
Unconscionability of Arbitration Clauses Restricting Class Actions, Opening Brief (CA)	Arbit App. F.1
Unconscionable Mandatory Arbitration Clauses in Consumer Credit Contracts	CLP5 Ch. 12.1.2

	Wells, et al. v. Chevy Chase Bank, F.S.B., et al. (Md. Ct. of App.), Arbitration Clause Added as a "Bill Stuffer"; Unconscionability; "Loser Pays Rule," Excessive Arbitration Fees, and Denial of Class Action Remedy (Two Briefs)	Arbit CD Extra
Auto Credit, Leases, Repos, Deficiencies	Appellate Brief: FTC Holder Rule Preserves Consumer Claims That Are Less Than Rescission	CLP8 Ch. 21.1
	Brief: Car Dealers' Truth in Lending Disclosures Must Be Given to the Consumer Before the Auto Sale Contract Is Signed	CLP8 Ch. 16.1
	Car Lease Arbitration Clause Attacked As Not Binding or Unconscionable	CLP7 Ch. 12.1
	Memoranda—Auto Contract Clause Choosing Distant Forum and Arguing Truth In Lending Statute of Limitations Tolled by Soldiers' and Sailors' Relief Act.	CLP8 Ch. 8.1
	Repossession Delay Discharges Obligation of Cosigner on Car Sale UCC	CLP6 Ch. 13.2
	Summary Judgment: Misrepresenting APR in Car Financing; Yield Spread Premium: TILA, UDAP, RISA, Car Titling Statute (MI)	CLP9 Ch. 2.1
Auto Fraud	Attorney Fees, Treble Damages Should be Recoverable on Dealer's Surety Bond: Appellant's Brief (*Helper*)	Auto CD Extra
	Attorney Fees, Treble Damages Should Be Recoverable on Dealer's Surety Bond: Appellant's Reply Brief (*Helper*)	Auto CD Extra
	Auto Dealer Interest Markups, Race Discrimination, ECOA, Nissan MAC	CLP7 Ch. 1.1, 1.2
	Auto Spot Delivery, Waiver Agreement Void, Odometer Act Violation	CLP7 Ch. 5.4
	Automobile Odometer Fraud and Threat of Violent Repossession, Summary Judgment Motion Brief	CLP5 Ch. 3.3
	Concealment of Address of Prior Owner Which Would Show Rough Use (*Yazzie v. Amigo Chevrolet, Inc.*)	CLP9 Ch. 5.4
	Dealer's Failure to Provide Title Certificate with Prior Owner's Address is Odometer Act Disclosure Violation, Summary Judgment Brief (*Yazzie*)	Auto CD Extra
	Dealer's Failure to Provide Title Certificate with Prior Owner's Address Is Odometer Act Disclosure Violation, Summary Judgment Reply Brief (*Yazzie*)	Auto CD Extra
	In Opposition to NMAC's Motion for Summary Judgment, Race Discrimination in Auto Finance Markup, ECOA	CD CD Extra
	In Support of Motion to Amend Complaint Auto Sales Fraud	CLP6 Ch. 9.2
	Opposing Motion to Dismiss in "Spot Delivery" Case	FCR CD Extra

	Salvaged Auto Fraud, Summary Judgment	CLP5 Ch. 6.1
	Summary Judgment: Misrepresenting APR in Car Financing; Yield Spread Premium: TILA, UDAP, RISA, car titling statute (MI)	CLP9 Ch. 2.1
	Undisclosed Sale of Salvaged vehicle	CLP2 Ch. 6.2.6
Banking, Electronic Fund Transfers	Amicus Brief: Banker's Setoff of Social Security Funds in Checking Accounts Violates Exemption in Social Security Act (9th Circuit)	CLP8 Ch. 17.1
	Bank Set-Off of Exempt Social Security Funds for Debt to Bank, Appellate Brief	CBPL CD Extra
	Bank Set-Off of Exempt Social Security Funds for Debt to Bank, Reply Brief	CBPL CD Extra
	Credit Union Wrongfully Setoff a Customer's Exempt Social Security Funds, Appellate Brief (D.N.M.)	CLP7 Ch. 13.5
	Creditor Garnishment of Exempt Social Security Funds	CBPL CD Extra
	West Virginia v. TeleCheck, Response to Amicus Brief	CBPL CD Extra
Credit Cards, Open-End Credit	In Support of Class Certification TIL, UDAP, and Breach of Contract Case—Credit Card Issuer's Failure to Refund Credit Balance (*Coe*)	CCA App. L.2
	Reply Memoranda in Support of Class Certification TIL, UDAP, and Breach of Contract Case—Credit Card Issuer's Failure to Refund Credit Balance (*Coe*)	CCA App. M.1
	Unconscionable Mandatory Arbitration Clauses in Consumer Credit Contracts	CLP5 Ch. 12.1.2
Credit Discrimination	Auto Dealer Interest Markups, Race Discrimination, ECOA, Nissan MAC	CLP7 Ch. 1.1, 1.2
	Auto Dealerships Alleging Race Discrimination and Rebate Theft	CLP3 Ch. 9.2.8
	Automobile Financing, Race Discrimination in Mark-Up, Amicus Brief of United States (*Cason v. Nissan Motors Acceptance Corp.*)	CD CD Extra
	Opposition to Finance Company's Motion to Dismiss in ECOA Notice Case (*Smith v. Regional Acceptance Corp.*)	CD CD Extra
	Reverse Redlining Case, Amicus Brief of United States (*Hargraves v. Capital City Mortgage Corp.*)	CD CD Extra
Credit Reporting	Excerpts from Chapter on Damages Resulting from Credit Reporting Errors	CLP10 Ch. 13.2
	Fair Credit Reporting Act Furnisher Liability Brief, Statute of Limitations	CLP10 Ch. 1.2
	Fair Credit Reporting Act Furnisher Liability Brief, Failure to Investigate	CLP10 Ch. 1.1

	Fair Credit Reporting Act Furnisher Liability Reply Brief, Statute of Limitations	CLP10 Ch. 1.3
	FCRA Unauthorized Release of Credit Report After Imposter Applied for Credit	CLP6 Ch. 10.3
	In Opposition to Dismissal: Preemption, Tort Claims, UDAP	CLP9 Ch. 9.6.4, 9.6.5, 9.6.6
	In Opposition to Dismissal/Summary Judgment— Unauthorized Access of Ex-Spouse to Credit Report	CLP9 Ch. 9.6.3
	Opposing Alleged Settlement Credit Reporting	CLP5 Ch. 1.2.6
	Opposing Defendant's Motion for Summary Judgment—FCRA § 1681s-2(b) (Failure to Conduct Reasonable Reinvestigation)	FCR CD Extra
	Opposing Motion for Judgment as Matter of Law in § 1681s-2(b) (Failure to Conduct Reasonable Reinvestigation)	FCR CD Extra
	Opposing Motion for Judgment as Matter of Law— FCRA § 1681s-2(b) (Failure to Conduct Reasonable Reinvestigation)	FCR CD Extra
	Opposing Motion to Dismiss Credit Repair Organization Statute against Car Dealer	CLP6 Ch. 2.4
	Opposing Motion to Dismiss in "Spot Delivery" Case	FCR CD Extra
Debt Collection, General	Appellate Brief: FTC Holder Rule Preserves Consumer Claims That Are Less Than Rescission	CLP8 Ch. 21.1
	Arguing that FDCPA Does Not Require Conduct to Be Intentional to Violate the Act	CLP4 Ch. 6.1
	Assignment of Debt After First Collector Lost Collection Suit, FDCPA	CLP7 Ch. 9.1
	Collection from Unobligated Spouse in Distant Forum, FDCPA	CLP7 Ch. 8.2
	Credit Union Wrongfully Setoff a Customer's Exempt Social Security Funds, Appellate Brief	CLP7 Ch. 13.5
	Debt Collector Is Not Exempt Governmental Official Just Because it Collects Debts for Government	CLP7 Ch. 9.3
	Excessive Charges and False Threats, Reply Memorandum for Partial Summary Judgment (CT)	CLP10 Ch. 3.4
	Excessive Charges and False Threats, Motion for Partial Summary Judgment (CT)	CLP10 Ch. 3.3
	Expert Witness Report on Fair Debt Collection Practices Act Damages; Qualifications	CLP8 Ch. 10.1, 10.2
	FCDPA Collecting Illegal Charges and the Bona Fide Error Defense Under the Fair Debt Collection Practices Act	CLP6 Ch. 12.1
	FDCPA: Summary Judgment Memoranda: Collector Pretended to Be Creditor; State Debt Collection Statute	CLP9 Ch. 3.3
	Illegal Charges by Private Collector of Property Tax	CLP9 Ch. 11.1

	In Support of Motion for Partial Summary Judgment Fair Debt Collection Practices Act	FDC App. J.1
	Invasion of Privacy, Intentional Infliction, Severe Distress, FDCPA, Memorandum of Law in Opposition to Summary Judgment (AL)	CLP10 Ch. 5.13
	Jurisdiction Exists Where Debt Collector Purposely Contacted State Resident	CLP7 Ch. 8.3
	Memoranda in Support of Motion to Compel Discovery of Operating Manual and Prices Paid to Purchase Debts	CLP8 Ch. 14.2
	Memoranda—Auto Contract Clause Choosing Distant Forum	CLP8 Ch. 8.3
	Prejudgment Garnishment of Bank Account Violates FDCPA	CLP7 Ch. 9.2
	Sale of Claim, after Prior Suits on Claim were Dismissed with Prejudice, Was FDCPA Violation	CLP9 Ch. 10
	Trial Brief, Fair Debt Collection Practices Act	FDC App. J.4
	Unlicensed Collecting, Contacting Represented Consumer, Excessive Amount, Time Barred Debt; Motion for Partial Summary Judgment (CT)	CLP10 Ch. 3.5
Debt Collection, Student Loans	Challenging Student Loan Garnishment and Other Collection Procedures, Appellant's Reply Brief	Stud CD Extra
	Challenging Student Loan Garnishment and Other Collection Procedures, Appellant's Brief	Stud CD Extra
	False Certification Discharge: Memo, Motion for Summary Judgment and in Opposition to Defendant's Motion for Summary Judgment	Stud CD Extra
	Reply Brief in Support of Motion for Summary Judgment, Challenge to Offset of Social Security for Old Student Loans (E.D.Mich)	Stud CD Extra
	Supplemental Summary Judgment Brief in Action Challenging Federal Benefit Offsets to Collect Old Student Loans	Stud CD Extra
	U.S. Defendant's Memorandum Supporting Motion to Dismiss Action Challenging Federal Collection Procedures, Calculation of Collection Fees (E.D. Cal.)	Stud CD Extra
	U.S. Defendant's Reply to Plaintiffs' Supplemental Brief—Challenge to Offset of Social Security for Old Student Loans (E.D.Mich)	Stud CD Extra
Deceptive Practices, Fraud, RICO	In Opposition to Defendant's Motion to Dismiss Predatory Mortgage Lending Involving Multiple Parties: RICO, TILA	CLP1 Ch. 7.5
	In Support of Class Certification TIL, UDAP, and Breach of Contract Case—Credit Card Issuer's Failure to Refund Credit Balance (*Coe*)	CCA App. L.2

Fringe Lenders: Pay Day Loans, Auto Pawn, Rent to Own, Refund Anticipation Loans	Injunction Opinion Auto Pawn Business Subject to Regulation under State Credit Statutes	CLP3 Ch. 4.2.4
	Payday loans, Amicus brief—Rental of bank charter, Goleta National Bank, Ace Cash Express (OH)	COC Supp. App. F.7
	Predatory Lending: History of Rise of High Cost Lending Cash Advances as Alleged Assignments of Tax Refunds, Amicus Brief	COC App. F.4
	Re Injunction, and Opinion: Pay Day Loan—Check Advance Transaction is Loan Under State Finance Act	CLP3 Ch. 4.1.3
	Rent to Own, Opposition to Motion for Summary Judgment	CLP2 Ch. 8.4
	Response to Motion to Dismiss—Payday Loan Suit	COC App. F.3
Installment Loans, Closed-End Credit, Usury	Payday loans, Amicus brief—Rental of bank charter, Goleta National Bank, Ace Cash Express (OH)	COC Supp. App. F.7
	Predatory Lending: History of Rise of High Cost Lending; Cash Advances as Alleged Assignments of Tax Refunds; Amicus Brief	COC App. F.4
	Repossession Delay Discharges Obligation of Co-signer on Car Sale UCC	CLP6 Ch. 13.2
	Response to Motion to Dismiss—Payday Loan Suit	COC App. F.3
Insurance	Adequacy of Capitalization of Restructured Insurer of Environmental Hazards	CLP7 Ch. 15.1
	HMO Health Maintenance Organizations for Delay in Authorizing and Paying for Cancer Treatment	CLP6 Ch. 5.2
Mortgages, Predatory Loans, Foreclosures	In Opposition to Defendant's Motion to Dismiss Predatory Mortgage Lending Involving Multiple Parties RICO TILA	CLP1 Ch. 7.5
	Mandatory Arbitration Clause Lacked Mutuality	CLP5 Ch. 12.2
	Mortgage Lender: Fraud, HOEPA, TILA	CLP9 Ch. 1.3.1
	Opposing Mortgage Lender's Motion for Summary Judgment, TIL Rescission	CLP9 Ch. 1.4.1, 1.4.2
	Opposition and Affidavit to Summary Judgment, Misrepresentation that Refinancing Would Lower Payments	CLP9 Ch. 7.1.6–7.1.7
	OTS Brief—Changes to AMPTA Regulations	COC CD Extra
	Preemption Not Available to Assignee National Bank Where Original Lender Lacked Preemption Status	CLP7 Ch. 10.1
	Preliminary Injunction to Prevent Foreclosure of Mortgages, Failure to Credit Payments, Enjoin Illegal Fees	CLP9 Ch. 6.2
Truth in Lending	Brief: Car Dealers' Truth in Lending Disclosures Must Be Given to the Consumer Before the Auto Sale Contract is Signed	CLP8 Ch. 16.1

	Consumers' Memo of Law on Consumer's Unclean Hands and Burden of Proof for TIL Claim (OR)	CLP10 Ch. 14
	In Support of Plaintiff's Motion for Summary Judgement TILA Rescission Bankruptcy Court	CLP1 Ch. 8.5
	In Support of Preliminary Injunction—TILA Rescission in Bankruptcy Court	CLP1 Ch. 8.3
	Memoranda—Auto Contract Clause Choosing Distant Forum and Arguing Truth In Lending Statute of Limitations Tolled by Soldiers' and Sailors' Relief Act.	CLP8 Ch. 8.1
	Mortgage Lender: Fraud, HOEPA, TILA	CLP9 Ch. 1.3.1
	Objections to Magistrate's Recommendations, Truth in Lending Rescission for HOEPA Violations Argued to be Not Subject to Arbitration	CLP8 Ch. 11.2
	Opposing Mortgage Lender's Motion for Summary Judgment, TIL Rescission	CLP9 Ch. 1.4.1, 1.4.2
	Truth in Lending Rescission by Recoupment	CLP3 Ch. 8.1
Utilities, Energy	Brief Against Municipal Water Utility for Shutting off Water of Tenants Without Notice (OH)	CLP10 Ch. 17.2
	Illegal Charges by Private Collector of Water/Sewer Bills	CLP9 Ch. 11.3–11.4
	Reply Brief Against Municipal Water Utility for Shutting off Water of Tenants Without Notice (OH)	CLP10 Ch. 17.3
Post-Trial Motions, Orders, Attorney Fee Documents *Arbitration*	Motion to Vacate Arbitration Award New Car Lemon Arbitration (NY)	Warr CD Extra
	Proposed Order for Injunction, Brief, Long Distance Telephone Company's Arbitration Clause is Unconscionable	CLP8 Ch. 1.5
Auto Fraud	Petition for Award of Attorney Fees	Auto App. L.2
	Questions for Expert Witness on Attorney Fees	Auto App. L.3
Auto Warranties, Lemon Law, Auto Repair	Attorney Fees Bifurcation Issue Lemon Law case	CLP4 Ch. 15.25
	Brief Requesting Attorney Fee—Repossession Civil Rights Police Assistance	CLP5 Ch. 8.1
	Federal Limitation in *Buckhannon* Should Not Be Imposed on Preexisting State Statute Awarding Attorney Fees	CLP9 Ch. 15
	Motion to Treble Damage Award: UDAP, Warranty	Warr App. M.10
	Motion to Vacate Arbitration Award New Car Lemon Arbitration (NY)	Warr CD Extra
Credit Discrimination	Action Against Subprime Lender Alleging Discriminatory Overcharges by Affiliated Mortgage Brokers, Consent Decree (*U. S. v. Long Beach Mortgage Co.*)	CD CD Extra

	Action Alleging Discrimination in Use of Credit Score Overrides (*U. S. v. Deposit Guaranty National Bank*)	CD CD Extra
	Action Alleging Discriminatory Credit Score Thresholds (*U. S. v. Associates National Bank*)	CD CD Extra
	Action Alleging Redlining and Marketing Discrimination Consent Decree (*U.S. v. Decatur FSLA*)	CD CD Extra
	Action Alleging Redlining By Use of Correspondent Lenders (*U. S. v. Albank, FSB*)	CD CD Extra
	ECOA and FHA Case Alleging Bank Refused to Lend to Native Americans, Consent Decree (*United States v. Blackpipe State Bank*)	CD CD Extra
	ECOA and Regulation B violations (*Franklin Acceptance*); Consent Decree	CD CD Extra
	Insurance Redlining (*United States v. Nationwide Mutual Insurance Company*); Consent Decree	CD CD Extra
	Redlining and Adverse Impact of Mortgage Lender's Business Practices, Consent Decree (*United States v. Chevy Chase Federal Savings Bank*)	CD CD Extra
	Subprime Lender Violation of FHA, ECOA, RESPA, TILA, Settlement Agreement (*United States v. Delta Funding Corp. and Delta Financial Corp.*)	CD CD Extra
Credit Reporting	Attorney Fee Motion Punitive Damage Claims Against Credit Reporting Agencies and Creditors for Identity Theft	CLP5 Ch. 1.1.14
	Consent Agreement with Credit Repair Agency—*FTC v. NCS Credit Network, Inc.*	FCR App. H.5
	Consent Agreements with Resellers of Consumer Reports: *First American Real Estate Solutions CREDCO*	FCR App. H.4.3
	Consent Agreements with Resellers of Consumer Reports: *I.R.S.C. Consent Order*	FCR App. H.4.2
	Consent Agreements with Resellers of Consumer Reports: *Inter-fact*	FCR App. H.4.1
	Consent Decree, FCRA, *United States v. Performance Capital Management*, Furnishers of Information	FCR CD Extra
	Consent Decree, FCRA, *United States v. DC Credit Services*	FCR CD Extra
	Equifax Enforcement Orders Excerpts from *In re Equifax, Inc.*	FCR App. H.2.2
	Equifax Enforcement Orders, Equifax Agreement	FCR App. H.2.3
	Equifax Enforcement Orders, *In re Equifax*	FCR App. H.2.5
	Equifax Enforcement Orders, *In re Equifax* (VT)	FCR App. H.2.6
	Equifax Enforcement Orders, *In re Equifax Credit Information Services, Inc.*, Analysis of Proposed Consent Order to Aid Public Comment	FCR App. H.2.4.2

	Equifax Enforcement Orders, *In re Equifax Credit Information Services, Inc.,* Agreement Containing Consent Order to Cease and Desist	FCR App. H.2.4.1
	Equifax Enforcement Orders, *US v. Equifax* (telephone access)	FCR App. H.2.5
	Experian Enforcement Orders FTC v. TRW now Experian], Inc.	FCR App. H.1.2
	Experian Enforcement Orders, *TRW Inc. now Experian] v. Morales*	FCR App. H.1.3
	Experian Enforcement Orders, *US v. Experian* (telephone access)	FCR App. H.1.4
	FCRA, Post Trial Motion—Opposition to Motion for JMOL, New Trial and Remittitur	FCR CD Extra
	FCRA, Settlement Agreement And Release	FCR CD Extra
	FTC Consent Order Against Quicken	FCR Supp. App. H.6
	FTC Enforcement Action Against Minor for Violation of Gramm-Leach-Bliley Act	FCR Supp. App. H.7
	FTC Settlement with Credit Repair Organization, ICR Services, Inc.	FCR CD Extra
	FTC v. Information Search Inc., Gramm-Leach-Bliley Act	FCR CD Extra
	Trans Union Enforcement Orders, *In re Trans Union Credit Information Co.* 102 F.T.C. 1109, 1121 (1983).	FCR App. H.3.2
	Trans Union Enforcement Orders, *In re Trans Union Corp.*	FCR App. H.3.4
	Trans Union Enforcement Orders, *In re Trans Union* (Targeted marketing lists)	FCR App. H.3.5
	Trans Union Enforcement Orders *U.S. v. Trans Union* (Consent Decree)	FCR App. H.3.6
	Trans Union Enforcement Orders, *Alabama v. Trans Union*	FCR App. H.3.3
	Trans Union Enforcement Orders, *In re Trans Union* (FTC Commission Opinion)	FCR App. H.3.7
	United States of America v. Equifax Information Services, Inc.	FCR Supp. App. H.8
Debt Collection, General	Application for Order of Contempt Against Check Collector (CA)	CLP10 Ch. 6.1
	Attorney Fees Motion, Memoranda: Where Offer of Judgment Silent, Fees Larger than Consumer's Recovery are Needed for Private Enforcement of FDCPA	CLP9 Ch. 14
	Challenging the Amount of Attorney Fees Awarded, Fair Debt Collection Practices Act	CLP4 Ch. 4.3
	Costs Should Not Be Taxed Against Consumer Who Lost FDCPA Suit	CLP7 Ch. 8.4
	Declaration in Support of Award of Attorney Fees, Fair Debt Collection Practices Act	FDC App. K.2

Mortgages, Predatory Loans, Foreclosures	Consumers' Response to Post-Trial Motions on Punitive Damages and Consumers' Unclean Hands (OR)	CLP10 Ch. 14.7
	Ex Parte Injunction to Stay Foreclosure	TIL Supp. E.6.4
	Judgment Home Improvement Fraud, Agency $28 Million Punitive Damages Award for Bank's Involvement	CLP1 Ch. 5.8
	Motion to Dispense with Bond or Security Requirement	TIL Supp. E.6.5
	Order Waiving Bond	TIL Supp. E.6.6
Truth in Lending	Attorney Fees Motion with Memorandum of Law and Attorney's Affidavit in Settled Truth in Lending Case	CLP1 Ch. 11.1
	Attorney Fees Petition for Successful Appeal of TIL Decision *(Rodash)*	CLP1 Ch. 11.3
	Expert's Affidavit in Case Seeking Appellate Attorney Fees *(Rodash)*	CLP1 Ch. 11.5
	Jury Instructions Proposed on Fraud and TIL Claims (OR)	CLP10 Ch. 14.6
	Legal Services Corp. Interpretation—Ability of LSC-Funded Offices to Co-Counsel with Private Attorney Seeking Attorney Fees (1999)	TIL CD Extra
	Legal Services Corp. Further Interpretation—Ability of LSC-Funded Offices to Co-Counsel with Private Attorney Seeking Attorney Fees (2003)	TIL CD Extra
	Order for Partial Summary Judgment for the Plaintiff Rescinding Mortgage Declaring Debt Unsecured Pursuant to TILA	CLP1 Ch. 8.7
	Order to Dismiss Overdraft Protection Complaint	TIL CD Extra
Class Actions, Articles	Appeal of Class Action Settlement: *Devlin v. Scardelletti* and Some Unanswered Questions, by Lisa Mezzetti, Margaret Farrell, Ashley Kushner	CCA CD Extra
	"Attorney Reports on the Impact of *Amchem* and *Ortiz* on Choice of a Federal or State Forum in Class Action Litigation: A Report to the Advisory Committee on Civil Rules Regarding a Case-based Survey of Attorneys," by Thomas E. Willging, Shannon R. Wheatman: Federal Judicial Center (2004)	CCA CD Extra
	"Effects of *Amchem/Ortiz* on the Filing of Federal Class Actions: Report to the Advisory Committee on Civil Rules," by Bob Niemic, Tom Willging: Federal Judicial Center (2002)	CCA CD Extra
	"Lawyer Advertising on the Internet: Ethical Quagmires and Global Opportunities"	CLP4 Ch. 10.1
	"Practioners Update on Case Law Addressing Rule 23(f)," by Michael Malakoff and Erin Brady with *Kennedy v. United Health Care, Blyler v. Agee*	CCA CD Extra
	"Quantifying Notice Results in Class Actions: The *Daubert/Kumho* Mandate," by Katherine Kinsella	CCA CD Extra

		"Separating the Wheat from the Chaff: How to Identify and Evaluate a Potential Class Action Lawsuit"	CLP4 Ch. 9.1
		"Taming the Uncommon Issues: What Role Should Subclasses Play in Rule 23(b)(3) Certification?"	CLP4 Ch. 9.2
		"The Truth, the Whole Truth, at this Point in Time: Lessons in Class Action Settlement Communications and the Infant Formula Settlements," by Richard Redfern	CCA CD Extra
		"Thoughts and Comments on Hybrid Class Actions; State v. National Certifications; Releases; and Cy Pres Remedies," by O. Rand Bragg	CCA CD Extra
		NACA Consumer Class Action Guidelines	CCA App. B
	Arbitration	"Nuts and Bolts of Arbitrating a Class Action," by Lynn Shecter	CCA CD Extra
		"Trying to Protect the Class Action from Mandatory Arbitration," by Jean Sternlight	CCA CD Extra
Class Actions, Authorization to Represent		Class Action Retainer Agreements	CCA App. C.1
		Co-Counsel Agreement with Fixed Percentage Distribution of Attorney Fees	CCA App. C.3.2
		Co-Counsel Agreement with Pro-Rate Distribution of Attorney Fees	CCA App. C.3.3
		Named Plaintiff's Statement of Duty to the Class	CCA App. C.2
Class Actions, Complaints	*Arbitration*	Arbitration Issues: *Ting v. AT&T*, Violation of the Consumer Legal Remedies Act, Unfair Business Practices Act (CA)	Arbit App. C
	Auto Credit, Leases, Repos, Deficiencies	Auto Lease Early Termination UDAP	CLP1 Ch. 9.1
		Class Complaint for Altering FTC Used Car Sticker (OH)	CLP10 Ch. 2.4
		Consumer Leasing Act and Deceptive Practices Case—Car Lease (*Shepherd*)	CCA App. D.7
		Repossession Failure to Give Required Notice of Sale: RISA, UDAP	CLP6 Ch. 4.1
	Auto Fraud	Auto Dealer, Finance Company, Federal Odometer Act, Consumer Fraud Act	Auto App. K.1
		Auto Dealer Overcharged for Extended Warranties: UDAP, RISA	CLP6 Ch. 6.1
		Auto Dealerships Alleging Race Discrimination and Rebate Theft; Discovery	CLP3 Ch. 9.2.1
		Odometer Fraud, Breach of Contract (*Potter*) (Unabridged)	Auto CD Extra
		Odometer Fraud; FTC Holder Notice Triggers Bank's Class Liability for Dealer's Fraud	CLP1 Ch. 3.1

	Odometer Rollback, Class Complaint	AF 1998 App. H.1
	Used Car Churning Scheme; RICO; and Memorandum—Motion to Dismiss	CLP3 Ch. 9.3.1
Auto Warranties, Lemon Law, Auto Repair	Class Complaint for Padding Repair Bills (OH)	CLP10 Ch. 2.3
Banking, Electronic Fund Transfers	Bank Practices Leading to Increased Bounced Check Fees	CBPL CD Extra
	Bank Practices Leading to Increased Bounced Check Fees (Amended Class Complaint)	CBPL CD Extra
Bankruptcy	Taxing Agency for Filing Baseless Chapter 13 Proofs of Claim, Discovery; Consent Decree	CLP3 Ch. 7.2
	Unlawful Collection of Debts Discharged in Bankruptcy Sears	CLP5 Ch. 2.1.1
Credit Discrimination	American with Disabilities Act to Improve the Accessibility of a Concert Facility to Wheelchairs	CLP4 Ch. 16.1
	Challenging Yield Spread Auto Loan Pricing Structure as ECOA Violation (NMAC)	CD App. F.5
	ECOA Adverse Action Notice Violation (with Jury Demand)	CD App. F.4
	ECOA Cosigner Violation in Class Action	CD App. F.3
Credit Reporting	FCRA, Impermissible Access	FCR CD Extra
	FCRA, Insurance Company Obtains Credit Reports with Impermissible Purposes, under False Pretenses, and Fails to Provide Adverse Action Notice	FCR CD Extra
	Improper Use of Credit Scoring, Against Insurance Company	FCR CD Extra
	Raising Car Insurance Premium Based on Credit Report	CLP9 Ch. 9.4
Debt Collection, General	Bank's Debt Collection Suits in Distant Forum are Abuse of Process Unfair Trade Practice Due Process Violation	CLP6 Ch. 14.1
	Collection Agency Litigation Abuses; also Motion for Class Certification, Brief	CLP2 Ch. 11.2.1
	Fair Debt Collection Case Involving Cy Pres Remedy, also Motion for Class Certification, Order Certifying Class and Approving Final Settlement	CLP3 Ch. 3.1
	Fair Debt Collection Practices Act: Collection of Debt Which Expired by the Passage of Time	CLP8 Ch. 15.1
	False Threat of Foreclosure: FDCPA, UDAP	CLP6 Ch. 3.1
	FDCPA, UDAP, and Tort Claims for a Collection Agency's Seeking Attorney Fees and Engaging in Unauthorized Practice of Law	CLP8 Ch. 19.1
	Federal Fair Debt Collection Case (*Boddie*)	CCA App. D.4

	Motion to Compel Rule 26(a) Disclosures: Fair Debt Collection Practices Act: Collection of Debt Which Expired by the Passage of Time	CLP8 Ch. 15.4
Debt Collection, Student Loans	Against Department of Education, Trade School's False Certification	Stud App. E.5.2.1
	Against School Officers, Related Parties	CLP2 Ch. 13.4
	Challenge to Department of Education's False Certification Discharge Procedures	Stud App. E.2.3
	Challenging Wage Garnishment Procedures, Student Loans	Stud App. E.4.1
	Class Action Complaint Seeking Remedies for Coercive Collection Practices Involving Discharged Debt	Bankr App. G #124
	School Officer, Related Parties, Trade School Fraud	Stud 2001 App. E.5.2.1
	Student Loan Collection Abuse, Discovery, Motion for Class Certification, Memorandum	CLP2 Ch. 14.1
	Suit to Enjoin U.S. Department of Education's Collection of Loans to Victims of a Fraudulent Vocational School, Discovery	CLP5 Ch. 9.1
Deceptive Practices, Fraud, RICO	Car Rental Company Including Illegal Limitations on its Insurance Coverage	CLP9 Ch. 17.1.2
	Compulsory Arbitration Denied in Class Action Alleging Home Repair Fraud, RICO and Unauthorized Insurance Practices; Discovery	CLP4 Ch. 1.1
	Deceptive Labeling of Calcium Supplement	CLP8 Ch. 23.1
	Hybrid Class Complaint under 23(b)(1)/(2)/(3) Seeking Injunctive and Declaratory Relief, Hawaii (*Kalima*)	CCA App. D.2
	Lenders for Campground Membership Fraud, RICO, Lender Liability, FTC Holder Rule	CLP1 Ch. 6.1
	RICO and Deceptive Practices Case—Lender's Failure to Include FTC Holder Notice (*Howard*)	CA99 App. D.6
	RICO, Deceptive Practices and Fraud Case—Revolving Repossessions (*Carr*)	CCA App. D.10
	Unconscionability of Standard Form Arbitration Agreement (*Ting*)	CCA App. D.3
Fringe Lenders: Pay Day Loans, Auto Pawn, Rent to Own, Refund Anticipation Loans	Auto Pawn Transactions Raising UDAP and TIL Claims, also Discovery, Memorandum in Support of Motion for Class Certification	CLP3 Ch. 4.3
Installment Loans, Closed-End Credit, Usury	Credit Overcharges Usury UDAP Mortgage Refinancing	CLP6 Ch. 6.2
	State Usury Case (*Adams*)	CCA App. D.9
Insurance	Deceptive Practices Case, Vendor's Single Interest Insurance (*Ortiz*)	CCA App. D.8

	Forced Placed Automobile Insurance Claims, also Discovery Memorandum in support of Class Certification	CLP5 Ch. 5.1
	Raising Car Insurance Premium Based on Credit Report	CLP9 Ch. 9.4
Mortgages, Predatory Loans, Foreclosures	HOEPA Creditor Extended Credit Without Regard to Consumer's Repayment Ability; Briefs	CLP4 Ch. 2.1.1
	Mortgage Servicer's Practices: Delays in Payment, Loan Advances, UDAP, Breach of Fiduciary Duty	CLP7 Ch. 11.1
	Predatory Lending by a Non-Bank Home Equity Lender (*Samuel*)	CCA App. D.1
	Predatory Mortgage Lending Abuses HOEPA	CLP6 Ch. 1.1
	RESPA Related Broker and Title Company	CLP6 Ch. 15.1
	RESPA Requirement to Use Particular Title Company	CLP6 Ch. 15.4
Truth in Lending	Consumer Leasing Act and Deceptive Practices Case—Car Lease (*Shepherd*)	CCA App. D.7
	TIL Disclosure Case, Hidden Finance Charge in Car Sale (*Willis*)	CCA App. D.5
	TIL Rescission and Deceptive Practices Case—Home Improvement Contract (*Mount*)	CCA99 App. D.2
	TIL Rescission Rights Exercised in a Class Action	CLP5 Ch. 10.1
	TIL Untimely Disclosure Case (*Diaz*)	CCA App. D.6
Utilities, Energy	Class Action Complaint, Electric Company Overcharges in a Deregulated Market	CLP8 Ch. 3.1
	Long Distance Phone Overcharges	CLP7 Ch.2.1
Class Actions, Discovery	Certificate that Parties are Unable to Resolve Dispute	CCA App. G.2
	Government's Notice of Motion, Motion to Intervene and Stay Civil Discovery, *In re Homestore.com*	CCA CD Extra
	Memorandum in Support of Plaintiff's Motion to Compel Discovery	CCA App. G.4
	Motion to Compel Discovery	CCA App. G.1
	Plaintiff's Opposition to Government Motion to Intervene and Stay Discovery, *In re Homestore.com*	CCA CD Extra
	Proposed Order Compelling Defendant to Respond to Plaintiff's Requests	CCA App. G.3
	Response to Defendant's Motion to Stay Discovery	CCA App. F
Auto Credit, Leases, Repos, Deficiencies	Auto Lease Early Termination UDAP	CLP1 Ch. 9.2
	Consumer Leasing Act and Deceptive Practices Case—Car Lease (*Shepherd*)	CCA App. E.2
	Repossession Failure to Give Required Notice of Sale: RISA, UDAP	CLP6 Ch. 4.2

	Auto Fraud	Class Action Interrogatories to Financing Entity	Auto App. K.5
		Odometer Fraud FTC Holder Notice Triggers Bank's Class Liability for Dealer's Fraud	CLP1 Ch. 3.1
	Debt Collection, General	Deposition Notice: Fair Debt Collection Practices Act: Collection of Debt Which Expired by the Passage of Time	CLP8 Ch. 15.3
		Fair Debt Collection Practices Act Case (*Boddie*)	CCA App. E.1
		Fair Debt Collection Practices Act, Class Discovery	FDC App. I.4
		False Threat of Foreclosure FDCPA UDAP	CLP6 Ch. 3.2
	Deceptive Practices, Fraud, RICO	Deceptive Labeling of Calcium Supplement	CLP8 Ch. 23.2
		Lenders for Campground Membership Fraud, also RICO, Lender Liability, FTC Holder Rule	CLP1 Ch. 6.2
		Opposition to Motion to Bar the Plaintiff's Expert: Deceptive Labeling of Calcium Supplement	CLP8 Ch. 23.11
	Installment Loans, Closed-End Credit, Usury	State Usury Case (*Adams*)	CCA App. E.4
	Insurance	Deceptive Practices Case—Vendor's Single Interest Insurance (*Ortiz*)	CCA App. E.3
	Mortgages, Predatory Loans, Foreclosures	Discovery Predatory Mortgage Lending Abuses HOEPA Production of Documents Subpoena	CLP6 Ch. 1.2
		Mortgage Servicer's Practices: Delays in Payment, Loan Advances, UDAP, Breach of Fiduciary Duty	CLP7 Ch. 11.2
		RESPA Related Broker and Title Company	CLP6 Ch. 15.2
Class Actions, Protective Orders		Brief in Support of Plaintiff's Motion to Restrict Defendant's Communications with Class Members	CCA App. I
		Class Action Sample Objection to Defendant's Document Request to Named Plaintiff	CCA App. J
		Motion and Order for Protection of Class Members' Files (State Court) (*Corral*)	CCA App. H.2
		Motion and Order for Protection of Class Members' Files (Federal Court) (*Samuel*)	CCA App. H.1
	Auto Fraud	Odometer Case, Memorandum in Support of Motion for Protective Order	Auto App. K.2.3
		Odometer Case, Motion for Protective Order and Other Relief	Auto App. K.2.2
Class Actions, Certification Pleadings		Answer in Opposition to Petition for Leave to Appeal Grant of Certification	CCA App. N.2
		Request for Certification under 23(b)(2), in Case Seeking Injunctive and Declaratory Relief (*Kalima*)	CCA App. K.1
	Auto Credit, Leases, Repos, Deficiencies	Auto Sale Lender Liability Where FTC Holder Notice Improperly Omitted	CLP1 Ch. 4.8

	Memorandum, Auto Lease, Early Termination, UDAP	CLP1 Ch. 9.3
Auto Fraud	Odometer Class Action, Motion to Certify Class with Supporting Memorandum (*Potter*) (Unabridged)	Auto CD Extra
	Odometer, Consumer Fraud; Motion to Certify Class with Supporting Memorandum	Auto App. K.3.2
	Odometer, Consumer Fraud; Reply Brief in Support of Class Certification	Auto App. K.3.3
	Odometer Fraud FTC Holder Notice Triggers Bank's Class Liability for Dealer's Fraud	CLP1 Ch. 3.1
	Odometer Rollback	Auto 1998 H.3
	Reply Brief in Support of Class Certification (*Potter*) (Unabridged)	Auto CD Extra
	Response to Objections—Evidence in Support of Class Certification (*Potter*)	Auto CD Extra
Credit Discrimination	Auto Dealer Interest Markups, Race Discrimination, ECOA, Nissan MAC	CLP7 Ch. 1.1, 1.2
	Discretionary Mark-Up with Racial Impact in Car Sales as ECOA Violation (NMAC)	CD CD Extra
Debt Collection, General	Confusing Debt Validation Notice, FDCPA	CLP7 Ch. 7.4
	Fair Debt Collection Practices Act (*Bauer*)	CCA99 App. K.1
	Fair Debt Collection Practices Act: Collection of Debt Which Expired by the Passage of Time	CLP8 Ch. 15.5
	FDCPA, UDAP, and Tort Claims for a Collection Agency's Seeking Attorney Fees and Engaging in Unauthorized Practice of Law	CLP8 Ch. 19.2
	Memorandum in Support of Certifying a FDCPA Statutory Damages Class (TX)	CLP10 Ch. 8.1
Debt Collection, Student Loans	Brief in Support of Petition to Appeal Denial of Rule 23(b)(3) Certification, Wage Garnishment (*Cliff*)	CCA Supp. App. N.1.2.2
	Challenge to Student Loan Collection Letters	Stud App. E.3.3
	Petition to Appeal Denial of Rule 23(b)(3) Certification, Wage Garnishment (*Cliff*)	CCA Supp. App. N.1.2.1
	School Officer, Related Parties, Trade School Fraud	Stud 2001 App. E.5.2.2
	Trade School, also Class Notice	CLP2 Ch. 13.8
Deceptive Practices, Fraud, RICO	Auto Finance Upcharge Cases: Class Certification Decision, *Coleman v. GMAC*	UDAP CD Extra
	Deceptive Labeling of Calcium Supplement	CLP8 Ch. 23.4
Insurance	Deceptive Practices Case— Vendor's Single Interest Insurance (*Ortiz*)	CCA App. K.4
Mortgages, Predatory Loans, Foreclosures	Predatory Mortgage Lending Abuses, HOEPA	CLP6 Ch. 1.6

		RESPA Requirement to Use Particular Title Company	CLP6 Ch. 15.4
	Truth in Lending	Motion for Class Certification TIL Rescission Rights Exercised in a Class Action	CLP5 Ch. 10.2
		TIL Disclosure Case—Hidden Finance Charge in Car Sale (*Willis*)	CCA App. K.2
		TIL Rescission and Deceptive Practices Case—Home Improvement Contract (*Mount*)	CCA99 App. K.2
		TIL Untimely Disclosure Case (*Diaz*)	CCA App. K.3
Class Actions, Class Notices		"Preliminary Suggestions for Lawyers to Consider in Drafting Class Action Notices," by the Federal Judicial Center	CCA CD Extra
		Model Notice of Proposed Class Action Settlement, Right of Exclusion and Hearing—*Smith v. XYZ Corp.*	CCA CD Extra
		Model Summary of Notice of Proposed Class Action Settlement, Right to Exclusion and Hearing—*Smith v. XYZ Corp.*	CCA CD Extra
		Notice of Proposed Class Action Settlement and Consent Decree—*Brown v. Equitable Life Assurance*; other cases	CCA CD Extra
		Notice of Proposed Class Action Settlement, Right to Exclusion, and Hearing (Sample Asbestos Case)	CCA CD Extra
		Notice of Proposed Class Action Settlement, Gasoline, NJ	CCA CD Extra
	Auto Fraud	Odometer Case, Class Action Notice	Auto App. K.4
	Credit Discrimination	Auto Dealer Interest Markups, Race Discrimination, ECOA, Nissan MAC	CLP7 Ch. 1.1, 1.2, 1.3
	Debt Collection, General	Combined Rule 23(c) and (e) Notice of Certification and Settlement Federal Fair Debt Collection Case (*Boddie*)	CCA99 App. N.3.2
	Deceptive Practices, Fraud, RICO	Notice of Certification Rule 23(c) RICO (*Hughes*)	CCA App. O.1
	Installment Loans, Closed-End Credit, Usury	Combined Rule 23(c) and (e) Notice of Certification and Settlement State Usury Case (*Adams*)	CCA App. O.3.4
	Mortgages, Predatory Loans, Foreclosures	Notice to the Complete Class, Predatory Lending by a Non-Bank Home Equity Lender (*Samuel*)	CCA App. O.3.1.1
		Special Notice to Subclass, Predatory Lending by a Non-Bank Home Equity Lender (*Samuel*)	CCA App. O.3.1.2
	Truth in Lending	Combined Rule 23(c) and (e) Notice of Certification and Settlement TIL Disclosure Case—Hidden Finance Charge in Car Sale (*Willis*)	CCA App. O.3.3
	Utilities, Energy	Notice of Pendency of Class Action Determination, Proposed Settlement and Date of Settlement Hearing (AT&T Wireless, NJ)	CCA CD Extra

Class Actions, Briefs, Memoranda		Notice of Proposed Class Action Settlement, Electric Company Overcharges in a Deregulated Market	CLP8 Ch. 3.8
		Short Class Notice: AT&T Wireless Consumer Class Action Litigation (NJ)	CCA CD Extra
		Certification in Case Under 23(b)(2) Seeking Injunctive and Declaratory Relief, Hawaii (*Kalima*)	CCA App. L.1
		Challenges to Rule 68 Offers of Judgment (*Colbert*)	CCA Supp. App. X
	Arbitration	Trial Brief, Class Action, Arbitration Issues: Unconscionability in Formation and Terms of Arbitration Agreement, *Ting v. AT&T*, (N.D.Ca)	Arbit CD Extra
	Auto Credit, Leases, Repos, Deficiencies	In Support of Class Certification Consumer Leasing Act and Deceptive Practices Case—Car Lease (*Shepherd*)	CCA App. L.5
		Reply Memoranda in Support of Class Certification: Consumer Leasing Act and Deceptive Practices Case—Car Lease (*Shepherd*)	CCA App. M.3
		Repossession Failure to Give Required Notice of Sale: RISA, UDAP, Summary Judgment	CLP6 Ch. 4.5
	Credit Cards, Open-End Credit	Challenging Mandatory Arbitration Clause Found in Credit Card "Stuffer"	CLP1 Ch. 1.2
		Challenging Mandatory Arbitration Clause Found in Credit Card "Stuffer"	CLP1 Ch. 1.3
	Credit Discrimination	Auto Dealer Interest Markups, Race Discrimination, ECOA, Nissan MAC, Brief in Support of Class Notice Proposal	CLP7 Ch. 1.3
		ECOA, Race Discrimination, Disgorge Unjust Enrichment, Auto Finance NMAC	CD CD Extra
		ECOA, Race Discrimination, Auto Sales, Motion to Dismiss Defendant's Counterclaims (*Ford Credit*)	CD CD Extra
		Opposing Summary Judgment in ECOA Notice Case (*Bank One*)	CD CD Extra
		Opposition to NMAC's Motion for Summary Judgment, Race Discrimination in Auto Finance Markup, ECOA	CD CD Extra
	Debt Collection, General	Bank's Debt Collection Suits in Distant Forum Are Abuse of Process Unfair Trade Practice Due Process Violation	CLP6 Ch. 14.2
		In Support of Class Certification Federal Fair Debt Collection Case (*Bauer*)	CCA99 App. L.1
		Motion for Partial Summary Judgment Challenging False Threat of Foreclosure: FDCPA, UDAP	CLP6 Ch. 3.4
		Offer of Judgment Does Not Moot FDCPA Class Action	CLP9 Ch. 12
		Offer of Judgment May Not Be Used to Moot FDCPA Class Action	CLP7 Ch. 14.1

	Reply Memoranda in Support of Class Certification, Federal Fair Debt Collection Case (*Bauer*)	CCA99 App. M.1
	Reply Memorandum Challenging False Threat of Foreclosure: FDCPA, UDAP	CLP6 Ch. 3.5
Debt Collection, Hospital	Reply Memoranda in Support of Class Certification: Hospital Collection Case (*Albino*)	CCA App. M.5
Debt Collection, Student Loans	Appeal of Denial of Class Certification on Numerosity, Discovery, and Class Definition; Refusal of Student Loan Debt Collector to Provide Pregarnishment Hearings	CLP9 Ch. 16
Deceptive Practices, Fraud, RICO	Brief in Opposition to Motion for Judgment Notwithstanding the Verdict: Deceptive Labeling of Calcium Supplement	CLP8 Ch. 23.16
	Lenders for Campground Membership Fraud RICO Lender Liability FTC Holder Rule	CLP1 Ch. 6.6
Installment Loans, Closed-End Credit, Usury	In Support of Class Certification State Usury Case (*Adams*)	CCA App. L.7
	Mandatory Arbitration Provision Is Not Enforceable	CLP1 Ch. 1.1
	Opposing Motion to Dismiss Credit Overcharges: Usury, UDAP, Mortgage Refinancing	CLP6 Ch. 6.3
Insurance	Forced Placed Insurance Auto Credit Sales	CLP1 Ch. 2.1
	In Support of Class Certification Forced Placed Insurance Auto Credit Sales	CLP1 Ch. 2.2
	In Support of Class Certification Deceptive Practices Case—Vendor's Single Interest Insurance (*Ortiz*)	CCA App. L.6
	Reply Memoranda in Support of Class Certification: Deceptive Practices Case—Vendor's Single Interest Insurance (*Ortiz*)	CCA App. M.4
Mortgages, Predatory Loans, Foreclosures	In Opposition of Motion to Dismiss: Predatory Mortgage Lending Abuses, HOEPA	CLP6 Ch. 1.4
Truth in Lending	In Support of Class Certification TIL Rescission and Deceptive Practices Case—Home Improvement Contract (*Mount*)	CCA99 App. L.3
	In Support of Class Certification: TIL, UDAP, and Breach of Contract Case—Credit Card Issuer's Failure to Refund Credit Balance (*Coe*)	CCA App. L.2
	In Support of Class Certification TIL Untimely Disclosure Case (*Diaz*)	CCA App. L.4
	In Support of Class Certification TIL Disclosure Case—Hidden Finance Charge in Car Sale (Willis)	CCA App. L.3
	Reply Memoranda in Support of Class Certification: TIL, UDAP, and Breach of Contract Case—Credit Card Issuer's Failure to Refund Credit Balance (*Coe*)	CCA App. M.1
	Reply Memoranda in Support of Class Certification: TIL Untimely Disclosure Case (*Diaz*)	CCA App. M.2

		Reply Memoranda in Support of Class Certification: TIL Rescission and Deceptive Practices Case, Home Improvement Contract (*Mount*)	CCA99 App. M.3
Class Actions, Pre-Trial Motions, Trial Practice	*Credit Discrimination*	Expert Report of Professor Ian Ayres, Disparate Racial Impacts in Finance Charge Markups, NMAC	CD CD Extra
		Expert Report on Impact of NMAC's Credit Policy on Hispanic Borrowers, by Mark Cohen	CD CD Extra
		Expert Report on Racial Impact of NMAC's Finance Charge Markup Policy by Mark Cohen, Ph.D.	CD CD Extra
		Motion for Preliminary Injunction (Nissan MAC)	CD CD Extra
	Debt Collection, General	Summary Judgment Motion: Fair Debt Collection Practices Act: Collection of Debt Which Expired by the Passage of Time	CLP8 Ch. 15.6
	Debt Collection, Student Loans	Summary Judgment Against Dept. of Education, Trade School Abuse	Stud App. E.5.2.2
	Deceptive Practices, Fraud, RICO	Car Rental Company Including Illegal Limitations on its Insurance Coverage, Summary Judgment	CLP9 Ch. 17.1.3, 17.1.4
		Jury Instructions, Jury Questions: Deceptive Labeling of Calcium Supplement	CLP8 Ch. 23.12
		Summary Judgment Motion: Deceptive Labeling of Calcium Supplement	CLP8 Ch. 23.7
Class Actions, Settlements		Memorandum in Support of Motion for Final Approval of Proposed Class Action Settlement—*In re Synthroid Marketing Litigation*	CCA CD Extra
		Memorandum Supporting Settlement Approval, Attorney Fees Award; Response to "Professional Objector Counsel"—*Baird v. Thompson Consumer Electronics*	CCA CD Extra
	Auto Credit, Leases, Repos, Deficiencies	Memoranda in Support of Final Approval of Class Settlement Consumer Leasing Act and Deceptive Practices Case—Car Lease (*Shepherd*)	CCA App. R.3
		Settlement Notice Dealer Law Violations Relating to Used Car Sales, Rule 23(e) (*Norris*)	CCA App. O.2.2
		Stipulations of Proposed Settlements Revolving Repossession Case (*Johnson*)	CCA99 App. O.4
		Stipulations of Proposed Settlements Consumer Leasing Act and Deceptive Practices Case—Car Lease (*Shepherd*)	CCA App. P.4
	Auto Fraud	Odometer Class Action, Final Order Approving Settlement	Auto App. K.6.3
		Odometer Class Action, Final Report of Plaintiff's Counsel with Affidavit	Auto App. K.6.2
		Odometer Class Action, Order Preliminarily Approving Settlement	Auto App. K.6.1

		Motion Seeking Additional Discovery as Part of Settlement Objection; Document Requests	CCA App. S.7
		Objection to Settlement and Intervention	CLP4 Ch. 12.1
	Auto Credit, Leases, Repos, Deficiencies	Attorney Affidavit Opposing Preliminary Approval of Class Action Settlement	CCA Supp. App. S.9.1
		Intervenors' Objections to Class Action Settlement (*H&R Block*)	CCA Supp. App. S.11
		Memorandum Opposing Preliminary Approval of Class Action Settlement	CCA Supp. App. S.9.2
		Opposition to Inadequate Consumer Class Action Settlement—Defective Post-Repossession Notices, Including Affidavits	CLP9 Ch. 13.1–13.3
	Auto Warranties, Lemon Law, Auto Repair	Response to Objections to Settlement—*Howard v. Ford Motor Company*	CCA CD Extra
	Credit Cards, Open-End Credit	Objections to Settlement Agreement (*Boehr*)	CCA App. S.2
	Debt Collection, General	Objections to Settlement Agreement (*Follansbee*)	CCA App. S.6
	Installment Loans, Closed-End Credit, Usury	Objections to Settlement (*Buchet*)	CCA App. S.5.1
		Objections to Settlement Agreement (*Reynolds*)	CCA App. S.3
	Insurance	Objections to Settlement Agreement (*Wilson*)	CCA App. S.1
	Utilities, Energy	Objections to Stipulation of Settlement by Boyd Objectors (*Dotson v. Bell Atlantic-MD, Inc./Fausto Scrocco, Mojan, Inc;. Sysnet, Inc., v. Bell Atlantic-MD, Inc. and Maryland PSC*)	CCA CD Extra
Class Actions, Cy Pres		Amicus Brief: Importance of *Cy Pres* Distribution to Obtaining Class Action Relief	CLP8 Ch. 18.1
		Amicus Brief in Support of Suggestion for *Cy Pres* Distribution of Property	CCA App. Q.3
		Cy Pres Memorandum—Distributing the Unclaimed Residue Damages in Class Actions as *Cy Pres* Distribution to Legal Aid and Advocacy Organizations	CLP5 Ch. 11.1
		Defendant's Motion and Memorandum for Order Approving Final Distribution of Settlement Fund, Including *Cy Pres* Award	CCA App. Q.2
		Memorandum of Law Supporting *Cy Pres* Award	CCA App. Q.1
	Credit Cards, Open-End Credit	*Cy Pres* Remedy *Beasley*—Late Fees, Memorandum, Court Orders	CLP1 Ch. 12.1
Class Actions, Attorney Fees		"Seeking Fees in Class Action Cases," by Robert Bramson	CCA CD Extra
		Memorandum in Support of State Catalyst Theory for Award After *Buckhannon* (*Farkas*/Kentucky)	CCA Supp. App. T.2

Auto Credit, Leases, Repos, Deficiencies		Memorandum in Support of Plaintiff's Motion for Attorney Fees and Reimbursement of Expenses (*Minnick*)	CCA Supp. App. T.1.2
		Motion for Award of Attorney Fees and Reimbursement of Expenses (*Minnick*)	CCA Supp. App. T.1.1
		Reply Memorandum, Motion for Award of Attorney Fees and Reimbursement of Expenses (*Minnick*)	CCA Supp. App. T.1.3
		Request for Attorney Fees Auto Sale Lender Liability Where FTC Holder Notice Improperly Omitted	CLP1 Ch. 4.14
Debt Collection, General		Attorney Fees Motion: Fair Debt Collection Practices Act: Collection of Debt Which Expired by the Passage of Time	CLP8 Ch. 15.9
Installment Loans, Closed-End Credit, Usury		Memorandum in Support of Counsel for Objectors' Request for Attorney Fees (*Buchet*)	CCA App. S.5.2
Insurance		Memorandum in Support of Final Approval of Settlement and Application for Award of Attorney Fees Forced Placed Insurance Auto Credit Sales	CLP1 Ch. 2.10
Mortgages, Predatory Loans, Foreclosures		Objections to Settlement and Request for Fees, Mortgages and RESPA (*Robinson*)	CCA App. S.4
Bankruptcy, Petitions, Schedules, Official Forms	*Bankruptcy*	Adversary Proceeding Cover Sheet	Bankr App. E
		Appearance of Child Support Creditor or Representative	Bankr App. E
		Bankruptcy Forms software from Law Disks—(Fill in petition/schedules using WordPerfect or Microsoft Word)	*Consumer Law in a Box* CD; *Bankruptcy* CD
		Disclosure of Compensation of Bankruptcy Petition Preparer	Bankr App. E
		Notice to Individual Consumer Debtor	Bankr App. E
		Official Bankruptcy Forms, Reproducible Official Forms	Bankr App. D
		Official Form 1. Petition in Bankruptcy	Bankr App. D
		Official Form 10. Proof of Claim	Bankr App. D
		Official Form 16. A, B Captions	Bankr App. D
		Official Form 16D. Captions Adversary Proceedings	Bankr App. D
		Official Form 17. Notice of Appeal	Bankr App. D
		Official Form 18. Discharge of Debtor in a Chapter 7 Case	Bankr App. D
		Official Form 20A. Notice of Motion or Objection	Bankr App. D
		Official Form 20B. Notice of Objection to Claim	Bankr App. D
		Official Form 21, Statement of Social Security Numbers	Bankr App. D

Bankruptcy, Initial Forms	Application and Order for Waiver of Miscellaneous Fees	Bankr App. G #7
	Application and Order for Additional Extension of Time to File Chapter 13 Schedules, Statement of Affairs, and Chapter 13 Plan	Bankr App. G #5
	Application and Order for Waiver of Filing Fee to Amend Debtor's Schedule of Creditors	Bankr App. G #20
	Application for Counsel Fees	Bankr App. G #22
	Chapter 13 Bankruptcy Checklist from Debtor's Attorney to Debtor	Bankr App. G #16
	Chapter 13 Debtor's Motion to Assume Lease	Bankr App. G #15
	Chapter 13 Plan Assuming Residential Lease	Bankr App. G #14
	Chapter 13 Plan Providing for Filing of Adversary Proceeding Involving Predatory Mortgage Lending Claims	Bankr App. G #13
	Chapter 13 Plan Providing for Liquidation of Debtor's Interest in Residence	Bankr App. G #12
	Chapter 7 Information Sheet from Attorney to Debtor	Bankr App. G #17
	Debtor's Amendment of Schedules	Bankr App. G #19
	Debtor's First Amended Chapter 13 Plan	Bankr App. G #18
	Debtors' Chapter 13 Plan	Bankr App. G #8
	Motion and Order for Extension of Time to File Schedules and Statement of Affairs	Bankr App. G #3
	Motion and Order for Extension of Time to File Chapter 13 Schedules, Statement of Affairs, and Chapter 13 Plan	Bankr App. G #4
	Motion for Payover Order in Chapter 13	Bankr App. G #10
	Motion to Keep Prior Name Confidential	Bankr App. G #6
	Notification to Creditor Seeking Information As to Account	Bankr App. G #2
	Order Confirming Chapter 13 Plan	Bankr App. G #9
	Order to Pay Wages to the Trustee in Chapter 13	Bankr App. G #11
	Pre-Filing Notification to Creditors of Representation	Bankr App. G #1
	Statement by Debtor's Attorney of Fees Charged	Bankr App. G #21
Bankruptcy, Automatic Stay	Answer to Application for Abandonment of Real Estate	Bankr App. G #34
	Answer to Motion for Relief from Automatic Stay	Bankr App. G #28
	Answer to Motion for Relief from Automatic Stay Raising Avoidability of Transfer to Plaintiff	Bankr App. G #31
	Answer to Motion of Landlord for Relief from Automatic Stay	Bankr App. G #30
	Complaint Seeking Contempt Remedies and Recovery of Property from IRS	Bankr App. G #27
	Complaint Seeking Damages for Violation of Automatic Stay and Unfair Trade Practices	Bankr App. G #24

	Debtor's Answer to Motion for Relief from Codebtor Stay	Bankr App. G #32
	Debtor's Objection to Relief from the Codebtor Stay	Bankr App. G #33
	Letter to Creditors Giving Notice of Stay	Bankr App. G #23
	Motion for Expedited Hearing on Contempt Motion	Bankr App. G #26
	Motion for Sanctions Pursuant to Rule 9011 for Baseless Motion for Relief from Automatic Stay	Bankr App. G #29
	Motion Seeking Relief for Violations of the Automatic Stay by Governmental Agency	Bankr App. G #25
	Motion to Reimpose Stay After Relief from Stay Has Been Granted	Bankr App. G #35
Bankruptcy, Turn-over of Property	Complaint Seeking Turnover of Property	Bankr App. G #37
	Letter Demanding Turnover of Property	Bankr App. G #36
	Motion for Enforcement of Turnover Order and to Hold Defendant in Contempt of Court	Bankr App. G #38
Bankruptcy, Utilities	Complaint Seeking Reconnection of Utility Service and Damages	Bankr App. G #42
	Complaint to Enjoin Termination of Utility Service for Nonpayment of Deposit by Debtor Current on Her Utility Payments	Bankr App. G #41
	Letter to Utility Company Giving Notice of Stay and Requirements of 11 U.S.C. § 366	Bankr App. G #39
	Letter to Utility Company Giving Notice of Conversion from Chapter 13 to Chapter 7	Bankr App. G #40
	Motion for Modification of Security Deposit for Utility Service	Bankr App. G #43
Bankruptcy, Steps After Filing	Chapter 13 Section 341(a) Meeting Questions	Bankr App. G #48
	Chapter 7 Section 341(a) Meeting Questions	Bankr App. G #45
	Debtor's Motion to Excuse Appearance and to Conduct Meeting of Creditors by Interrogatories	Bankr App. G #50
	Interrogatories to Debtor in Lieu of Attendance at Meeting of Creditors	Bankr App. G #51
	Letter Advising Belatedly-Added Creditor of Meeting of Creditors	Bankr App. G #44
	Report of Trustee	Bankr App. G #52
	Section 341(a) Questions from United States Trustee Chapter 7 Handbook	Bankr App. G #46
	Section 341(a) Questions from United States Trustee Chapter 13 Handbook	Bankr App. G #49
	Statement of Information Required by 11 U.S.C. § 341	Bankr App. G #47

	Motion to Avoid Non-Possessory, Non-Purchase Money Security Interest	Bankr App. G #76
	Order Avoiding Lien on Residential Real Estate	Bankr App. G #75
	Order Avoiding Non-Possessory, Non-Purchase Money Security Interest	Bankr App. G #77
Bankruptcy, Litiga-tion Generally	Appellant's Election Form	Bankr App. G #105
	Application for Default Judgment	Bankr App. G #93
	Brief: Sovereign Immunity Defense is Not Available Unless Student Loan Agency Proves it is "Arm of the State" Student Loan Dischargeability	CLP6 Ch. 7.2.1
	Class Action Complaint Unlawful Collection of Debts Discharged in Bankruptcy May Dept Stores	CLP5 Ch. 2.2
	Complaint Bankruptcy *Ex parte Young* Seeking Injunction and Declaratory Judgment that State Officials Violated Federal Law	CLP6 Ch. 7.1.1
	Complaint: Class Action Adversary Proceeding Raising Claims Under Stay, Discharge, and Exemption Provisions As Well As 42 U.S.C. § 1983	Bankr App. G #83
	Complaint Consumer Law Claims in Bankruptcy Court, TILA Rescission, Fraud, Discovery, Memoranda	CLP4 Ch. 14.1
	Complaint in Bankruptcy Court Objecting to Secured Claim TILA Rescission	CLP1 Ch. 8.2
	Complaint Raising School's Fraud in Bankruptcy Proceedings	CLP2 Ch. 13.6
	Complaint Seeking Damages in Non-Core Adversary Proceeding Against a Non-Creditor for Unfair Debt Collection Practices	Bankr App. G #87
	Complaint Seeking Restoration of Driver's License	Bankr App. G #86
	Complaint Seeking Review of Administrative Action	Bankr App. G #85
	Complaint to Prohibit Eviction from Public Housing Based upon Dischargeable Debt for Rent	Bankr App. G #84
	Complaints: Article: "Primer on Bankruptcy and the Sovereign Immunity of States: When You Can't Sue State Agencies, When You Can Sue State Officials"	CLP6 Ch. 7.1.2
	Debtor's Motion for Expedited Discovery	Bankr App. G #89
	Default Judgment by Clerk	Bankr App. G #96
	Defendant's Request for Admissions	Bankr App. G #91
	In Forma Pauperis Order	Bankr App. G #82
	Memorandum in Support of Plaintiff's Motion for Summary Judgement, TILA Rescission in Bankruptcy Court	CLP1 Ch. 8.5
	Memorandum In Support of Preliminary Injunction TILA Rescission Bankruptcy Court	CLP1 Ch. 8.3
	Motion for Abandonment of Property by Trustee	Bankr App. G #88

Motion for Determination That Proceeding Is a Core Proceeding	Bankr App. G #99
Motion for Leave to Appeal Interlocutory Order	Bankr App. G #102
Motion for Leave to Proceed In Forma Pauperis	Bankr App. G #81
Motion for Stay of Order Pending Appeal	Bankr App. G #103
Notice of Removal	Bankr App. G #97
Objecting to Secured Claim in Bankruptcy, also Discovery, Memorandum, Chapter 13 Plan, Attorney Fee Request	CLP2 Ch. 3.3
Order for Default Judgment	Bankr App. G #94
Order for Partial Summary Judgment for the Plaintiff Rescinding Mortgage Declaring Debt Unsecured Pursuant to TILA	CLP1 Ch. 8.7
Petition for Writ of Habeas Corpus	Bankr App. G #92
Plaintiff's Motion for Withdrawal of Proceeding to the District Court	Bankr App. G #98
Plaintiff's Objections to Findings of Fact and Conclusions of Law	Bankr App. G #101
Plaintiff's Request for Documents	Bankr App. G #90
Request for Default Judgment by Clerk	Bankr App. G #95
Rescission Letter TILA Bankruptcy Court	CLP1 Ch. 8.1
Stipulation for Appeal to Bankruptcy Appellate Panel	Bankr App. G #104
Stipulation That Matter May Be Determined by Bankruptcy Court	Bankr App. G #100

Bankruptcy, Discharge and Reaffirmation

Application for Approval of Reaffirmation Agreement	Bankr App. G #116
Brief Amicus Curiae Bankruptcy Private Right of Action for Violation of Discharge Injunction. Cox First Circuit case	CLP6 Ch. 16.3
Brief Bankruptcy Private Right of Action for Violation of Discharge Injunction.	CLP6 Ch. 16.1
Brief Bankruptcy Student Loan Undue Hardship	CLP6 Ch. 7.2.1
Class Action Complaint Seeking Remedies for Coercive Collection Practices Involving Discharged Debt	Bankr App. G #124
Class Action Complaint Unlawful Collection of Debts Discharged in Bankruptcy Sears	CLP5 Ch. 2.1.1
Class Action Settlement Agreement Sears Unlawful Collection of Debts Discharged in Bankruptcy	CLP5 Ch. 2.1.2
Complaint Challenging Misapplication of Mortgage Payments in Chapter 13 Case	Bankr App. G #127
Complaint Seeking Contempt Remedies for Violation of the Automatic Stay and Discharge Injunction	Bankr App. G #120
Complaint to Determine Dischargeability of Student Loan	Bankr App. G #106

Complaint to Determine Dischargeability of Student Loan	Stud App. E.6.1
Complaint to Enjoin Discriminatory Denial of Guaranteed Student Loan	Bankr App. G #121
Complaint to Recover SSI Benefits Collected by State As Reimbursement for Pre-bankruptcy Welfare Debt	Bankr App. G #119
Credit Card Debts, Constructive Fraud, Implied Representation, Amicus Brief, Fifth Circuit	CLP7 Ch. 17.1
Debtor's Answer to Complaint Seeking Determination of Nondischargeability	Bankr App. G #107
Debtor's Application for a Hardship Discharge	Bankr App. G #112
Declaration in Support of Reaffirmation Agreement	Bankr App. G #115
Defendant's Interrogatories in Dischargeability Case Based on Credit Card Fraud	Bankr App. G #110
Defendant's Requests for Admissions in Dischargeability Case Based on Credit Card Fraud	Bankr App. G #111
Defendant's Requests for Production of Documents in Dischargeability Case Based on Credit Card Fraud	Bankr App. G #109
Dischargeability Complaint Raising School's Fraud	Stud App. E.6.2
Interrogatories Directed to Lender Regarding Debtor's Alleged False Financial Statement(s)	Bankr App. G #108
Letter to Client After Discharge	Bankr App. G #118
Letter to Creditor Concerning Proposed Reaffirmation Agreement	Bankr App. G #113
Motion for Order Declaring Mortgage Loan Current	Bankr App. G #125
Motion for Preliminary Relief in Complaint to Enjoin Discriminatory Denial of Guaranteed Student Loan	Bankr App. G #122
Order Approving Reaffirmation Agreement	Bankr App. G #117
Order Declaring Mortgage Loan Current	Bankr App. G #126
Proposed Order for Preliminary Relief in Complaint to Enjoin Discriminatory Denial of Guaranteed Student Loan	Bankr App. G #123
Reaffirmation Agreement	Bankr App. G #114

Bankruptcy, Plan Conversion, Modification, Dismissal

Debtor's Amended Plan Permitting Mortgage Refinancing to Pay Off Plan	Bankr App. G #132
Debtor's Motion to Convert Chapter 7 Case to Chapter 13	Bankr App. G #135
Debtor's Motion to Dismiss Chapter 7 Case	Bankr App. G #137
Debtor's Motion to Dismiss Chapter 13 Case	Bankr App. G #136
Debtor's Motion to Reopen Case	Bankr App. G #138
Debtor's Notice to Convert Case from Chapter 13 to Chapter 7	Bankr App. G #133
Motion to Modify Plan to Terminate Plan	Bankr App. G #129

Pleadings by Subject

The following listing is organized first by the subject area of the pleading and then, within a given subject area, by the type of pleading. This listing is particularly useful for those interested in various types of pleadings within a subject area. Those needing a specific type of pleading, irrespective of the subject area, will find more useful the listing found at Pleadings by Type, *supra*.

The subject area headings are:

- Arbitration
- Auto Credit, Leases, Repos, Deficiencies
- Auto Fraud
- Auto Warranties, Lemon Law, Auto Repair
- Banking, Electronic Fund Transfers
- Bankruptcy
- Credit Cards, Open-End Credit
- Credit Discrimination
- Credit Reporting
- Debt Collection, General
- Debt Collection, Hospital
- Debt Collection, Student Loans
- Deceptive Practices, Fraud, RICO
- Fringe Lenders: Pay Day Loans, Auto Pawn, Rent to Own, Refund Anticipation Loans
- Installment Loans, Closed-End Credit, Usury
- Insurance
- Mobile Homes, Landlord-Tenant
- Mortgages, Predatory Loans, Foreclosures
- Truth in Lending
- Utilities, Energy

The cross-references are:
Arbit = Consumer Arbitration Agreements
Auto = Auto Fraud
Bankr = Consumer Bankruptcy Law and Practice
CBPL = Consumer Banking and Payments Law
CCA = Consumer Class Actions
CD = Credit Discrimination
CLP = Consumer Law Pleadings (Numbers One through Ten)
COC = Cost of Credit
FCRA = Fair Credit Reporting Act
FDC = Fair Debt Collection
Repo = Repossessions and Foreclosures
Stud = Student Loan
TIL = Truth in Lending
UDAP = Unfair and Deceptive Acts and Practices
Warr = Consumer Warranty Law

Briefs, Memoranda	*Cardegna v. Buckeye Check Cashing, Inc.*—Reply Brief Fla Sup Ct since Payday Lending Contract Is Criminal under State Law and Void *Ab Initio*, an Arbitration Clause Embedded in the Contract May Not Be Enforced	Arbit CD Extra
	Dunlap v. Friedman's Jewelers—Brief Opposing Certiorari to the U.S. Sup. Ct., Supporting State Supreme Court Decision Which Strikes Arbitration Clause That Bans Punitive Damages, Effectively Bars Class Actions and Is Non-mutual.	Arbit CD Extra
	Eastman v. Conseco Finance Servicing Corp—Brief Wis Sup Ct, Federal Arbitration Act Does Not Preempt State Consumer Protection Laws; Issues: Non-mutual Arbitration Clause, Bar to Consumer Class Actions, Injunctive Relief or Punitive Damages	Arbit CD Extra
	Hill v. MBNA America Bank, NACBA Amicus Brief, Second Circuit, Bankruptcy Code Supercedes FAA.	Arbit CD Extra
	Raymond James Financial Services, Inc. v. Saldukas (FL Sup Ct), Brief, Party Need Not Prove Prejudice Before it Can Establish Waiver of Other Party's Right to Compel Arbitration	Arbit CD Extra
	Jevne v. Superior Court of Los Angeles County, et al (CA Sup. Ct.)—Amicus Brief: CA's Statutory Ethics Rules Requiring Arbitrators to Disclose Conflicts of Interest Are Not Preempted by the SEC Act or FAA	Arbit CD Extra
	Cardegna v. Buckeye Check Cashing, Inc. Opening Brief Fla Sup Ct. Since Payday Lending Contract Is Criminal under State Law and Void *Ab Initio*, an Arbitration Clause Embedded in the Contract May Not Be Enforced	Arbit CD Extra
	Boghos v. Certain Underwriters at Lloyd's of London, Appellee Answer Brief, Insurer's Arbitration Clause Unconscionable, Excessive Costs to Disability Claimant, Insurer Consented to Court Jurisdiction over Coverage Claims, CA Sup. Ct.	Arbit CD Extra
	Boghos v. Certain Underwriters at Lloyds, Brief Cal App. Ct, Disability Insurer's Arbitration Clause Foreclosed Suit on Failure to Pay Claims; Unconscionable Based on Non-mutuality and Cost Requirements.	Arbit CD Extra
	BDO Seidman LLP v. Hottle, Amicus Brief, CT Sup. Ct., Arbitration Clause Is Unenforceable If Three Accounting Partners Resolve All Disputes Between Firm and Employees	Arbit CD Extra
	Leonard v. Terminix—Amicus Brief: Ala. Sup. Ct., Arguing That the Court Did Not Violate the Federal Arbitration Act by Striking down an Arbitration Clause That Effectively Barred Class Actions	Arbit CD Extra
	Luke v. Baptist Medical Center-Princeton—(11th Cir.) Brief: Employer's Arbitration Clause Is Unenforceable Where Employee Repeatedly Refused to Sign Clause	Arbit CD Extra
	Objections to Magistrate's Recommendations, Truth in Lending Rescission for HOEPA Violations Argued to be Not Subject to Arbitration	CLP8 Ch. 11.2

Mintze v. American General Finance, Inc.—(3d Cir.) Brief: Bankruptcy Code Supercedes FAA	Arbit CD Extra
Wells, et al. v. Chevy Chase Bank, F.S.B., et al., (Md. Ct. of App.), Arbitration Clause Added as a "Bill Stuffer"; Unconscionability; "Loser Pays Rule," Excessive Arbitration Fees, and Denial of Class Action Remedy (Two Briefs)	Arbit CD Extra
Unconscionability of Arbitration Clause, Brief Opposing Petition for Writ of Certiorari *American General Finance, Inc. v. Branch*, Ala. Sup Ct.	Arbit CD Extra
Unconscionability Based on Bias of National Arbitration Forum, *Toppings v. Meritech Mortgage Services, Inc.*, W.Va. Sup. Ct., Reply Brief	Arbit CD Extra
Nagrampa v. MailCoups, Inc.—(9th Cir.). Brief: Requiring Arbitration in Boston, Excessive Costs, and Appear Before the American Arbitration Association Is Unconscionable under California Law	Arbit CD Extra
Trial Brief, Class Action, Arbitration Issues Unconscionability in Formation and Terms of Arbitration Agreement, *Ting v. AT&T*, (N.D.Ca)	Arbit CD Extra
Sanderson Farms, Inc. v. Gatlin, Miss. Sup. Ct. Supplemental Authority: High Arbitration Costs as Grounds to Void Arbitration Agreement	Arbit CD Extra
Nagrampa v. MailCoups, Inc.—(9th Cir.) Reply Brief: Requiring Arbitration in Boston, Excessive Costs, and Appear Before the American Arbitration Association Is Unconscionable under California Law.	Arbit CD Extra
McDougle v. Silvernell, (Ala. Sup. Ct.), Brief of Appellees: Arbitration Clause Unilaterally Added to Agreement after Consummation	Arbit CD Extra
Limit on Punitive Damages Makes Arbitration Clause Unenforceable, Brief in Opposition to Petition for Writ of Certiorari, *Cavalier Manufacturing, Inc. v. Jackson*, Ala. Sup. Ct.	Arbit CD Extra
High Arbitration Fees Thwarting Vindication of Federal Statutory Rights, *Green Tree Financial Corp. v. Randolph* (U.S. Sup. Ct.)	Arbit CD Extra
Enforceability of Arbitration Clause in Agreement Void *ab initio*, *Burden v. Check Into Cash of Kentucky*, Petition for Writ of Certiorari, U.S. Sup. Ct.	Arbit CD Extra
Arbitration, Employment Contract, Forum in Philippines is Unconscionable, *Bautisa v. Star Cruises and Norwegian Cruise Line, Ltd.*, Amicus brief, Eleventh Circuit	Arbit CD Extra
Car Lease Arbitration Clause Attacked As Not Binding or Unconscionable	CLP7 Ch. 12.1
Mandatory Arbitration Clause Lacked Mutuality	CLP5 Ch. 12.2
Unconscionable Mandatory Arbitration Clauses in Consumer Credit Contracts	CLP5 Ch. 12.1.2

	Magnuson-Moss Warranty Act Conflict with Federal Arbitration Act, *Abela v. General Motors Corp.*, Mich. Ct. of App.	Arbit CD Extra
Briefs, Memoranda	Arbitration, Unconscionable High Costs; Waiver By: Company's Breach of Agreement, *Sanderson Farms, Inc. v. Gatlin*, Miss. Sup. Ct.	Arbit CD Extra
	Unconscionability Based on Bias of National Arbitration Forum, *Toppings v. Meritech Mortgage Services, Inc.*, W. Va. Sup. Ct.	Arbit App. H
	Magnuson-Moss Warranty Act's Prohibition on Predispute Binding Arbitration Clauses, Petition for Certoriari, *Abela v. General Motors Corp.*, U.S. Sup. Ct.	Arbit App. G
	Unconscionability of Arbitration Clauses Restricting Class Actions, Amicus Brief: *Hayes v. County Bank* (NY)	Arbit App. F.3
	Unconscionability of Arbitration Clauses Restricting Class Actions, Reply Brief (CA)	Arbit App. F.2
	Unconscionability of Arbitration Clauses Restricting Class Actions, Opening Brief (CA)	Arbit App. F.1
	Arbitration Costs, Damage Limitations, and Unconscionability, Reply Brief	Arbit App. E.2
	Arbitration Costs, Damage Limitations, and Unconscionability, Opening Brief	Arbit App. E.1
	Challenging Mandatory Arbitration Clause Found in Credit Card "Stuffer"	CLP1 Ch. 1.2
	Opposing Compulsory Arbitration, Home Repair Fraud	CLP4 Ch. 1.4
	Mandatory Arbitration Provision Is Not Enforceable	CLP1 Ch. 1.1
	Consumers' Brief Opposing Enforcement of Arbitration Clause As Unconscionable (OR)	CLP10 Ch. 14.3
	Consumers' Affidavit in Support of Opposition to Arbitration (OR)	CLP10 Ch. 14.4
Post-Trial Motions, Orders, Attorney Fee Documents	Proposed Order for Injunction, Brief, Long Distance Telephone Company's Arbitration Clause Is Unconscionable	CLP8 Ch. 1.5
	Motion to Vacate Arbitration Award New Car Lemon Arbitration (NY)	Warr CD Extra
Class Actions, Articles	"Trying to Protect the Class Action from Mandatory Arbitration," by Jean Sternlight	CCA CD Extra
	"Nuts and Bolts of Arbitrating a Class Action," by Lynn Shecter	CCA CD Extra
Class Actions, Complaints	Arbitration Issues: *Ting v. AT&T*, Violation of the Consumer Legal Remedies Act, Unfair Business Practices Act (CA)	Arbit App. C
Class Actions, Briefs, Memoranda	Trial Brief, Class Action, Arbitration Issues: Unconscionability in Formation and Terms of Arbitration Agreement, *Ting v. AT&T* (N.D. Ca.)	Arbit CD Extra

Auto Credit, Leases, Repos, Deficiencies	*Complaints, Answers, Counterclaims*	Against Auto Dealership Alleging Hidden Credit Charges by Its Alter Ego Finance Company	CLP3 Ch. 9.1.2
		Injunction against Boat's Repossession Sale and Claim for Damages Relating to Sale Abuses	CLP2 Ch. 12.2
		Commercially Unreasonable Sale as Defense to Automobile Creditor's Deficiency Action	CLP2 Ch. 12.3
		Auto Sale, Lender Liability Where FTC Holder Notice Improperly Omitted	CLP1 Ch. 4.2
		Answer Repossession Delay Discharges Obligation of Cosigner on Car Sale UCC	CLP6 Ch. 13.1
		Failure to Honor Credit Life Insurance after Debtor Died, Repossession, UCC	CLP7 Ch. 16.1
		Auto Spot Delivery, Repossession, Conversion, Fraud, Violation of UCC 9-504	CLP7 Ch. 5.2
		Misrepresenting APR in Car Financing; Yield Spread Premium: TILA, UDAP, RISA, Car Titling Statute, (MI)	CLP9 Ch. 2.1
		Complaint, Failure to Disclose that a Trade-in was Given in a Car Lease	CLP8 Ch. 5.1
		Sample Consumer Leasing Act Complaint	TIL Supp. E.7
		Answer Counterclaim Discovery Usury Retail Installment Sales Act, Car Credit Sale	COC App. E.1
		Repossession Deficiency Action	Repo App. D.1
		Counterclaims and Defenses Based on UCC § 9-615(f)	Repo App. D.2
		Repossession, Enjoin Sale	Repo App. D.3
		Repossession, Violation of 42 U.S.C. § 1983, Conversion, Breach of Peace	Repo App. D.4
	Discovery, Interrogatories and Document Requests	Failure to Honor Credit Life Insurance after Debtor Died, Repossession, UCC	CLP7 Ch. 16.2
		Auto Repossession	CLP4 Ch. 4.1
		Auto Sale Lender Liability Where FTC Holder Notice Improperly Omitted	CLP1 Ch. 4.5
		Auto Fraud Alleging Hidden Credit Charges by Dealer's Alter Ego Finance Company	CLP3 Ch. 9.1.3
		Misrepresenting APR in Car Financing; Yield Spread Premium: TILA, UDAP, RISA, Car Titling Statute (MI)	CLP9 Ch. 2.2–2.7
		Automobile Repossession Deficiency Suit	Repo App. E.1
	Discovery, Interrogatories	Sample Consumer Leasing Act Interrogatories	TIL Supp. F.6
		Repossession, Dealer-Only Auto Auction Deficiency Suit	Repo App. E.3
	Discovery, Document Requests	Sample Consumer Leasing Act Request for Production of Documents	TIL Supp. App. F.7
	Discovery, Requests for Admissions	Repossession Vehicle Valuation after Repossession	Repo App. E.5

Pleadings by Subject

		Repossession Failure to Give Required Notice of Sale: RISA, UDAP, Summary Judgment	CLP6 Ch. 4.5
	Class Actions, Settlements	Memoranda in Support of Final Approval of Class Settlement Consumer Leasing Act and Deceptive Practices Case—Car Lease (*Shepherd*)	CCA App. R.3
		Settlement Notice Dealer Law Violations Relating to Used Car Sales, Rule 23(e) (*Norris*)	CCA App. O.2.2
		Stipulations of Proposed Settlements Consumer Leasing Act and Deceptive Practices Case—Car Lease (*Shepherd*)	CCA App. P.4
		Stipulations of Proposed Settlements Revolving Repossession Case (*Johnson*)	CCA99 App. O.4
	Class Actions, Objections to Settlement	Opposition to Inadequate Consumer Class Action Settlement—Defective Post-Repossession Notices, Including Affidavits	CLP9 Ch. 13.1–13.3
		Attorney Affidavit Opposing Preliminary Approval of Class Action Settlement	CCA Supp. App. S.9.1
		Memorandum Opposing Preliminary Approval of Class Action Settlement	CCA Supp. App. S.9.2
		Intervenors' Objections to Class Action Settlement (*H&R Block*)	CCA Supp. App. S.11
	Class Actions, Attorney Fees	Motion for Award of Attorney Fees and Reimbursement of Expenses (*Minnick*)	CCA Supp. App. T.1.1
		Reply Memorandum, Motion for Award of Attorney Fees and Reimbursement of Expenses (*Minnick*)	CCA Supp. App. T.1.3
		Memorandum in Support of Plaintiff's Motion for Attorney Fees and Reimbursement of Expenses (*Minnick*)	CCA Supp. App. T.1.2
		Request for Attorney Fees Auto Sale Lender Liability Where FTC Holder Notice Improperly Omitted	CLP1 Ch. 4.14
Auto Fraud	*Demand Letters, Notices, Retainers, Forms*	Settlement Letter: Undisclosed Sale of Lemon Buy-Back RV (OH)	CLP10 Ch. 2.1.8
		Client Letter—Settlement: Undisclosed Sale of Lemon Buy-Back RV (OH)	CLP10 Ch. 2.1.7
	Complaints, Answers, Counterclaims	Undisclosed Sale of Lemon Buy-Back	CLP2 Ch. 6.1.1
		Undisclosed Defects and Excessive Price Leading to Car's Repossession	CLP2 Ch. 6.3.1
		Undisclosed Sale of Salvaged vehicle	CLP2 Ch. 6.2.1
		Dealer for Car's Prior Use (*Giles*) (Unabridged)	Auto CD Extra
		Concealed Wreck (*Petrie*)	Auto CD Extra
		Odometer and Concealed Wreck (*Malone*)	Auto CD Extra
		Auto Dealer for Concealment of Salvage Branded Title (*Summers*) (Unabridged)	Auto CD Extra
		Fraud and Civil Conspiracy in the Sale of Wrecked Vehicle (*Dallas*)	Auto CD Extra

	Rebuilt Wreck Complaint (OH)	CLP10 Ch. 2.2
	Automobile Odometer Fraud and Threat of Violent Repossession	CLP5 Ch. 3.1
	Auto Fraud Sales Practices	CLP6 Ch. 9.1
	Auto Spot Delivery, Odometer Act, TILA, Conversion, UDAP	CLP7 Ch. 5.1
	Auto Spot Delivery, Repossession, Conversion, Fraud, Violation of UCC 9-504	CLP7 Ch. 5.2
	Auto Dealer for Concealment of Car's Prior Use	Auto App. G.7
	Lemon Buyback Case	Auto App. G.6
	Auto Dealer and Financer, Undisclosed Wreck History	Auto App. G.5
	Auto Dealer for Concealment of Salvage Branded Title	Auto App. G.4
	Auto Dealer and Lender—Odometer Misrepresentations, Lender's Information Sent to Credit Reporting Agency	Auto App. G.3
	Auto Dealers for Tampering, False Statements, and False Disclosures	Auto App. G.2
	Undisclosed Sale of Lemon Buy-Back RV Complaint (OH)	CLP10 Ch. 2.1.1
	Concealment of Car's Prior Use by Car Rental Agency	CLP9 Ch. 5.3
	Concealment of Salvage Title	CLP9 Ch. 5.2
	Concealment of Wreck, and Prior Owner, Rental Agency	CLP9 Ch. 5.1
	Misrepresenting APR in Car Financing; Yield Spread Premium: TILA, UDAP, RISA, Car Titling Statute, (MI)	CLP9 Ch. 2.1
	Complaint, Failure to Disclose That a Trade-in Was Given in a Car Lease	CLP8 Ch. 5.1
Discovery, Interrogatories and Document Requests	Undisclosed Defects and Excessive Price Leading to Car's Repossession	CLP2 Ch. 6.3.2
	Undisclosed Sale of Salvaged Vehicle	CLP2 Ch. 6.2.2
	Net Worth Discovery	Auto App. H.4
	Auto Spot Delivery	CLP7 Ch. 5.3
	Undisclosed Sale of Lemon Buy-Back RV, Second Set of Discovery to Manufacturer (OH)	CLP10 Ch. 2.1.6
	Undisclosed Sale of Lemon Buy-Back RV, Discovery Directed to Bank (OH)	CLP10 Ch. 2.1.4
	Undisclosed Sale of Lemon Buy-Back RV, Discovery Directed to the Manufacturer (OH)	CLP10 Ch. 2.1.3
	Undisclosed Sale of Lemon Buy-Back RV, Discovery Directed to the Dealer (OH)	CLP10 Ch. 2.1.2
	Undisclosed Sale of Lemon Buy-Back	CLP2 Ch. 6.1.2
	Misrepresenting APR in Car Financing; Yield Spread Premium: TILA, UDAP, RISA, Car Titling Statute (MI)	CLP9 Ch. 2.2–2.7
Discovery, Interrogatories	Undisclosed Damage History	Auto App. H.2.2

	Lemon Laundering, Interrogatories to Manufacturer	Auto App. H.3.4
	Odometer Fraud	Auto App. H.1.2
	Lemon Laundering, Interrogatories to Dealer	Auto App. H.3.2
	Dealer—Undisclosed Wreck History	Auto 2002 App. F.2.5
Discovery, Document Requests	Initial Document Requests—Concealed Wreck	Auto CD Extra
	Undisclosed Auto Repair History, Manufacturer	Auto 1998 Appx F.4.3
	Undisclosed Auto Repair History, Lender	Auto 1998 Appx F.4.4
	Undisclosed Auto Repair History, Dealer	Auto 1998 Appx F.4.2
	Undisclosed Sale of Lemon Buy-Back RV, Second Document Request to Dealer (OH)	CLP10 Ch. 2.1.5
	Floor Plan Financier, Document Requests	Auto Supp. App. H.6
	Lemon Laundering, Document Request to Dealer	Auto App. H.3.3
	Lemon Laundering, Document Request to Manufacturer	Auto App. H.3.5
	Odometer Fraud	Auto App. H.1.3
	Undisclosed Damage History	Auto App. H.2.3
	Dealer—Undisclosed Wreck History	Auto 1998 Appx F.2.2
Discovery, Requests for Admissions	Odometer Fraud	Auto App. H.1.4
	Undisclosed Damage History	Auto App. H.2.4
Discovery, Depositions	Outline for Deposition of Car Dealer in Concealed Wreck Damage Case	Auto App. H.2.5
	Deposition Outline: Immediate, Remote Sellers, Undisclosed Wrecked Cars	Auto CD Extra
	Deposition of Former Used Car Manager about the Resale of a Wrecked Car (MO)	CLP10 Ch. 18.2
	Deposition (With Comments) of Business Manager Regarding Sale of a Rebuilt Wreck (MO)	CLP10 Ch. 18.3
	Deposition of Used Car Manager Regarding Resale of Wrecked Car (MO)	CLP10 Ch. 18.1
Discovery, Discovery Motions	Consumer's Access to Other Cars Sold by Dealer	Auto App. H.5
Pre-Trial Motions, Trial Practice	Jury Instructions in Wrecked Car Case	Auto App. I.9
	Expert Report of Professor Ian Ayres, Disparate Racial Impacts in Finance Charge Markups, NMAC	CD CD Extra

Expert Report on Racial Impact of NMAC's Finance Charge Markup Policy by Mark Cohen, Ph.D.	CD CD Extra
Motion for Preliminary Injunction (NMAC)	CD CD Extra
Jury Instruction Regarding Missing Evidence	Auto App. I.10
Mediation Presentation: Undisclosed Sale of Lemon Buy-Back RV (OH)	CLP10 Ch. 2.1.9
Undisclosed Sale of Lemon Buy-Back RV Repair History, Trial Parts and Labor Comparison Chart (OH)	CLP10 Ch. 2.1.10
Response to Motion to Dismiss and Plaintiffs' Motion for Partial Summary Judgment, FTC Holder Rule (*Potter*)	Auto CD Extra
Jury Instructions Automobile Odometer Fraud and Threat of Violent Repossession	CLP5 Ch. 3.4
Jury Instructions in Odometer Case	Auto App. I.8
Opening Statement to Jury Rebuilt Car Litigation (*Sloan*)	Auto CD Extra
Voir Dire, Wreck Damage Case	Auto App. I.2
Jury Instructions, Misrepresentation of Vehicle Characteristics (*MacArthur*)	Auto CD Extra
Motion in Limine and for Bifurcation	Auto App. I.7
Verdict Form, Misrepresentation of Vehicle Characteristics (*MacArthur*)	Auto CD Extra
Motion for Summary Judgment, Material Facts, Memorandum, Failure to Disclose That a Trade-in Was Given in a Car Lease	CLP8 Ch. 5.2
Outline for Questioning of Expert Witness on Condition of Vehicle	Auto App. I.6
Voir Dire Outline, Rebuilt Wreck	Auto App. I.3
Opening Statement to Jury, Federal Odometer Act	Auto App. I.4
Auto Fraud, Sample Motions and Briefs (List)	Auto App. J
Closing Argument to Jury, Federal Odometer Act	Auto App. I.5
Special Verdict Form in Wrecked Car Case	Auto App. I.11
Jury Instructions Undisclosed Sale of Salvaged vehicle	CLP2 Ch. 6.2.7
Plaintiff's Motion for Summary Judgment in "Spot Delivery" Case	FCR CD Extra
Briefs, Memoranda Undisclosed Sale of Salvaged vehicle	CLP2 Ch. 6.2.6
Auto Spot Delivery, Waiver Agreement Void, Odometer Act Violation	CLP7 Ch. 5.4
Summary Judgment: Misrepresenting APR in Car Financing; Yield Spread Premium: TILA, UDAP, RISA, car titling statute (MI)	CLP9 Ch. 2.1
Concealment of Address of Prior Owner Which Would Show Rough Use (*Yazzie v. Amigo Chevrolet, Inc.*)	CLP9 Ch. 5.4
Auto Dealer Interest Markups, Race Discrimination, ECOA, Nissan MAC	CLP7 Ch. 1.1, 1.2
In Support of Motion to Amend Complaint Auto Sales Fraud	CLP6 Ch. 9.2

	Salvaged Auto Fraud, Summary Judgment	CLP5 Ch. 6.1
	Automobile Odometer Fraud and Threat of Violent Repossession, Summary Judgment Motion Brief	CLP5 Ch. 3.3
	Dealer's Failure to Provide Title Certificate with Prior Owner's Address is Odometer Act Disclosure Violation, Summary Judgment Reply Brief (*Yazzie*)	Auto CD Extra
	Dealer's Failure to Provide Title Certificate with Prior Owner's Address Is Odometer Act Disclosure Violation, Summary Judgment Brief (*Yazzie*)	Auto CD Extra
	Attorney Fees, Treble Damages Should be Recoverable on Dealer's Surety Bond: Appellant's Reply Brief (*Helper*)	Auto CD Extra
	Attorney Fees, Treble Damages Should be Recoverable on Dealer's Surety Bond: Appellant's Brief (*Helper*)	Auto CD Extra
	In Opposition to NMAC's Motion for Summary Judgment, Race Discrimination in Auto Finance Markup, ECOA	CD CD Extra
	Opposing Motion to Dismiss in "Spot Delivery" Case	FCR CD Extra
Post-Trial Motions, Orders, Attorney Fee Documents	Questions for Expert Witness on Attorney Fees	Auto App. L.3
	Petition for Award of Attorney Fees	Auto App. L.2
Class Actions, Complaints	Odometer Fraud, Breach of Contract (*Potter*) (Unabridged)	Auto CD Extra
	Odometer Rollback, Class Complaint	AF 1998 App. H.1
	Used Car Churning Scheme; RICO; and Memorandum—Motion to Dismiss	CLP3 Ch. 9.3.1
	Auto Dealerships Alleging Race Discrimination and Rebate Theft; Discovery	CLP3 Ch. 9.2.1
	Odometer Fraud; FTC Holder Notice Triggers Bank's Class Liability for Dealer's Fraud	CLP1 Ch. 3.1
	Auto Dealer, Finance Company, Federal Odometer Act, Consumer Fraud Act	Auto App. K.1
	Auto Dealer Overcharged for Extended Warranties: UDAP, RISA	CLP6 Ch. 6.1
Class Actions, Discovery	Odometer Fraud FTC Holder Notice Triggers Bank's Class Liability for Dealer's Fraud	CLP1 Ch. 3.1
	Class Action Interrogatories to Financing Entity	Auto App. K.5
Class Actions, Protective Orders	Odometer Case, Memorandum in Support of Motion for Protective Order	Auto App. K.2.3
	Odometer Case, Motion for Protective Order and Other Relief	Auto App. K.2.2
Class Actions, Certification Pleadings	Odometer Fraud FTC Holder Notice Triggers Bank's Class Liability for Dealer's Fraud	CLP1 Ch. 3.1

		Response to Objections—Evidence in Support of Class Certification (*Potter*)	Auto CD Extr
		Reply Brief in Support of Class Certification (*Potter*) (Unabridged)	Auto CD Extra
		Odometer Class Action, Motion to Certify Class with Supporting Memorandum (*Potter*) (Unabridged)	Auto CD Extra
		Odometer, Consumer Fraud; Motion to Certify Class with Supporting Memorandum	Auto App. K.3.2
		Odometer, Consumer Fraud; Reply Brief in Support of Class Certification	Auto App. K.3.3
		Odometer Rollback	Auto 1998 H.3
	Class Actions, Class Notices	Odometer Case, Class Action Notice	Auto App. K.4
	Class Actions, Settlements	Order Approving Settlement Odometer Fraud FTC Holder Notice Triggers Bank's Class Liability for Dealer's Fraud	CLP1 Ch. 3.12
		Odometer Class Action, Final Order Approving Settlement	Auto App. K.6.3
		Odometer Class Action, Final Report of Plaintiff's Counsel with Affidavit	Auto App. K.6.2
		Odometer Class Action, Order Preliminarily Approving Settlement	Auto App. K.6.1
Auto Warranties, Lemon Law, Auto Repair	*Demand Letters, Notices, Retainers, Forms*	Letter to National Highway Traffic Safety Administration for Preliminary Evaluation File	CLP4 Ch. 15.13
		Notice That Consumer Is Deducting Damages From the Outstanding Balance	Warr App. J.2
		Notice of Rejection or Revocation of Acceptance	Warr App. J.1
	Complaints, Answers, Counterclaims	New Car Lemon Case	CLP2 Ch. 5.1
		New Car Lemon Law Suits, Discovery, Lemon Law Tools	CLP4 Ch. 15.1
		Gray Market Vehicle Sales Motorcycle	CLP6 Ch. 11.1
		New Car Lemon Suit (TN)	CLP8 Ch. 7.1
		Combustion of a Recalled Car	CLP8 Ch. 6.1
		Lemon Law, New Car (TN)	Warr CD Extra
		Mobile Home Case (MI)	Warr CD Extra
		New Car Lemon Law, Magnuson-Moss Act (VA)	Warr CD Extra
		Dealer and Manufacturer of Defective Mobile Home	Warr App. K 6
		Damages for Breach of Implied Warranty of Merchantability	Warr App. K.2.2
		For Damages for Breach of Implied Warranty of Fitness for a Particular Purpose	Warr App. K.2.3
		For Damages for Breach of Express Warranty	Warr App. K.2.4
		Revocation of Acceptance	Warr App. K.2.5

	Used Car Sale	Warr App. K.3
	New Car Lemon Case	Warr App. K.5
	Dealer and Financer for Improper Setup of Mobile Home	Warr App. K.7
Discovery, Interrogatories and Document Requests	New Car Lemon Case	CLP2 Ch. 5.2
	Gray Market Vehicle Sales Motorcycle	CLP6 Ch. 11.2
	Mobile Home, Requests for Production of Documents, Interrogatories to Dealer, Finance Co. (Discovery in Arbitrated Matter)	Warr CD Extra
	Combined Discovery Request to Manufacturer New Car Lemon Case	Warr App. L.5.1
	Combined Discovery Request to Dealer New Car Lemon Case	Warr App. L.5.3
Discovery, Interrogatories	New Car Lemon Suit (TN)	CLP8 Ch. 7.3
	Combustion of a Recalled Car	CLP8 Ch. 6.2
	For Used Car Sale	Warr App. L.6
	Expert Witness Interrogatories to Defendant	Warr App. L.5.5
	Lemon Law Case (TN)	Warr CD Extra
	For New Car Lemon Law Case	Warr App. L.5
	To Lender Concerning Its Relationship to Seller	Warr App. L.4
	To the Seller	Warr App. L.2
Discovery, Document Requests	New Car Lemon Suit (TN)	CLP8 Ch. 7.2
	Lemon Law Case (TN)	Warr CD Extra
	To Mobile Home Manufacturer	Warr App. L.7
	Warranty Document Requests	Warr App. L.3
Discovery, Requests for Admissions	To Manufacturer New Car Lemon Case	Warr App. L.5.2
Pre-Trial Motions, Trial Practice	Jury Verdict Form, Automobile Lemon case: UCC, Magnuson-Moss Warranty Act, Michigan Lemon Law, Motor Vehicle Service and Repair Act, Misrepresentation, UDAP	CLP9 Ch. 8
	Jury Instructions for Magnuson-Moss Warranty Act Claims	CLP5 Ch. 6.3
	Motion to Exclude Discussion of Attorney Fees (CA)	Warr CD Extra
	Motion to Enjoin Repossession (OH)	Warr CD Extra
	Jury Instructions: Title, Vehicle Defects (OH)	Warr CD Extra
	Motion to Exclude Disparagement of Attorney (OH)	Warr CD Extra
	Verdict Form New Car Case	Warr App. M.9.2
	Verdict Form Used Car Case	Warr App. M.9.1
	Jury Instructions, Lemon Law	Warr App. M.8.4

		Jury Instructions: Substantial Impairment and Shaken Faith Doctrine	Warr App. M.8.3
		Jury Instructions: Rejection, Revocation, Merchantability, Fitness for a Particular Purpose and Disclaimer	Warr App. M.8.2
		Jury Instructions: Express Warranty, Merchantability, Revocation and Magnuson-Moss Warranty Act	Warr App. M.8.1
		Jury Instructions: Warranty	Warr App. M.8
		Closing Argument Before a Jury and Excerpt of Rebuttal	Warr App. M.7
		Direct Examination Outline: Buyer in Case Involving Breach of Warranty, Fraud	Warr Supp. App. M.6a
		Direct Examination of Consumer's Expert	Warr App. M.6
		Opening Statement Before Jury	Warr App. M.5
		Voir Dire, Car Warranty case	Warr App. M.4
		Trial Brief, New Car Case	Warr App. M.3
		Pre-Trial Statement—New Car Case	Warr App. M.2
		Verdict Form, Auto Lease (MI)	Warr CD Extra
	Post-Trial Motions, Orders, Attorney Fee Documents	Attorney Fees Bifurcation Issue Lemon Law case	CLP4 Ch. 15.25
		Federal Limitation in *Buckhannon* Should Not Be Imposed on Preexisting State Statute Awarding Attorney Fees	CLP9 Ch. 15
		Brief Requesting Attorney Fee—Repossession Civil Rights Police Assistance	CLP5 Ch. 8.1
		Motion to Treble Damage Award: UDAP, Warranty	Warr App. M.10
		Motion to Vacate Arbitration Award New Car Lemon Arbitration (NY)	Warr CD Extra
	Class Actions, Complaints	Class Complaint for Padding Repair Bills (OH)	CLP10 Ch. 2.3
	Class Actions, Objections to Settlement	Response to Objections to Settlement—*Howard v. Ford Motor Company*	CCA CD Extra
Banking, Electronic Fund Transfers	*Complaints, Answers, Counterclaims*	FDCPA Against Attorney for Seizing Exempt Bank Account Funds	CLP2 Ch. 12.1
		Credit Union Wrongfully Setoff a Customer's Exempt Social Security Funds (D.N.M.)	CLP7 Ch. 13.1
		West Virginia v. TeleCheck	CBPL CD Extra
		Creditor Garnishment of Exempt Social Security Funds	CBPL CD Extra
	Pre-Trial Motions, Trial Practice	Credit Union Wrongfully Setoff a Customer's Exempt Social Security Funds, Motion for Summary Judgment (D.N.M.)	CLP7 C.13.2

	Briefs, Memoranda	Amicus Brief: Banker's Setoff of Social Security Funds in Checking Accounts Violates Exemption in Social Security Act (9th Circuit)	CLP8 Ch. 17.1
		Bank Set-Off of Exempt Social Security Funds for Debt to Bank, Appellate Brief	CBPL CD Extra
		Bank Set-Off of Exempt Social Security Funds for Debt to Bank, Reply Brief	CBPL CD Extra
		Creditor Garnishment of Exempt Social Security Funds	CBPL CD Extra
		West Virginia v. TeleCheck, Response to Amicus Brief	CBPL CD Extra
		Credit Union Wrongfully Setoff a Customer's Exempt Social Security Funds, Appellate Brief (D.N.M.)	CLP7 Ch. 13.5
	Class Actions, Complaints	Bank Practices Leading to Increased Bounced Check Fees (Amended Class Complaint)	CBPL CD Extra
		Bank Practices Leading to Increased Bounced Check Fees	CBPL CD Extra
Bankruptcy	*Demand Letters, Notices, Retainers, Forms*	Notice of TILA Rescission	CLP9 Ch. 19.1
	Complaints, Answers, Counterclaims	Mortgage Servicer for Disregarding Chapter 13 Plan Provisions	CLP3 Ch. 7.1
		Mortgage Adversary Complaint: TIL Rescission in Bankruptcy, RESPA, UDAP, Yield Spread Premium	CLP9 Ch. 19.2
	Discovery, Interrogatories and Document Requests	Bankruptcy Proceeding to Determine Dischargeability of Student Loan	Stud App. F.3
	Class Actions, Complaints	Taxing Agency for Filing Baseless Chapter 13 Proofs of Claim, Discovery; Consent Decree	CLP3 Ch. 7.2
		Unlawful Collection of Debts Discharged in Bankruptcy Sears	CLP5 Ch. 2.1.1
	Class Actions, Settlements	Agreement of Sears, Unlawful Collection of Debts Discharged in Bankruptcy	CLP5 Ch. 2.1.2
	Bankruptcy, Petitions, Schedules, Official Forms	Official Form 6. Schedule B, Personal Property	Bankr App. D
		Official Form 16D. Captions Adversary Proceedings	Bankr App. D
		Official Form 6. Schedule C, Exempt Property	Bankr App. D
		Official Form 6. Schedule D, Creditors Holding Secured Claims	Bankr App. D
		Official Form 16. A, B Captions	Bankr App. D
		Third-Party Summons	Bankr App. E
		Official Form 10. Proof of Claim	Bankr App. D
		Official Form 1. Petition in Bankruptcy	Bankr App. D
		Sample Completed Bankruptcy Schedules to Institute Case	Bankr App. F
		Official Form 20B. Notice of Objection to Claim	Bankr App. D
		Summons in an Adversary Proceeding	Bankr App. E

	Official Form 6. Schedule H, Codebtors	Bankr App. D
	Bankruptcy Forms software from Law Disks—(Fill in petition/schedules using WordPerfect or Microsoft Word)	*Consumer Law in a Box* CD; *Bankruptcy* CD
Bankruptcy, Initial Forms	Chapter 13 Plan Providing for Liquidation of Debtor's Interest in Residence	Bankr App. G #12
	Application and Order for Waiver of Miscellaneous Fees	Bankr App. G #7
	Order Confirming Chapter 13 Plan	Bankr App. G #9
	Motion for Payover Order in Chapter 13	Bankr App. G #10
	Order to Pay Wages to the Trustee in Chapter 13	Bankr App. G #11
	Motion to Keep Prior Name Confidential	Bankr App. G #6
	Chapter 13 Plan Providing for Filing of Adversary Proceeding Involving Predatory Mortgage Lending Claims	Bankr App. G #13
	Chapter 13 Plan Assuming Residential Lease	Bankr App. G #14
	Application for Counsel Fees	Bankr App. G #22
	Statement by Debtor's Attorney of Fees Charged	Bankr App. G #21
	Application and Order for Waiver of Filing Fee to Amend Debtor's Schedule of Creditors	Bankr App. G #20
	Debtor's Amendment of Schedules	Bankr App. G #19
	Pre-Filing Notification to Creditors of Representation	Bankr App. G #1
	Debtor's First Amended Chapter 13 Plan	Bankr App. G #18
	Application and Order for Additional Extension of Time to File Chapter 13 Schedules, Statement of Affairs, and Chapter 13 Plan	Bankr App. G #5
	Motion and Order for Extension of Time to File Chapter 13 Schedules, Statement of Affairs, and Chapter 13 Plan	Bankr App. G #4
	Chapter 13 Debtor's Motion to Assume Lease	Bankr App. G #15
	Notification to Creditor Seeking Information As to Account	Bankr App. G #2
	Motion and Order for Extension of Time to File Schedules and Statement of Affairs	Bankr App. G #3
	Chapter 13 Bankruptcy Checklist from Debtor's Attorney to Debtor	Bankr App. G #16
	Chapter 7 Information Sheet from Attorney to Debtor	Bankr App. G #17
	Debtors' Chapter 13 Plan	Bankr App. G #8
Bankruptcy, Automatic Stay	Answer to Application for Abandonment of Real Estate	Bankr App. G #34
	Debtor's Objection to Relief from the Codebtor Stay	Bankr App. G #33
	Debtor's Answer to Motion for Relief from Codebtor Stay	Bankr App. G #32
	Answer to Motion for Relief from Automatic Stay Raising Avoidability of Transfer to Plaintiff	Bankr App. G #31
	Letter to Creditors Giving Notice of Stay	Bankr App. G #23
	Complaint Seeking Damages for Violation of Automatic Stay and Unfair Trade Practices	Bankr App. G #24

Pleadings by Subject

	Complaint to Recover SSI Benefits Collected by State As Reimbursement for Pre-bankruptcy Welfare Debt	Bankr App. G #119
	Defendant's Interrogatories in Dischargeability Case Based on Credit Card Fraud	Bankr App. G #110
	Proposed Order for Preliminary Relief in Complaint to Enjoin Discriminatory Denial of Guaranteed Student Loan	Bankr App. G #123
	Motion for Preliminary Relief in Complaint to Enjoin Discriminatory Denial of Guaranteed Student Loan	Bankr App. G #122
	Letter to Creditor Concerning Proposed Reaffirmation Agreement	Bankr App. G #113
	Class Action Settlement Agreement Sears Unlawful Collection of Debts Discharged in Bankruptcy	CLP5 Ch. 2.1.2
	Complaint to Enjoin Discriminatory Denial of Guaranteed Student Loan	Bankr App. G #121
	Complaint Seeking Contempt Remedies for Violation of the Automatic Stay and Discharge Injunction	Bankr App. G #120
	Class Action Complaint Unlawful Collection of Debts Discharged in Bankruptcy Sears	CLP5 Ch. 2.1.1
	Defendant's Requests for Admissions in Dischargeability Case Based on Credit Card Fraud	Bankr App. G #111
	Debtor's Application for a Hardship Discharge	Bankr App. G #112
	Brief Bankruptcy Student Loan Undue Hardship	CLP6 Ch. 7.2.1
	Complaint to Determine Dischargeability of Student Loan	Stud App. E.6.1
	Dischargeability Complaint Raising School's Fraud	Stud App. E.6.2
Bankruptcy, Plan Conversion, Modification, Dismissal	Debtor's Notice to Convert Case from Chapter 13 to Chapter 7	Bankr App. G #133
	Motion to Modify Plan After Confirmation	Bankr App. G #128
	Motion to Modify Plan to Terminate Plan	Bankr App. G #129
	Motion to Modify Plan to Surrender Vehicle	Bankr App. G #130
	Motion to Modify Plan to Permit Mortgage Refinancing to Pay Off Plan	Bankr App. G #131
	Debtor's Amended Plan Permitting Mortgage Refinancing to Pay Off Plan	Bankr App. G #132
	Debtor's Motion to Reopen Case	Bankr App. G #138
	Supplemental Schedule of Debts Arising After Filing of the Petition, But Prior to Conversion to Chapter 7	Bankr App. G #134
	Debtor's Motion to Convert Chapter 7 Case to Chapter 13	Bankr App. G #135
	Debtor's Motion to Dismiss Chapter 13 Case	Bankr App. G #136
	Debtor's Motion to Dismiss Chapter 7 Case	Bankr App. G #137
Bankruptcy, Farm Reorganization	Order Authorizing Debtor-in-Possession to Apply for ASCS Programs	Bankr App. G #140
	Debtor's Motion for Permission to Apply for ASCS Programs	Bankr App. G #139

		Disposable Income Affidavit for Chapter 12 Cases	Bankr App. G #145
		Motion for Authority to Obtain Secured Credit	Bankr App. G #141
		Cash Collateral Stipulation	Bankr App. G #142
		Chapter 12 Plan	Bankr App. G #143
		Order Confirming Chapter 12 Plan	Bankr App. G #144
	Bankruptcy, Consumers as Creditors	Discovery, Bankruptcy Litigation with High Rate Mortgage Lender	CLP7 Ch.6.2
		Complaint Seeking Subordination of Secured Creditor's Claims	Bankr App. G #154
		Bankruptcy Complaint to Recover Transferred Property Chapter 11 Merchant	CLP1 Ch. 10.8
		In Forma Pauperis Petition and Memorandum of Law in Support	Bankr App. G #147
		Objection to Confirmation of Chapter 11 Plan	Bankr App. G #153
		Objection to Chapter 11 Disclosure Statement	Bankr App. G #152
		Objections to Chapter 11 Plan of High Rate Mortgage Lender	CLP7 Ch. 6.1
		Procedures for Consumer Creditor Claims Against Merchant in Chapter 11 Bankruptcy	CLP1 Ch. 10.1
		Complaint to Establish Priority over Lien Creditor Consumer Creditor Claims Against Merchant in Chapter 11 Bankruptcy	CLP1 Ch. 10.7
		Motion for Relief from Stay by Tenant to Raise Counterclaims to Eviction	Bankr App. G #146
		Complaint to Determine Dischargeability of Tenant's Claims Against Landlord	Bankr App. G #148
		Motion for Appointment of Committee of Tenants	Bankr App. G #149
		Statement of Attorney Pursuant to Rule 2019	Bankr App. G #151
		Expedited Motion for Appointment of Committee of Consumer Creditors	Bankr App. G #150
Credit Cards, Open-End Credit	*Complaints, Answers, Counterclaims*	Credit Cards Failure to Recognize Defense, also Discovery	CLP2 Ch. 9.1
		Fair Credit Billing Act	TIL App. E.5
	Discovery, Interrogatories	Defendant's Interrogatories in Dischargeability Case Based on Credit Card Fraud	Bankr App. G #110
		Fair Credit Billing Act	TIL App. F.4
	Discovery, Document Requests	Defendant's Requests for Production of Documents in Dischargeability Case Based on Credit Card Fraud	Bankr App. G #109
	Discovery, Requests for Admissions	Defendant's Requests for Admissions in Dischargeability Case Based on Credit Card Fraud	Bankr App. G #111
	Pre-Trial Motions, Trial Practice	Opposition to Demurrer—Unconscionable Mandatory Arbitration Clauses in Consumer Credit Contracts	CLP5 Ch. 12.1.1

		Expert Analysis, Illusory Benefit of Secured Credit Card	CLP10 Ch. 12.2
	Briefs, Memoranda	In Support of Class Certification TIL, UDAP, and Breach of Contract Case—Credit Card Issuer's Failure to Refund Credit Balance (*Coe*)	CCA App. L.2
		Reply Memoranda in Support of Class Certification TIL, UDAP, and Breach of Contract Case—Credit Card Issuer's Failure to Refund Credit Balance (*Coe*)	CCA App. M.1
		Unconscionable Mandatory Arbitration Clauses in Consumer Credit Contracts	CLP5 Ch. 12.1.2
	Class Actions, Briefs, Memoranda	Challenging Mandatory Arbitration Clause Found in Credit Card "Stuffer"	CLP1 Ch. 1.2
		Challenging Mandatory Arbitration Clause Found in Credit Card "Stuffer"	CLP1 Ch. 1.3
	Class Actions, Objections to Settlement	Objections to Settlement Agreement (*Boehr*)	CCA App. S.2
	Class Actions, Cy Pres	Cy Pres Remedy *Beasley*—Late Fees, Memorandum, Court Orders	CLP1 Ch. 12.1
Credit Discrimination	*Complaints, Answers, Counterclaims*	Auto Dealerships Alleging Race Discrimination and Rebate Theft	CLP3 Ch. 9.2.1
		Violations of the FHA and ECOA in Marketing of Lending Products and Services (*U.S. v. Mid America Bank*), also Consent Order	CD CD Extra
		Lending Discrimination Against Native Americans (*U.S. v. First National Bank of Gordon*), also Consent Order	CD CD Extra
		Discrimination in Mobile home Purchase Loans (*U.S. v. First National Bank of Dona Ana County*), also Settlement Agreement	CD CD Extra
		Discrimination in Collection of Subprime Credit Card Accounts (*U.S. v. Fidelity Federal Bank*), also Settlement Agreement	CD CD Extra
		ECOA Notice Violations and Violations of the Federal Fair Credit Reporting Act (*Cleaver v. Greater Mid-Atlantic Finance Co., Inc.*)	CD CD Extra
		ECOA Notice Violations (*Lane v. Southside Bank*)	CD CD Extra
		Car Dealer Discrimination Against Mandarin Speakers (state law claims) (*A. v. Wondries Associates, Inc.*)	CD CD Extra
		Subprime Lender Violation of FHA, ECOA, RESPA, TILA (*United States v. Delta Funding Corp. and Delta Financial Corp.*)	CD CD Extra
		Reverse Redlining, Gender (*Eva v. MidwestNational Mortgage Banc*)	CD CD Extra
		Redlining and Adverse Impact of Mortgage Lender's Business Practices (*United States v. Chevy Chase Federal Savings Bank*)	CD CD Extra

	Insurance Redlining (*United States v. Nationwide Mutual Insurance Company*)	CD CD Extra
	Fair Housing Act Violation, Segregation, Dual Housing Market *(Honorable v. The Easy Life Real Estate Systems)*	CD CD Extra
	ECOA and Regulation B Violations (*Franklin Acceptance*)	CD CD Extra
	ECOA and FHA Case Alleging Bank Refused to Lend to Native Americans (*United States v. Blackpipe State Bank*)	CD CD Extra
	Action Alleging Redlining By Use of Correspondent Lenders (*U. S. v. Albank, FSB*)	CD CD Extra
	Action Alleging Redlining and Marketing Discrimination (*U. S. v. Chevy Chase Federal Savings Bank*)	CD CD Extra
	Action Alleging Redlining and Marketing Discrimination (*U.S. v. Decatur FSLA*)	CD CD Extra
	Action Alleging Discriminatory Credit Score Thresholds (*U. S. v. Associates National Bank*)	CD CD Extra
	Action Alleging Discrimination in Use of Credit Score Overrides (*U. S. v. Deposit Guaranty National Bank*)	CD CD Extra
	Action Against Subprime Lender, Discriminatory Overcharges by Affiliated Mortgage Brokers (*U. S. v. Long Beach Mortgage Co.*)	CD CD Extra
	ECOA Notice Provisions, also TILA, FCRA	CD Supp. App. F.6
	ECOA Cosigner Violation	CD App. F.2
	Denial of Home Mortgage and Discriminatory Appraisal Practices as ECOA, Fair Housing and Civil Rights Violations	CD App. F.1
Discovery, Interrogatories and Document Requests	ECOA Notice Case (*Cleaver v. Greater Mid-Atlantic Finance Co., Inc.*)	CD CD Extra
Discovery, Interrogatories	ECOA Zip Code Redlining	CD App. G.3
	ECOA Cosigner Violation	CD App. G.2
	ECOA Adverse Action Notice Violation	CD App. G.1
	Reverse Redlining Case, Gender, Defendant Midwest National, Document Requests(*Eva v. Midwest National Mortgage Banc*)	CD CD Extra
	Reverse Redlining, Gender, Defendant Thomas Butzer, Document Requests (*Eva v. Midwest National Mortgage Banc*)	CD CD Extra
	Reverse Redlining, Gender, Defendant USMR, Document Requests (*Eva v. Midwest National Mortgage Banc*)	CD CD Extra
Discovery, Document Requests	Fair Housing Case, Segregation, Dual Market	CD App. G.4
	Fair Credit Reporting Act, to Furnisher	FCR Supp. App. I.3.3

Pre-Trial Motions, Trial Practice	Reverse Redlining, Gender, Surreply in Opposition to 12(b)(6) Motions *(Eva v. Midwest National Mortgage Banc)*	CD CD Extra
	Pre-Trial Order Including Jury Instructions in ECOA Notice Case *(Cleaver v. Greater Mid-Atlantic Finance Co., Inc)*	CD CD Extra
	Reverse Redlining, Gender, Opposition to Defendant's Motions for Judgment on the Pleadings *(Eva v. Midwest National Mortgage Banc)*	CD CD Extra
	Segregation, Dual Housing Market, Fair Housing Act Violation, Opposing Motion for Summary Judgment *(Honorable v. The Easy Life Real Estate Systems)*	CD CD Extra
Briefs, Memoranda	Auto Dealer Interest Markups, Race Discrimination, ECOA, Nissan MAC	CLP7 Ch. 1.1, 1.2
	Automobile Financing, Race Discrimination in Mark-Up, Amicus Brief of United States *(Cason v. Nissan Motors Acceptance Corp.)*	CD CD Extra
	Reverse Redlining Case, Amicus Brief of United States *(Hargraves v. Capital City Mortgage Corp.)*	CD CD Extra
	Auto Dealerships Alleging Race Discrimination and Rebate Theft	CLP3 Ch. 9.2.8
	Opposition to Finance Company's Motion to Dismiss in ECOA Notice Case *(Smith v. Regional Acceptance Corp.)*	CD CD Extra
Post-Trial Motions, Orders, Attorney Fee Documents	Subprime Lender Violation of FHA, ECOA, RESPA, TILA, Settlement Agreement *(United States v. Delta Funding Corp. and Delta Financial Corp.)*	CD CD Extra
	Redlining and Adverse Impact of Mortgage Lender's Business Practices, Consent Decree *(United States v. Chevy Chase Federal Savings Bank)*	CD CD Extra
	Insurance Redlining *(United States v. Nationwide Mutual Insurance Company)*; Consent Decree	CD CD Extra
	ECOA and Regulation B violations *(Franklin Acceptance)*; Consent Decree	CD CD Extra
	ECOA and FHA Case Alleging Bank Refused to Lend to Native Americans, Consent Decree *(United States v. Blackpipe State Bank)*	CD CD Extra
	Action Alleging Redlining By Use of Correspondent Lenders *(U. S. v. Albank, FSB)*	CD CD Extra
	Action Alleging Redlining and Marketing Discrimination Consent Decree *(U.S. v. Decatur FSLA)*	CD CD Extra
	Action Alleging Discriminatory Credit Score Thresholds *(U. S. v. Associates National Bank)*	CD CD Extra
	Action Alleging Discrimination in Use of Credit Score Overrides *(U. S. v. Deposit Guaranty National Bank)*	CD CD Extra
	Action Against Subprime Lender Alleging Discriminatory Overcharges by Affiliated Mortgage Brokers, Consent Decree *(U. S. v. Long Beach Mortgage Co.)*	CD CD Extra

	Class Actions, Complaints	American with Disabilities Act to Improve the Accessibility of a Concert Facility to Wheelchairs	CLP4 Ch. 16.1
		ECOA Cosigner Violation in Class Action	CD App. F.3
		ECOA Adverse Action Notice Violation (with Jury Demand)	CD App. F.4
		Challenging Yield Spread Auto Loan Pricing Structure as ECOA Violation (NMAC)	CD App. F.5
	Class Actions, Certification Pleadings	Auto Dealer Interest Markups, Race Discrimination, ECOA, Nissan MAC	CLP7 Ch. 1.1, 1.2
		Discretionary Mark-Up with Racial Impact in Car Sales as ECOA Violation (NMAC)	CD CD Extra
	Class Actions, Class Notices	Auto Dealer Interest Markups, Race Discrimination, ECOA, Nissan MAC	CLP7 Ch. 1.1, 1.2, 1.3
	Class Actions, Briefs, Memoranda	Opposing Summary Judgment in ECOA Notice Case *(Bank One)*	CD CD Extra
		ECOA, Race Discrimination, Disgorge Unjust Enrichment, Auto Finance NMAC	CD CD Extra
		ECOA, Race Discrimination, Auto Sales, Motion to Dismiss Defendant's Counterclaims *(Ford Credit)*	CD CD Extra
		Opposition to NMAC's Motion for Summary Judgment, Race Discrimination in Auto Finance Markup, ECOA	CD CD Extra
		Auto dealer interest markups, Race discrimination, ECOA, Nissan MAC, Brief in Support of Class Notice Proposal	CLP7 Ch. 1.3
	Class Actions, Pre-Trial Motions, Trial Practice	Expert Report of Professor Ian Ayres, Disparate Racial Impacts in Finance Charge Markups, NMAC	CD CD Extra
		Expert Report on Racial Impact of NMAC's Finance Charge Markup Policy by Mark Cohen, PhD.	CD CD Extra
		Motion for Preliminary Injunction (Nissan MAC)	CD CD Extra
		Expert Report on Impact of NMAC's Credit Policy on Hispanic Borrowers, by Mark Cohen	CD CD Extra
Credit Reporting	*Demand Letters, Notices, Retainers, Forms*	Client Retainer Forms	CLP4 Ch. 8.1
		Repeatedly Obtaining Credit Reports Without an Authorized Purpose	CLP9 Ch. 17.2.1
		Sample Letter Explaining Damages and Legal Theories to Opposing Counsel	FCR CD Extra
		Sample Request for Consumer's Credit Report	FCR CD Extra
	Complaints, Answers, Counterclaims	Information Suppliers and Multiple Reporting Agencies, also Discovery	CLP2 Ch. 10.3
		Information Furnishers (Mistaken Identity)	CLP2 Ch. 10.4
		FCRA Suit Against Multiple Reporting Agencies, also Discovery, Memorandum in Opposition to Motion to Dismiss	CLP2 Ch. 10.2

	Equifax Enforcement Orders Excerpts from *In re Equifax, Inc.*	FCR App. H.2.2
	Equifax Enforcement Orders, Equifax Agreement	FCR App. H.2.3
	Equifax Enforcement Orders, *In re Equifax Credit Information Services, Inc.,*Agreement Containing Consent Order to Cease and Desist	FCR App. H.2.4.1
	Equifax Enforcement Orders, *In re Equifax Credit Information Services, Inc.,* Analysis of Proposed Consent Order to Aid Public Comment	FCR App. H.2.4.2
	Equifax Enforcement Orders, *In re Equifax*	FCR App. H.2.5
	Equifax Enforcement Orders, *US v. Equifax* (telephone access)	FCR App. H.2.5
	Equifax Enforcement Orders, *In re Equifax* (VT)	FCR App. H.2.6
	Trans Union Enforcement Orders, *In re Trans Union Credit Information Co.* 102 F.T.C. 1109, 1121 (1983).	FCR App. H.3.2
	Trans Union Enforcement Orders, *Alabama v. Trans Union*	FCR App. H.3.3
	Trans Union Enforcement Orders, *In re Trans Union Corp.*	FCR App. H.3.4
	Trans Union Enforcement Orders, *In re Trans Union* (Targeted marketing lists)	FCR App. H.3.5
	Trans Union Enforcement Orders *U.S. v. Trans Union* (Consent Decree)	FCR App. H.3.6
	Trans Union Enforcement Orders, *In re Trans Union* (FTC Commission Opinion)	FCR App. H.3.7
	Consent Agreements with Resellers of Consumer Reports: *Inter-fact*	FCR App. H.4.1
	Consent Agreements with Resellers of Consumer Reports: *I.R.S.C. Consent Order*	FCR App. H.4.2
	Consent Agreements with Resellers of Consumer Reports: *First American Real Estate Solutions CREDCO*	FCR App. H.4.3
	Consent Agreement with Credit Repair Agency—*FTC v. NCS Credit Network, Inc.*	FCR App. H.5
	FTC Consent Order Against Quicken	FCR Supp. App. H.6
	FTC Enforcement Action Against Minor for Violation of Gramm-Leach-Bliley Act	FCR Supp. App. H.7
	United States of America v. Equifax Information Services, Inc.	FCR Supp. App. H.8
	Experian Enforcement Orders FTC v. TRW [now Experian], Inc.	FCR App. H.1.2
Class Actions, Complaints	Raising Car Insurance Premium Based on Credit Report	CLP9 Ch. 9.4
	FCRA, Impermissible Access	FCR CD Extra
	Improper Use of Credit Scoring, Against Insurance Company	FCR CD Extra

Pleadings by Subject

		FCRA, Insurance Company Obtains Credit Reports with Impermissible Purposes, under False Pretenses, and Fails to Provide Adverse Action Notice	FCR CD Extra
	Class Actions, Settle-ments	FCRA Class Action Settlement, Consumer Erroneously Reported as "Included" in Bankruptcy	FCR CD Extra
Debt Collection, General	*Demand Letters, Notices, Retainers, Forms*	Collecting and Failing to Verify Old Identity Theft Claim, Client's Contact Log	CLP10 Ch. 4.4
		Demand Letter, Fair Debt Collection Practices Act	CLP7 Ch. 4.1
		Demand Letter, Seizure of Exempt Funds in Bank Account	CLP8 Ch. 2.1
	Complaints, Answers, Counterclaims	Adding FDCPA Claim to Tort Claims, Amended Complaint (AL)	CLP10 Ch. 5.3
		Invasion of Privacy, Intentional Infliction, Severe Distress, Amended Complaint Adding Party (AL)	CLP10 Ch. 5.2
		Attorney for Seizing Exempt Bank Account Funds	CLP2 Ch. 12.1
		Attorney for Allowing Collector to Use Attorney's Name, also Discovery, Brief	CLP2 Ch. 11.1
		Complaint Seeking Damages for Violation of Automatic Stay and Unfair Trade Practices	Bankr App. G #24
		Invasion of Privacy, Intentional Infliction, Severe Distress, Complaint (AL)	CLP10 Ch. 5.1
		Collecting and Failing to Verify Old Identity Theft Claim, Complaint	CLP10 Ch. 4.1
		Credit Union Wrongfully Setoff a Customer's Exempt Social Security Funds	CLP7 Ch. 13.1
		Harassment; Unauthorized Practice of Law by Debt Collector, FDCPA	CLP7 Ch. 3.1
		Confusing Debt Validation Notice, FDCPA	CLP7 Ch. 7.1
		Complaint Seeking Damages in Non-Core Adversary Proceeding Against a Non-Creditor for Unfair Debt Collection Practices	Bankr App. G #87
		FDCPA: Collector Pretending to be Creditor, state debt collection statutes	CLP9 Ch. 3.1
		Answer, Counterclaim in Second Suit for Continuing to Dun and Harass Consumer After the Creditor's Claims Had Been Settled in First Suit	CLP8 Ch. 12.1
		FDCPA Suit in Federal Court vs. Attorneys Who Sued Consumer a Second Time after First Suit Settled	CLP8 Ch. 12.2
		Abusive Debt Collection Complaint	CLP8 Ch. 13.1
		Conversion, Breach of Contract and Negligence—Seizure of Exempt Funds in Bank Account	CLP8 Ch. 2.2
		Tort Suit for Outrageous Debt Collection Practices	CLP8 Ch. 20.1
		Fair Debt Collection Including Both Federal and State Causes of Action	FDC App. H.1
		Fair Debt Collection Practices Act	FDC App. H.2

Discovery, Interrogatories and Document Requests	Harassment; Unauthorized Practice of Law by Debt Collector, FDCPA	CLP7 Ch. 3.1
	Confusing Debt Validation Notice, FDCPA	CLP7 Ch. 7.2
	Collecting and Failing to Verify Old Identity Theft Claim, Request to Inspect Premises	CLP10 Ch. 4.3
	Collecting and Failing to Verify Old Identity Theft Claim, Combined Discovery Request	CLP10 Ch. 4.2
	Motion to Compel Discovery of Operating Manual and Prices Paid to Purchase Debts; Memorandum	CLP8 Ch. 14.1
	Tort Suit for Outrageous Debt Collection Practices	CLP8 Ch. 20.3
	FDCPA: Collector Pretending to be Creditor, State Debt Collection Statutes	CLP9 Ch. 3.2
	Fair Debt Collection Practices Act	FDC App. I.1
Discovery, Interrogatories	Invasion of Privacy, Intentional Infliction, Severe Distress, Interrogatories (AL)	CLP10 Ch. 5.4
Discovery, Document Requests	Invasion of Privacy, Intentional Infliction, Severe Distress, Fourth Request for Production of Documents (AL)	CLP10 Ch. 5.10
	Invasion of Privacy, Intentional Infliction, Severe Distress, Request for Production of Documents (AL)	CLP10 Ch. 5.6
	Invasion of Privacy, Intentional Infliction, Severe Distress, Second Request for Production of Documents (AL)	CLP10 Ch. 5.8
	Invasion of Privacy, Intentional Infliction, Severe Distress, Third Request for Production of Documents (AL)	CLP10 Ch. 5.9
Discovery, Requests for Admissions	Invasion of Privacy, Intentional Infliction, Severe Distress, Admissions (AL)	CLP10 Ch. 5.5
Discovery, Depositions	Deposition of Collection Lawyer/Owner (CT)	CLP10 Ch. 3.2
	Deposition of Collection Lawyer (CT)	CLP10 Ch. 3.1
	Invasion of Privacy, Intentional Infliction, Severe Distress, Deposition of Collection Agency Employee (AL)	CLP10 Ch. 5.11
	Invasion of Privacy, Intentional Infliction, Severe Distress, Deposition of Collection Agency Owner (AL)	CLP10 Ch. 5.12
	Invasion of Privacy, Intentional Infliction, Severe Distress, Notice of Taking Deposition	CLP10 Ch. 5.7
	Deposition of FDCPA Class Representative	CLP10 Ch. 4.5
	Deposition of Debt Collection Employee Representing the Debt Collection Agency (TX)	CLP10 Ch. 8.2
Discovery, Discovery Motions	To Compel Discovery, Fair Debt Collection Practices Act	CLP4 Ch. 4.2
Pre-Trial Motions, Trial Practice	Motion to Strike Affirmative Defenses, Fair Debt Collection Practices Act	CLP7 Ch. 4.2
	Credit Union Wrongfully Setoff a Customer's Exempt Social Security Funds, Motion for Summary Judgment	CLP7 C.13.2

	Excessive Charges and False Threats, Motion for Partial Summary Judgment (CT)	CLP10 Ch. 3.3
	Arguing that FDCPA Does Not Require Conduct to Be Intentional to Violate the Act	CLP4 Ch. 6.1
	Prejudgment Garnishment of Bank Account Violates FDCPA	CLP7 Ch. 9.2
	Trial Brief, Fair Debt Collection Practices Act	FDC App. J.4
	In Support of Motion for Partial Summary Judgment Fair Debt Collection Practices Act	FDC App. J.1
Post-Trial Motions, Orders, Attorney Fee Documents	Attorney Fees Motion, Memoranda: Where Offer of Judgment Silent, Fees Larger than Consumer's Recovery are Needed for Private Enforcement of FDCPA	CLP9 Ch. 14
	Harassment; Unauthorized Practice of Law by Debt Collector, FDCPA	CLP7 Ch. 3.1
	Costs Should Not Be Taxed Against Consumer Who Lost FDCPA Suit	CLP7 Ch. 8.4
	Memoranda—Defendant's Motion to Preclude Expert Witness Report on Fair Debt Collection Practices Act Damages; Qualifications	CLP8 Ch. 10.3
	Invasion of Privacy, Intentional Infliction, Severe Distress, FDCPA, Consent Judgment (AL)	CLP10 Ch. 5.14
	Application for Order of Contempt Against Check Collector (CA)	CLP10 Ch. 6.1
	Memorandum of Law in Support of Contempt Against Check Collector (CA)	CLP10 Ch. 6.2
	Reply Memorandum of Law in Support of Contempt Against Check Collector (CA)	CLP10 Ch. 6.3
	Draft Order of Contempt Against a Check Collector (CA)	CLP10 Ch. 6.4
	Challenging the Amount of Attorney Fees Awarded, Fair Debt Collection Practices Act	CLP4 Ch. 4.3
	Motion for Award of Attorney Fees, Affidavit, Brief, Order, Fair Debt Collection Practices Act	FDC App. K.1
	Declaration in Support of Award of Attorney Fees, Fair Debt Collection Practices Act	FDC App. K.2
	Order Awarding Attorney Fees, Fair Debt Collection Practices Act	FDC App. K.3
	Memorandum in Support of Award of Attorney Fees, Fair Debt Collection Practices Act	FDC App. K.4
	Opinion: *Couston v. United Service Bureau, Inc.,* Clearinghouse No. 27718C (D. Idaho Oct. 15, 1979)	FDC CD Extra
	Fulton v. Metropolitan Hospitals, Inc. (D. Or. April 5, 1982)	FDC CD Extra
	Opinion: *Grammatico v. Sterling,* Clearinghouse No. 47976 (N.D. N.Y. Dec. 27, 1991)	FDC CD Extra
	Opinion: *Kimberly v. Great Lakes Collection Bureau, Inc.,* Clearinghouse No. 50431A (D. Conn. June 2, 1993)	FDC CD Extra

Pleadings by Subject

	Opinion: *Kimberly v. Great Lakes Collection Bureau, Inc.*, Clearinghouse No. 50431B (D. Conn. Sept. 26, 1996)	FDC CD Extra
	Opinion: *Merchant v. Nationwide Collection Service, Inc.* (Fla. Cir. Ct. Marion Cty March 18, 1985)	FDC CD Extra
	Opinion: *Nunez v. Interstate Corporate Systems, Inc.*, Clearinghouse No. 36186 (D.Ariz. Sept. 26, 1983)	FDC CD Extra
	Opinion: *Page v. Checkrite, Ltd.*, Clearinghouse No. 45759 (D. Neb. Sept. 10, 1984)	FDC CD Extra
Class Actions, Complaints	Motion to Compel Rule 26(a) Disclosures: Fair Debt Collection Practices Act: Collection of Debt Which Expired by the Passage of Time	CLP8 Ch. 15.4
	Fair Debt Collection Practices Act: Collection of Debt Which Expired by the Passage of Time	CLP8 Ch. 15.1
	Federal Fair Debt Collection Case (*Boddie*)	CCA App. D.4
	FDCPA, UDAP, and Tort Claims for a Collection Agency's Seeking Attorney Fees and Engaging in Unauthorized Practice of Law	CLP8 Ch. 19.1
	Fair Debt Collection Case Involving Cy Pres Remedy, also Motion for Class Certification, Order Certifying Class and Approving Final Settlement	CLP3 Ch. 3.1
	Bank's Debt Collection Suits in Distant Forum are Abuse of Process Unfair Trade Practice Due Process Violation	CLP6 Ch. 14.1
	Collection Agency Litigation Abuses; also Motion for Class Certification, Brief	CLP2 Ch. 11.2.1
	False Threat of Foreclosure: FDCPA, UDAP	CLP6 Ch. 3.1
Class Actions, Discovery	False Threat of Foreclosure FDCPA UDAP	CLP6 Ch. 3.2
	Fair Debt Collection Practices Act Case (*Boddie*)	CCA App. E.1
	Deposition Notice: Fair Debt Collection Practices Act: Collection of Debt Which Expired by the Passage of Time	CLP8 Ch. 15.3
	Fair Debt Collection Practices Act, Class Discovery	FDC App. I.4
Class Actions, Certification Pleadings	Confusing Debt Validation Notice, FDCPA	CLP7 Ch. 7.4
	Fair Debt Collection Practices Act (*Bauer*)	CCA99 App. K.1
	FDCPA, UDAP, and Tort Claims for a Collection Agency's Seeking Attorney Fees and Engaging in Unauthorized Practice of Law	CLP8 Ch. 19.2
	Fair Debt Collection Practices Act: Collection of Debt Which Expired by the Passage of Time	CLP8 Ch. 15.5
	Memorandum in Support of Certifying a FDCPA Statutory Damages Class (TX)	CLP10 Ch. 8.1
Class Actions, Class Notices	Combined Rule 23(c) and (e) Notice of Certification and Settlement Federal Fair Debt Collection Case (*Boddie*)	CCA99 App. N.3.2
Class Actions, Briefs, Memoranda	Bank's Debt Collection Suits in Distant Forum are Abuse of Process Unfair Trade Practice Due Process Violation	CLP6 Ch. 14.2

		In Support of Class Certification Federal Fair Debt Collection Case (*Bauer*)	CCA99 App. L.1
		Offer of Judgment May Not Be Used to Moot FDCPA Class Action	CLP7 Ch. 14.1
		Reply Memorandum Challenging False Threat of Foreclosure: FDCPA, UDAP	CLP6 Ch. 3.5
		Motion for Partial Summary Judgment Challenging False Threat of Foreclosure: FDCPA, UDAP	CLP6 Ch. 3.4
		Reply Memoranda in Support of Class Certification, Federal Fair Debt Collection Case (*Bauer*)	CCA99 App. M.1
		Offer of Judgment Does Not Moot FDCPA Class Action	CLP9 Ch. 12
	Class Actions, Pre-Trial Motions, Trial Practice	Summary Judgment Motion: Fair Debt Collection Practices Act: Collection of Debt Which Expired by the Passage of Time	CLP8 Ch. 15.6
	Class Actions, Settlements	Stipulations of Proposed Settlements Federal Fair Debt Collection Case (*Boddie*)	CCA App. P.1
	Class Actions, Objections to Settlement	Objections to Settlement Agreement (*Follansbee*)	CCA App. S.6
	Class Actions, Attorney Fees	Attorney Fees Motion: Fair Debt Collection Practices Act: Collection of Debt Which Expired by the Passage of Time	CLP8 Ch. 15.9
Debt Collection, Hospital	*Complaints, Answers, Counterclaims*	State Public Assistance Agency Payment of Hospital Bill	CLP8 Ch. 4, X
		Answer, Counterclaims, Hospital Collection Suit	CLP8 Ch. 4, VI
		Third-Party Complaint Against Health Insurer	CLP8 Ch. 4, IX
		Article: "Defending Hospital Collection Cases, 2001"	FDC CD Extra
	Discovery, Interrogatories and Document Requests	Hospital Collection Suit, Interrogatories, Bill of Particulars	CLP8 Ch. 4, IV
	Discovery, Depositions	Deposition Outline, Hospital Employee Witness	CLP8 Ch. 4, XI
	Pre-Trial Motions, Trial Practice	Medicaid Patient, Illegal Collection, FDCPA, Motion for Summary Judgment	CLP7 Ch. 8.1
		Voir Dire Questions, Hospital Collection Suit	CLP8 Ch. 4, XIII
		Jury Instructions, Closing Argument, Hospital Suit	CLP8 Ch. 4, XIII
		Trial Memorandum, Hospital Collection Suit	CLP8 Ch. 4, XIII
		Motion for Summary Judgment, Hospital Suit	CLP8 Ch. 4, XII
		Motion to Dismiss Hospital Collection Suit	CLP8 Ch. 4, IV
	Class Actions, Briefs, Memoranda	Reply Memoranda in Support of Class Certification: Hospital Collection Case (*Albino*)	CCA App. M.5
Debt Collection, Student Loans	*Demand Letters, Notices, Retainers, Forms*	Student Loans Request for Reasonable and Affordable Repayment Agreement	CLP2 Ch. 13.1

	Seeking Declaratory Relief That School's Fraud is Defense on the Student Loan	CLP2 Ch. 13.5
	Complaints: *Article*: "Primer on Bankruptcy and the Sovereign Immunity of States: When You Can't Sue State Agencies, When You Can Sue State Officials"	CLP6 Ch. 7.1.2
	Complaint to Determine Dischargeability of Student Loan	Bankr App. G #106
	Complaint to Enjoin Discriminatory Denial of Guaranteed Student Loan	Bankr App. G #121
	Action Challenging Private Student Lender Practices	Stud CD Extra
	State Court Complaint Against Trade School	Stud CD Extra
	Individual Case Challenging Denial of Disability Discharge	Stud CD Extra
	For Declaratory Relief that School's Fraud Is Defense on the Student Loan	Stud 2001 E.5.3
	To Enjoin Discriminatory Denial of Guaranteed Student Loan	Stud App. E.6.3
	Dischargeability Complaint Raising School's Fraud	Stud App. E.6.2
	Dischargeability of Student Loan	Stud App. E.6.1
	Trade School Abuse, Complaint and Demand for Jury Trial	Stud Supp. App. E.5.2.3
	Trade School Abuse, State Court Complaint Against School	Stud App. E.5.1
	Challenging Federal Benefit Offsets to Collect Old Student Loans	Stud App. E.4.2
	Challenge to Student Loan Collection Letters	Stud App. E.3.1
	Challenge to Disability Discharge Denial	Stud App. E.2.4
	Challenging Denial of False Certification Discharge	Stud CD Extra
Discovery, Interrogatories and Document Requests	To Trade Schools	CLP2 Ch. 13.7
	Challenge to Student Loan Collection Letters	Stud App. E.3.2
	Directed to Trade Schools	Stud App. F.2
	Case Challenging Administrative Offset to Collect Old Student Loans	Stud App. F.1.2
	Case Challenging Student Loan Collection Letters	Stud App. F.1.1
Pre-Trial Motions, Trial Practice	Motion for Preliminary Relief in Complaint to Enjoin Discriminatory Denial of Guaranteed Student Loan	Bankr App. G #122
	Proposed Order for Preliminary Relief in Complaint to Enjoin Discriminatory Denial of Guaranteed Student Loan	Bankr App. G #123
	Motion for Preliminary Injunction in Case Challenging Denial of Disability Discharge	Stud CD Extra
Briefs, Memoranda	False Certification Discharge: Memo, Motion for Summary Judgment and in Opposition to Defendant's Motion for Summary Judgment	Stud CD Extra

	Challenging Student Loan Garnishment and Other Collection Procedures, Appellant's Reply Brief	Stud CD Extra
	Challenging Student Loan Garnishment and Other Collection Procedures, Appellant's Brief	Stud CD Extra
	U.S. Defendant's Memorandum Supporting Motion to Dismiss Action Challenging Federal Collection Procedures, Calculation of Collection Fees (E.D. Cal.)	Stud CD Extra
	U.S. Defendant's Reply to Plaintiffs' Supplemental Brief—Challenge to Offset of Social Security for Old Student Loans (E.D.Mich)	Stud CD Extra
	Reply Brief in Support of Motion for Summary Judgment, Challenge to Offset of Social Security for Old Student Loans (E.D.Mich)	Stud CD Extra
	Supplemental Summary Judgment Brief in Action Challenging Federal Benefit Offsets to Collect Old Student Loans	Stud CD Extra
Post-Trial Motions, Orders, Attorney Fee Documents	Requests for Attorney Fees, EAJA Motion and Brief	CLP2 Ch. 13.9
	Group Discharge Letters from Dept. of Education, Various Schools	Stud CD Extra
Class Actions, Complaints	Class Action Complaint Seeking Remedies for Coercive Collection Practices Involving Discharged Debt	Bankr App. G #124
	Suit to Enjoin U.S. Department of Education's Collection of Loans to Victims of a Fraudulent Vocational School, Discovery	CLP5 Ch. 9.1
	Student Loan Collection Abuse, Discovery, Motion for Class Certification, Memorandum	CLP2 Ch. 14.1
	Against School Officers, Related Parties	CLP2 Ch. 13.4
	Challenge to Department of Education's False Certification Discharge Procedures	Stud App. E.2.3
	Challenging Wage Garnishment Procedures, Student Loans	Stud App. E.4.1
	Against Department of Education, Trade School's False Certification	Stud App. E.5.2.1
	School Officer, Related Parties, Trade School Fraud	Stud 2001 App. E.5.2.1
Class Actions, Certification Pleadings	Brief in Support of Petition to Appeal Denial of Rule 23(b)(3) Certification, Wage Garnishment (*Cliff*)	CCA Supp. App. N.1.2.2
	Petition to Appeal Denial of Rule 23(b)(3) Certification, Wage Garnishment (*Cliff*)	CCA Supp. App. N.1.2.1
	Trade School, also Class Notice	CLP2 Ch. 13.8
	Challenge to Student Loan Collection Letters	Stud App. E.3.3
	School Officer, Related Parties, Trade School Fraud	Stud 2001 App. E.5.2.2

	Class Actions, Briefs, Memoranda	Appeal of Denial of Class Certification on Numerosity, Discovery, and Class Definition; Refusal of Student Loan Debt Collector to Provide Pregarnishment Jearings	CLP9 Ch. 16
	Class Actions, Pre-Trial Motions, Trial Practice	Summary Judgment against Dept. of Education, Trade School Abuse	Stud App. E.5.2.2
Deceptive Practices, Fraud, RICO	*Demand Letters, Notices, Retainers, Forms*	Car Rental Company Including Illegal Limitations on its Insurance Coverage	CLP9 Ch. 17.1.1
	Complaints, Answers, Counterclaims	Theft of Identity by Salesman at Auto Dealership	CLP3 Ch. 5.1
		Theft of Identity by Unknown Person; Discovery	CLP3 Ch. 5.2
		Rescission of Deed in Sale Leaseback Scheme	CLP3 Ch. 1.3
		Befriending Scam, also Discovery	CLP3 Ch. 1.2
		Scheme to Defraud Elderly Homeowner	CLP3 Ch. 1.1
		Storage of Consumer's Possessions	CLP2 Ch. 7.2
		Furniture Non-Delivery	CLP2 Ch. 7.1
		Auto Lease Early Termination UDAP	CLP1 Ch. 9.1
		Predatory Mortgage Lending Involving Multiple Parties RICO TILA	CLP1 Ch. 7.1
		Home Improvement Fraud, Agency $28 Million Punitive Damages Award for Bank's Involvement	CLP1 Ch. 5.1
		Travel Agency Who Recommended Insolvent Tour Operator	CLP4 Ch. 5.1
		Travel Agent Alleging Failure to Investigate Reliability of Tour Operator	CLP4 Ch. 5.2
		Travel Club and Tour Operator Alleging that Tour Operator Was Insolvent	CLP4 Ch. 5.3
		Infertility Program, Unfair and Deceptive Practices	CLP4 Ch. 13.1
		Home Construction Claims, Discovery	CLP5 Ch. 7.1
		Home Repair Contractor Assignee, Fair Credit Reporting Act, Truth in Lending Act, UDAP	CLP6 Ch. 17.1
		Credit Repair Organization Statute Fraud Claims against Car Dealer	CLP6 Ch. 2.2
		False Threat of Foreclosure, FDCPA, UDAP	CLP6 Ch. 3.1
		TIL Rescission and Deceptive Practices Case—Home Improvement Contract (*Mount*)(Class Action)	CCA99 D.2
		Auto Finance Upcharge Cases GMAC Links:	UDAP CD Extra
		Auto Finance Upcharge Cases: NMAC Links	UDAP CD Extra
	Discovery, Interrogatories and Document Requests	Deceptive Practices Case—Vendor's Single Interest Insurance (*Ortiz*)(Class Action)	CCA App. E.3
		Home Repair Contractor Assignee, Fair Credit Reporting Act, Truth in Lending Act, UDAP	CLP6 Ch. 17.2

		Opposition to Motion to Bar the Plaintiff's Expert: Deceptive Labeling of Calcium Supplement	CLP8 Ch. 23.11
		Deceptive Labeling of Calcium Supplement	CLP8 Ch. 23.2
	Class Actions, Certification Pleadings	Deceptive Labeling of Calcium Supplement	CLP8 Ch. 23.4
		Auto Finance Upcharge Cases: Class Certification Decision, *Coleman v. GMAC*	UDAP CD Extra
	Class Actions, Class Notices	Notice of Certification Rule 23(c) RICO (*Hughes*)	CCA App. O.1
	Class Actions, Briefs, Memoranda	Brief in Opposition to Motion for Judgment Notwithstanding the Verdict: Deceptive Labeling of Calcium Supplement	CLP8 Ch. 23.16
		Lenders for Campground Membership Fraud RICO Lender Liability FTC Holder Rule	CLP1 Ch. 6.6
	Class Actions, Pre-Trial Motions, Trial Practice	Jury Instructions, Jury Questions: Deceptive Labeling of Calcium Supplement	CLP8 Ch. 23.12
		Summary Judgment Motion: Deceptive Labeling of Calcium Supplement	CLP8 Ch. 23.7
		Car Rental Company Including Illegal Limitations on its Insurance Coverage, Summary Judgment	CLP9 Ch. 17.1.3, 17.1.4
	Class Actions, Settlements	Settlement Notice Lender's Liability for Campground's Law Violations Rule 23(e) (*Hughes*)	CCA App. O.2.1
Fringe Lenders: Pay Day Loans, Auto Pawn, Rent to Own, Refund Anticipation Loans	*Complaints, Answers, Counterclaims*	Auto Pawn Business Subject to Regulation under State Credit Statutes	CLP3 Ch. 4.2
		Pay Day Loan—Check Advance Transaction is Loan Under State Finance Act	CLP3 Ch. 4.1
		Rent to Own	CLP2 Ch. 8.1
		Rent-to-Own Company—Usurious Interest, Discovery, Briefs	CLP4 Ch. 11.1
		Payday Loans, Ace Cash Express, MD	COC Supp. App. F.6
		Complaint Against Payday Lender for Disguising its Loans as Sales of Internet Access (FL)	CLP10 Ch. 9
		Payday Loan also Opposition to Motion to Dismiss, Discovery, Usury, Small Loan Act, RICO, Truth In Lending, and UDAP	COC App. F.1
	Discovery, Interrogatories and Document Requests	Rent to Own	CLP2 Ch. 8.2

	Briefs, Memoranda	Rent to Own, Opposition to Motion for Summary Judgment	CLP2 Ch. 8.4
		Re Injunction, and Opinion: Pay Day Loan—Check Advance Transaction is Loan Under State Finance Act	CLP3 Ch. 4.1.3
		Injunction Opinion Auto Pawn Business Subject to Regulation under State Credit Statutes	CLP3 Ch. 4.2.4
		Response to Motion to Dismiss—Payday Loan Suit	COC App. F.3
		Predatory Lending: History of Rise of High Cost Lending Cash Advances as Alleged Assignments of Tax Refunds, Amicus Brief	COC App. F.4
		Payday loans, Amicus brief—Rental of bank charter, Goleta National Bank, Ace Cash Express (OH)	COC Supp. App. F.7
	Class Actions, Complaints	Auto Pawn Transactions Raising UDAP and TIL Claims, also Discovery, Memorandum in Support of Motion for Class Certification	CLP3 Ch. 4.3
Installment Loans, Closed-End Credit, Usury	*Complaints, Answers, Counterclaims*	Loan Flipping	CLP3 Ch. 2.6
		Rent-to-Own Company—Usurious Interest, Discovery, Briefs	CLP4 Ch. 11.1
		Auto Sale Lender Liability Where FTC Holder Notice Improperly Omitted	CLP1 Ch. 4.2
		Answer Repossession Delay Discharges Obligation of Cosigner on Car Sale UCC	CLP6 Ch. 13.1
		Payday Loans, Ace Cash Express, MD	COC Supp. App. F.6
		Refund Anticipation Loan Debt Collection Case	COC Supp. App. G.1
		Payday Loan Opposition to Motion to Dismiss, and Discovery also: Usury, Small Loan Act, RICO, Truth in Lending, and UDAP	COC App. F.1
		Small Loan Usury	COC App. E.3
		Answer Counterclaim Discovery Usury Retail Installment Sales Act, Car Credit Sale	COC App. E.1
	Discovery, Interrogatories and Document Requests	Auto Sale Lender Liability Where FTC Holder Notice Improperly Omitted	CLP1 Ch. 4.5
	Discovery, Interrogatories	Refund Anticipation Loan Debt Collection Case, to Bank	COC Supp. App. G.2
		Refund Anticipation Loan Debt Collection Case, to Tax Preparation Firm	COC Supp. App. G.4
	Discovery, Document Requests	Refund Anticipation Loan Debt Collection Case, to Bank	COC Supp. App. G.3
		Refund Anticipation Loan Debt Collection Case, to Tax Preparation Firm	COC Supp. App. G.5

Discovery, Requests for Admissions	Small Loan Usury	COC App. E.3
Pre-Trial Motions, Trial Practice	Affidavit: Broker's Fee as a Hidden Finance Charge	COC App. E.5
	Affidavit: Interest Calculation Broker Fee Usury	COC App. E.5
	Expert Testimony in *Besta v. Beneficial Finance*—Insurance Packing	COC App. E.6.1
	Expert Report on the Economic Cost of Debt Consolidation	COC App. E.6.2
	Expert Report on the Spiraling Costs and Profits to Lenders Due to Multiple Refinancings	COC App. E.6.3
	Motion for Summary Judgment: RESPA, Unearned Referral Fee, Delta Funding, PA	COC Supp. App. H.1
	Jury Instructions in Case Alleging Fraud by Mortgage Lender and by Investment Banker Who Securitized the Paper	COC CD Extra
	Verdict Form, *Austin v Chisick, Lehman Brothers, MBIA*	COC CD Extra
Briefs, Memoranda	Repossession Delay Discharges Obligation of Cosigner on Car Sale UCC	CLP6 Ch. 13.2
	Response to Motion to Dismiss—Payday Loan Suit	COC App. F.3
	Predatory Lending: History of Rise of High Cost Lending; Cash Advances as Alleged Assignments of Tax Refunds; Amicus Brief	COC App. F.4
	Payday loans, Amicus brief—Rental of bank charter, Goleta National Bank, Ace Cash Express (OH)	COC Supp. App. F.7
Class Actions, Complaints	State Usury Case (*Adams*)	CCA App. D.9
	Credit Overcharges Usury UDAP Mortgage Refinancing	CLP6 Ch. 6.2
Class Actions, Discovery	State Usury Case (*Adams*)	CCA App. E.4
Class Actions, Class Notices	Combined Rule 23(c) and (e) Notice of Certification and Settlement State Usury Case (*Adams*)	CCA App. O.3.4
Class Actions, Briefs, Memoranda	Mandatory Arbitration Provision Is Not Enforceable	CLP1 Ch. 1.1
	In Support of Class Certification State Usury Case (*Adams*)	CCA App. L.7
	Opposing Motion to Dismiss Credit Overcharges: Usury, UDAP, Mortgage Refinancing	CLP6 Ch. 6.3
Class Actions, Settlements	Stipulations of Proposed Settlements State Usury Case (*Adams*)	CCA App. P.5
Class Actions, Objections to Settlement	Objections to Settlement (*Buchet*)	CCA App. S.5.1
	Objections to Settlement Agreement (*Reynolds*)	CCA App. S.3

	Class Actions, Attorney Fees	Memorandum in Support of Counsel for Objectors' Request for Attorney Fees (*Buchet*)	CCA App. S.5.2
Insurance	*Complaints, Answers, Counterclaims*	Home Repair Fraud, RICO and Unauthorized Insurance Practices	CLP4 Ch. 1.1
		HMO Health Maintenance Organizations for Delay in Authorizing and Paying for Cancer Treatment	CLP6 Ch. 5.1
		Failure to Honor Credit Life Insurance after Debtor Died, Repossession, Constructive Fraud	CLP7 Ch. 16.1
		Third-Party Complaint Against Health Insurer, in Hospital Collection Suit	CLP8 Ch. 4, IX
	Discovery, Interrogatories and Document Requests	Failure to Honor Credit Life Insurance after Debtor Died, Repossession, Constructive Fraud	CLP7 Ch. 16.2
	Briefs, Memoranda	Adequacy of Capitalization of Restructured Insurer of Environmental Hazards	CLP7 Ch. 15.1
		HMO Health Maintenance Organizations for Delay in Authorizing and Paying for Cancer Treatment	CLP6 Ch. 5.2
	Class Actions, Complaints	Deceptive Practices Case, Vendor's Single Interest Insurance (*Ortiz*)	CCA App. D.8
		Forced Placed Automobile Insurance Claims, also Discovery Memorandum in support of Class Certification	CLP5 Ch. 5.1
		Raising Car Insurance Premium Based on Credit Report	CLP9 Ch. 9.4
	Class Actions, Discovery	Deceptive Practices Case—Vendor's Single Interest Insurance (*Ortiz*)	CCA App. E.3
	Class Actions, Certification Pleadings	Deceptive Practices Case— Vendor's Single Interest Insurance (*Ortiz*)	CCA App. K.4
	Class Actions, Briefs, Memoranda	In Support of Class Certification Deceptive Practices Case— Vendor's Single Interest Insurance (*Ortiz*)	CCA App. L.6
		Reply Memoranda in Support of Class Certification: Deceptive Practices Case—Vendor's Single Interest Insurance (*Ortiz*)	CCA App. M.4
		Forced Placed Insurance Auto Credit Sales	CLP1 Ch. 2.1
		In Support of Class Certification Forced Placed Insurance Auto Credit Sales	CLP1 Ch. 2.2
	Class Actions, Objections to Settlement	Objections to Settlement Agreement (*Wilson*)	CCA App. S.1
	Class Actions, Attorney Fees	Memorandum in Support of Final Approval of Settlement and Application for Award of Attorney Fees Forced Placed Insurance Auto Credit Sales	CLP1 Ch. 2.10
Mobile Homes, Landlord-Tenant	*Complaints, Answers, Counterclaims*	Real Estate Broker Fraud, also Motion for Class Certification (Class Action)	CLP2 Ch. 4.2

		Mobile Home Sale Complaint for Damages and Cancellation	CLP2 Ch. 4.1
		Mobile Home Conversion of Mobile Home Park; Retaliatory Eviction; Tie-In of Home Purchase to Park Space, also Discovery & Briefs	CLP2 Ch. 2.2
		Mobile Home Uninhabitable Park Conditions, also Discovery & Briefs	CLP2 Ch. 2.1
		Mobile Home Constructive Eviction Through Utility Shut Off	CLP2 Ch. 1.3
		Uninhabitability Defense to Eviction	CLP2 Ch. 1.2
		Landlord-Tenant Challenging Lease Provisions	CLP2 Ch. 1.1
		Answer to Motion of Landlord for Relief from Automatic Stay	Bankr App. G #30
		Nursing Home—Quality of Care, Discovery	CLP4 Ch. 3.1.1
		Nursing Home—Unlawful Business Practices, Memorandum	CLP4 Ch. 3.2.1
		Mobile Home Dealer and Manufacturer	CLP5 Ch. 4.2.1
		Complaint to Prohibit Eviction from Public Housing Based upon Dischargeable Debt for Rent	Bankr App. G #84
		Complaint to Determine Dischargeability of Tenant's Claims Against Landlord	Bankr App. G #148
		Damages for Breach of Implied Warranty of Merchantability	Warr App. K.2.2
		Dealer and Financer for Improper Setup of Mobile Home	Warr App. K.7
	Discovery, Interrogatories and Document Requests	Manufactured Home Dealer and Financer	CLP5 Ch. 4.1.2
		Mobile Home, Requests for Production of Documents, Interrogatories to Dealer, Finance Co. (Discovery in Arbitrated Matter)	Warr CD Extra
	Pre-Trial Motions, Trial Practice	Motion for Relief from Stay by Tenant to Raise Counterclaims to Eviction	Bankr App. G #146
Mortgages, Predatory Loans, Foreclosures	*Demand Letters, Notices, Retainers, Forms*	Veteran's Letter to VA Concerning Mortgage Foreclosure	CLP2 Ch. 3.1
		Qualified Written Request Under RESPA to Obtain Mortgage Loan Information	Bankr App. G #69
		Notice of TILA Rescission	CLP9 Ch. 19.1
		Rescission Notice Truth in Lending Act	TIL App. D
		Sample Qualified Written Request Under RESPA	Repo Supp. O.5.1
		Sample Qualified Written Request Under RESPA After Bankruptcy Filing	Repo Supp. O.5.2
	Complaints, Answers, Counterclaims	RESPA Litigation: Yield Spread Premiums; Briefs, Discovery	CLP3 Ch. 6.1

Pleadings by Subject

	Foreclosure Answer with TILA and RESPA Affirmative Defenses	Repo Supp. O.2.1
	Complaint Against Lender for Fraud Against Non-English Speakers and Truth in Lending Violations (OR)	CLP10 Ch. 14.1
	Action to Enjoin Foreclosure and Bring Affirmative Causes of Action	Repo Supp. O.3.1
	Home Improvement Contractor, Fraud	Repo Supp. O.4
	Home Improvement Case	Warr App. K.4
Discovery, Interrogatories and Document Requests	Mortgage Servicer's Practices: Delays in Payment, Loan Advances, UDAP, Breach of Fiduciary Duty	CLP7 Ch. 11.2
	Mortgage Adversary Complaint: TIL Rescission in Bankruptcy, RESPA, UDAP, Yield Spread Premium	CLP9 Ch. 19.3
	Predatory Mortgage Lending Involving Multiple Parties: RICO , TILA	CLP1 Ch. 7.2
	Home Improvement Fraud, Agency, $28 Million Punitive Damages Award for Bank's Involvement	CLP1 Ch. 5.4
	Foreclosure Defense: Motion for Entry of Document Preservation Order	CLP8 Ch. 22.4
	RESPA Litigation: Yield Spread Premiums; Excerpts from Depositions of Defendants	CLP3 Ch. 6.5
	Foreclosure Defense: Discovery Requests and Request to Admit	Repo Supp. O.2.2
	Foreclosure Defense, Interrogatories and Requests for Production of Documents from Broker	Repo Supp. O.3.3
Discovery, Document Requests	Request for Production of Predatory Lender's Loan Documents and Policies (OR)	CLP10 Ch. 14.2
Discovery, Discovery Motions	Motion to Compel Discovery, Extend Time, and for Sanctions, Misrepresentation that Refinancing Would Lower Payments	CLP9 Ch. 7.1.2–7.1.4
Pre-Trial Motions, Trial Practice	Summary Judgment Memoranda and Draft Order, Mortgage Loan Claims for TIL Rescission and for Illegal Yield Spread Premium	CLP9 Ch. 19.4.2, 19.5
	Mortgage Servicer's Practices: Delays in Payment, Loan Advances, UDAP, Breach of Fiduciary Duty, Motion to Dismiss, Brief	CLP7 Ch. 11.6
	Motion to Preclude Lender's Evidence—Due Diligence	CLP9 Ch. 1.5
	Mortgage Lender Fraud: Undisputed Material Facts	CLP9 Ch. 1.3.2
	Expert's Exhibits—Interest Rates, Home's Loss of Value, by Mark Leymaster	CLP9 Ch. 1.2
	Mortgage Lender Fraud: Fraud, HOEPA, TILA, Pretrial Memo, Jury Instructions	CLP9 Ch. 1.1
	Expert Witness Affidavit Corporate Identity Home Improvement Fraud, Agency $28 Million Punitive Damages Award for Bank's Involvement	CLP1 Ch. 5.6

		Predatory Lending by a Non-Bank Home Equity Lender (*Samuel*)	CCA App. D.1
		RESPA Requirement to Use Particular Title Company	CLP6 Ch. 15.4
		RESPA Related Broker and Title Company	CLP6 Ch. 15.1
		Mortgage Servicer's Practices: Delays in Payment, Loan Advances, UDAP, Breach of Fiduciary Duty	CLP7 Ch. 11.1
	Class Actions, Discovery	RESPA Related Broker and Title Company	CLP6 Ch. 15.2
		Discovery Predatory Mortgage Lending Abuses HOEPA Production of Documents Subpoena	CLP6 Ch. 1.2
		Mortgage Servicer's Practices: Delays in Payment, Loan Advances, UDAP, Breach of Fiduciary Duty	CLP7 Ch. 11.2
	Class Actions, Certification Pleadings	RESPA Requirement to Use Particular Title Company	CLP6 Ch. 15.4
		Predatory Mortgage Lending Abuses, HOEPA	CLP6 Ch. 1.6
	Class Actions, Class Notices	Special Notice to Subclass, Predatory Lending by a Non-Bank Home Equity Lender (*Samuel*)	CCA App. O.3.1.2
		Notice to the Complete Class, Predatory Lending by a Non-Bank Home Equity Lender (*Samuel*)	CCA App. O.3.1.1
	Class Actions, Briefs, Memoranda	In Opposition of Motion to Dismiss: Predatory Mortgage Lending Abuses, HOEPA	CLP6 Ch. 1.4
	Class Actions, Settlements	Stipulation of Settlement (*Morales, et al v. Associates First Capital Corp., et al.*)	CCA CD Extra
		Memoranda in Support of Final Approval of Class Settlement TIL Rescission Case—Home Improvement Contract (*Ogden*)	CCA App. R.2
		Predatory Lending by a Non-Bank Home Equity Lender (*Samuel*)	CCA App. R.1
		Order Certifying Settlement Class, Approving Class Action Settlement, and Awarding Attorney Fees (*Morales v. Citigroup*)	CCA CD Extra
		Predatory Lending by a Non-Bank Home Equity Lender (*Samuel*)	CCA App. P.1
		Mortgage Servicer's Practices: Delays in Payment, Loan Advances, UDAP, Breach of Fiduciary Duty, Settlement Motion, Agreement, Order	CLP7 Ch. 11.8
	Class Actions, Attorney Fees	Objections to Settlement and Request for Fees, Mortgages and RESPA (*Robinson*)	CCA App. S.4
Truth in Lending	*Demand Letters, Notices, Retainers, Forms*	Notice of TILA Rescission	CLP9 Ch. 19.1
		Rescission Letter TILA Bankruptcy Court	CLP1 Ch. 8.1
		Rescission Notice Truth in Lending Act	TIL App. D
		HOEPA Points and Fees Worksheet	TIL App. H

Pleadings by Subject

Post-Trial Motions, Orders, Attorney Fee Documents	Attorney Fees Motion With Memorandum of Law and Attorney's Affidavit in Settled Truth in Lending Case	CLP1 Ch. 11.1
	Attorney Fees Petition for Successful Appeal of TIL Decision *(Rodash)*	CLP1 Ch. 11.3
	Expert's Affidavit in Case Seeking Appellate Attorney Fees *(Rodash)*	CLP1 Ch. 11.5
	Order for Partial Summary Judgment for the Plaintiff Rescinding Mortgage Declaring Debt Unsecured Pursuant to TILA	CLP1 Ch. 8.7
	Jury Instructions Proposed on Fraud and TIL Claims (OR)	CLP10 Ch. 14.6
	Order to Dismiss Overdraft Protection Complaint	TIL CD Extra
	Legal Services Corp. Further Interpretation—Ability of LSC-funded Offices to Co-Counsel with Private Attorney Seeking Attorney Fees (2003)	TIL CD Extra
	Legal Services Corp. Interpretation—Ability of LSC-funded Offices to Co-Counsel with Private Attorney Seeking Attorney Fees (1999)	TIL CD Extra
Class Actions, Complaints	Consumer Leasing Act and Deceptive Practices Case—Car Lease *(Shepherd)*	CCA App. D.7
	TIL Untimely Disclosure Case *(Diaz)*	CCA App. D.6
	TIL Disclosure Case, Hidden Finance Charge in Car Sale *(Willis)*	CCA App. D.5
	TIL Rescission Rights Exercised in a Class Action	CLP5 Ch. 10.1
	TIL Rescission and Deceptive Practices Case—Home Improvement Contract *(Mount)*	CCA99 App. D.2
Class Actions, Certification Pleadings	Motion for Class Certification TIL Rescission Rights Exercised in a Class Action	CLP5 Ch. 10.2
	TIL Rescission and Deceptive Practices Case—Home Improvement Contract *(Mount)*	CCA99 App. K.2
	TIL Untimely Disclosure Case *(Diaz)*	CCA App. K.3
	TIL Disclosure Case—Hidden Finance Charge in Car Sale *(Willis)*	CCA App. K.2
Class Actions, Class Notices	Combined Rule 23(c) and (e) Notice of Certification and Settlement TIL Disclosure Case—Hidden Finance Charge in Car Sale *(Willis)*	CCA App. O.3.3
Class Actions, Briefs, Memoranda	In Support of Class Certification TIL Disclosure Case—Hidden Finance Charge in Car Sale (Willis)	CCA App. L.3
	In Support of Class Certification TIL Untimely Disclosure Case *(Diaz)*	CCA App. L.4
	Reply Memoranda in Support of Class Certification: TIL, UDAP, and Breach of Contract Case—Credit Card Issuer's Failure to Refund Credit Balance *(Coe)*	CCA App. M.1
	Reply Memoranda in Support of Class Certification: TIL Untimely Disclosure Case *(Diaz)*	CCA App. M.2

		In Support of Class Certification: TIL, UDAP, and Breach of Contract Case—Credit Card Issuer's Failure to Refund Credit Balance (*Coe*)	CCA App. L.2
		In Support of Class Certification TIL Rescission and Deceptive Practices Case—Home Improvement Contract (*Mount*)	CCA99 App. L.3
		Reply Memoranda in Support of Class Certification: TIL Rescission and Deceptive Practices Case, Home Improvement Contract (*Mount*)	CCA99 App. M.3
	Class Actions, Settlements	Stipulations of Proposed Settlements with Dealer; Assignee, TIL Disclosure Case—Hidden Finance Charge in Car Sale (*Willis*)	CCA App. P.3
Utilities, Energy	*Demand Letters, Notices, Retainers, Forms*	Letter to Utility Company Giving Notice of Stay and Requirements of 11 U.S.C. § 366	Bankr App. G #39
	Complaints, Answers, Counterclaims	Complaint to Enjoin Termination of Utility Service for Nonpayment of Deposit by Bankrupt Current on Her Utility Payments	Bankr App. G #41
		Complaint Seeking Reconnection of Utility Service and Damages after Bankruptcy	Bankr App. G #42
		Long Distance Phone Overcharges	CLP7 Ch.2.1
		Complaint—Inadequacy of Utility Allowance	AUS CD Extra
		Long Distance Company Rates NARUC, NCLC and Others' Petition to FCC to Impose Notice Requirement	AUS CD Extra
		Long Distance Telephone Company's Arbitration Clause is Unconscionable	CLP8 Ch. 1.1
		Complaint Against Municipal Water Utility Shutting off Water of Tenants without Notice (OH)	CLP10 Ch. 17.1
	Pre-Trial Motions, Trial Practice	Long Distance Phone Overcharges, Opposition to Motion to Dismiss	CLP7 Ch.2.2
		Motion for Modification of Security Deposit for Utility Service in Bankruptcy	Bankr App. G #43
	Briefs, Memoranda	Illegal Charges by Private Collector of Water/Sewer Bills	CLP9 Ch. 11.3–11.4
		Brief Against Municipal Water Utility for Shutting off Water of Tenants Without Notice (OH)	CLP10 Ch. 17.2
		Reply Brief Against Municipal Water Utility for Shutting off Water of Tenants Without Notice (OH)	CLP10 Ch. 17.3
	Class Actions, Complaints	Class Action Complaint, Electric Company Overcharges in a Deregulated Market	CLP8 Ch. 3.1
		Long Distance Phone Overcharges	CLP7 Ch.2.1
	Class Actions, Class Notices	Short Class Notice: AT&T Wireless Consumer Class Action Litigation (NJ)	CCA CD Extra
		Notice of Proposed Class Action Settlement, Electric Company Overcharges in a Deregulated Market	CLP8 Ch. 3.8

	Notice of Pendency of Class Action Determination, Proposed Settlement and Date of Settlement Hearing (AT&T Wireless, NJ)	CCA CD Extra
Class Actions, Settlements	Motion for Preliminary Approval of Settlement Agreement, Electric Company Overcharges in a Deregulated Market	CLP8 Ch. 3.2
	Order and Final Judgment, Electric Company Overcharges in a Deregulated Market	CLP8 Ch. 3.5
Class Actions, Objections to Settlement	Objections to Stipulation of Settlement by Boyd Objectors (*Dotson v. Bell Atlantic-MD, Inc./Fausto Scrocco, Mojan, Inc;. Sysnet, Inc., v. Bell Atlantic-MD, Inc. and Maryland PSC*)	CCA CD Extra

Pleadings by Title

This listing specifies all NCLC pleadings found in the bound volumes in the Consumer Credit and Sales Legal Practice Series. The listing is organized first by title and then by chapter or appendix of each title. More information on the pleadings found in the ten volumes of *Consumer Law Pleadings* can also be found in "Description of Pleadings." The contributors to those ten volumes can be found by using the listing in "Contributors by Title."

The titles are in the following order:

Automobile Fraud
Consumer Arbitration Agreements
Consumer Bankruptcy Law and Practice
Consumer Class Actions
Consumer Law Pleadings Number One
Consumer Law Pleadings Number Two
Consumer Law Pleadings Number Three
Consumer Law Pleadings Number Four
Consumer Law Pleadings Number Five
Consumer Law Pleadings Number Six
Consumer Law Pleadings Number Seven
Consumer Law Pleadings Number Eight
Consumer Law Pleadings Number Nine
Consumer Law Pleadings Number Ten
Consumer Warranty Law
Cost of Credit
Credit Discrimination
Fair Credit Reporting Act
Fair Debt Collection
Repossessions and Foreclosures
Student Loan Law
Truth in Lending

Automobile Fraud

Appendix G   Sample Complaints

       G.1 Complaints in the Appendix and on the CD-Rom

       G.2 Sample Complaint Against Two Dealers for Tampering, False Statements, and False Disclosures

       G.3 Sample Complaint Against Dealer and Lender Relating to Odometer Misrepresentations and Lender's Supply of Information to Credit Reporting Agency

       G.4 Sample Complaint Against Dealer for Concealment of Salvage Branded Title

       G.5 Sample Complaint Against Dealer and Financer for Undisclosed Wreck History

       G.6 Sample Complaint in a Lemon Buyback Case

       G.7 Sample Complaint Against Dealer for Concealment of Car's Prior Use

Consumer Arbitration Agreements

Consumer Bankruptcy Law and Practice

Consumer Class Actions

Consumer Law Pleadings Number One (1994)

Consumer Law Pleadings Number Two (1995)

Consumer Law Pleadings Number Three (1997)

Pleadings by Title

Consumer Law Pleadings Number Four (1998)

Consumer Law Pleadings Number Five (1999)

Consumer Law Pleadings Number Six (2000)

Consumer Law Pleadings Number Seven (2001)

Pleadings by Title

Consumer Law Pleadings Number Eight (2002)

Consumer Law Pleadings Number Nine (2003)

Consumer Law Pleadings Number Ten (2004)

Pleadings by Title

Consumer Warranty Law

Cost of Credit

Credit Discrimination

Fair Credit Reporting

Fair Debt Collection

Repossessions and Foreclosures

Student Loan Law

Truth in Lending

Pleadings by Title

Description of Pleadings

This listing describes all of the pleadings found in *Consumer Law Pleadings with Disk*, Numbers One through Ten, in volume and chapter order. This listing is best utilized in conjunction with one of the other listings in this volume. Use the *other* listing to pinpoint a particular pleading. Then use this listing to read a brief overview of that pleading, its context, and related information. Based on that information, one can determine whether to utilize the pleading itself, found on the companion CD-Rom.

Consumer Law Pleadings With Disk, Number One (1994)

Chapter 1 Avoiding Mandatory Arbitration

One of today's most important consumer law issues is whether consumers, instead of pressing their claims against creditors in a court action, can be required by the credit agreement to arbitrate those claims before a panel of one or more arbitrators. Consumer lenders are increasingly inserting boilerplate language in their credit agreements (or sending out amendments to those agreements stuffed in with billing statements) that require consumers to arbitrate any claim of any type they have against the creditor—sometimes even though the creditor is not required to arbitrate its collection action against the consumer.

Consumer attorneys are concerned with this trend because it makes it difficult, if not impossible to pursue a case as a class action, for a consumer to recover statutory, multiple or punitive damages, or for the consumer to recover attorney fees even though the statute being utilized provides for those fees. Moreover, consumers lose their constitutional right to a jury determination, and arbitrators (particularly those participating in a creditor-created arbitration program) may be less sympathetic to Congressionally mandated consumer protections than a judge or jury. (An arbitrator ruling against a creditor is unlikely to ever be picked by the creditor again to handle its arbitration.)

Discovery is also often critical to pursuit of a consumer claim because the facts will reside almost exclusively in the creditor's possession, but arbitrators are unlikely to allow extensive discovery. Consumers also generally lose their right to appeal arbitration decisions, even if the arbitrator

has misapplied federal or state law, as clearly enunciated by court decisions or statutes. Moreover, arbitration may be more costly for a consumer than a court action, and it may be more difficult for the consumer to proceed in the arbitration *in forma pauperis*.

This chapter presents sample briefs and pleadings relating to arbitration issues in two different cases. The first case was initiated in a California Superior Court as a consumer class action challenging certain insurance practices by ITT Financial. ITT answered that its mandatory arbitration provision found in its credit agreements required that the matter be handled through arbitration. The superior court found that the case could proceed in court because ITT's arbitration clause was unconscionable *inter alia* because it was inserted in adhesion contracts, appeared to require arbitration in Minneapolis, and required payment of a large fee.

ITT appealed this decision, and reprinted as § 1.1, *infra* is the plaintiff/appellee's brief asking the California middle level appellate court to uphold the trial court decision. The decision was eventually upheld in *Patterson v. ITT Consumer Financial Corp.*, 14 Cal. App. 4th 1659 (1993) rev den., cert den, 114 S.Ct. 1217 (1994). Consumers in other states might succeed in a similar challenge based either upon an unconscionability theory, or some related approach, such as a violation of the state's unfair and deceptive acts and practices (UDAP) statute. Although ITT has reportedly changed some of the terms of its arbitration provision to allow waiver of the fee and to make clearer that the arbitration need not take place in Minneapolis, many contracts containing the older provision are still in place.

This chapter also reprints three documents from *Badie v. Bank of America*. In that case, several individuals, Consumer Action, and the California Trial Lawyers Association affirmatively challenged the Bank of America's practice of including a mandatory arbitration provision stuffed into the monthly billing statement sent to its credit card customers. The complaint, reprinted as § 1.2, *infra*, presents several theories to affirmatively challenge a creditor's mandatory arbitration provision. This is distinguished from *Patterson* where the consumers challenged ITT's insurance practices (not the arbitration provision), and the issue in the case became whether the dispute over ITT's insurance practices must be submitted to binding arbitration. The consumers' pre-trial brief in *Badie* is reprinted at § 1.3 and the post-trial brief is reprinted at § 1.4, *infra*. The plaintiffs lost at the trial level, but have appealed the case to the California Court of Appeals.

The documents reprinted in this chapter retain the names of all the plaintiffs and defendants, but the addresses of consumers have been changed, and the first names of the consumer plaintiffs have been deleted or changed. Certificate of process, attorney signature blocks, and similar material have been deleted.

Chapter 2 Lenders Pay $125 Million For Their Overreaching Conduct

To recover as much as $125 million for defrauded consumers is indeed rare for a consumer attorney, but this is exactly what Mark Chavez and other consumer attorney accomplished in successfully settling a series of class actions concerning creditors' sale of forced placed automobile insurance. For example, a Ford Motor Credit Co. subsidiary settled a force-placed insurance case in September, 1993 for $58.3 million; Barnett Banks settled for $19 million in October, 1993; and First Interstate Bancorp settled for $16 million in 1992. Other settlements include $9 million with BankAmerica Corp., $3.7 million with Bank of the West, $3.5 million with Nissan Motor Acceptance Co., and $1.1 million with Wells Fargo & Co.

Keys to the success of the litigation in this area were that major financial institutions were caught red handed improperly taking huge sums of money from consumers. As a result, the class sizes were large, the amount of out-of-pocket damage of each class member was significant, and the defendants both could pay large judgments and were concerned with their public image.

A number of other class actions are still being pursued around the country concerning force-placed automobile insurance, and there is a continuing potential for abuse in this area because creditors are purchasing expensive insurance to be paid by the consumer without first obtaining the consumer's permission. Automobile creditors typically require consumers to purchase automobile collision and theft coverage to protect the collateral. The credit contract will authorize the creditor to purchase such insurance on behalf of the consumer if the consumer does not present evidence of continuous coverage or if the coverage ever lapses during the term of the loan. Usually the auto insurance that the creditor purchases for the consumer—called "force-placed" or collateral protection insurance—will be vendor single-interest insurance, meaning that the coverage only protects the creditor's interest in the car and does not protect the consumer's equity in the car.

There are a number of abuses related to force-placed insurance. Allegations in various lawsuits indicate that the following creditor practices may be widespread:

- Purchasing additional coverages for the consumer other than collision or theft, such as skip or deficiency insurance, and not disclosing this to the consumer—these purchases are not authorized by the credit contract and only benefit the creditor, not the consumer;

- Purchasing force-placed insurance even though the consumer already had adequate coverage;

- Purchasing force-placed insurance at prices that include potential rebates if a creditor's experience is good (as high as 14% of the premium) and not passing this rebate on to the consumer;

- Receiving commissions for the force-placed insurance even though the creditor is not licensed to act as an agent for those coverages;

- Failing to disclose that only single interest insurance was being purchased to protect the creditor's interest in the car, but not the consumer's equity interest;

- Disadvantageous financing of the force-placed insurance premiums—such insurance should be financed at lower rates than the car loan because the creditor can easily obtain from the insurer a full rebate of unearned insurance premiums after a car's repossession;

- Using the creditor's address and not the consumer's address as the garaging address, thus generally increasing the cost of the automobile insurance that is rated in part by such designation;

- Purchasing force-placed insurance or beginning the financing for the insurance starting at a date before the creditor actually purchased the insurance; and

- Purchasing a form of single interest insurance whose coverages had unusually restrictive requirements disadvantageous to consumers—such as forcing consumers to turn in their cars as total losses even after only minor damage.

The materials in this chapter reprint many of the pleadings from one of Mr. Chavez's successful forced-placed insurance settlements—*Reed v. Bank of America*. The complaint seeking monetary damages and injunctive relief is reprinted at § 2.1, *infra*. Reprinted at § 2.2 is the memorandum of points and authorities supporting the motion for class certification. In part because of the unique nature of California class action procedure, the plaintiffs immediately sought before class certification an order approving a class notice and allocating the cost of the notice to the defendant. See § 2.3, *infra*.

The remaining documents relate to the settlement of the case. § 2.4 is the memorandum in support of approving the settlement, certifying the class, and providing notice to the class. Also reprinted is the proposed order certifying the settlement class, the preliminary approval order, a class notice briefly summarizing the proposed settlement, and the more detailed class notice of the proposed settlement, at §§ 2.5, 2.6, 2.7, 2.8, 2.9 respectively. The plaintiffs also sought injunctive relief, and this was part of the settlement as well, as indicated by the order for injunctive relief reprinted at § 2.10, *infra*. § 2.11 reprints the memorandum in support of final approval of settlement and application for award of attorney fees. The actual settlement agreement for $9.1 million has not been reprinted, because it is quite long, fact-specific, and summarized in the other documents.

In the interest of privacy, the plaintiffs' first names have been changed. Also not included are certificates of process, attorney signature blocks, and other non-essential items.

Chapter 3 FTC Holder Notice Triggers Bank's Class Liability for Dealer's Fraud

One of the most important and misunderstood aspects of consumer law is the operation of the FTC Holder Notice, as set out in 16 C.F.R. 433.[1] The notice in consumer credit agreements states that the holder of the note is subject to all claims and defenses the consumer has against the seller. The FTC Holder Notice is explained in detail at National Consumer Law Center, *Unfair and Deceptive Acts and Practices* § 6.6 (5th ed. 2001).

One of the more important applications of the FTC Holder Notice is where a car dealer, home improvement contractor, or other merchant engages in a pattern of widespread fraud, but where the merchant is likely to be judgement proof, if not before a class action is filed, then certainly by the time a final order of judgement is issued. The presence of the FTC Holder Notice in financing contracts related to the fraudulent sales transactions means that consumers can raise their claims against the note holder, and not just against the fraudulent merchant. Where one or two creditors has financed all the consumer loans for a particular merchant, then a class action against those creditors based solely on the merchant's fraud is a viable option.

An excellent example of such an approach is presented in the materials in this chapter from *Johnson v. First National Bank in Alamogordo*. A used car dealer had systematically rolled back odometers and then gone out of business. Because the First National Bank financed all the dealer's car loans, the plaintiffs brought in federal court an odometer tampering class action complaint against the bank, the car dealer, and several individuals connected with the auto dealer. See § 3.1, *infra*. The complaint alleges that the dealer violated the federal Odometer Act, engaged in unfair and deceptive practices, and breached its common law duties and various warranties. The complaint further alleges that the bank is subject to all the class' claims against the dealer. The plaintiffs followed up their complaint with a first set of interrogatories to the bank, reprinted at § 3.2, *infra*.

The next aspect of the case was certifying a class against the bank. The motion, memorandum, reply memorandum, and proposed order are reprinted *infra* at §§ 3.3, 3.4, 3.5, and 3.6 respectively. After the class was conditionally certified,

---

1 Reprinted at National Consumer Law Center, Unfair and Deceptive Acts and Practices Appx. B.2 (3d ed. 1991).

the plaintiffs moved for partial summary judgment, primarily on the issue that the bank was liable for the dealer's misconduct pursuant to the FTC Holder Notice. The motion, memorandum, and reply memorandum are reprinted *infra* at §§ 3.7, 3.8, and 3.9, respectively. The memoranda provide an excellent discussion of why the lender is subject to the consumers' claims against the dealer because of the operatio of the FTC Holder Rule. While the legal issue is straightfoward, it is one with which many defendants and courts are not familiar, and consumer attorneys should anticipate in their cases the necessity of the type of "educational" briefs as presented in *Johnson*.

The court certified the class and ruled for the class on the partial summary judgment issue, leaving the bank little choice but to settle the case. The bank eventually paid out over $300,000 to 76 class members and paid the class' attorney for all his time pursuing the case and for subsequently administering the settlement distribution to the class. The proposed order preliminarily approving the settlement of the class action is reprinted at § 3.10, *infra*. Also included in the materials is the final report of the plaintiff's counsel with accompanying affidavit concerning distribution of the class settlement (at § 3.11, *infra*) and the proposed final order approving settlement of the class action (at § 3.12, *infra*).

The first names of the named plaintiffs have been deleted for privacy purposes, as have the names of individual class members from the affidavit concerning distribution of the settlement. Also not reprinted are certificates of process, attorney signature blocks, and other non-essential information.

Chapter 4 Lender Liability Where FTC Holder Notice Improperly Omitted

The previous chapter sets out pleadings in a successful class action based on the presence of the FTC Holder Notice in the loan documents. Because the notice was part of the loan agreement, the consumers could raise their claims relating to a car dealer against the financing bank. This is critical in most class action situations because a small dealer is unlikely to repay a large judgement, while a major financial institution will have no choice.

In some situations though, the FTC Holder Notice should have been inserted in the loan documents, but it is not. When this is the case, the legal basis for the consumers' rights to raise claims against the note holder are more complex. For a detailed discussion, see National Consumer Law Center, *Unfair and Deceptive Acts and Practices* § 6.6 (5th ed. 2001). Nevertheless, it is still imperative in many cases to include the creditor as a defendant if the consumers' injury is to ever be remedied.

An interesting example of a class action where the FTC Notice is not in the promissory notes is *Brown v. Lasalle*

Northwest National Bank, where the auto dealer referred customers to an insurance agent who then referred the customers to the bank. The bank's loan documents did not include the FTC Holder Notice, since the bank claimed not to have any arrangement or relationship to the dealer. The plaintiffs, on the other hand, claimed that the three-way relationship was enough to establish a business relationship between the dealer and bank, so that the FTC Holder Notice should have been included in the loan agreements. Moreover, the plaintiffs alleged that the bank was engaged in a RICO violation and an unfair and deceptive trade practice by attempting to evade the application of the FTC Holder Notice.

The court at 820 F. Supp. 1078 (N.D. Ill. 1993) denied the bank's motion to dismiss, holding that the plaintiffs had alleged a sufficient business relationship between bank and dealer to trigger the FTC Holder Notice and that the plaintiffs properly alleged RICO and deceptive practices violation based on this failure to include the notice.

The materials in this chapter should also be compared with those found at chapter 6, *infra* where the FTC Holder Notice was not included in loan agreements relating to the purchase of interests in campgrounds. The plaintiffs in the materials found in chapter 6 also argued that the FTC Holder Rule should apply and that the failure to include the notice renders the bank liable for damages resulting from the campground's misconduct.

The class attorneys in *Brown v. Lasalle Northwest National Bank* generated many documents in the case. We have presented here a number of the more important ones. First is reprinted at § 4.1, *infra*, the consumer attorney's initial demand letter to the bank. The consumer's subsequent complaint was dismissed because the RICO count was not pled with sufficient particularity. Reprinted at § 4.2, *infra* is the plaintiff's request to file an amended complaint. The amended complaint itself is found at § 4.3, *infra*. The plaintiff's memorandum in opposition to the defendant's motion to dismiss is found at § 4.4, *infra*. The court granted the consumer leave to amend the complaint and rejected the motion to dismiss at 820 F. Supp. 1078 (N.D. Ill. 1993).

The next three sections deal with discovery in the case. The plaintiff's first request for admissions, interrogatories, and document requests is found at § 4.5, *infra*. Supplemental interrogatories are reprinted at § 4.6, and the plaintiff's response to the defendant's discovery request is found at § 4.7, *infra*.

The plaintiffs in *Brown* moved for class certification, and produced an accompanying memorandum, and then a reply memorandum. These are reprinted at §§ 4.8, 4.9, and 4.10, respectively. When the class was certified, the defendant requested the court to reconsider its ruling, and the plaintiff's response to this request is found at § 4.11, *infra*. The notice to the class of the pendency of the action is reprinted at § 4.12, *infra*.

The case was then settled. The plaintiff's memorandum in

support of the settlement with accompanying settlement issues is found at § 4.13, *infra*. The class was awarded approximately $350,000, and a program was set up so that the relationship between the lender and insurance agent was not sufficient to trigger the FTC Holder Notice. Class attorneys were paid an amount determined by the court not to exceed $150,000. Included at § 4.14, *infra*, is one of the class attorney's affidavit in support of the fee request. Not reprinted is an essentially similar declaration from another class attorney.

The materials in this chapter have changed the names and addresses of the plaintiffs, and have not included certificates of process, attorney signature blocks, or other non-essential information.

Chapter 5 $28 Million Punitive Damages Award for Bank's Involvement in Home Improvement Fraud

Many of the cases in this volume relate to consumer class actions where the class recovers hundreds of thousands or even millions of dollars. But the case in this volume involving the largest consumer recovery is *Baker v. Harper*, an action on behalf of five individuals, where the jury awarded $45 million in actual and punitive damages (later remitted to $28 million). This is a dramatic example of the potential utility of individual consumer cases seeking punitive damages. Typically, such cases are based on basic common law tort principles, and a state jury is asked to assess actual and punitive damages. Ordinary citizens with experiences with used car dealers, home improvement contractors, and debt collectors are asked to send major corporations a message about their improper practices.

Another key to the *Harper* case was that the plaintiffs did not just sue the home improvement contractor, but also the lender for punitive damages. Probably no judgment of any size could ever have been recovered from the home improvement contractor, but the lender was a sizeable corporation. Nevertheless, even that corporation might find its assets stretched to pay a $28 million judgment. Fortunately, the plaintiffs had investigated the lender's parent corporation, a major international bank, and obtained an agreement that the parent would pay for any judgement awarded against the subsidiary.

The facts in *Harper* were that a home improvement contractor sold its services door to door, offering to take care of the financing. The home improvement work was shoddy or non-existent, and the financing disadvantageous to the consumers. The consumers were also promised additional proceeds from the loan that they could use for other purposes, although they actually received very little. The consumers also signed completion certificates on the day the contracts were signed and were instructed to say that the work was done satisfactorily if someone called. All the financing was with Union Mortgage, and no contracts were signed if Union did not approve of a loan. Union was in turn owned by a major foreign bank.

The complaint, reprinted at § 5.1, *infra*, was brought in state court on behalf of five homeowners against the home improvement contractor and the mortgage company. The mortgage company's parent corporations were later added as defendants. The major claim was one for common law fraud, and the plaintiffs alleged that the home improvement contractor was acting as agent for and under the control of the mortgage company and that there was a conspiracy among the various defendants. The case later concentrated on the agency claim. A jury trial was requested, and the plaintiffs requested compensatory and punitive damages without specifying an amount. A default judgment was entered into against the home improvement contractor, as shown at § 5.2, *infra*, and the case thus focused on Union Mortgage.

Another important aspect of the case was establishing the parent bank's liability for any judgment against Union Mortgage. A few documents relating to discovery from the parent foreign bank are reprinted at § 5.4, *infra*. An example of the plaintiffs' response to discovery from the foreign bank is reprinted at § 5.5, *infra*. § 5.6, *infra*, is an affidavit from the plaintiff's expert attesting that Union Mortgage and the parent foreign bank are to all intents and purposes one and the same entity. The plaintiffs' brief in response to the foreign bank's motion to dismiss is found at § 5.3, and this is the major document in the case outlining the bank's liability for the acts of the mortgage company. Eventually, the parent foreign bank signed an agreement stating it would indemnify Union Mortgage for any judgment against Union. *See* § 5.7, *infra*. Consequently, the plaintiffs had now narrowed the case to what was Union's degree of liability for the acts of the home improvement contractor. Any subsequent judgment would be recoverable against a major international bank.

The eventual jury award in the case was a stunning $9 million for *each* of the five plaintiffs. The order and judgment is reprinted at § 5.8, *infra*. Not surprisingly, the defendant filed various motions after the judgment and the plaintiffs' (successfully) drafted an order denying all those motions, as reprinted at § 5.9, *infra*, except that the amount was remitted to $28 million.

Certain materials have not been reprinted from this case. The names and addresses of consumers have been changed, and certificates of service, notarizations, attorney signature blocks, and the like have not been included. Also not reprinted are a series of motions to compel documents and responses as well as motions for sanctions and for dismissal, as the defendants were being extremely uncooperative during discovery. There were also many similarities in plaintiffs' various requests for production and plaintiffs' requests for admission, and the chapter only includes a small sample of these documents.

Chapter 6 Class Litigation Against Lenders for Campground Membership Fraud

A widespread and serious form of consumer abuse is the high pressure and deceptive marketing of interests in campgrounds, and this chapter reprints pleadings from three of a series of campground cases brought by the law firm of Malakoff Doyle & Finberg. To date these cases have resulted in the recovery of over $10 million in settlements.

This campground litigation is instructive because it not only demonstrates how to successfully challenge in a class action a widespread pattern of sales abuse, but also because it shows how banks and other lenders can be found liable to a class for a seller's misconduct. As such, the materials in this chapter present another variant to the documents found in chapters 3 and 4, and to a lesser extent chapter 5. In some of the campground cases, the FTC Holder Notice is found in the loan agreements, and then the issues are similar to those found in chapter 3. See § 6.7, *infra*. In others, the FTC Notice was missing from the documents, and then the issues are more analogous to chapter 4, although the theories of lender liability are somewhat different. See §§ 6.1, 6.6, *infra*.

This chapter also focuses on some issues not found in the other chapters, such as the interrelation of a seller's chapter 11 reorganization and claims against the related lenders. See § 6.7, *infra*. The materials in this chapter also present an excellent series of discovery requests to support a class-wide challenge to a deceptive marketing scheme where the lender is to be found liable for the seller's misconduct. See §§ 6.2, 6.3, 6.4, and 6.5, *infra*. Those interested in sample RICO materials will also find items of interest in this chapter.

The first pleading presented is a complaint against a bank for fraud relating to a campground's sales practices even though the FTC Holder Notice is not in the loan documents. See § 6.1, *infra*. Then a series of discovery in the same case is reprinted—the First Set of Interrogatories, the First Request for Production of Documents, the Second Set of Interrogatories, and the Second Request for Production of Documents at §§ 6.2, 6.3, 6.4, and 6.5, respectively.

The chapter also reprints at § 6.6, *infra* a brief in support of a motion for class certification in a similar campground case where the FTC Notice is also omitted. The final document is from a third campground case, one where the FTC Holder Notice was in the loan documents. § 6.7, *infra* is the plaintiffs' brief in opposition to a summary judgment motion filed by one of the defendants. Beside dealing with lender liability, the brief also addresses issues concerning the interrelationship of the campground's bankruptcy reorganization and the class action against the lenders.

The names and addresses of class members have been changed in these documents. In addition, certificates of service, attorney signature blocks and similar items have not been reprinted. Moreover, these materials represent the most interesting pleadings from a series of related cases, and do not reprint all the pleadings filed in any particular case.

Description of Pleadings

Chapter 7 Overreaching Loan Scheme Involving Multiple Parties

Recent years have seen a growth of predatory lending practices aimed at unsophisticated and relatively low income homeowners. Typical is the participation of numerous parties, such as lenders, home improvement contractors, brokers, and attorneys, in a scheme to provide homeowners with extremely disadvantageous second mortgages, and often to then refinance that mortgage with an even less advantageous mortgage. The final resolution of these practices too often is for consumers to lose both their homes and their built up equity in their homes.

The materials found in this chapter provide an excellent example of a legal challenge on behalf of three elderly, relatively unsophisticated low income homeowners of Boston's inner city. They allege that various lenders, closing attorneys, loan brokers, and home improvement contractors worked together to provide extraordinarily disadvantageous mortgages to these homeowners, and then to arrange for the loans to be refinanced at even worse terms. The homeowners' legal theories include the state unfair and deceptive practices statute, RICO, breach of fiduciary duty, fraud, negligence, breach of contract and warranty, Truth in Lending disclosure violations, and Truth in Lending rescission.

Reprinted at § 7.1, *infra*, is a complaint on behalf of three homeowners against multiple defendants—various interrelated lenders, loan brokers, home improvement contractors, and closing attorneys. The plaintiffs then sent similar requests for production of documents to several of these defendants, and § 7.2, *infra* reprints one of these requests.

The plaintiffs brought this case in state court and utilized state law theories, even using the Massachusetts Truth in Lending statute instead of the federal one. But the defendants were able to remove the case to federal court because of the federal RICO claim. The plaintiffs (unsuccessfully) attempted to remand the case to state court, and §§ 7.3 and 7.4, *infra*. reprint the motion and accompanying memorandum seeking remand of the action back to state court.

One of the defendant's then filed a motion to dismiss, and § 7.5, *infra*, reprints the plaintiffs' memorandum in opposition to that motion. That memorandum is a good summary of the legal bases for the plaintiffs' claims.

The names of the plaintiffs and defendants have been changed in all of these pleadings. In addition, certificates of service, attorney's signature blocks, and similar non-essential information has not been included.

Chapter 8 Truth In Lending Rescission in Bankruptcy Court

One of the most potent ways of protecting a homeowner against a foreclosure on a mortgage (other than a mortgage used to purchase the home) is through Truth in Lending rescission. This converts the secured obligation to an unsecured one, and also can radically reduce the consumer's indebtedness. For more details, see National Consumer Law Center, *Truth in Lending* ch.6 (4th ed. 1999 and Supp.).

TIL rescission is particularly effective when coupled with a chapter 13 bankruptcy filing. The bankruptcy filing automatically stays the foreclosure, and the amount owed on the mortgage can be paid over the life of the plan or longer. Moreover, if the mortgage is successfully rescinded under Truth in Lending, the consumer's obligation to tender back to the creditor is an unsecured obligation that may be discharged after the consumer has paid only a fraction of the amount owed. The bankruptcy proceeding also provides a convenient forum to bring all other claims against the creditor or other parties relating to the mortgage. For more on the bankruptcy aspects of saving a home from a second mortgage, see National Consumer Law Center, *Consumer Bankruptcy Law and Practice* (6th ed. 2000 and Supp.).

The materials in this chapter provide an excellent example of an attempt to save a consumer's home and radically reduce the consumer's indebtedness through Truth in Lending rescission and a chapter 13 bankruptcy filing. The first document, § 8.1, *infra*, is a letter to the creditor rescinding a mortgage pursuant to Truth in Lending. This is an essential first step to any Truth in Lending rescission action and should generally precede the bankruptcy filing.

After the homeowner rescinded, the homeowner filed a chapter 13 bankruptcy. For sample chapter 13 pleadings, see National Consumer Law Center, *Consumer Bankruptcy Law and Practice* Appxs. D, E, F, and G (6th ed. 2000 and Supp.). Despite the homeowner having rescinded the mortgage, the creditor filed a secured claim in the bankruptcy proceeding, in effect denying the effect of the rescission letter. The homeowner's complaint in bankruptcy court objecting to the secured claim is reprinted as § 8.2, *infra*. This complaint seeks additional relief, including enforcement of the rescission remedy and damages against the creditor pursuant to Truth in Lending and other causes of action. The homeowner then sought injunctive relief from the bankruptcy court to allow the consumer to refinance the rescinded mortgage with a new creditor at a sharply reduced interest rate. *See* § 8.3, *infra*.

Also included in the materials at §§ 8.4, 8.5, and 8.6 *infra* are the plaintiff's motion for partial summary judgment on the Truth in Lending rescission issues, the accompanying memorandum, and the homeowner's affidavit, respectively. A proposed order for the bankruptcy judge is included at § 8.7, *infra*.

The names of all the parties have been changed in these materials. In addition, non-essential information such as certificates of process and attorney signature blocks have not been included.

Chapter 9 Automobile Lease Case

Automobile leasing is an increasingly important area of consumer law. The number of consumers who lease their cars instead of purchasing them is growing rapidly. But, because litigation under the federal Consumer Leasing Act (CLA) is still much less frequent than under Truth in Lending, lessors frequently fail to comply with this federal disclosure statute. Moreover, it is very common for consumers to terminate their leases early, not only because they default on their payments, but because for a host of reasons they voluntarily wish to switch cars or turn in their leased car before the normal lease term. But lessors often charge astronomical early termination charges—charges that can successfully be challenged under the CLA.

There are a number of attractive aspects of CLA litigation concerning automobile leases. Even one disclosure violation results in recovery of $1000 plus actual damages plus attorney fees. The one year statute of limitations runs from lease termination, not consummation. Unlike TIL, which has been "simplified," any disclosure violation leads to statutory damages. Moreover, the CLA prohibits unreasonable early termination penalties, and violation of this standard should also result in $1000 plus actual damages plus attorney fees. Any leasing case should also consider other causes of action, including deception, retail installment sales acts, common law contract claims, warranty claims, and the like.

Automobile leasing cases are often susceptible to class action treatment because what is typically at issue is the standard form lease contract and the leasing company's standard procedure for enforcing its contract provisions. The amount at stake for each class member is significant, and the class size will be fairly large—depending on whether the class is statewide or nationwide. Lessors or their assignees also generally have deep pockets.

For more detail on automobile leasing, the federal Consumer Leasing Act, and other legal theories to challenge leasing practices, see National Consumer Law Center, *Truth in Lending* ch. 9 (4th ed. 1999 and Supp.). This newly revised chapter explains the various potential disclosure violations, and explores when a lease early termination charge is unreasonable. Appendix P of the 1989 Second Edition also reprints the CLA, FRB Regulation M on Leasing, and the FRB Commentary on Leasing.

Nevertheless, not all automobile leasing cases will focus on the federal Consumer Leasing Act. The materials reprinted *infra* are from a recent automobile leasing class action where the class attorneys decided to use alternative theories other than the CLA. They wanted to stay in state court, the statute of limitations under state theories was better than under the CLA, and the plaintiffs in that case encountered certain CLA scope problems. The CLA does not apply to leases where total payments exceed $25,000 nor to leases for business as opposed to consumer purposes.

This chapter reprints at § 9.1 a class action complaint in state court that is *not* brought under the CLA, but instead is brought solely under various state law theories. (The model Truth in Lending complaint at NCLC's *Truth in Lending* Appendix D (4th ed 1999 and Supp.) will be helpful in drafting a complaint that includes a CLA count.)

The discovery materials found at § 9.2, *infra,* will be relevant not only for actions under state theories, but also for CLA auto leasing cases as well. The discovery materials include requests for admission, interrogatories, and requests for production of documents. § 9.3 contains a class certification motion in that case, and § 9.4 is the accompanying memorandum.

The names of the parties have been changed in this pending case. In addition, certificates of process, signature blocks for attorneys, and other nonessential information has not been included.

Chapter 10 Recovering on Consumer Claims From Merchant in Bankruptcy

Consumer attorneys too often view consumer claims as worthless where a merchant or other defendant has filed for bankruptcy. The materials in this chapter show how aggressive representation on behalf of a group of consumers can result in a significant recovery from a merchant in bankruptcy, while the consumer attorney's fees are paid for out of the merchant's bankruptcy estate.

For more detailed analysis of a consumer's rights as a creditor in a merchant's or landlord's bankruptcy, see National Consumer Law Center, *Consumer Bankruptcy Law and Practice* ch. 17 (6th ed. 2000 and Supp.). In addition, see forms that manual's Appendix G.13, which are also available on the Companion CD-Rom.

The materials in this chapter are from a case handled by legal services attorneys involving a bankrupt furniture store. Lawyers at Community Legal Services in Philadelphia (CLS) were first approached by a number of consumers who had paid large deposits for furniture that was never delivered. The consumers had been organized with the assistance of the Consumers Education and Protection Association (CEPA), a local consumer group. Upon investigation, the consumers learned that the owner had owned a previous furniture store which had also gone out of business after taking deposits from hundreds of customers.

After attending the creditors meeting, at which the owner took the Fifth Amendment in response to all questions, consumers sought to have the United States Trustee appoint a committee of consumer creditors. Although they had been invited to serve on the general unsecured creditors committee, the consumers and their attorneys felt that there would be a conflict of interest since they had, in large part, priority claims under section 507(a)(6) of the Bankruptcy Code. They were concerned that their claims take precedence over the claims of other unsecured creditors and the consumers did not wish to undertake a fiduciary duty to represent the interests of those other creditors.

When the United States Trustee declined to appoint an official committee of consumer creditors, the consumers filed a motion requesting that the court order the trustee to appoint such a committee. See § 10.1, *infra*. The motion was granted and a number of the consumer creditors were appointed to the official committee. The committee, in turn, filed an application to retain CLS as its counsel. See § 10.2, *infra*.

After doing further investigation, the official committee filed an adversary complaint against the debtor furniture store and the creditor with a first lien on all of the assets of the company, AT&T Commercial Finance Corporation. See § 10.7, *infra*. The complaint sought recovery against the creditor or subordination of the creditor's lien to the consumers' rights on several theories based on the creditor having financed the business knowing from experience of the owner's unscrupulous practices. (A predecessor of the same creditor had financed the owner's previous business.) The official committee's legal theories included general equitable subordination principles, the Uniform Commercial Code's rights given to a purchaser of identifiable goods in the debtor's warehouse as against the secured creditor, fraudulent transfer theories and lender liability theories. Ultimately, this adversary proceeding was settled by an agreement that the consumer creditors would get 60% of the proceeds of the lender's lien and the lender would agree to support only a chapter 11 plan to which the consumer creditors did not object.

Another novel provision of the settlement agreement provided that the debtor's inventory would be disposed of by allowing those consumers who had ordered identifiable furniture to complete their purchases if they wished. Afterwards, a private sale would be held at which all consumer creditors would be permitted to purchase the inventory at a 65% discount. Finally a public auction would be held of whatever furniture remained. This allowed consumer creditors an option to recoup some portion of their claims through the bankruptcy sale process.

In the meantime, the debtor filed a chapter 11 plan which the consumer creditors felt was grossly deficient, proposing to continue the furniture sales to those consumers where it would be profitable, having some unknown entity advance the money to complete the sales, and eliminating the claims of any consumers who did not go through with the contracts assumed by the debtor. The consumer creditors committee objected to this plan on a wide variety of grounds. *See* § 10.4, *infra*. The committee argued that the plan was not feasible since there was no known source of financing. Moreover the plan did not propose to pay the consumer priority claims in full, and the assumed executory contracts would not have been promptly performed according to their original terms. The consumer creditors objected to the debt-

or's disclosure statement on similar grounds, as well as various misleading statements it contained. *See* § 10.3, *infra*.

The official committee of consumer creditors then moved to terminate the exclusivity period for filing a chapter 11 plan so it could file a chapter 11 plan as well. This motion was granted and the consumer creditors committee filed a chapter 11 plan and disclosure statement. See §§ 10.5, 10.6, *infra*.

An innovative provision of the plan provided that those consumers who purchased goods at the private sale conducted by the secured creditor would have their claims reduced by the amounts of the discounts they received. This was proposed so that those consumers who did not have the money to purchase furniture at the private sale, or did not wish to purchase that furniture because they had already purchased replacement furniture, could have greater dividends from the proceeds of the sale.

The consumers' disclosure statement was approved, as was the debtor's disclosure statement after some changes were made in it. Both disclosure statements and plans were mailed out to all creditors. The result of the voting was that every class of creditors voted against the debtor's plan and all but two consumer priority creditors voted in favor of the consumer creditors committee's plan. However, since the consumer creditors committee plan needed the votes of all priority creditors, in that it did not assure full payment of priority claims, the consumer creditors committee plan could not be confirmed at the initial confirmation hearing scheduled by the court.

Because they were uncertain whether or not their plan would be confirmed, the consumer creditors committee joined in the motion of the secured creditor for relief from the automatic stay so that at a minimum the consumers would share in the proceeds of AT&T's lien. After relief from the stay was granted, notice was sent to all consumer creditors that a private sale would be held at which they could obtain a 65% discount. The notice contained detailed provisions worked out by the official committee of consumer creditors so that those who had lost the most money and had waited the longest for their furniture had the first chance to purchase furniture at the sale. Ultimately, the private sale was held and approximately $100,000 was realized. A large percentage of the consumers took advantage of the sale provisions.

After the private sale, the consumer creditors committee learned that the two priority creditors who had voted against the plan had both misunderstood the terms of the plan and in fact were in favor of the plan. A motion was filed to allow them to change their votes and ultimately, over the objections of the debtor, the consumer creditors committee's plan was approved. In accordance with that plan, roughly $100,000 realized for the consumers from the sale of the inventory is being distributed to those consumers who had claims remaining after the sale. They will receive approximately 54% of their claims from this distribution. The costs of the committee's counsel were also paid from these proceeds.

The next steps in the case involved adversary proceedings against the debtor's principals and some of the creditors to recover fraudulent transfers and preferences. *See* § 10.8, *infra*. It is hoped that the funds recovered for the estate through these proceedings will pay administrative expenses, such as attorney's fees for the committee's counsel as well as additional dividends for the consumer creditors and perhaps other creditors as well.

The accompanying pleadings change the names and addresses of individual consumer creditors and certain individuals related to the corporation in bankruptcy. The materials also delete certificates of service, attorney signature blocks, and other non-essential information.

Chapter 11 Seeking Attorney Fees Pursuant to Fee Shifting Statute

A number of consumer protection statutes provide attorney fees for a prevailing consumer. See, e.g. National Consumer Law Center, *Truth in Lending* ch. 8 (4th ed. 1999 and Supp.), National Consumer Law Center, *Fair Debt Collection* § 6.8 (4th ed. 2000), National Consumer Law Center, *Fair Credit Reporting Act* § 11.6 (4th ed. 1998 and Supp.), National Consumer Law Center, *Credit Discrimination* § 11.6 (2d ed. 1998 and Supp.), National Consumer Law Center, *Unfair and Deceptive Acts and Practices* Ch. 8 (5th ed. 2001), *Consumer Class Actions: A Practical Litigation Guide* Ch. 15 (4th ed. 1999).

The materials in this chapter provide examples of fee petitions in two different Truth in Lending cases. (For model attorney fee pleadings developed in cases under the Fair Debt Collection Practices Act, see National Consumer Law Center, *Fair Debt Collection* Appx. G (2000 4th ed. and Supp.).) Both the cases in this chapter involving Truth in Lending attorney fees were brought on behalf of an individual, and were not class actions. The attorneys in both cases were legal services attorneys, and in both cases fees are being sought at a rate of $200 an hour. In one case fees of $51,000 were sought even though the case had settled. The federal magistrate recommended that the plaintiffs receive an attorney fee award for all amounts sought, and the fees were subsequently settled for somewhat less than this amount. In the other case, fees of $29,000 were sought for work in handling the appeal before the Eleventh Circuit. The Eleventh Circuit approved a fee award, but remanded to the trial court the determination of the size of the fee award.

In § 11.1, *infra*, the consumer's attorney in *Montiel* presents a motion for fees after the case had settled with an accompanying memorandum. An affidavit from the attorney describing in detail the work performed in that case is reprinted at § 11.2, *infra*. In § 11.3, *infra*, the consumer's attorney in *Rodash* presents a similar petition for fees to the

Eleventh Circuit for work before the Eleventh Circuit in successfully appealing the trial court's adverse ruling on a Truth in Lending issue. Accompanying that petition is the attorney's affidavit (found at § 11.4, *infra*), and also an affidavit from an expert supporting the fee request (found at § 11.5, *infra*).

The first name of the consumer plaintiffs have been deleted for privacy purposes. The caption has been simplified to delete reference to the counterplaintiff and counterdefendant. Also deleted are certificates of service, notary and signature blocks and related information not central to the pleadings.

Chapter 12 *Cy Pres* Remedy

Whenever a fund is created for payment to class members, there is the potential for a residue of money not distributed to class members. There are various reasons why this can be the case—where class members cannot be located, where those entitled to payment do not request payment or do not cash payment checks, where an agreed-upon fund is larger than the amount payable to individual class members, and the like. Counsel for the class must be prepared to propose a plan for this residue. Returning the money to the defendant will not benefit the class and will not deter future misconduct.

The *cy pres* remedy uses this residue for a purpose or purposes consistent with the interests of the class, but where the money is not distributed to individual class members. Good examples of the use of the *cy pres* remedy are found in *Beasley v. Wells Fargo Bank* and *Kovitz v. Crocker National Bank*, companion class actions before the California Superior Court in San Francisco, where over $3 million in *cy pres* awards were made to the California office of Consumers Union, the Volunteer Legal Services Program of the Bar Association of San Francisco, San Francisco Neighborhood Legal Assistance Foundation, Consumer Action, and Consumer Credit Counseling Services to perform various specified projects of benefit to California consumers.

The jury in *Beasley* awarded $5.2 million in favor of the class of consumer credit card customers who had been assessed excessive late and overlimit fees. *Kovitz* was then settled for $3.78 million. Only about $6 million of these amounts could be returned to individual card customers. The court ordered that half the residue be distributed through prospective credits to existing cardholders and the other half used for a *cy pres* remedy. Because of accrued interest and other adjustments, this amount equalled approximately $3 million.

This chapter reprints the memorandum in support of approval of the *cy pres* remedy at § 12.1, *infra*, the orders for the *cy pres* remedy at §§ 12.2 and 12.3, *infra*, and an example of a memorandum of understanding from one of the recipient organizations at § 12.4, *infra*. One of the interesting aspects of the *Beasley* and *Kovitz cy pres* remedy is that the bank proposed that much of the *cy pres* money go to consumer credit counseling instead of being awarded to consumer education and advocacy groups. The documents found in this chapter indicate how the class attorney and the court dealt with this issue—awarding some money for credit counseling but with certain restrictions and conditions on the way the credit counseling organization could use the money.

The first names of the named plaintiffs have been deleted to protect their privacy. In addition, certificates of service, attorney signature blocks, and similar items have been deleted from the reprinted documents.

Consumer Law Pleadings With Disk, Number Two (1995)

Chapter 1 Evictions and Other Landlord-Tenant Disputes

Consumer law has important applications to landlord-tenant relations, particularly concerning evictions, lease provisions, habitability, utilities, security deposits, and lessor and agent oral representations. More and more attorneys specializing in housing law are discovering the utility of consumer law.

This chapter provides samples of consumer law pleadings addressing common landlord-tenant problems. Section 1.1 reprints an answer and counterclaims to the landlord's claim for back rent. The tenants used a state deceptive practices act and a state landlord-tenant act to challenge the terms of the lease as being void, unenforceable and as illegal penalties. The suspect lease provisions required the tenants' fastidious maintenance of dwelling as well as lawn and shrubbery; which allowed the landlord to re-enter and reserve possession of the property by force; and which accelerated the balance of the lease for problems of noise or littering. The consumers sought actual and statutory damages and attorney fees.

The pleadings found in § 1.2 demonstrate a variety of claims, including state deceptive practices claims, where the landlord has failed to maintain the premises in habitable condition. Suits of this sort not only deter grossly negligent and appalling behavior by landlords, but can result in substantial damage awards for the tenants. For example, in *Haddad v. Gonzalez*, 410 Mass. 855, 576 N.E. 2d 658 (1991), the court affirmed an award of $61,475 to a tenant whose landlord had rented an uninhabitable apartment, refused to repair it, and threatened and abused the tenant. The tenant won treble damages because a state deceptive practices claim had been pleaded.

The pleadings in § 1.2 present an uninhabitability defense and counterclaims to an eviction action, as well as a pro-posed finding of facts and conclusion of law. The section also presents two appellate brief, the first focusing primarily on the substantive issues, and the other on the size of the attorney fee award.

Consumer law claims also are important when a landlord acts unfairly in terminating the tenancy. A recurrent problem is landlord attempts to lock tenants out or shut off their utilities in lieu of a proper eviction. Section 1.3 is an example of a tenant's suit for damages and injunctive relief against an effort to force the tenant out by shutting off the utilities. The tenants also sought a temporary restraining order requiring the landlord to refrain from further disconnection or threats to disconnect the tenant's electricity as well as to refrain from actual or constructive eviction, reprinted at § 1.3.2. Section 1.3.3 provides the trial brief that lays out the claims in more detail concerning wrongful eviction, trespass and unfair and deceptive trade practice stemming from the landlord's attempt to evict the tenants by disconnecting their water and electricity. Although not pled in that case, where the lockout or shut-off is an attempt to collect back rent, state debt collection statutes or debt collection regulations may provide an additional cause of action.

The final set of pleadings reprinted at § 1.4 relate to a landlord's persistent abuse of the eviction process to collect rent that was not owed and to evict tenants who were current on rent. The plaintiffs assert Fair Debt Collection Practices Act and deceptive practices act claims against the landlord's attorney, as well as allege that the landlord and related agents charged excessive rent and terminated tenancies in violation of the lease, the state deceptive practices statute, the U.S. Housing Act and HUD regulations.

Chapter 2 Mobile Home Parks

A significant number of Americans live in mobile home parks. In general, these consumers own their own mobile home, and rent from the park owner the site where the home is affixed. While the park residents may have one year leases or even be tenants at will, their homes are typically not very mobile. This puts tenants at a special disadvantage when dealing with the park owner—once the consumer affixes the home to the park space, the consumer has few options, no matter what the park conditions and the park rent levels. For example, some mobile home parks have inadequate water and sewer systems or other severe problems affecting habitability.

To compound this problem, local zoning laws often discourage mobile home parks, and there is a severe shortage of park space in many areas of the country. This has led some park owners to tie the offering of park space with the consumer having to purchase the home from the park owner or a related party.

Tenant associations or individuals attempting to rectify abuses are threatened with retaliatory evictions or utility shut-offs. Park owners also face few restrictions as to their ability at will to change park rules, alter services, or increase rents. If the park owner decides to convert to a shopping center or other non-park use, tenants are also provided minimal leverage.

Consumer law provides certain remedies in all of these situations. This chapter provides a series of pleadings dealing with these park abuses. Section 2.1 reprints pleadings from a class action on behalf of the tenants at a mobile home park who had been living for years with contaminated water and a defective sewer system. The tenants secured injunctive relief and the appointment of a receiver to correct these conditions; the conditions have now finally been corrected and their damage claims are awaiting trial. The section contains the complaint for injunctive and damage relief, as well as documents relating to the request for a temporary restraining order, a preliminary injunction, and other preliminary relief. Also included are interrogatories and requests for production of documents. Individual defendants sought to be removed from the case as not responsible for the corporation's conduct. The section reprints at § 2.1.6 the class' brief in opposition to this motion to dismiss.

The plaintiffs then sought class certification as well as court protection from retaliatory eviction for tenants who withheld rent during the pendency of the lawsuit. See § 2.1.7, *infra*. The accompanying memorandum is found at § 2.1.8.

The second mobile home park case excerpted in this chapter focuses on park conversions, tie-ins of the sale of homes to park space, and retaliatory evictions. When the owners of a mobile home park sought to sell the park, state law required them to offer it for sale to the park residents. When the park residents put together a financing package to buy the park, the owners backed out of the deal. A few months later, the owners simultaneously offered the park for sale again at a higher price, and told the residents that the park was being converted to a condominium and they could either buy their lots or move out.

The Attorney General filed suit because of these deceptive and confusing steps by the owners, and the park residents intervened in the suit. The park residents' intervention complaint, included here at § 2.2.1, raises a number of issues, including a deceptive practices claim because of the unlawful threat of eviction of residents who did not buy their lots, and a claim for specific performance of the original sale of the park to the residents. An individual resident also asserted a challenge to a tie-in requirement that the park imposed, refusing to rent him a lot unless he bought a mobile home from the park.

Subsection 2.2.2 includes a motion and memorandum for partial summary judgment concerning the illegal eviction claim. Subsection 2.2.3 reprints the consumer's brief in opposition to the defendant's motion for summary judgment on the tie-in issue. The consumer's brief provides a good overview of the legal basis for finding the tie-in to be a state UDAP violation.

The court ruled that the residents could not be required to purchase their lots or be evicted, and the park withdrew its plan to sell the park or convert it into a condominium. However, the court refused to grant specific performance of the original agreement to sell the park. It also denied the claim that the park's deceptive and confusing notices violated the state deceptive practices statute, and dismissed the tie-in claim. These issues are now on appeal, and the tenants' appellate brief and reply brief on all of these issues are included as §§ 2.2.4 and 2.2.5.

Chapter 3 Home Foreclosures

Home foreclosure rates have increased nationally by more that 200% since 1980 and show no signs of abatement. More than 600,000 homes were foreclosed in 1989. Each foreclosure of a residential mortgage is a personal, social and financial tragedy for the household facing foreclosure.

Families faced with a threatened foreclosure have a number of legal strategies to not only delay, but permanently prevent the foreclosure. These are set out in National Consumer Law Center, *Repossessions and Foreclosures* ch. 13 (4th ed. 1999). This chapter reprints materials dealing with three of the more effective approaches to stopping a foreclosure.

Section 3.1 provides a form letter that sets out the various defenses to foreclosure or a deficiency on a VA mortgage. The letter is signed by the homeowner, does not require an attorney, and is an effective first step to dealing with VA mortgage foreclosure issues. The homeowner need only check the appropriate defenses on the letter and mail it to the VA.

Section 3.2 reprints pleadings relating to the defense of a complaint seeking a foreclosure on a FHA-insured mortgage. Section 3.2.1 sets out the consumer's answer alleging that prior to foreclosure the loan provider failed to service the loan as required by HUD. Section 3.2.2 reprints the homeowner's request for production of documents in a similar FHA foreclosure action where the defense relates to the issue of failure to service the loan. Section 3.2.3 sets out a brief in opposition to the lender's motion for summary judgment on the issue of failure to service the loan as a defense to foreclosure.

Section 3.3 involves another important area of foreclosure defense, using a chapter 13 bankruptcy filing to respond to a foreclosure on a second mortgage where the second mortgage company engaged in questionable business practices. While homeowners defrauded by a second mortgage company may have valid claims for damages, it may be difficult to use these claims to stop the foreclosure. On the other hand, a bankruptcy filing immediately stays any attempt at foreclosure, and allows homeowners to regroup,

all their claims against the mortgage company or
ies. The bankruptcy can then restructure any re-
indebtedness, allowing the homeowner to cure past
and spread out future payments.

The consumer in Section 3.3 responded to a television
advertisement for second mortgages. She was told that while
she did not qualify for the advertised second mortgage,they
would refer her to another second mortgage company, which
approved her loan. The loan required monthly *interest only*
payments at a variable rate between 18% and 36% for a term
of three years and a balloon in the amount of the original
principal amount due at the end of the term. The loan also
required the homeowner to borrow $5,760 beyond the basic
loan to fund an escrow account to be held by the sole
stockholder and soled director for the mortgage company.

Section 3.3.1 is a complaint in bankruptcy objecting to the
lender's mortgage on the home, claiming the loan is void
and unenforceable based on violations of consumer protection statutes. Interrogatories addressed to the lender are set
out at § 3.3.2. Section 3.3.3 is a cross motion and accompanying memorandum for partial summary judgment and an
objection to the lender's motion for summary judgment,
arguing that the lender inflated the principal amount by
adding interest in advance, that the terms of the loan were
misleading and deceptive, and that the lender violated state
debt collection, UDAP, mortgage, fair trade and consumer
statutes.

Section 3.3.4 lists the witnesses and documentary evidence to be used by the debtor, and § 3.3.5 proposes findings
of fact and rulings of law. Section 3.3.6 addresses whether
"charges" refers to interest rates only or whether it addresses penalties and other charges which lenders add in
excess of the base interest rate ceiling.

Section 3.3.7 is a trial memorandum on liability which
addresses what amount, if any, the homeowner must pay to
the lender in the course of her chapter 13 plan if the
bankruptcy court were to find the lender in violation of the
law and the promissory note to be void. The reply memo on
damages in section 3.3.8 urges the court to find the promissory note void. Finally, section 3.3.9 presents the homeowner's chapter 13 plan, which allows her to avoid foreclosure and keep her home.

Chapter 4 Home Sales, Brokerage, and Repairs

A consumer's home is generally the consumer's most
important tangible asset, and consumer problems with the
home thus have an especial importance. This chapter deals
with problems of home sales, real estate brokers, and home
repairs. Additional information

Section 4.1 deals with a dependent child receiving a small
inheritance with which she decides to purchase a mobile
home for her mentally impaired mother and herself. The
vendor assured the plaintiffs that they could afford the

mobile home and even quoted affordable terms. Plaintiffs
then paid almost $15,000 to the vendor as a down payment.
It was only after the down payment that the consumers were
asked to sign a contract materially different from the terms
previously quoted. The contract terms made the mobile
home unaffordable to the plaintiffs and the vendors were
well aware that the consumers could no longer afford the
mobile home under the new terms. Afraid they would have
no mobile home and lose their $15,000, the consumers
signed the contract. The consumer then sued the seller and
lender for damages and to cancel the sale.

Section 4.2 presents a class action litigation against systematic real estate broker fraud. The broker promised rent-
to-own homeownership to consumers who had past credit
problems. After securing a four hundred dollar down payment from consumers, the broker promises to find rental
property with the option of homeownership. The consumers
who were actually shown homes found them to be unsafe,
uninhabitable or in some cases unavailable due to the fact
that the broker could not locate the owner.

The plaintiffs proceeded as a class of approximately three
hundred people. Section 4.2 consists of a Complaint, Motion
for Class Certification, a Proposed Order, and a Memorandum in Support of Class Certification.

Section 4.3 deals with an elderly woman suffering from
dementia who was solicited for home improvements. As is
often the case, the "improvements" were shoddy, incomplete and over-priced. The plaintiff properly rescinded her
contract and brought this action to recover the fees paid,
damages for breach of fiduciary duty, and statutory damages. The home improvement contractor had arranged financing with an originating lender who had then sold the
loan to a bank.

Section 4.3.1 reprints a complaint against both the originating lender and its assignee. The rest of the section
contains two sets of discovery, one for the originating lender
and one for the assignee presently holding the note. Each set
includes interrogatories, requests for production of documents, and requests for admissions.

Section 4.4 also deals with shoddy and incomplete home
improvements. However, the plaintiffs in § 4.4 are con-
fronted with home improvement contractors who attempt to
shield themselves from liability by hiding behind a dis-
solved corporation. The complaint focuses on the plaintiffs'
attempt to pierce the corporate veil by showing that the
contractor was in sole control of the corporation and that the
contractor commingled his personal funds with the corporate funds.

Chapter 5 New Car Lemon Case

All fifty states now have new car lemon laws which
provide certain statutory warranty rights for new car buyers.
Many lawyers are familiar with consumer complaints con-

cerning new car defects, and some attorneys now specialize in this area, and obtain excellent results for their clients, including statutory attorney fees.

This chapter provides a sample complaint and sample discovery for a new car warranty case. The complaint at § 5.1 sets out claims for violations of the state lemon law and the federal Magnuson-Moss Act and for negligent automobile repair. Next are presented three different sets of discovery, each including interrogatories and requests for production of documents. One set is to the car manufacturer; one set is drafted for the auto dealer who sold the car; the third set is propounded to the auto dealer that did the actual repair work. The second two sets of interrogatories and document requests would be merged if the same dealer sold the car and did all of the repairs.

More on state lemon laws, the Magnuson-Moss Act, UCC, warranty law, and automobile repairs can be found at National Consumer Law Center, *Consumer Warranty Law* (2d ed. 2001). All fifty states' lemon laws are summarized and key Magnuson-Moss Act materials are reprinted.

Chapter 6 Used Car Fraud

Used car fraud is perhaps the most common consumer law case. A wide array of possible cases could have been included in this chapter. The three cases reprinted here have special relevance to current used car fraud practices, provide excellent samples of discovery, and contain several types of pleadings not found elsewhere in this volume.

More on used car fraud can be found in several NCLC manuals. *Unfair and Deceptive Acts and Practices* (5th ed. 2001) discusses the FTC Used Car Rule, misrepresentations about prior use and other characteristics, service contracts, pricing misrepresentations, deposits, warranties, and cancellations. *Automobile Fraud* (1998 ed. and Supp.) covers not only odometer rollbacks, but also sale of salvaged vehicles and other fraud issues. *Consumer Warranty Law* (2d ed. 2001) examines state used car lemon laws and other special state statutes, the FTC Used Car Rule, UCC warranty law, common law fraud, and the federal Magnuson Moss Act.

Section 6.1, *infra* examines a type of used car fraud that is much more pervasive than many realize—the undisclosed sale to consumers of low-mileage used cars that had previously been returned to the manufacturer under state lemon laws. It is axiomatic that all the many returned lemon cars have to go somewhere, and the path of greatest profit is not to junk them, but to sell them as demonstrators or executive trade-ins. See National Consumer Law Center, *Unfair and Deceptive Acts and Practices* § 5.4 (5th ed. 2001). Tracing a car's title can usually provide indication of a returned lemon because title goes back to the manufacturer before proceeding again to the consumer through a dealer.

Section 6.1.1 consists of a complaint against a car manufacturer, a dealer, and an auto auction relating to the sale to a consumer of a car previously returned to the manufacturer as a lemon, and where the dealer sold the car without repairing defects, disclosing the defects to the purchaser, and without making proper title disclosures to the registry of motor vehicles. The consumer alleged fraud and willful violation of state law concerning return of lemon buy-backs. Section 6.1 also includes two sets of discovery, one to the selling dealer and one to the manufacturer. Each set includes interrogatories and requests for production of documents.

Section 6.2 involves another common type of used car fraud the undisclosed sale of a salvaged vehicle, that is a vehicle with a major, unrevealed collision history. As an added bonus, the case also involves odometer law violations. The complaint reprinted at § 6.2.1 alleges fraud, breach of express and implied warranties, and violation of federal and state odometer statutes, the state deceptive practices statute, state titling requirements, and the federal Magnuson-Moss Act. The complaint seeks significant actual, minimum, multiple, and punitive damages, as well as attorney fees. Also reprinted from the case are interrogatories, requests for production of documents, an expert's report on the vehicle, pre-trial disclosures, a trial brief alleging recklessness in odometer representations, and jury instructions adopted by the court.

Perhaps the bread and butter used car case is one where the dealer sells the consumer a car with undisclosed defects for more than what the car is worth even without the defects, and at disadvantageous financing terms. The car breaks down, the consumer refuses to pay, the dealer repossesses the car and sells it for less than its actual worth, and seeks a deficiency from the consumer. Section 6.3 presents such a case.

Section 6.3.1 reprints a complaint against a used car dealer for violations of Truth in Lending, the FTC Used Car Rule, and the state deceptive practices statute, breach of express and implied warranties, fraud, negligence, and a commercially unreasonable disposition of the repossessed car under UCC Article 9. The complaint seeks actual, statutory, and punitive damages. (Note that Article 9 statutory damages are 10% of the cash price and the full finance charge.) Also reprinted from the case are interrogatories, requests for admission, and requests for the production of documents.

The names of the parties have been changed throughout this chapter. Also deleted are attorney signature blocks, certificates of service, and similar non-germane parts of the pleadings.

Chapter 7 Furniture Sales and Storage

While most consumer litigation concerns homes, home repair, cars, credit, collection, and insurance, consumer abuse is not limited to these areas. For example, the sale and storage of furniture often results in consumer complaints.

This chapter reprints materials concerning furniture non-delivery and problems relating to the storage of furniture and other personal items.

Section 7.1 contains a complaint against a furniture company and an individual officer for failure to deliver furniture. Claims involve breach of contract and warranty, fraud, and deceptive practices. While the cost of the furniture is only a few thousand dollars, the complaint seeks significant additional actual and punitive damages, making the case a significant one even though brought as an individual action.

Section 7.2 reprints a complaint against a storage company and an auction company for wrongfully attempting to enforce a warehouseman's lien on the consumer's stored property. When the consumers moved to New York, they asked the mover to arrange storage for part of their belongings. It is alleged that the storage company failed to provide the consumers with invoices and other notices, that they assessed charges greater than agreed upon, and that the warehouse then attempted to auction off the consumers' stored items. The complaint alleges violations of the state deceptive practices statute, the state's "Truth in Storage" statute, and UCC Article 7, and seeks to enjoin any sale of the property and requests significant actual and statutory damages and attorney fees.

Chapter 8   Rent to Own Transactions

Rent-to-own companies are a significant area of concern for those representing low-income families. Offering furniture, television sets, VCRs, and appliances on a weekly rental plan, they lure people through aggressive advertising, door-to-door canvassing, and the promise of an easy way to acquire goods without credit checks. The consumer becomes the owner of the goods after completing all the "rental" payments, plus, in some cases, a final ownership payment.

The weekly rental payments typically total two to five times the usual retail sales price of the goods. Moreover, the rent-to-own company claims to be exempt from state retail installment sales laws that protect the consumer from excessive charges and precipitous repossession. If the consumer misses a payment, the company claims the right to retake the property, and the consumer lose all built-up equity in the item.

Consumers' attorneys and state consumer protection offices have sued rent-to-own companies in many states, challenging these practices as violations of the state retail sales laws and UDAP statutes. In response, rent-to-own companies have gone to state legislatures and won passage of industry-sponsored rent-to-own laws. These laws typically require disclosures of the unbelievably bad terms of rent-to-own transactions, but do little or nothing to reform those terms.

The pleadings in this chapter demonstrate that it is still possible to attack the underlying unconscionability of rent-to-own transactions, even in states like Illinois that have passed an industry-sponsored rent-to-own law. The complaint starts with the rent-to-own company's violation of the state RTO statute's disclosure requirements, and seeks as damages the amount by which the actual total of payments exceed the disclosed total. Such disclosure errors may be fairly common, given the temptation to understate their out-of-line prices that rent-to-own companies must face. The complaint then strikes at the more fundamental inequities in the transaction, asserting price unconscionability claims under the sales and rental articles of the Uniform Commercial Code (Articles 2 and 2A). By asserting that both the non-disclosure and the unconscionability claims constitute violations of the state's deceptive practices (UDAP) statute, the complaint invokes the additional remedies that many UDAP statutes allow.

Also included at §§ 8.2 and 8.3 are interrogatories, a document request, and a deposition notice that seek information regarding the rent-to-own company's financial status, the identity of witnesses, its history of consumer complaints, and an explanation of the charges imposed on the consumer under the contract. Financial information about the rent-to-own company may be important since certain companies have few assets (while others are major corporations). Some may be independently incorporated but connected in some way to a larger network of rent-to-own companies; if there is reason to suspect this, discovery should also explore the company's relationship to any parent corporation or franchisor.

Also reprinted at § 8.4 is the consumer's brief in opposition to the RTO companies motion to summary judgment on the issue of compliance with the RTO statute's disclosure requirements. The brief presents useful background information about the RTO industry and RTO practices as well as the legal argument concerning disclosure requirements.

Depending on the circumstances, it might also be possible to assert claims based on warranty law, UCC Article 2A, or on the state law that provides a cooling-off period for door-to-door sales in a rent-to-own case. For a complete discussion of litigation against rent-to-own companies, see National Consumer Law Center, *Unfair and Deceptive Acts and Practices* § 5.7.4 (5th ed. 2001); National Consumer Law Center, *Repossessions and Foreclosures* § 19.3 (4th ed. 1999).

Chapter 9   Credit Card Issuer's Failure to Recognize Defense to Card Payment

Federal law provides a number of valid defenses to credit card payment, such as another party's unauthorized use of the card, merchant or creditor error, and the consumer's defenses against the merchant. The federal Fair Credit Billing Act and other provisions in the federal Truth in Lending Act specify procedures for consumers to raise these defenses, and procedures that the card issuer must take in response. For more on these requirements, see National Consumer Law Center, *Truth in Lending* Ch. 5 (4th ed. 1999 and Supp.).

Considering the millions of credit card customers and the billions of card transactions a year, it is not uncommon for the consumer to dispute the amount the card issuer claims is the consumer's obligation to pay. Despite the dispute, card issuers may aggressively pursue consumers for the amount the card issuer claims is due.

The materials in this chapter provide a sample consumer complaint, interrogatories, and request for production of documents where the card issuer's own in-house collection department harassed the consumer despite the consumer's valid defense to card payment. The card issuer had failed to recognize the consumer's claim that the card was stolen or lost, and the charges were thus unauthorized. The card issuer's in-house collection arm pursued the consumer for years, and the consumer finally turned around and sued the card issuer for harassment.

Of special note is the consumer's claim against the card issuer for violations of the federal Fair Debt Collection Practices Act (FDCPA). While the FDCPA generally only applies to independent collection agencies, and not to a creditor's in-house collection arm, the creditor is liable under the FDCPA if its in-house collector identifies itself by a name that would indicate that a third party is collecting on the debt. See National Consumer Law Center, Fair Debt Collection § 4.2.3 (4th ed. 2000 and Supp.).

Other claims in the consumer's complaint against the card issuer include violations of the Fair Credit Billing Act, the state deceptive practices act, the state debt collection practices act, and tort claims for infliction of emotional distress and invasion of privacy. These claims in addition to the FDCPA are especially valuable in claims against a creditor (where the FDCPA does not usually apply) or where the consumer is seeking damages beyond those available under the FDCPA (such as punitive or treble damages).

Chapter 10 Fair Credit Reporting

Studies have found extremely high error rates in consumer credit reports—perhaps every other report contains at least one error. About 90% of American adults have credit reports, about 20 billion pieces of information is added to credit records a year, and about half a billion credit reports are sold a year. It may be that as many as 200 million credit reports a year contain inaccurate information. It is no wonder that credit reporting is viewed by consumers as such a significant problem. A detailed treatise covering all credit reporting issues is found at National Consumer Law Center, *Fair Credit Reporting Act* (4th ed. 1998).

This chapter contains four different sets of pleadings concerning credit reporting. Section 10.1 is a relatively

simple action against one reporting agency for violations of the federal Fair Credit Reporting Act (FCRA). One aspect of the case of especial note is the inclusion of various counts under a state credit reporting statute, an increasingly important remedial approach. The materials include a complaint, interrogatories, and a request for production of documents.

One problem with straightening out a credit report with one reporting agency is that most Americans have files with at least the "Big Three" reporting agencies, TRW, Trans Union, and Equifax. All three may be reporting the same erroneous information. Section 10.2 is a FCRA case against the Big Three reporting agencies as well as against Merchants Association Credit Bureau. Essentially similar counts are brought against all four agencies for intentional and negligent reporting practices. Damages and an injunction are sought under the FCRA. Also included are interrogatories and requests for production of documents.

Even correcting all three credit reports may not be enough where a creditor or other supplier of credit information continues to report erroneous information. Moreover, it may be that a credit reporting agency is not liable under the FCRA's standards for certain inaccurate information, but that the supplier of the information was negligent in providing it to the reporting agency. Although there are significant legal hurdles in suing a supplier of information (see National Consumer Law Center, *Fair Credit Reporting Act* Ch. 10 (4th ed. 1998)), this is certainly an important option. Section 10.3 reprints portions of a case against the major reporting agencies and also against a major creditor for its practices in supplying information to the reporting agencies.

Section 10.3 includes a complaint and multiple discovery against different defendants. Interrogatories against the supplier of information and two different reporting agencies are reprinted. Similarly, there are two requests for production of documents from a supplier of information, two requests for documents from one of the reporting agencies (TRW) and one request of another reporting agency. The section also reprints a request for admissions from the supplier of information and from three of the reporting agencies.

Section 10.4 presents another type of reporting case, solely against the supplier of information, with no joinder of a reporting agency. A complaint against the supplier using various state law theories is reprinted.

Chapter 11 Fair Debt Collection Practices Act Litigation

Fair Debt Collection Practices Act (FDCPA) litigation is one of the most active areas of consumer law, and a number of private consumer attorneys have developed practices concentrating on the FDCPA. Most consumers in default have insufficient income to pay all their obligations, and it is the job of private collection agencies to convince consumers to pay certain, generally unsecured debts ahead of other (and usually more pressing) debts, such as rent, home mortgages, car payments, utilities, and food. The FDCPA specifies detailed standards for acceptable conduct by private collection agencies, and provides statutory and actual damages and attorney fees for any violation of those standards.

The materials in this chapter are from two of the most experienced and successful FDCPA litigators, and provide a good sample of the type of documents that those litigators have found effective. Additional FDCPA pleadings can be found in National Consumer Law Center, *Fair Debt Collection* (4th ed. 2000 and Supp.) and on its companion CD-Rom.

Section 11.1 deals with a FDCPA suit against an attorney who allegedly allowed a collection agency to use the attorney's name in correspondence threatening debtors even though the attorney had no real involvement or knowledge of the individual dispute. Section 11.1 reprints the FDCPA complaint, interrogatories, request for production of documents, and requests for admissions.

One key issue in the case was whether the attorney was on the collector's in-house staff or was in private practice, retained by the collector. Subsection 11.1.5 reprints the consumer's motion and memorandum to compel discovery of the means of compensation and other contractual matters between the collection agency and the attorney, which the attorney had refused to divulge. Subsection 11.1.6 is the consumer's summary judgment motion, and § 11.1.7 is the consumer's appellate brief before the Second Circuit, which provides a useful analysis of the legal issues involved.

Section 11.2 is a FDCPA federal court class action against a collection agency's litigation abuses, that include suing debtors in a distant forum in violation of the FDCPA, engaging in the unauthorized practice of law by filing suit in its own name on the basis of a contingency assignment, and collecting in litigation unreasonable and unlawful excessive charges and fees. The section reprints the class action complaint, interrogatories and request for production of documents.

An important issue in any FDCPA case, but particularly in a class action, is whether the collector can bring a counterclaim on the underlying debt. Subsections 11.2.3 and 11.2.4 provide a motion to dismiss such a counterclaim, along with the accompanying memorandum and the plaintiff's reply brief, all of which provide an excellent analysis of the issue. Subsection 11.2.5 reprints the motion and memorandum in support of class certification, and § 11.2.6 the plaintiff's motion and memorandum in support of partial summary judgment. The plaintiff's reply brief is found at § 11.2.7.

Chapter 12 Seizure of Consumer's Bank Account or Personal Property

Any court judgement against an individual can lead to seizure of that individual's bank account or other property to satisfy the judgement. Even where the court judgment does not involve a consumer debt, consumer law provides various protections for the judgment debtor. Other property can be seized when a secured debt is in default. Again, consumer law offers important consumer safeguards.

This chapter reprints materials form three very different cases dealing with the seizure of consumer property. Section 12.1 involves the seizure of a consumer's bank account pursuant to a court judgment. The complaint seeks damages from an attorney for using various deceptive techniques to seize the account, and for failing to release funds from that account that are exempt by law from garnishment. The complaint alleges violations of the federal Fair Debt Collection Practices Act and the state deceptive practices act.

Section 12.2 reprints a complaint and request for a temporary restraining order to enjoin the repossession sale of a boat, where the boat proved defective and the dealer seized the boat while the parties were disputing the matter. At issue is not only the consumer's damages, but also whether the boat should be sold and in what manner. The complaint alleges numerous theories, including breach of express and implied warranties, rejection and revocation of acceptance, rescission, breach of duty of good faith, violation of the state deceptive practices statute, fraud, conversion, replevin, violation of the state lien law, and negligence. The request for a temporary restraining order attempts to stop the repossession sale until the respective rights of the parties can be established.

Often repossessed collateral is sold before the consumer takes legal action. In that case, an important issues is whether the sale was commercially reasonable and the notice of sale proper. This is particularly critical where the creditor seeks a deficiency.

Comprehensive pleadings containing numerous different types of defenses and counterclaims to a deficiency action are found at National Consumer Law Center, *Repossessions* (4th ed. 1999). Reprinted in this volume at § 12.3 is a shorter, directed response to a deficiency action, dealing solely with commercially unreasonable disposition and notice, and where the creditor is a subsidiary of an automobile manufacturer. Also included for such a case are interrogatories and requests for production of documents targeted to the issues of commercially unreasonable sale and notice problems. Again, this discovery is shorter and more targeted than the discovery available in the *Repossessions* manual.

Chapter 13 Trade School Fraud as Basis for Non-Payment of Student Loans

Literally millions of students are in default on their student loans because for-profit trade schools failed to provide the promised path to a job and stable earnings, resulting in students been unable and unwilling to pay for their "education." Victims of shoddy trade schools are now being dunned by the government, being assessed 42% collection fees, having their wages garnished without court process, their earned income tax credits and other refunds intercepted, their credit rating ruined, and their eligibility for new educational loans and grants denied.

This chapter illustrates a number of the steps that can be taken to help students who have been victimized by fraudulent trade schools. The first step may be to provide the student some breathing room by arranging a minimal repayment schedule.

A consumer in default on a student loan has a statutory right to obtain a repayment agreement that is reasonable and affordable based on the consumer's total financial circumstances. This does not reduce the amount owed (and in fact interest continues to accrue), but this does stop tax intercepts, wage garnishments, collection suits and contacts, and, after six payments, the student reestablishes eligibility for new loans and grants. Obtaining a payment plan with payments as low as $5 a month gives the consumer breathing room while other approaches are considered, as set out below.

Regulations now specify the consumer's right to a reasonable and affordable payment plan, and these are described in National Consumer Law Center, *Student Loan Law* (2001). But there is no standard form for seeking such a repayment plan. What follows at § 13.1 is one such request. The request should clearly specify that the consumer is requesting a reasonable and affordable payment plan to establish renewed eligibility. Many loan holders take the position that they can offer high repayment plans (e.g. $150 a month) unless the consumer specifically requests a reasonable and affordable plan to renew eligibility.

Another approach to putting collection efforts on hold is to consolidate the defaulted loan into a Federal Direct Student Loan with income contingent repayment. How to do this, with an application form, is set out at National Consumer Law Center, *Student Loan Law* (2001). This consolidation, though, may limit a consumer's ability to later raise substantive defenses related to the old loan.

Congress has provided victimized students with two ways to discharge their loans. The first is the closed school discharge, which forgives all remaining indebtedness and reimburses all past loan payments if the school closed while the student was in attendance or where the student had been in attendance within 90 days of the closure date. See National Consumer Law Center, *Student Loan Law* (2001). The student simply fills out a form provided the student by the Department of Education or the state guaranty agency.

The other statutory basis for a loan discharge is if the school falsely certified the student as eligible for the loan. The Department of Education has interpreted this as limiting the discharge to situations where the school has falsified the students ability to benefit from the course or where the school has forged the consumer's signature. See *Student Loan Law* (2001).

The "ability to benefit" or "ATB" false certification relates to the requirement that schools determine a student's ability to benefit from a course (e.g. by giving a standardized test) where that student does not have a high school degree. If the school does not properly determine this for a student who has not graduated high school, then the student may have a grounds for seeking a loan discharge.

The Department of Education in mid-1995 adopted a form application for seeking a false certification discharge. The material that follows at § 13.2 preceded that form application, and it is much more detailed than what the application requires. Nevertheless, the Department is extremely stingy in granting false certification discharges, and the most effective approach may be to work up detailed information about a particular school on behalf of a large number of students, as set out at § 13.2.

Another approach for remedying trade school misconduct is for the student (or a group of students) to bring a damage action against the school for fraud, breach of contract, and related claims. Section 13.3 reprints such a state court complaint against a school for fraud, state deceptive practices act violations, conversion, misrepresentation, and breach of contract.

This approach may be successful for an individual action against a school still in business, but often trade schools are insolvent by the time a student brings an action, or by the time the student attempts to collect a judgement. Where a class action is brought against a school for significant damages, it is particularly likely that a favorable judgement will spur the school to close before the judgement can be collected.

An alternative strategy is set out at § 13.4, where a federal court RICO class action is brought against individual owners, officers, and others responsible for the school's fraud, who may remain solvent even if the school goes out of business. This complaint also seeks class-wide relief against the Department of Education on two theories: first, that the 1992 amendments to the Higher Education Act require the students' loan debts to be forgiven; and, second, that the close relationship between the trade school and the lenders allows students to assert fraud claims in defense of the loan debts.

Yet another approach is to seek a declaration that the student or a class of students are not required to repay their loans to lenders, guarantors, or the Department of Education because of their school-related claims. That is, the students would allege that the lenders are subject to school-related claims and defenses because of their close relationship with the school, and that the guaranty agencies and the Department of Education are in the same shoes as the lenders, being their assignees. This has the advantage of the student not having to try to collect a money judgement, and it consolidates the issue of school fraud and the student's obligation to pay the loan into one proceeding.

A student's ability to raise school-related claims as a

defense on a loan is generally straightforward for Perkins Loans, Federal Direct Student Loans, and for those Guaranteed Student Loans (GSL's) entered into after January 1, 1994. See National Consumer Law Center, *Student Loan Law* (2001).

For GSLs prior to 1994, the law is still unsettled. Section 13.5 reprints a complaint seeking a declaration that the student's school-based defenses satisfy a pre-1994 GSL. Some of the theories set out in that complaint are probably now not as effective as other possible approaches. The complaint relies heavily on the "origination" theory, but an attorney today might select instead an agency theory or a state deceptive practices claim for failure to include the FTC Holder Notice. See National Consumer Law Center, *Student Loan Law* (2001).

A disadvantage of a class action for declaratory relief is that the law is so unsettled that the case can drag on for years, with no interim relief for the affected students. Seeking the same relief in a bankruptcy proceeding is one possible solution to this problem because bankruptcy courts tend to resolve issues relating to the bankruptcy more rapidly than an affirmative action in state or federal court.

Student loans are not dischargeable in bankruptcy unless they were first due at least seven years before the date of the bankruptcy filing or unless payment would cause a financial hardship. The student who does not meet the seven year standard can claim that repayment of the loan will cause substantial hardship, and that the school's inability to train the student is one reason the repayment of the loan would lead to such a hardship.

In addition, in the bankruptcy proceeding, the student can raise the school's fraud as a defense to the lender's proof of claim, and the bankruptcy court is then likely to rule speedily on whether the student in fact does owe the disputed amount. In at least some cases, lenders have not opposed the consumer's hardship discharge as settlement of the consumer's school-related defenses.

Section 13.6, *infra,* requests both a hardship discharge and raises school-related defenses. This pleading relates to a guaranteed student loan taken out prior to January 1, 1994, and, as with the complaint set out at § 13.5, relies heavily on the origination theory as the basis for lender liability. A bankruptcy filing today might instead rely on other theories of lender liability, as discussed above.

No matter whether the defendant is a school, an officer, or a lender, the student will have to prove the school's misconduct. For example, even if a lender is liable for the school's misconduct, the consumer must still prove the school's misconduct to raise this as a defense on the loan. As with most lawsuits, discovery is key to proving school misconduct. Section 13.7 provides two sets of discovery directed to a trade school, including both interrogatories and requests for production of documents.

Similarly, no matter who the student decides to sue, a class action is often the preferable route because of the

relatively small amounts at stake for each individual student and because of the similarity of treatment of each class member. Section 13.8.1 reprints a proposed order, motion, and memorandum concerning certification of a class of trade school students, and § 13.8.2 provides a class notice.

One of the impediments to litigation seeking a declaration that a loan amount is not due is the difficulty for the student's attorney in recovering fees for the case. The students rarely have the ability to pay for an attorney and there is unlikely to be a common fund created, only a declaration that amounts owed are no longer owed. It may also be difficult to recover statutory attorney fees from the lender. Section 13.9.1 reprints a request for attorney fees from the United States under the Equal Access to Justice Act with an accompanying memorandum. Section 13.9.2 contains the students' reply brief.

Chapter 14 Student Loan Collection Abuse

Literally millions of student loan obligations have been contracted out to private debt collection agencies on a commission basis by the U.S. Department of Education and by state guaranty agencies. These collection agencies are asked not only to contact the students, but to assist the Department of Education relating to other of the student's statutory rights and obligations.

When the student asks, pursuant to statute, for a reasonable and affordable payment plan based on the student's total financial circumstances, so that the student can renew eligibility for student assistance, it is the collection agency that determines the payment amount. When the student asks for a closed school or false certification discharge, the first point of contact for the student is likely to be a collection agency. Collection agencies may also be involved in nonjudicial wage garnishments and tax intercept hearings. Not surprising, there have been widespread allegations of deception and misinformation coming out of these collection agencies, which may solely be paid on a commission basis to service a large number of defaulted student accounts.

The fact that the United States Department of Education or a state agency has hired the collection agency does not immunize the private collector from liability under the federal Fair Debt Collection Practices Act (FDCPA). The collection agency is liable for its own collection practices that violate the FDCPA. More on collectors' liability for student loan collection abuse can be found in National Consumer Law Center, *Student Loan Law* (2001).

An effective approach to challenging student loan collection abuse is by a class action because the collector is likely to engage in a pattern of FDCPA violations not only for one, but for thousands of students from whom it is collecting, and because some of the violations may even be found in form letters. One complication though to FDCPA litigation against student loan collectors is determining which of the illegal collection practices are engaged in by the private collector and which by the U.S. Department of Education. The federal government is not subject to the FDCPA, and other theories would have to be used in suing the government directly.

This chapter reprints documents from such a class action against a student loan collection agency hired by the U.S. Department of Education. Section 14.1 is the class action complaint alleging FDCPA violations. § 14.2 contains requests for admission, interrogatories, and requests for production of documents for the collection agency, § 14.3 is a motion for class certification, and § 14.4 is the accompanying memorandum. The name of the parties are fictitious, and attorney signature blocks, certificates of service and related materials have been deleted.

Chapter 15 Hospital Collection Defenses

Hospital bills can present consumers with unexpected, extremely large, and unaffordable debt obligations. For many practitioners, it may be a surprise to learn that consumers have a number of viable defenses to such obligations, and that aggressive advocacy can often result in very favorable settlements.

Hospital patients almost never enter into a written agreement with the hospital specifying the amount the patient will pay for designated services. Instead, the hospital unilaterally, and after the fact, establishes an amount it seeks for the services. Hospitals typically specify an amount for a service that is higher than the amount negotiated with insurers and HMOs or specified by Medicare or Medicaid for the same service.

If a consumer challenges the basis for the hospital's claim for payment, the hospital will have to ground its bill on an implied agreement to pay a reasonable price for services rendered. The burden of proof in most jurisdictions is on the hospital to establish that the charges are reasonable.

When the hospital's complaint states that the amount sought is a reasonable price for the services rendered, then the consumer need only deny this in the answer. The burden is then on the hospital to prove its claim. Do not raise the unreasonableness of the amount claimed by way of an affirmative defense, because this would muddy the question of burden of proof.

Particularly where the consumer has requested a jury trial, the hospital may then have great difficulty proving its case since it must prove as reasonable each component of the bill. Juries will be impressed that the same hospital charges less for the same services where the patient is covered through insurance, and HMO, Medicare, or Medicaid. Section 15.3 details various forms of discovery that can assist the consumer in disputing the reasonableness of the price for the services rendered—notice of deposition, two sets of interrogatories, a request for production of documents, and a

freedom of information act request from the state agency that monitors hospital rates.

Hospital collection actions may attempt to avoid these issues by seeking a recovery based on an account stated, which would require no proof on their part of the value of the services rendered, since the claim would be based on an agreed amount between hospital and patient. The response to this claim is that there is no account stated, since there was no agreement as to price. Subsections 15.1.1 and 15.1.2 reprint a consumer's motion to dismiss and accompanying memorandum because the hospital obligation is not based on an account stated as stated in the hospital's complaint. Subsection § 15.1.3 provides interrogatories designed to establish that there is no account stated.

Other times, hospitals may present such a vague or cursory complaint that it is impossible to tell under what theory it is seeking payment, thus complicating the consumer's defense. The response in such a case is to request more particulars. Section 15.2 presents a demand for more particulars, with an accompanying motion and memorandum of law.

Another possible consumer defense in a hospital collection case is based on the hospital's Hill-Burton obligation to provide certain free assistance in return for past receipt of certain federal money. Subsection 15.4.1 presents a consumer's application to a hospital for reduced fees under the hospital's Hill-Burton obligations. Subsection 15.4.2 outlines use of a hospital's non-compliance with the Hill-Burton Act as a defense in the hospital's collection effort. Subsections 15.4.3 through 15.4.5 provide interrogatories, requests for production of documents, and a memorandum of law relating to Hill-Burton issues. Finally, § 15.4.6 gives an example of an administrative complaint concerning a hospital's failure to comply with its Hill-Burton obligations.

Consumers before hospitalization may discuss with hospital staff their inability to pay for the services to be rendered. Hospital staff may make certain promises that the patient need not make payment or need make only partial payment. Such statements may be binding on the hospital. An example of use of such statements as an affirmative defense is found at § 15.5, *infra*.

A patient may be eligible for Medicaid or Medicare, but for various reasons the hospital may not process an application for payment under those programs, but instead seek repayment from the patient. Section 15.6 presents various affirmative defenses to the hospital's collection effort based on its failure to process a Medicare or Medicaid application. The section also sets out interrogatories and memoranda of law relating to a hospital's failure to process a Medicare or Medicaid claim.

In some cases a consumer's obligation on a hospital bill is based on the failure of another party to pay the bill, such as the consumer's insurer, employer health plan, or a state agency. Sections 15.7 and 15.8 present third party complaints against an insurer and employee health plan for failure to pay the consumer's bill, and section 15.9 provides a sample complaint against a state agency.

More on defending hospital bills can be found in another NCLC manual. See National Consumer Law Center, *Fair Debt Collection* Ch. 14 (4th ed. 2000 and Supp.). As with most of the materials in this volume, the names in the pleadings are fictitious. Signature blocks, certificates of services, and similar material has been deleted.

Consumer Law Pleadings With Disk, Number Three (1997)

Chapter 1 Elder Financial Exploitation

Although older Americans represent only ten percent of the nation's population, it is estimated that they represent thirty percent of all victims of consumer fraud. This chapter provides sample pleadings addressing financial scams targeting elderly homeowners. For additional pleadings dealing with predatory lending practices aimed at unsophisticated and low-income homeowners, see National Consumer Law Center, *Consumer Law Pleadings with Disk*, *Number One*, Ch. 7 (1994) and *Consumer Law Pleadings with Disk*, *Number Two*, Ch. 4 (1995).

The factual scenario in the first case is not unusual. An elderly homeowner with limited income and substantial equity in her home is in need of financial assistance to make repairs to her home and pay back taxes. She approaches a mortgage company about obtaining a modest loan. The mortgage company quickly assesses the situation and determines that her equity in the home and her lack of financial sophistication make her a perfect target for one of their scams. They persuade the homeowner to borrow thousands of dollars more than she planned, based on the misrepresentation that she could convert her home into rental apartments which would generate income to pay the loan and provide her additional income.

The complaint reprinted at § 1.1.1 describes the events which predictably followed. The mortgage company referred the homeowner to a construction firm it knew would perform shoddy work and in short order, her home was rendered uninhabitable forcing her to find shelter elsewhere. The defendants never completed construction of the property, the homeowner was unable to pay the mortgage, and the defendants ultimately acquired title to the property at a foreclosure sale.

The complaint includes RICO claims alleging an enterprise between the mortgage company, construction firm and their agents and officers. Since the case settled quickly on confidential terms favorable to the plaintiff, there are no other pleadings provided for this case.

The next case at § 1.2 involves a "befriending" scam where a home improvement company representative ini-

tially convinced an elderly homeowner to have work done on her home. Taking advantage of her physical and mental disabilities, he and several accomplices befriended the plaintiff by making promises to repair her home and provide her financial assistance. Over the course of a year, the defendants eventually convinced her to transfer a joint tenancy interest in her home to one of the defendants and obtain a $143,000 mortgage, with a substantial portion of the loan proceeds paid to another defendant for improvements which were never made to her home.

Subsection 1.2.1 contains the complaint filed against the individual defendants and the finance companies involved in the scheme. The complaint alleges TIL rescission, quiet title, and negligent lending claims and several variations on fraud-type claims. The pleadings also include a request for a temporary restraining order at § 1.2.2 and the preliminary injunction which was entered is found at § 1.2.3. Also reprinted from the case are interrogatories and document requests. The case was eventually tried before a jury and a judgment reflecting the jury verdict, including awards against several of the defendants on the fraud counts, is found at § 1.2.7.

The final case in this chapter also involves a befriending scam in which the defendants offered to help the plaintiff who was facing a foreclosure on her home. After convincing the plaintiff that her situation was desperate, the defendants then tricked her into signing documents transferring her home to them at a fraction of its a value in a sale/leaseback scam. The complaint reprinted at § 1.3.1 contains many of the claims found in the previous case as well as a claim against the notary (and some claims which are unique to California law).

Chapter 2 Loan Flipping

This case was settled very shortly after the complaint was filed on confidential terms favorable to this elderly client.[2] Because of the quick settlement, there were no other useful discovery documents or briefs to supplement the complaint. But since the case takes a direct hit at the insidious practice of "flipping," in a particularly egregious case, we thought it might be useful to readers to get an idea of the kind of analysis that went into the case before the attorneys made a decision as to their representational approach.

---

2 This introduction was prepared by Kathleen Keest, presently with the Iowa Attorney General's Office. Kathleen was an NCLC staff attorney from 1985 to 1996 specializing in Truth in Lending, usury, and other credit laws. Before that for nine years she was an attorney specializing in consumer law with the Legal Services Corporation of Iowa. She is the author of National Consumer Law Center, The Cost of Credit: Regulation and Legal Challenges (1995 and Supp.), co-author of National Consumer Law Center, Usury and Consumer Credit Regulation (1987) and National Consumer Law Center, Truth in Lending (2d ed. 1989 and 3d ed. 1995), and a contributor to National Consumer Law Center, Credit Discrimination (1993 and Supp.).

It has long been known that finance companies view refinancing current customers as an avenue to greater profits. To some extent, there are reasonable, defensible reasons for this. For example, there are lower "search" costs involved in keeping existing customers than in seeking out new ones, and a past relationship means the creditor has familiarity with the client's payment record.

But for the customer, there are significant differences in being a repeat customer at a finance company than at other businesses. First, a continual relationship with a finance company means continually being in debt. Second, it means continually being in debt at rates which, even on the face of things, are very high. Third, the process of repeatedly renewing the relationship insidiously ratchets up the price considerably in ways that are by no means evident and in ways that few average consumers understand.

The industry's practice of aggressively seeking repeated renewals is called "flipping." Like its analogues in other industries—"twisting" in insurance sales and "churning" in securities sales—it is ripe for challenge because it is rife with abuse. And like those unsavory practices, it involves what economists call "information asymmetries" because these are all particularly complex products and services. The sellers know a lot more than the buyers, and the nature of the products make it difficult for the ordinary buyer to protect themselves from unethical sellers.

When [Plaintiff] came in, it was quite clear to his advocates that what the finance company did to him was outrageous. Less apparent was what to do about it. Analyzing these cases can be like peeling off several layers of an onion. Examining the outer layers, and looking at each transaction in isolation, may show that there are readily apparent violations of Truth in Lending or the state credit code on the face of at least the most recent transaction, and perhaps others. That certainly should be done, for often Truth in Lending rescission is available.[3] But it can be well worth the advocate's time and effort to peel away the outer layers to get to the core of the harm done to the client, for that may suggest a greater array of legal claims from which to chose the most promising strategy.

Chapter 3 Fair Debt Collection Class Litigation Involving *Cy Pres* Remedy

In general, consumer attorneys have identified several drawbacks to pursuing class actions under the FDCPA. First, damages recoverable by consumers are capped at the lesser of 1% of the collector's net worth or $500,000. 15 U.S.C. § 1692k(a)(2)(B). Second, there have been several decisions

stating that injunctive relief is not available for private parties as the FDCPA does not expressly provide for injunctive relief for private parties as it does for FTC actions.[4] Third, pursuing a class action may require the commitment of extensive staff and resources for class notices.

The case in this chapter suggests that a different class action approach may avoid these problems. Class actions for declaratory relief may be sought which ask the court to declare that a practice by a collector violates the FDCPA. Declaratory relief class actions are considered Federal Rule of Civil Procedure 23(b)(2) actions in that their principle relief is not for damages. There are less rigorous notice requirements in a Rule 23(b)(2) class action than in a Rule 23(b)(3) class action for damages. In a Rule 23(b)(3) class action, notice to class members of pendency of the action is required and the cost of the notice is borne by class representatives pursuant to *Eisen v. Carlisle & Jacquelin*, 417 U.S. 156 (1974).[5]

This approach also avoids the cases that prohibit FDCPA actions for injunctive relief. In addition, statutory damages are still available under Rule 23(b)(2) class actions for declaratory relief, thus preserving the potential deterrent factor that larger damage recoveries and attorney fee awards serve by requiring that collectors take notice of their FDCPA violations and change their actions.

This case illustrates how a practitioner may put this type of class action into practice. The complaint alleged that the defendant sent a debt collection letter to the plaintiff and others similarly situated implying that the collector was vouched for or was affiliated with the federal and state government. The court found the plaintiff met the general requirements for a class action under Rule 23(a) of numerosity, questions of law or facts common to the class, typicality of the representative plaintiff, and adequacy of representation. (The class certification decision in this case is found at *Gammon v. GC Services Ltd. Partnership*, 162 F.R.D. 313 (N.D. Ill. 1995)).

After assessing the potential statutory damage recovery, however, the plaintiff sought a no-notice, non-opt out class action pursuant to Fed. R. Civ. P. 23(b)(2), contending that declaratory relief predominated over the other claims for relief. Due to the number of potential class members and the FDCPA damage cap, the statutory class damages that could be recovered was 13 cents or less per class member. This recovery would be less than the cost of the postage needed to distribute it. Since statutory damages were so low per class member and discretionary in any event, plaintiff's counsel argued that the predominate relief was declaratory relief. The court certified the class action concluding, "the request for non-monetary relief predominates over the request for dam-

---

3   *See generally* National Consumer Law Center, Truth in Lending (4th ed. 2000 and Supp). *See also* For examples of rescission case pleadings, see also National Consumer Law Center, Consumer Law Pleadings With Disk, Number 1 Ch. 8 (1994) and Consumer Law Pleadings, With Disk, Number 2 Ch. 4 (1995).

4   *See* National Consumer Law Center, *Fair Debt Collection* (4th ed. 2000 and Supp.)

5   *See* National Consumer Law Center, *Fair Debt Collection* (4th ed. 2000 and Supp).

ages."[6] Even where the FDCPA class is limited to the state in which the named plaintiffs reside, the declaratory relief may still predominate.[7]

The defendant expressed concern that if the court certified the class, individual class members would forego up to $1,000 in statutory damages. (It should be noted that the final settlement order at § 3.6 does not bar class members from seeking actual damages). Since Rule 23(b)(2) actions are no-notice, non-opt out class actions, the court noted this with concern but stated that the FDCPA contemplated class actions for statutory damages, without regard to the minimum statutory damage recovery, and that the disgorgement of illegal gains from wrongdoers was an important function of class actions that should not be defeated by unfiled, hypothetical individual claims.

In lieu of direct payments to consumers, the final settlement reached in this case established a *cy pres* fund in an amount slightly less than the maximum statutory damages which would have been available to the class. In cases where there is a small class and a defendant with a high net worth, the recovery would be sufficient that class counsel would ordinarily seek a direct payment to class members. But if class distribution costs exceed the statutory damages, as in this case, then the court may use the *cy pres* doctrine to distribute the award to the next best purpose to benefit the class, for example, funding for legal services. In addition, the possibility of a *cy pres* remedy may be a factor used by the court to find that a class action is superior to denying class certification and permitting only an individual action.[8]

NCLC recognizes that these types of settlements may be controversial and by publishing the pleadings in this chapter, we are neither endorsing nor criticizing this approach. There are many different factors that consumer attorneys should consider in pursuing class actions and fashioning class settlements. For a discussion of these issues, attorneys may wish to review a recent publication of the National Association of Consumer Advocates, "Standards and Guidelines for Litigating and Settling Consumer Class Actions" (Oct. 8, 1997).

Chapter 4 Avoiding Credit Regulation: Payday and Auto Pawn Loans

Since the inception of usury laws and other credit regulation, there have been schemes designed to avoid their coverage. Today, the number of "fringe lenders" such as check cashing outlets, pawnshops, rent-to-own businesses, and tax refund anticipation lenders continues to grow. These businesses aggressively seek out individuals who are not served by the regular banking system.

This chapter provides samples of pleadings addressing these schemes to avoid credit regulation. Section 4.1 reprints the pleadings in a case brought against a check cashing establishment that was making "payday" loans by advancing money, generally for a period of 14 days, against checks drawn on the customer's checking account. The typical transaction resulted in a charge to the customer of 28% of the amount advanced, resulting in interest payments far in excess of the state usury limits.

Although the amended complaint found at § 4.1.1 was brought by the Virginia Attorney General, the factual allegations and the formulation of the causes of action in the complaint should nevertheless assist attorneys in pursuing a private action. To get a sense of how these businesses attract customers, readers may wish to review the advertising scripts reprinted as Exhibit 1 to the complaint in § 4.1.1.

The pretrial brief reprinted at § 4.1.2 sets out the legal arguments in support of the claim that "check advancements" should be treated as loans subject to the state small loan statute. The brief also includes strong arguments in favor of finding the corporate officers of the company personally liable for the wrongful conduct. Subsection 4.1.4 contains the favorable decision of the trial court in which the attorney general's arguments are largely adopted. In addition to injunctive and declaratory relief finding the loans to be void, substantial money judgments were entered against the company and its principals.

Section 4.2 concerns another type of fringe banking involving an "auto-pawn" company that was making loans against auto titles while permitting borrowers to keep possession of the auto, or as they would say in the business: "Pawn your title, keep your car." The question this case poses is whether the lending activity constitutes a legitimate "pawn" transaction under state law. In the decision found at § 4.2.5, the trial court resolves this issue against the lender finding that it was not engaging in a *bona fide* pawnbroking business and therefore was not entitled to the pawnbroker exemption under the state usury statute.

The final case in this chapter found at § 4.3 also involves auto pawn transactions but is brought as a private class action using different legal theories. Unlike the case in § 4.1, a state law had been enacted effectively legalizing these so-called pawn transactions. Thus, in the complaint reprinted at § 4.3.1, plaintiffs allege that the transactions violate TIL and the state UDAP statute, and that the charges imposed on consumers are in excess of those permitted by the pawn statute. Subsections 4.3.2, 4.3.3 and 4.3.4 contain useful discovery materials. The plaintiffs' class certification motion, reprinted at § 4.3.5, is currently before the court.

---

6   *Gammon v. GC Services Ltd. Partnership*, 162 F.R.D. 313, 321 (N.D. Ill. 1995).

7   *See* Mace v. Van Ru Credit Corp., 109 F.3d 338 (7th Cir. 1997) (FDCPA class action against interstate debt collector may be limited to class of single state's consumers).

8   *See* National Consumer Law Center, *Consumer Law Pleadings, Number 1* Ch. 12 (1994) for additional pleadings relating to the *cy pres* remedy. *But cf.* Mace v. Van Ru Credit Corp., 109 F.3d 338 (7th Cir. 1997) (cy pres may be used only in unusual circumstances).

Chapter 5 Theft of Identity

Given the massive amounts of information about consumers exchanged between credit reporting agencies and creditors, and the ease with which this information may be accessed, it should come as no surprise that credit information is occasionally used for an illegal purpose. The materials in this chapter involve cases where an unsuspecting consumer's credit identity is literally stolen and used by the thief in a scheme to fraudulently obtain credit or property.

It is not uncommon for businesses which rely upon consumer credit reports for credit screening purposes to have a pre-existing relationship with a credit reporting agency where a dedicated computer terminal is provided with a direct link to the agency. The business needs only to certify to the credit reporting agency that it has a legitimate purpose for the information and that it will not misuse the information provided. Credit information can then be accessed from the computer terminal simply by typing in a potential customer's first and last name.

Because some businesses have little or no safeguards to ensure that such terminals are used only by authorized personnel, an unscrupulous employee or anyone else having physical access to the terminal can pull up a credit report on a potential victim. The thief may then obtain credit in the name of the victim by submitting credit applications using the victim's personal credit information obtained from the report.

In the first case of this chapter, the "theft of identity" was accomplished by a car salesman who was easily able to access the dealership's credit agency terminal. Having obtained the plaintiff's personal and credit information, he then submitted numerous credit applications and was able to purchase thousands of dollars of goods and services on the various credit card accounts, loans and checking accounts he subsequently opened in the plaintiff's name.

The second case illustrates that theft of identity cases may be brought even where the identity of the thief cannot be determined conclusively prior to filing. In this case, the plaintiff suspected that a student at a college he had attended had obtained his personal and credit information by stealing his mail.

In using these pleadings, practitioners should be aware that extensive amendments to the FCRA were enacted by the passage of the "Consumer Credit Reporting Reform Act of 1996." Some of the new substantive provisions strengthen consumer protections while others weaken rights available under prior law. Most of the Act's changes went into effect on September 30, 1997. For a comprehensive analysis of the changes, see NCLC REPORTS, 15 Consumer and Credit & Usury Ed. 5 (Sept./Oct. 1996) and 16 Consumer and Credit & Usury Ed. 17 (Mar./Apr. 1997).

One frequently occurring abuse is the repeated reintroduction of inaccurate information after it has been previously deleted in response to a consumer dispute. This is the kind of problem a victim of identity theft is likely to face when attempting to remove erroneous information and regain their former credit identity. The consumers in both of these cases were clearly frustrated in their attempts to get the inaccurate information permanently removed from their reports.

The new law is more explicit in requiring agencies to maintain procedures to prevent the reappearance of disputed information. More importantly, the new law requires that before deleted information can be reinserted, the person who furnishes the information must now certify to the agency that it is complete and accurate. In addition, the consumer must now be notified in writing that the disputed information has been reinserted. See National Consumer Law Center, Fair Credit Reporting Act (4th ed. 1998 and Supp.).

Chapter 6 RESPA Litigation: Yield Spread Premiums

A yield spread premium is a lender's payment to a mortgage broker for increasing the loan interest to a rate above "par," which is a rate higher than the rate at which the lender would otherwise be willing to make the loan. This payment generally supplements the fee already being paid by the borrower to the broker for the broker's services. While the payment provides benefits to lenders and brokers, it clearly does not improve the consumer's position and instead inflates the costs of homeownership. In most cases, consumers are not even aware that their loan has been "upsold" as the yield spread premium is usually disclosed on the HUD-1 settlement statement with such cryptic notations as "P.O.C. YSP." This chapter contains the pleadings from one of the pending class action lawsuits which allege that yield spread premiums violate RESPA's prohibition against kickbacks and referral fees.

This practice has sparked much controversy. While regulatory and statutory changes are being considered on this issue, the district courts which have thusfar issued opinions on the legality of the charges are divided. For a review of the current case law, see NCLC REPORTS, 16 Consumer Credit & Usury Ed. 7 (Sept./Oct. 1997).

In addition to claims under RESPA, the amended complaint at § 6.1 alleges claims for intentional interference with a contractual relationship, breach of fiduciary duty, restitution for money had and received, and fraud by concealment. Interrogatories and production requests directed to the lender are found at § 6.2 and § 6.3.

The plaintiff also conducted depositions of several key witnesses which were used in her motion for summary judgment found at § 6.4 and reply brief reprinted at § 6.10. Since these depositions provide an in depth look at the industry practice, excerpts from the depositions have been reprinted at §§ 6.5 through 6.9. In addition, a copy of the actual "Broker's Fee Agreement" in this case is copied as an exhibit to § 6.4. Based on the documents and deposition testimony, the plaintiff has determined that under a program made available to broker's by the lender, a yield spread premium of 4% of the net loan amount is typically paid by the lender for an interest rate increase of one full percentage point.

As reflected by the plaintiff's response at § 6.11, the defendants have also filed a motion for summary judgment. The parties are currently awaiting a decision from the court on the dispositive motions.

Chapter 7 Challenging Creditors' Overcharges In Bankruptcy Claims

Consumer bankruptcy attorneys who represent homeowners in chapter 13 cases often encounter inflated secured claims filed by mortgage lenders, servicers and their attorneys. Errors in secured claims can undermine the success of debtors' chapter 13 plans and prevent them from obtaining a fresh start.

While some errors are not surprisingly inadvertent, others appear to be deliberate or reflect a general pattern and practice of the creditor resulting in excessive interest and escrow charges affecting hundreds if not thousands of consumer debtors. In such cases, creditor abuses may not only violate confirmation orders or discharge injunctions entered in debtors' bankruptcy cases but may also give rise to claims under state UDAP statutes and usury laws. The materials in this chapter show how debtors' counsel may challenge such abusive practices, including the use of class actions in bankruptcy court. (For a more detailed discussion of class actions in bankruptcy, see National Consumer Law Center, Consumer Bankruptcy Law and Practice § 13.7 (6th ed. 2000 and Supp.)).

One of the initial problems facing debtors' counsel in these cases is determining whether there has been an overcharge. A little-known provision of the Real Estate Settlement Procedures Act, known as the "Servicer Act," places an obligation on the holder or servicer of a mortgage to respond to inquiries concerning the loan from the borrower within a specified time period. This can be a valuable tool for bankruptcy attorneys in determining whether secured claims filed by mortgage servicers are inflated. (For a more detailed discussion of this provision, see National Consumer Law Center, The Cost of Credit (2d ed. 2000 and Supp.).

In the first case in this chapter found at Section 7.1, the debtors completed their chapter 13 plans providing for full payment of all pre-bankruptcy arrears on their home mortgages. Soon after they received their discharge and their bankruptcy cases were closed, the debtors began receiving letters from the mortgage servicer threatening foreclosure, claiming that their mortgage payments were in arrears or that they had failed to make payment on alleged "escrow adjustments." Despite numerous attempts by their counsel

to obtain an accounting showing the alleged default, the mortgage servicer persisted with foreclosure proceedings.

Section 7.1.1 is a class action complaint which was filed against the mortgage servicer alleging that the servicer engaged in the practice of deliberately disregarding the provisions of debtors' confirmed chapter 13 plans. The case resulted in a favorable settlement for the class providing for injunctive relief requiring the servicer to adjust its accounting procedures, including requiring it to properly treat ongoing post-petition payments as current even though outstanding pre-petition arrears are being cured through payments under the plan. The servicer was also required to conduct reviews of all class members mortgage accounts using the new accounting procedures, credit debtors with any overcharges and suspend foreclosure proceedings in cases involving overcharges.

Section 7.2 involves a case challenging the policy of a state taxing authority to file estimated proofs of claim in all chapter 13 cases where the agency has no record that the debtor filed tax returns, even where the agency has no actual knowledge that a debt is owed. In the named plaintiff's case, she was not required to file returns for the years in question because she did not have any taxable income. The practice of filing such estimated claims often results in delays in confirmation of debtors' chapter 13 plans as they struggle to get the creditor to file corrected claims.

Section 7.2.1 is a class action complaint that was filed in the debtor's bankruptcy case. Other pleadings in this section include a set of interrogatories and document requests. Section 7.2.3 contains a motion and memorandum seeking class certification by the bankruptcy court. The remaining documents relate to the settlement which was reached in the case.

Chapter 8 Truth in Lending Rescission by Recoupment

Perhaps the most important aspect of the Truth in Lending Act's extended rescission right for consumers is its value as a defense to foreclosure. Though there is a three year limitation on the right to affirmatively cancel a mortgage, courts have applied traditional common law principles of recoupment to allow rescission even after the three year period as a foreclosure defense.

When Congress amended the Truth in Lending Act in 1995, it gave considerable support to the consumer position on this issue. Although the banking industry lobbied strongly for a legislative overruling of the favorable court decisions, Congress actually provided, for the first time, statutory authority for the right to rescind certain mortgage loans by way of recoupment. The specific statutory language enacted provides that "[n]othing in this subsection affects a consumer's right of rescission in recoupment under State law." 15 U.S.C. § 1635(i)(3).

This chapter contains briefs from one of the first circuit court cases to review the rescission by recoupment issue and the impact of the 1995 amendments. The case involved an elderly homeowner who had invoked her right of rescission in defense to the creditor's foreclosure action by filing an adversary proceeding in a chapter 13 bankruptcy case. Although the creditor did not contest the homeowner's grounds for asserting rescission under TILA, it argued that her claim for rescission was barred by the statute of limitations. The bankruptcy court specifically addressed the new statutory language and concluded that the homeowner was entitled to rescind the mortgage after the statutory period since recoupment was permitted under state law. *Botelho v. Citicorp Mortgage Inc. (In re Botelho)*, 195 B.R. 558 (Bankr. D. Mass. 1996). For an analysis of the decision, see "Rescission by Recoupment Under the 1995 TILA Amendments," 15 NCLC Reports, Consumer Credit and Usury Edition, 23 (May/June 1997).

The District Court for the District of Massachusetts then affirmed the bankruptcy court's decision and the creditor appealed to the First Circuit Court of Appeals. The materials in this chapter include the brief of the appellee homeowner filed in the Court of Appeals. The brief contains a thorough review of prior court decisions on the rescission by recoupment issue and persuasive arguments on the effect of the new statutory language. This brief should be a valuable resource to advocates litigating this issue.

Reflecting the mortgage lending industry's extreme dissatisfaction with the lower court decisions in this case, an *amicus curiae* brief was filed by at least eight different banking groups urging reversal. The industry apparently views this as a test case on the issue, arguing that the ruling will undermine the secondary mortgage market and result in huge losses to the lending industry. To counter these alarmist claims, an *amicus curiae* brief was filed by the National Association of Consumer Advocates, which is found at section 8.2.

Although the Table of Contents and the Table of Authorities for the Appellant's Brief have been included, they have been omitted for the Amicus Brief.

Chapter 9 Auto Fraud

Consumer fraud is so pervasive throughout the auto sale and leasing industry that it is often reported as the number one consumer complaint. Auto fraud pleadings are found at National Consumer Law Center, *Consumer Law Pleadings with Disk, Number One* Ch. 9 (1994) and *Consumer Law Pleadings with Disk, Number Two* Chs. 5, 6 (1995). See also the discussion of discovering dealer documents and various auto fraud abuses at NCLC's *Unfair and Deceptive Acts and Practices* § 5.4 (5th ed. 2001) and *Automobile Fraud* (1998 and Supp.). Pleadings related to three new emerging auto frauds are included in this chapter.

Section 9.1, *infra* involves a fast growing trend among auto dealerships of targeting their advertising and sales practices to consumers with poor credit histories by offering their own "guaranteed" financing with no credit checks, regardless of prior credit history. In the case highlighted in this section, the dealership established a separate used car lot to make these sales and incorporated a finance company located across the street to handle the financing transactions.

The plaintiffs' amended complaint, found at § 9.1.2, *infra*, alleges that cars were sold at inflated prices with the dealer dictating the terms of the loan agreements, and that this created a hidden finance charge in violation of Truth in Lending. Plaintiffs also raised state UDAP, fraud, and RICO claims. The plaintiff's original complaint was filed in state court but was removed to federal court. Section 9.1.1 reprints plaintiff's attempt to have the case remanded to state court.

The first, second and third set of interrogatories directed to the dealership in that case are found at §§ 9.1.3, 9.1.4 and 9.1.5 respectively. Two additional sets of interrogatories reprinted at § 9.1.6 and § 9.1.7 attempt to probe the relationship between the dealership and the finance company. The plaintiffs' attempts to compel discovery are also provided at § 9.1.8 and § 9.1.9.

In response to a motion to dismiss, the plaintiffs have argued that the finance company is not a true assignee covered by TIL's limited assignee liability provision and that the transactions do not involve an arms length sale of commercial paper. The court has not yet ruled on this motion to dismiss.

Section 9.2, *infra* reprints pleadings from a case that initially began as a class action regarding a dealer's rebate theft, but as the plaintiff's attorney discovered more about the defendants' sales practices, the case was expanded to include race discrimination claims on behalf of a class of minority customers. Both the rebate and discrimination claims were significantly aided by the fact that several African-American former sales representatives at the dealerships approached the class' attorney concerning employment discrimination claims against the dealership. As discussed in plaintiff's class action memorandum found at § 9.2.8, plaintiff's obtained over a thousand "washout" sheets or buyer's orders from the former salesmen providing financial information about the sales they handled. Comparing this information with rebate documents obtained from the defendants in discovery, plaintiffs were able to analyze 249 sales transactions.

The statistical evidence compiled from this sample established an overwhelming pattern and practice of fraudulent conduct. Of the 249 sales reviewed, 90% (223) of the customers did not receive all or part of the rebate they were entitled to. The total amount stolen from these 223 customers was $279,100.00, an average of more than $1,250 per customer. Plaintiff's counsel estimates that approximately $1.7 million had been stolen from the overall class.

Plaintiffs also amassed substantial witness testimony from customers and former salesmen establishing that the defendant's management team directed its salesmen to treat black customers differently because of their race. The testimony revealed an atmosphere within the defendants' dealerships, evidenced by the use of racist language, which promoted discrimination against minority customers. A statistical comparison of former salesmen's buyers' orders with information obtained through discovery indicated that the average profit on black customers was two to three times greater than the profit derived from white customers.

Subsections 9.2.2 through 9.2.5 reprint the four sets of document requests which were sent to the dealership. Another request for production directed to the non-party auto manufacturer was issued pursuant to a state discovery statute and is reprinted at § 9.2.7. The plaintiffs' refiled motion for class certification is found at § 9.2.7, and plaintiffs are currently awaiting a decision on class certification.

The final set of pleadings reprinted at § 9.3 challenges a used car repossession churning scheme. The particular pleadings were contributed by Phillip Rogers and Rand Bragg. Several of their documents were based on pleadings in a similar case brought by Kieron Quinn.

In Mr. Quinn's case, an auto dealership with nine retail outlets marketed high-mileage cars primarily to personnel from local military bases. After the buyer's default, the dealer would buy back the loans from the lender for the amount the consumer owed and a subsidiary of the dealer then repossessed the car. The loan was then assigned to another subsidiary of the dealer which pursued state court collection and garnishment proceedings. The dealer would then sell the car to another consumer, often for close to the original sale price. Mr. Quinn reports that one car was sold to five different class members during a 40 month period.

Suit was filed against the dealer and the finance company alleging claims similar to those found in the complaint at § 9.3.1. A settlement was reached with the dealer for the sum $400,000 distributed among 2,501 class members. The dealer's affiliated collection firm also agreed to forego collection on $10.5 million in judgments against class members. Claims against the finance company have not as yet been resolved. The Fourth Circuit has reversed the trial court's grant of a motion to dismiss, and the trial court's grant of a second motion to dismiss is currently pending before the Fourth Circuit.

Attorneys Rogers and Bragg filed a similar action against a churning scheme, and that complaint is reprinted at § 9.3.1. Plaintiff's counsel reports that representatives of the repossession company provided many of factual details after they became dissatisfied with their business arrangement with the dealer. The case has settled with approximately $5 million being paid to class members.

Chapter 10 Land Installment Sales

This case involves the sale of homes through the use of land installment sales contracts by a variety of corporate entities all controlled by one defendant. The primary defendant's office sign gives an indication of the nature of the sales: "Money Tax Refund, Use it Wisely. You don't have to keep renting. We have 'owner financed' homes. No credit. Good credit. Poor credit. Stop paying your money on rent. With no bank qualifying, it is possible."

Because of the treatment of the corporate structure and class aggregation issues in this case, the pleadings are relevant even in states where land installment sales are not authorized or the practice is not followed.

The complaint found at § 10.1 reflects the incredible pre-filing investigation conducted by plaintiff's attorneys in tracking the many corporate entities involved in these transactions and establishing their common control.[9] Post-filing discovery reprinted at § 10.2 attempts to further untangle the complex web of corporate structures.

Plaintiff's counsel reports that a motion for class certification found at § 10.3 was denied by the court. Briefs in support of summary judgment are provided at § 10.5 and § 10.6. The case subsequently settled on terms favorable to the plaintiff.

Consumer Law Pleadings With Disk, Number Four (1998)

Chapter 1 Compulsory Arbitration Denied in Class Action Alleging Home Repair Fraud and Unauthorized Insurance Practices

This is a consumer class action brought on behalf of victims of an allegedly deceptive home improvement financing scheme that was designed and implemented by defendant Green Tree Financial Corporation ("Green Tree"). Green Tree allegedly developed, promoted and implemented a deceptive marketing scheme in which it recruited home improvement contractors as Green Tree dealers to obtain high-interest rate second mortgage loans from homeowners by means of deceptive and materially omissive in-home, direct marketing and advertising solicitations. As part of the scheme, Green Tree allegedly conducted demonstrations and "educational" presentations for dealer-contractors on how to market themselves as "FHA-approved" dealers and, in turn, generate loan contracts that would be assigned to Green Tree or a subsidiary. The

---

9 It should be noted that NCLC's Elizabeth Renuart was a staff attorney at St. Ambrose Housing Aid Center at the time this case was filed and she contributed to the drafting of the initial complaint.

consumers alleged that Green Tree provided the dealer-contractors with Green Tree loan forms, marketing kits, discount schedules and loan product information, all purportedly designed to help the dealer- contractors "increase customer sales." In part as a result of these deceptive marketing practices, Green Tree's home improvement loan originations grew exponentially after 1990, with a 35% increase to $627 million in 1995 alone.

It is alleged that the Defendants routinely targeted unsophisticated, low- to middle-income and senior citizen homeowners. Each of the Dealer-Contractors used false and misleading advertisements, fliers and high-pressure in-home sales solicitations to obtain from plaintiffs high-interest rate home improvement contracts secured by so-called "secondary mortgages." A consistent pattern of the defendants' deceptive marketing scheme was the misleading implication or outright misrepresentation that the home improvement program and financing were directed, sponsored, promoted or funded by government agencies such as the Federal Housing Authority (the "FHA"), the U.S. Department of Housing and Urban Development ("HUD") and others. The Dealer-Contractor would not perform the construction work that was promised or would perform the work in such an unsatisfactory and shoddy manner that virtually nothing of value was received by the homeowner. Having been deceived and taken advantage of, many homeowners, including plaintiffs, received nothing of value but were left with a sizeable debt secured by a mortgage on their homes. Due to fear, lack of knowledge, and the absence of funds, plaintiffs were forced to continue paying on these contracts, or to forgo other remedies, rather than risking the loss of their residence.

After the complaint was filed, the defendant asserted that the consumers' claims were governed by the compulsory arbitration clause on the back of their contract and that clause required that the consumers' claims be arbitrated. In addition to complaint at § 1.1, *infra*, this chapter contains the consumers' interrogatories at § 1.2, *infra*, motion to produce documents at § 1.3, *infra* and plaintiff's memorandum of law in opposition to defendant's motion to compel arbitration at § 1.4, *infra*. The defendant's motion to compel arbitration was denied on Dec. 16, 1997 and an appeal was taken.

Chapter 2 High Rate Home Equity Loans— HOEPA Litigation

The Home Ownership and Equity Protection Act of 1994 (HOEPA) was enacted by Congress in response to certain well-documented predatory lending practices in the high rate home equity lending industry. While HOEPA does not limit interest rates, it creates a special class of high rate and excessive cost loans which are more closely regulated. In addition to enhanced disclosure requirements which supplement those provided under TILA, HOEPA contains specific prohibitions against certain abusive loan terms and lender practices, including limitations on prepayment penalties, balloon payments, and negative amortization, as well as the lender practice of making loans without consideration of the borrower's ability to pay. The effective date of HOEPA was October 1, 1995.

In both of these cases, plaintiffs' counsel alleged that at least one of the two triggering mechanisms for coverage of HOEPA had been met. Briefly, to be subject to HOEPA, the lender must have (1) imposed a high interest rate, which the Act defines as an annual percentage rate of 10 percentage points greater than the yield on treasury securities having comparable maturities at the time the loan was made, or (2) charged total points and fees in excess of 8% of the total loan amount. (For a more detailed discussion of HOEPA, see National Consumer Law Center, Truth in Lending Ch. 10 (4th ed. 1999 and Supp.).

In the first case found at § 2.1, the complaint reprinted at § 2.1.1 describes the practice of a large national lender, in conjunction with a network of home improvement dealers, of steering consumers seeking home improvement loans into high cost first mortgage loan consolidations. Consumers were typically denied lower cost loans, which would have been subject to consumer protections available under the state home improvement loan statute, and instead offered more expensive first mortgage loans, resulting in additional fees and charges in some cases of up to 50% of the actual cost of the home improvements.

The complaint alleges that the loans were subject to HOEPA under the "points and fees" trigger, and that the lender failed to give borrowers the additional required HOEPA disclosures three days prior to consummation as provided under 15 U.S.C. § 1639(b)(1). The suit also attempts to attack the predatory lending practice of making mortgage loans based primarily on borrowers' equity in their homes without regard to their ability to repay the loans. Under HOEPA, the plaintiffs must establish that the lender engaged in a "pattern or practice" in order to prevail on this count.

Interestingly, the complaint also includes a claim under the Equal Credit Opportunity Act alleging that the lender's offer of credit to class members was effectively a counteroffer to their initial requests for home improvement loans, thereby requiring the lender to provide class members with a written notice of adverse action under 15 U.S.C. § 1691(d). (For more information on the ECOA, see National Consumer Law Center, Credit Discrimination (2d ed. 1998 and Supp.). In addition to the HOEPA and ECOA claims, the complaint alleges class claims under the state home improvement loan and UDAP statutes. Finally, various TIL disclosure violation and rescission claims are raised on behalf of individual plaintiffs.

In the brief filed in objection to the lender's motion to dismiss, reprinted at § 2.1.3, plaintiffs' counsel provide a thorough response to lender's argument that claims under the state home improvement loan statute should be dismissed. Essentially, the plaintiffs argue that the lender has characterized the transactions as loans rather than installment sales in order to evade the consumer protections in the state statute. This "direct loan" fiction analysis should be helpful to attorneys litigating similar state law coverage issues. The brief also addresses the lender's arguments relating to preemption of the state home improvement statute under DIDA, and the adverse action notification requirements under the ECOA.

In the second case found at § 2.2, the lender initially induced the plaintiff, an elderly woman who was beginning to experience the effects of Alzheimer's Disease, to enter into a mortgage transaction by claiming that her monthly payment would be reduced. Needless to say, her payment under the new mortgage actually increased to an amount which exceeded her monthly income from Social Security. The lender then convinced the plaintiff to enter into a series of renewals. In the complaint reprinted at § 2.2.1, plaintiff's counsel demonstrates how the "flipping" of these mortgages was clearly not in the plaintiff's economic interest and was intended by the lender to skim the equity in plaintiff's home. (For additional pleadings and a detailed analysis of a "flipping" case, see National Consumer Law Center, Consumer Law Pleadings No. 3, Ch. 2).

The complaint alleges that the lender violated HOEPA by failing to provide the additional disclosures, by extending credit to the plaintiff without considering her ability to repay the debt, and by including in the mortgage documents a provision for prepayment penalties. Claims based on the state UDAP statute and on fraud and misrepresentation theories are also included. Other pleadings in this case include a set of interrogatories found at § 2.2.2 and document requests found at § 2.2.3.

Chapter 3   Suit for Failure of Nursing Home to Fulfill Contract for Care and Suit Against Nursing Home for Seeking Unlawful Third Party Guarantees and Excessive Charges

The complaint at § 3.1.1 alleges that nursing home residents and their families were given verbal and written promises of care, which, among other things, promised a safe, secure and pleasant environment, a program affirming the dignity of the individual, a professional and well-trained staff, a reassuring environment in which residents and families could experience improved quality of life, and other promises regarding the high quality of care. The nursing home in fact was alleged to be understaffed, unsanitary, disease ridden, and substandard.

In the complaint at § 3.1.1, the plaintiffs seek certification of a class for the following claims:

- Third-party beneficiary claim for breach of the annual Medicare and Medicaid contracts;
- Breach of the contracts for services;
- Claim for intentional interference with the class members' contract rights;
- Claim for fraudulent misrepresentation; and
- Claim for negligence *per se* for failure to abide by the applicable statutes and rules for providing care to their nursing home residents.

Individual UDAP and promissory estoppel claims were also stated.

- The case was certified as class action consisting of a class of residents who had lived in the nursing home for the previous four and a half years and two subclasses, one consisting of private paying residents and the other consisting of medicare and medicaid residents.[10] The principal relief sought was a refund of the fees paid by the residents to the nursing home. The court refused to allow class relief for emotional distress damages as requiring individual proof and denied class injunctive and declarative relief as it was not actively pursued by the class. The court did not address the claim for punitive damages in its opinion on class certification.

- The discovery materials for this case contain several sets of interrogatories and requests for production of documents in § 3.1.3, *infra*. The Plaintiffs' Offer of Proof in section 3.1.4, *infra*, supports the request for class certification by discussing the factual basis for the claims and why they are appropriate for class relief. The National Consumer Law Center's treatise, Unfair and Deceptive Acts and Practices (5th ed. 2001) analyzes claims for substandard nursing home care claims under UDAP, civil RICO, and the Federal False Claims Act.[11]

- The second complaint at § 3.2.1 alleges two unlawful business practices. First it alleges that a nursing home required third party guarantees of payment, although such guarantees were expressly forbidden by federal nursing home law. Second it alleged that the nursing home overcharged nursing home residents by amounts often in the hundreds of dollars per resident per month. Specifically, the nursing home assessed a staggering array of unjustified "extra" charges for such items as unsterile gloves, vinyl examination gloves, barrier pads, chux, underpads, tolfa pads, bedside commodes, bed pans, trapeze bars, Kleenex, gowns, sheets, pillowcases, towels, disposable razors, syringes, bed side trays, humidifier bottles, powder, lotion, mouthwash, measurement cans, tape, hydrogen peroxide, cotton-tipped applicators, enema administration units, catheters, iodine swabsticks, lemon glycerine swabs, green sleeves, and electric beds. The nursing home's admissions agreement did not authorize such charges and

---

10   Burns v. Grancare, Inc., Clearinghouse No. , (Colo. Distr. Ct. 1998).

11   *See also* E. Carlson, "Illegal Guarantees in Nursing Homes," 30 Clearinghouse Rev. 33 (May 1996).

indicated that extra charges would only be imposed for extraordinary items. The charges for the extra items were also alleged to be grossly in excess of the items' cost.

- The complaint seeks restitution of moneys paid, an injunction against continuation of the unlawful business practices, and reasonable attorney fees.
- Section 3.2.2 is a memorandum of law in a similar case seeking summary judgment on the first alleged unlawful business practice—requiring illegal third party guarantees of payment.

Chapter 4 Repossession and Fair Debt Collection Discovery and Attorney Fee Materials

This Chapter contains materials to aid in discovery and in obtaining statutory attorney fees. Section 4.1.1 is the first set of interrogatories from an automobile repossession case. Section 4.1.2 is the motion to produce documents in the same case. Section 4.2 is a motion to compel and the memorandum of law in support of the motion to produce from a Fair Debt Collection Practices Act[12] case. The memorandum of law in support of the motion to compel deals with the issues of burdensomeness, client privilege, work product, and trade secrets—issues that frequently arise in a wide variety of consumer cases.[13] Section 4.3 is a brief in a case which successfully sought reversal of a district court decision providing for an inadequate award of attorney fees in a civil rights case complaining of a wrongful repossession.[14]

Chapter 5 Travel Frauds

This chapter contains three complaints against travel providers for the failure of a travel tour operator to provide the hotel, travel or entertainment services promised. The first complaint at § 5.1 is against the travel agency which recommended an insolvent tour operator which failed to provide any of the lodging or touring paid for by the consumers. Three of the four causes of action in that case survived a motion to dismiss. *Marcus v. Zenith Travel, Inc.,* N.Y. Law J. p.25, col. 3 (Nov. 19, 1990) (N.Y. Sup. Ct.), *aff'd*, 178 A.D. 372, 577 N.Y.S.2d 820 (N.Y.A.D. 1991). The second at § 5.2 is against a travel agency which booked the consumers for a scam travel tour without investigating its reliability. The third complaint at 5.3 is a class complaint against a club and the tour operator that the club promoted when the operator was insolvent. The claims sound in

negligence, breach of fiduciary responsibility, misrepresentation, promissory estoppel, UDAP, breach of contract, breach of warranty, suppression, civil RICO, among others.

Chapter 6 Fair Debt Collection Practices Act

The following brief argues that a collection lawyer's demand for payment of illegal charges added to a debt violated the FDCPA even if the attorney did not know that the creditor added the illegal charges. The brief points out that most provisions of the FDCPA provide for strict liability for violations of the Act. However, the Act provides a defense for unintentional errors which occur despite the maintenance of procedures to avoid such errors, although the brief argues that the error must not be an error of law. This brief was filed seeking United States Supreme Court review of *Jenkins v. Heintz*, 124 F.3d 824 (7th Cir. 1997) which held that a collection lawyer was not responsible for the addition of illegal charges to the loan balance by the creditor when he allegedly did not know the nature of the charges. The charges involved premiums for force placed insurance which comprised most of the claim. This brief should be helpful to lawyers who are faced with arguments based on the Seventh Circuit decision.

Chapter 7 Claim for Unauthorized Use of a Credit Report under the Federal Fair Credit Reporting Act

The Federal Fair Credit Reporting Act strictly limits the purposes for which a consumer's credit report may be used in order to protect the consumer's privacy and financial security.[15] Nevertheless individuals sometimes gain illicit access to another's credit report, often using an employer's or friend's employer's account with a credit reporting agency to gain that access. In such situations the employer may be responsible for not preventing the employee's illicit access to the credit report.[16] This illicit access may be instigated by a spouse in a messy divorce proceeding, by an attorney in a lawsuit, by a supervisor in an employment dispute, by a tax collector before tax liability has been determined, or by a salesperson regarding a prospect before any business negotiations have started.[17] Following is a complaint, interrogatories, and a memorandum of law used in a case for unauthorized use of a credit report under the Federal Fair Credit Reporting Act.[18] The claim is filed in either state or federal court for actual damages (including damages for injury to the consumer's credit reputation),

---

12 15 U.S.C. § 1692.

13 *See also* Artese v. Academy Collection Service, Inc., 1997 WL 509404 (D. Conn. 1997) (a decision dealing with compelling discovery in a FDCPA case).

14 Orchano v. Advanced Recovery, Inc., 107 F.3d 94 (2nd Cir. 1997).

---

15 National Consumer Law Center, Fair Credit Reporting Act (4th ed. 1998 and Supp.).

16 *Id.*

17 *Id.*

18 15 U.S.C. § 1692q.

punitive damages, and reasonable attorney fees.[19] The access to the account may be established by the consumer's credit report itself which generally reflects who has had access to the report. The lack of a lawful reason for the access is generally established by the lack of any relationship between the consumer and company that provided the access to the credit reporting agency. The memorandum of law in section 7.1, *infra*, also deals with the court's long arm jurisdiction over the defendant where it does not regularly conduct business in the consumer's state.

Chapter 8 Client Retainer Forms

This chapter contains three forms—a pre-retainer statement at § 8.1, an hourly retainer agreement at § 8.2, and a contingent fee retainer agreement at § 8.3. The pre-retainer statement is designed to be given to the client before there is an agreement to provide legal services. The choice of an hourly or contingency fee retainer is most commonly indicated by the nature of the claim and the financial resources of the client.

Chapter 9 Consumer Class Action Pointers

This chapter contains two articles by Mr. Malakoff on consumer class actions. Section 9.1 contains an article on the basic legal and practical requirements for a successful consumer class action. The second article at § 9.2 deals with using subclasses in consumer class actions to avoid problems of meeting the commonality, adequacy of representation and other class action requirements, particularly as affected by recent Supreme Court decisions.

Chapter 10 Lawyer Advertising on the Internet

Mr. Snyder's article examines such issues as when a lawyer's web page becomes an advertisement, interstate bar regulation of web pages, the potential waiver of the client privilege of confidentiality by using email, and unauthorized practice of law by lawyers on the internet.

Chapter 11 Class Action Against Rent-to-Own Company for Charging Usurious Interest

Section 11.1 contains pleadings from a statewide class action against one of the nation's largest rent-to-own companies alleging violation of New Jersey's usury law. The case was on appeal at the time of this writing. The pleadings

---

19 *See* National Consumer Law Center, Fair Credit Reporting Act Ch. 11 (4th ed. 1998 and Supp.).

include the amended complaint and several sets of interrogatories and motions to produce documents.

Sections 11.2 and 11.3 include two memoranda of law in support of the consumer's motion for summary judgment in *Fogie v. Thorn Americas, Inc.*, 1995 WL 649575 (D. Minn. 1995) (RTO contracts are credit sales for all purposes, and are subject to general contract usury ceiling), *aff'd, Fogie v. Thorn Americas, Inc.*, 95 F.3d 645 (8th Cir. 1996) (state court appeal pending after remand).

Rent-to-own transactions are also analysed in National Consumer Law Center, Unfair and Deceptive Acts and Practices § 5.7.4 (5th ed. 2001); National Consumer Law Center, The Cost of Credit: Regulation and Legal Challenges (2d ed. 2000); National Consumer Law Center, Truth in Lending § 2.2.4.3.4 (4th ed. 1999 and Supp.); Consumer Bankruptcy Law and Practice § 11.8 (6th ed. 2000); National Consumer Law Center, Repossessions and Foreclosures § 19.3 (4th ed. 1999 and Supp.); National Consumer Law Center, Consumer Law Pleadings With Disk, Number Two Ch. 8 (1995).

Chapter 12 Objections to Consumer Class Action Settlement

Section 12.1 is an Objection to a Class Action Settlement and Intervention on the basis that the relief proposed to the consumer class was too small and burdensome and the attorney fees to class counsel and the release to the defendant were excessive. The settlement proposed to provide a coupon to the class members who completed a proof of claim and submitted it to the court. The coupon could be used to obtain $15 off the cost of refinancing a mortgage with the defendant bank if used within two years. The objection focused on the requirement that the consumers must do business again with the wrongdoer to obtain any benefit from the settlement and that most class members would not want to do that. It also points out the inadequacies of the notice of settlement and the excessiveness of the class action attorney fee and of overbreadth of the release of unrelated claims provided to the defendant by the settlement. Section 12.2 contains the Class Action Guidelines of the National Association of Consumer Advocates ("NACA") which support many of the grounds urged for rejecting such a class action settlement. Section 12.3 is an affidavit filed in a different case by an NCLC attorney in support of an Objection to a Class Action Settlement. It makes many of the same points.

Chapter 13 Complaint for Unfair and Deceptive Infertility Program Practices

Section 13.1 is a class action complaint asserting that an infertility medical program engaged in a deceptive, fraudulent, misleading and flagrantly illegal course of conduct over a long period of years in connection with their dissemination of false, exaggerated and unsubstantiated laudatory misrepresentations as to their success rates in treating infertility problems and concealment and misrepresentation of significant health risks, high miscarriage rates, failure rates approaching 90%, excessive neonatal deaths and physical disability problems of infants born as a result of treatment by defendants, as well as the use of dangerous drugs in the treatment program. The complaint contains counts for unfair and deceptive acts and practices in violation of N.Y. Gen. Bus. L. § 349, false advertising in violation of N.Y. Gen. Bus. L. § 350, fraudulently omitting to reveal material facts regarding the success and failure rates of their IVF program and attendant medical risks, using informed consent forms violative of N.Y. Public Health Law 2805-d(1), violating fiduciary medical obligations and the implied contractual obligation of good faith and fair dealing, and unjust enrichment. The complaint seeks actual and punitive treble damages, and attorney fees. This chapter also includes the interrogatories used in the case.

Chapter 14 Litigating Consumer Law Claims in Bankruptcy Court

While litigating consumer claims in bankruptcy court has many advantages, it is particularly effective in response to a home foreclosure. The automatic stay which accompanies the bankruptcy filing prevents the mortgage lender from proceeding with foreclosure and provides the homeowner the opportunity to litigate potential consumer law claims. When coupled with Truth in Lending rescission, the homeowner may treat the mortgage obligation as an unsecured claim, which may significantly reduce the consumer's indebtedness and provide a means to satisfy TIL's tender obligations. *See* National Consumer Law Center, Truth in Lending § 6.11 (4th ed. 1999 and Supp.).

The homeowner in this case filed a Chapter 13 petition in order to stop a foreclosure sale of her home. The mortgage lender submitted a proof of claim in the bankruptcy case seeking payment as a secured claim. In response, the homeowner initiated an adversary proceeding against the lender alleging that the mortgage had been rescinded under TIL. An "adversary proceeding" is essentially a lawsuit within the bankruptcy case, subject to rules that parallel the Federal Rules of Civil Procedure. *See* National Consumer Law Center, Consumer Bankruptcy Law and Practice Ch. 13 (6th ed. 2000). The consumer's complaint in the adversary proceeding is reprinted at § 14.1.

The complaint alleged that the mortgage broker and lender were effectively "shell" corporations and that the individual defendant was each corporation's sole owner, officer and shareholder. It alleges that the defendants acted jointly in a fraudulent mortgage lending scheme in violation of TIL and the state's UDAP statute. The main a under TIL was that the lender failed to disclose the fee as a finance charge. Since the mortgage was m to the effective date of the TIL broker's fee rule (September 30, 1996), which provides that brokers' fees are generally considered part of the finance charge, the relationship between the corporate entities in this case was the focus of the consumer's TIL claim.

The pleadings include the consumer's opposition to a motion to dismiss, found at § 14.2, in which defendants' argue that the extended right of rescission under TIL is not available beyond the three year statutory period by way of recoupment. Although the consumer in this case was successful in defeating the defendant's claim, based on the decision in *Botelho v. Citicorp Mortgage, Inc. (In re Botelho)*, 195 B.R. 558 (Bankr. D. Mass. 1996), a different result may have been likely in light of the recent Supreme Court decision in *Beach v. Ocwen Federal Bank*, 118 S. Ct. 1408 (1998).

Also included is extensive discovery concerning the corporate structure of the defendants. The results of this discovery are detailed in the plaintiff's pre-trial memorandum, proposed findings of fact and post-trial memorandum which are also provided.

This case was tried before a bankruptcy judge resulting in a favorable decision for the homeowner. Finding sufficient evidence to "pierce the corporate veil," the judge largely adopted the plaintiff's proposed findings of fact and concluded that the broker's fee should have been treated as a finance charge. This TIL violation was also found to be a violation of the state UDAP statute. The judge ultimately denied relief under the plaintiff's other claims. Plaintiff's counsel reports that the plaintiff's primary goal of rescinding the mortgage and eliminating any further liability on the claim was accomplished.

Chapter 15 Tools for New Car Lemon Law Suits

The materials in this chapter have been developed by Mr. Burdge for his new car lemon law clients over the last twenty years. The complaint in § 15.1 contains an Ohio Lemon Law count,[20] a Magnuson-Moss Warranty Act claim,[21] and a claim under the Ohio Consumer Sales Act for unfair and deceptive acts and practices.[22] The complaint seeks actual and statutory damages, attorney fees, and equitable relief including alternative relief of rescission of the contract.

The discovery materials included are a combined discovery request to the manufacturer (interrogatories and request for

---

20   *See generally* National Consumer Law Center, Consumer Warranty Law (2d ed. 2001).

21   *See generally* National Consumer Law Center, Consumer Warranty Law (2d ed. 2001).

22   *See generally* National Consumer Law Center, Consumer Warranty Law § 11.1 (2d ed. 2001) and National Consumer Law Center, Unfair and Deceptive Acts and Practices (5th ed. 2001).

production of documents) at § 15.2, request for admissions at § 15.3, combined discovery request to the car dealer at § 15.4, combined discovery request on fraud damages to the car dealer at § 15.5, interrogatories to defendant's expert witness at § 15.6.

Form letters included in this chapter are a letter at § 15.7 to the client setting out the client's initial responsibilities in the case. Section 15.8 is a letter advising the client to forward the funds required to demand a jury trial. Section 15.9 is a letter asking the client to complete an attached form for providing information about the car. A letter to the client requesting the client complete a form providing a history of the client's complaints about the car is at § 15.10. A letter to the car dealer requesting information about the repairs to the car and requesting Technical Service Bulletin indices on the car is at § 15.11. A letter to the client indicating the fees to research information about the client's car and requesting payment for the research is at § 15.12. A letter requesting information on the motor vehicle from the National Highway Traffic Safety Administration is at § 15.13. A letter advising the client to retain an automotive expert and to pay a deposit on the expert's fee is at § 15.14. Section 15.15 is a letter advising the defense attorney of the consumer's damages and requesting correction without offering settlement. Section 15.16 invites a settlement offer prior to the pretrial conference. Section 15.17 is a letter to the client setting out the key data in the case and requesting the client's authorization to settle the case. A letter to defense counsel making a settlement offer follows at § 15.18. Section 15.19 is a letter to client explaining the defendants' settlement offer, and § 15.20 is a letter to the client recommending acceptance of the defendants' settlement offer. Section 15.21 is a computation of the settlement disbursements.

A number of motions are included. A request for judicial notice of an Ohio court decision is at § 15.22. A demand for judgement setting out the damages claimed in the case is at § 15.23. Section 15.24 is the consumer's pretrial statement. A motion to bifurcate the issue of reimbursement of attorney fees from general liability and damages is at § 15.25.

Chapter 16   Class Complaint under the American with Disabilities Act to Improve the Accessibility of a Concert Facility to Wheelchairs

Section 16.1 is a complaint under the Americans with Disabilities Act[23] to improve the safety and integration of handicapped facilities in a concert facility. The complaint seeks equitable relief, damages, and attorney fees. Section 16.2 is the Report of the Parties' Rule 26(f) Planning Meeting.

---

23   15 U.S.C. § 1281, et seq.

Consumer Law Pleadings With Disk, Number Five (1999)

Chapter 1   Punitive Damage Claims Against Credit Reporting Agencies and Creditors for Identity Theft

Identity theft is a terrible and increasingly more common fraud and crime. The perpetrator finds enough personal information about the victim to start assuming their identity for the purpose of establishing credit in the victims' name. The credit is used by the imposter to purchase goods and services. The bills are sent to the imposter who does not pay them, and the victims' credit report is ruined.[24]

The claim in the first case in § 1.1 was brought in a Mississippi state court by Michael Lewis against a credit reporting agency for actual and punitive damages arising from the agency's repeated failure to remove and block adverse credit information generated by an imposter from reappearing in the consumer's credit report. The claims were for defamation, breach of contract, and for willful or negligent violation of the Fair Credit Reporting Act.[25] In May 1998, the jury in the case awarded actual damages of $50,000 and $4.47 million in punitive damages (about 1% of the credit reporting agency's net worth). This chapter contains the complaint (§ 1.1.1), interrogatories (§ 1.1.2), two requests to produce documents (§§ 1.1.3, 1.1.6), a motion to compel discovery and a supporting brief (§§ 1.1.4, 1.1.5), the pretrial order (§ 1.1.7), the trial brief (§ 1.1.8), a motion in limine (§ 1.1.9) and supporting memorandum (§ 1.1.10), jury instructions (§ 1.1.11), a brief opposing the agency's motion for post trial relief (§ 1.1.12), and the motion for an award for the consumer's attorney fees (§ 1.1.14) and supporting memorandum of law (§ 1.1.15).

The second case also involves the repeated failure of several credit reporting agencies to keep an imposter's information from a consumer's credit reports and was filed by James Fishman, David Szwack, and Michael Lewis in a New York state court. This case also sought actual and punitive damages and statutory attorney fees alleging numerous claims, including defamation, breach of contract, and for willful or negligent violation of the Fair Credit Reporting Act. Section 1.2.1 and 1.2.2 are interrogatories and requests for production. Section 1.2.3 is the memoranda opposing the defendants' discovery objections. In this case the claims against the credit granter defendants were dismissed for failure to state a claim, and sections 1.2.4 and

---

24   *See generally* National Consumer Law Center, Fair Credit Reporting Act (4th ed. 1998 and Supp.); National Consumer Law Center, Consumer Law Pleadings With Disk, Number Three, Ch. 5 (1997).

25   15 U.S.C. § 1681. *See generally* National Consumer Law Center, Fair Credit Reporting Act (4th ed. 1998).

1.2.5 are the briefs filed in the unsuccessful appeal of that dismissal.[26] One of the remaining defendant credit reporting agencies unsuccessfully sought to enforce settlement negotiations which had broken down by alleging that a settlement agreement had been reached. Section 1.2.6 is the consumers' opposing memoranda of law with attached affidavits showing that there was no agreement and pointing out that oral settlement agreements are not enforceable in any event. The memoranda of law also deals with the consumers' desire to avoid a confidentiality clause in the settlement agreement—the negotiating point at which settlement negotiations broke down. The discussion of confidentiality may be useful to others wishing to avoid these odious clauses in their settlements.[27]

Chapter 2 Unlawful Collection of Debts Discharged in Bankruptcy

This chapter contains materials from two suits dealing with chain stores's efforts to collect debts which its customers sought to discharge in bankruptcy. Often by threatening repossession of household goods based on an alleged purchase money security interest, the retailers were successful in getting many customers to enter into reaffirmation agreements. The Bankruptcy Code contains very specific rules for reaffirming debts involved in a consumer bankruptcy.[28] For example, either the debtor's attorney must file a statement that a reaffirmation is in the debtor's best interest or a hearing will be held before a bankruptcy judge, and the agreement must be filed with the bankruptcy court.[29] These suits charged that the retailers ignored the law by failing to properly file reaffirmation agreements, rendering them void, and thereafter seeking payments on discharged debts.

From the first suit, in § 2.1.1 is the Amended Complaint seeking injunctive and declaratory relief, damages, and attorney fees for the class. The claims are based on the Bankruptcy Code, civil Rico,[30] the Massachusetts UDAP statute,[31] and Truth in Lending.[32] In § 2.1.2 is the stipulation and agreement of compromise and settlement. The settlement resulted in one of the largest restitution awards in a consumer class action, with approximately $172 million being returned to class members. The settlement was also unique in that approximately 80,000 class members were not required to file a proof of claim as they were identified by the defendant and automatically sent a refund check.

From the second suit in § 2.2.1 is plaintiffs' motion for classwide preliminary injunction, in § 2.2.2 is the memorandum in support of plaintiffs' motion for classwide preliminary injunction, and in § 2.2.3 is the plaintiffs' reply in support of motion for classwide preliminary injunction. In § 2.2.4 is plaintiffs' opposition to defendants' motion to dismiss. In § 2.2.5 is plaintiffs' memorandum in support of motion for preliminary approval of settlement agreement.

Chapter 3 Automobile Odometer Fraud and Threat of Violent Repossession

Section 3.1 is a complaint for damages brought on behalf of a young Navajo couple who purchased a used Chevy Blazer from a used car dealer in Farmington, N.M. The dealer did not properly disclose that the odometer had more than 167,262 miles on it disclosing only the mileage as 67,262. The complaint alleged that the dealer represented that the engine had been overhauled and that the 4-wheel drive worked. Soon after the sale the car stopped working. The complaint alleges that the financer of the transaction sent a collection notice with a picture showing two repossession men brandishing weapons and standing over a debtor in a pool of blood lying halfway into a garbage can. A jury awarded the consumers $669,000, including $450,000 punitive damages. Part of the award could be trebled by the court under the state unfair and deceptive acts and practices (UDAP) statute.

Section 3.2 is the plaintiff's first set of discovery seeking the identity of the people involved in the sale and production of all of the sales documents (current and previous) involving the vehicle as well as correspondence to the plaintiff, copies of all transactions during the year, and of bonds and insurance policies. Section 3.3 contains the consumers' motion for partial summary judgment, and their brief and reply brief supporting the motion. Section 3.4 contains the jury instructions approved by the court.

Chapter 4 Manufactured Homes: Warranties, Deception, and Financing Issues

Manufactured or mobile homes often involve compromises in the quality of their construction to make them affordable to lower income households and profitable to the manufacturer and seller. It is difficult to move a manufactured home without causing structural damage which further compromises its quality. Because of these issues, manufactured housing is closely regulated.[33]

---

26 *See* Polzer v. TRW, Inc., 682 N.Y.S.2d 194 (N.Y. App. Div. 1998).

27 *See also* www.tlpj.org for the internet web site of the Trial Lawyers for Public Justice which contains memorandum of law opposing confidentiality of class action settlement terms.

28 *See* National Consumer Law Center, Consumer Bankruptcy Law and Practice (6th ed. 2000 and Supp.).

29 *Id.*

30 18 U.S.C.A. §§ 1961–1968. *See generally* National Consumer Law Center, Unfair and Deceptive Acts and Practices (5th ed. 2001).

31 M.G.L. ch. 93A. *See generally* National Consumer Law Center, Unfair and Deceptive Acts and Practices (5th ed. 2001).

32 15 U.S.C.A. § 1601 et seq. *See generally* National Consumer Law Center, Truth in Lending (4d ed. 1999 and Supp.).

---

33 *See generally* National Consumer Law Center, Unfair and Deceptive Acts and Practices (5th ed. 2001); National Consumer Law

Section 4.1.1 is a Motion for Judgment in a suit against a manufactured home dealer and financer where the manufactured home was wrecked by the seller when the seller dropped one end of the manufactured home when bringing the home to the site for set up. The contract provided that the seller was responsible for the set up. The Motion for Judgment (which is readily adaptable as a complaint) alleges that after it was dropped the home was worthless. The seller also allegedly charged for $92.35 of sales taxes that were not due and financed this hidden finance charge for 30 years at 9% interest. The Motion for Judgment alleges breach of warranty, revocation of acceptance, violation of the Magnuson Moss Warranty Act,[34] violation of the state unfair and deceptive acts and practices (UDAP) statute, fraud,[35] and Truth in Lending violations.[36] Actual, punitive and statutory damages and attorney fees were sought. In addition, several sets of interrogatories, motions to produce, and requests for admissions to the seller and financer are included.

Section 4.2.2 is a complaint against a mobile home dealer and manufacturer for damages arising from selling a used manufactured home as new and failing to set up the mobile home properly with the result of severe structural damage. The complaint alleges breach of contract, breach of warranty, violation of the Magnuson Moss Warranty Act, violation of the state unfair and deceptive acts and practices (UDAP) statute, and fraud. Actual, punitive and statutory damages and attorney fees were sought. Section 4.2 also includes interrogatories and motion to produce.

Chapter 5 Forced Placed Automobile Insurance Claims

Section 5.1 is the amended complaint against an automobile finance company and an insurance company for providing replacement or forced placed property insurance at an inflated premium and with excessive coverage.[37] The retail installment contracts required the consumer to maintain property insurance on the car purchased and authorized the finance company to purchase replacement insurance if the consumer failed to maintain the insurance, but the replacement insur-

ance exceeded what was indicated in the contract. The complaint alleges violation of the New Mexico unfair and deceptive trade practice statute, the New Mexico unfair insurance practices act, the New Mexico motor vehicle sales finance act, breach of contract, breach of fiduciary duty, fraudulent concealment, and tortious interference with contractual relations. Also included in Chapter 5 are a set of interrogatories and request for production of documents to each defendant and the memorandum in support of class certification.

Chapter 6 Salvaged Automobile Fraud

This chapter contains two memoranda of law from a case where a wrecked car was sold without a salvaged car title and with misrepresentations about the car's history.[38] One memorandum is in support of summary judgment for the consumer and the other opposes summary judgment for the insurance company which should have obtained the salvaged car title. The memoranda discuss liability under the Michigan salvaged car title law, for breach of express warranty, for fraud, for revocation of acceptance, for breach of the warranty of title, for violation of the Magnuson-Moss Warranty Act, and the Michigan unfair and deceptive acts and practices statute. Section 6.3 contains jury instructions for the Magnuson-Moss Warranty Act claims.

Chapter 7 Home Construction Claims

Section 7.1 is a multiplaintiff complaint for the defective construction of prefabricated homes so that the units suffered excessive interior moisture accumulation resulting in fungus spores and airborne toxins greatly reducing the resalability of the units.[39] The complaint alleges claims for strict liability, negligence, nuisance, negligent misreprsentation, and deceit. The complaint seeks actual damages, punitive damages, and attorney fees.[40] Also included from this case in § 7.2 are interrogatories to a manufacturer of insulating barrier paper that was believed to cause the accumulation of interior moisture. Section 7.3 is the consumers' discovery, motion and case management memorandum.

Center, Consumer Warranty Law (2d ed. 2001); National Consumer Law Center, Consumer Law Pleadings With Disk, Number Two Ch. 2 (1995).

34 *See generally* National Consumer Law Center, Consumer Warranty Law (2d ed. 2001).

35 *See generally* National Consumer Law Center, Unfair and Deceptive Acts and Practices (5th ed. 2002).

36 *See generally* National Consumer Law Center, Truth in Lending (4th ed. 1999 and Supp.).

37 *See generally* National Consumer Law Center, Unfair and Deceptive Acts and Practices (5th ed. 2001); National Consumer Law Center, The Cost of Credit: Regulation and Legal Challenges (2d ed. 2000 and Supp.); National Consumer Law Center, Truth in Lending (4th ed. 1999 and Supp.); National Consumer Law Center, Consumer Law Pleadings With Disk, Number One Ch. 2 (1994).

38 *See generally* National Consumer Law Center, Automobile Fraud §§ 1.4.3, 2.1.4, 2.4.5.4, 6.2.1 (1998); National Consumer Law Center, Consumer Warranty Law (2d ed. 2001).

39 *See generally* National Consumer Law Center, Unfair and Deceptive Acts and Practices (5th ed. 2001).

40 Summary judgment in favor of the defendant insureds was reversed in Leverence v. United States Fidelity and Guaranty, 158 Wis. 2d 64 (Wis. Ct. App. 1990).

Chapter 8 Repossession Civil Rights Attorney Fee Request

This chapter contains a successful[41] brief requesting adequate statutory attorney fees from the U.S. Court of Appeals for the Second Circuit after the second inadequate award of statutory attorney fees by the district court. The case involved a civil rights claim arising from a wrongful repossession.[42] Last year's *Consumer Law Pleadings*, § 4.4, contained the prior brief in this case which successfully obtained the first reversal of a district court decision providing for an inadequate award of attorney fees.

Chapter 9 Suit to Enjoin U.S. Department of Education's Collection of Loans to Victims of a Fraudulent Vocational School

Section 9.1.1 is a class action complaint filed by victims of a fraudulent vocational school against the U.S. Department of Education seeking declaratory and injunctive relief and attorney fees. The complaint alleges that the plaintiffs' student loans should have been discharged and collection abandoned because the loans were obtained as a result of the school's false certification that the students would benefit from the vocational training. A federal statute mandated the discharge of student loans obtained by a false certification. The claims are based on the school's commissioned sales people getting drug addicts to sign student loan forms for a token $25 or $35 payment without any intention that they would ever enroll in the school. The Department of Education denied the recovered addicts' administrative request to discharge the loans. This action is based on the Administrative Procedures Act and The Higher Education Act. Attorney fees are sought pursuant to the Equal Access for Justice Act. Section 9.1.2 is the first set of interrogatories and request for production of documents in the case. A memorandum of law in support of a student's motion for summary judgment from a similar case is included as § 9.1.3.

Section 9.2.1 is a request to the U.S. Department of Education (DOE) for a discharge of all students of a fraudulent vocational because the school's pattern of admitting students without regard to their ability to benefit (ATB) from the vocational instruction offered. Samples of extensive exhibits attached to the request are included here. Section 9.2.2 is student's request and the DOE's ruling that the student's loan should be discharged because of the school's false ATB certification. Section 9.2.3 is a student's affidavit detailing some of abuses of the school's sales force. Section 9.2.4 is a DOE letter explaining its ATB certification requirements.

Chapter 10 Exercising TIL Rescission Rights in a Class Action

Where a home mortgage lender has engaged in systematic practices affecting numerous consumers, the question arises whether consumers' rescission rights may be enforced in a class action. Although there are few reported decisions, some courts have certified such a class where the plaintiffs have sought only declaratory relief establishing class members entitlement to seek rescission. *See* National Consumer Law Center, Truth in Lending, § 6.15 (4th ed. 1999 and Supp.).

In this class action, the plaintiffs allege a scheme between a home improvement contractor and a lender to deprive class members of meaningful TIL disclosures and the right of rescission by violating the delay in performance rule. The challenged practice is described in the complaint reprinted at § 10.1 as the "two-contract scheme." *See* National Consumer Law Center, Truth in Lending Ch. 6 (4th ed. 1999 and Supp.).

In a decision dated November 23, 1998 (*Williams v. Empire Funding Corp. et al.*, 183 F.R.D. 428 (E.D. Pa.)), the judge conditionally certified a class under Rule 23(b)(2) for the purpose of determining whether plaintiffs are entitled to a declaration that each member of the class may seek rescission under TIL. Plaintiffs' counsel reports that the defendants have sought an order redefining the class (the response to defendants' motion is reprinted at § 10.6). This chapter also includes: Plaintiff's Motion for Class Certification at § 10.2; Plaintiff's Memorandum in Support of Motion for Class Certification at § 10.3; Plaintiff's Reply Memorandum In Support of Motion for Class Certification at § 10.4; and Order Certifying Class at § 10.5.

Chapter 11 Distributing the Unclaimed Residue Damages in Class Actions as Cy Pres Distribution to Legal Aid and Advocacy Organizations

After the distribution of the damages in a class action there is generally an undistributed residue of the funds because of deceased or unlocated class members. A cy pres remedy is often fashioned by the courts to avoid the anomaly of these funds remaining with the wrongdoer.[43] Section 11.1 is the memorandum of law in support of a

---

41 *See* O'Sullivan v. Advanced Recovery, Inc., www.tourolaw.edu/2ndCircuit/November98/S98-7321.html (2nd Cir. 1998).

42 O'Sullivan v. Advanced Recovery, Inc., 107 F.3d 94 (2nd Cir. 1997).

43 *See, e.g.*, Six Mexican Workers v. Arizona Citrus Growers, 904 F.2d 1301 (9th Cir. 1990); In re Agent Orange Product Liability Litigation, 818 F.2d 187 (2d Cir. 1986). *See also* www.naca.net/Members%20+%20Library/Funding%20Advocacy.htm.

motion for approval of a cy pres remedy in a California state court.[44] Section 11.2 is an application of the National Consumer Law Center has used to apply for a cy pres distribution in a consumer class action. Section 11.3 is an application of the National Association of Consumer Advocates has used to apply for a cy pres distribution in a consumer class action.

Chapter 12 Unconscionable Mandatory Arbitration Clauses in Consumer Credit Contracts

Increasingly consumer credit providers are inserting compulsory arbitration clauses into their contracts in a way that would undermine substantial consumer remedies if the clauses were enforced.[45] This chapter contains material from two cases in which there were recent decisions for consumers by courts refusing to enforce a compulsory arbitration clause.

Section 12.1 contains materials in a case filed in state court in which an attempt to add an arbitration clause amendment to a bank's credit card and deposit account agreements was attacked as unconscionable. The amendment was included in credit card and deposit statements as a stuffer. The consumers alleged that the bank knew from past studies that only about 4% of its customers would read the stuffer. The language of the arbitration clause amendment was complicated and ambiguous. The trial court's judgment for the bank finding no unconscionability was reversed by the state court of appeal which found there was no consent by consumers to the amendment.[46] Some of the case materials from this case were published in National Consumer Law Center, Consumer Law Pleadings With Disk, Number One (1994): the complaint (§ 1.2), the trial brief (§ 1.3), and plaintiffs' post-trial brief (§ 1.4). In this edition are: the consumers' successful opposition to demurrer and motion to strike (§ 12.1.1), plaintiffs' post-trial brief re preemption (§ 12.1.2), opening appellate brief of plaintiffs/appellants (§ 12.1.3), reply brief of plaintiffs/appellants (§ 12.1.4), and answer to petition for review of plaintiffs/respondents (§ 12.1.5).

Section 12.2 is a brief filed in the Virginia Supreme Court of Appeals successfully arguing that a mandatory arbitration clause in predatory lender's home equity loan contract was so

one sided as to be unconscionable as a matter of law.[47] It argues that the question of the arbitration clause was properly decided by a court and that the clause was so one sided as to lack mutuality because it provided that the consumer gave up not only access to the courts, any jury or appeal but also the rights to punitive, treble or consequential damages or class action relief while the lender was left free to use the courts to collect the debt or foreclose the mortgage.

The brief in Section 12.2 also successfully argued that the loan broker was a credit services organization which must disclose its services in writing and give the consumer the opportunity to cancel the transaction.[48] The brief also argued that the loan broker breached its fiduciary duties, an issue that was determined to require fact finding and which was remanded by the Virginia Supreme Court of Appeals.

Consumer Law Pleadings With Disk, Number Six (2000)

Chapter 1 Predatory Mortgage Lending Abuses—HOEPA Litigation

This case is one of the first class actions brought under the Home Ownership and Equity Protection Act (HOEPA). In an important initial ruling in the case, a federal court granted a preliminary injunction to homeowners whose homes were to be sold at foreclosure sales. Since the lender had not treated the loans as covered by HOEPA, plaintiffs first hurdle to overcome was establishing that the loans met the "points and fees" trigger under the statute. HOEPA is applicable if the total "points and fees" charged by the lender exceeds 8% of the "total loan amount." (For a detailed discussion of this trigger, see National Consumer Law Center, Truth in Lending, 4th ed. 1999 at § 10.2.4).

In the complaint (§ 1.1), and the expert's report (§ 1.5), the plaintiffs sought to prove that several of the closing charges financed as part of the loan counted towards the "points and fees" trigger even though they would ordinarily be excluded from the finance charge under Regulation Z § 226.4(c)(7). To do this, plaintiffs needed to show that the lender received some *direct or indirect* compensation in connection with the charges, or that an affiliate of the creditor received part of the charges. *See* Regulation Z § 226.32(b)(iii). Based on the proof presented at the preliminary injunction hearing, the court found that a $700 closing attorney fee should be included in the "points and fees" trigger because the lender received

44   *See also* National Consumer Law Center, Consumer Law Pleadings With Disk, Number Three Ch. 3 (1997); National Consumer Law Center, Consumer Law Pleadings With Disk, Number One Ch. 12 (1994).

45   *See generally* National Consumer Law Center, Unfair and Deceptive Acts and Practices § 7.7 (5th ed. 2001); National Consumer Law Center, Consumer Law Pleadings With Disk, Number One Ch. 1 (1994) and Consumer Law Pleadings With Disk, Number Four Ch. 1 (1998).

46   Garciaparra v. Bank of America, __ Cal. App. 3d Supp. __ (1998).

47   Arnold v. United Companies Lending, Corp., __ S.E.2d __ (W. Va. 1998).

48   *See also* Sannes v. Jeff Wyler Chevrolet, Case No. 97CV000916 (Ohio Common Pleas, Clermont County Feb. 11, 1999) and Hall v. Jack Walker Pontiac, Case No. 97-6565 (Ohio Common Pleas Court, Montgomery County March 11, 1999) (car dealer were covered by the Ohio Credit Services statute when they arrange credit for a car buyer).

either direct or indirect compensation based on the close relationship between the attorney and the lender. *See* Lopez v. Delta Funding Corp., No. CV-98-7204 (CPS) (E.D.N.Y., decided Dec. 23, 1998), Clearinghouse No. 52,140. With the assistance of the expert report of NCLC's Gary Klein in performing the calculations, the court found that the plaintiffs' loans were subject to HOEPA when the attorney fee was included with the loan broker fees and other charges.

The discovery documents (§§ 1.2 and 1.3) are instructive in attempting to sort out the interrelationships between the various players in the sub-prime market: the originating lender, its mortgage brokers, the trust that purchases the loans as part of a securitization transaction, and the trustee. The plaintiffs' memorandum (§ 1.4) is also helpful in responding to defense dismissal motions in TIL/HOEPA cases based on the *Rooker/Feldman* doctrine where there has been a prior state court foreclosure or eviction judgment entered against the plaintiff.

Chapter 2　Credit Repair Organization Complaints

This chapter demonstrates the creative application of credit repair organization statutes to automobile dealers and other credit sellers. The Federal Credit Repair Organizations Act, 15 U.S.C. § 1679 *et. seq.*, applies, *inter alia*, to "any person who uses any instrumentality of interstate commerce or the mails to sell, provide, or perform . . . any service, in return for the payment of money or other valuable consideration, for the express or implied purpose of (i) improving any consumer's credit record, credit history, or credit rating, or (ii) providing advice or assistance [for these purposes]." This statute, which requires special disclosures and affords the consumer a three-day right to cancel, should be applicable to the many low-end used car dealers that advertise that they can help improve the consumer's credit rating.[49]

Many state credit repair organization statutes go beyond the federal statute and cover not only organizations that advertise credit repair services but also those that promise to arrange an extension of credit for the buyer.[50] These statutes potentially apply to all car dealers, home improvement companies, and other retailers who arrange financing for credit sales, unless they are insulated by some specific statutory exemption.[51] (Many state credit repair statutes include exemptions for licensed, regulated extenders of

credit, and after a court ruled that Ohio's statute covered car dealers that arrange credit the legislature added an exemption for them.)[52] Another advantage of state credit repair laws is that many delete the requirement that the credit repair activities be the "express or implied purpose" of the transaction, although they usually retain the requirement that the credit repair services or credit extension be "in return for" the consumer's payment.

This chapter first reproduces a complaint (§ 2.1) that alleges that a car dealer violated Ohio's credit repair organizations statute by arranging credit as part of the sale of a vehicle. The complaint also includes causes of action based on an Ohio UDAP rule, the FTC used car window sticker rule, and fraud. Another complaint that raises state credit repair organization claims, this time against a home improvement contractor, is found in Chapter 17, *infra*. A set of interrogatories, document requests, and requests for admissions is included as § 2.2.[53] Section 2.3 is a brief opposing a dealer's motion for summary judgment, focusing on the question of whether the state statute requires the consumer's payment to be earmarked for the credit repair service, and § 2.4 is a sample affidavit in support of a motion by the consumer for summary judgment.

In *Hall v. Jack Walker Pontiac*,[54] an Ohio trial court found that a motor vehicle dealer that arranged credit was covered by Ohio's credit repair organization statute. In *Midstate Siding & Window Co. v. Rogers*,[55] an Illinois intermediate appellate court found a home repair contractor covered by that state's statute. Even though the assistance was not specified as a term of the written agreement, it was understood to be part of the agreement between the parties. Consideration for this assistance was the consumers' signing the sales agreement.

State and federal credit repair organization laws are discussed in National Consumer Law Center, *Fair Credit Reporting Act* Ch. 8 (4th ed. 1998 and Supp.) and *Unfair and Deceptive Acts and Practices* § 5.1.16.6 (5th ed. 2001).

Chapter 3　Class Action Complaint Challenging False Threat of Foreclosure

This chapter contains a class action complaint challenging a collection attorney's false threat of foreclosure on a home for a hospital bill. Under Ohio law, a lien on a home for a hospital bill can be enforced only when the home is sold or transferred, so foreclosure is precluded. The complaint also includes claims that the defendant omitted the notice re-

---

49　*See, e.g.*, Hall v. Jack Walker Pontiac, 1999 Ohio Misc. Lexis 65 (Ohio C.P. March 1, 1999). In that decision the court describes the auto dealer's marketing of its credit arrangement and credit repair services (*e.g.*, "If anyone can help you build (or reestablish) your credit . . . THE CREDIT GENIE can!")

50　*See, e.g.*, Ind. Code Ann. § 25-5-15-2; Ohio Rev. Code § 4712.01(c)(1); Ok. Stat. Ann. tit. 24, § 132(2)(a); 73 Pa. Stat. § 2182.

51　These statutes may also cover loan brokers unless there is a specific exclusion for them.

52　Ohio Rev. Code § 4712.01, as amended effective Sept. 29, 1999.

53　These discovery requests include some questions that relate primarily to class action issues but which might also be proper in an individual action to help show pattern or practice, intent, knowledge, absence of mistake or accident, or similar issues.

54　1999 Ohio Misc. Lexis 65 (Ohio C.P. March 1, 1999).

55　1999 Ill. App. Lexis 652 (Ill. App. Ct. Feb. 1, 2000) (modified opinion). This decision is now on appeal to the Illinois Supreme Court.

Description of Pleadings

quired by 15 U.S.C. § 1692e(11) regarding the debt collection purpose of the letters. *See* National Consumer Law Center, Fair Debt Collection §§ 5.5.7, 5.5.12, 5.5.13 (4th ed. 2000).

The complaint (§ 3.1) raises claims under both the Fair Debt Collection Practices Act and the Ohio UDAP statute. Since the statute of limitations is longer for the Ohio UDAP claim, the complaint defines a larger class for that claim. Section 3.2 is a set of requests for admissions and interrogatories and § 3.3 is a set of requests for production of documents. Both focus on the facts necessary to establish liability and certify the case as a class action. A motion for summary judgment on the FDCPA claims, a supporting brief, and a reply brief are included as §§ 3.4, 3.5, and 3.6. The reply brief deals extensively with a unique issue raised by the defendant: that the threat of foreclosure was not an FDCPA violation because the state law prohibiting foreclosure for hospital bills was unconstitutional.

The court declined to certify the class, but in a separate opinion, *Lewis v. Marlin*, Clearinghouse No. 53021 (S.D. Ohio 1999), ruled in favor of the plaintiffs on the merits of the FDCPA claim. The court held that a threat of foreclosure was the clear import of the statements in the collection letters that the creditor's available remedies "include foreclosure and sale of your home" and that the defendant would be "forced to proceed with any and all of the remedies available" unless the debtor made payment arrangements within seven days. These threats of action that the defendant could not take and did not intend to take violated the FDCPA. The falsity of the defendant's threat to foreclose was unaffected by his claim that the statute prohibiting foreclosure was unconstitutional, since he had not challenged the constitutionality of the statute before sending the threatening letters.

Chapter 4 Class Action to Return Car Seller's Deficiency Recoveries for Failure to Give Required Notice of Repossession Sale Rights

One of the most common claims filed against consumers is a deficiency claim resulting from the shortfall produced by a repossession sale of a car. It is the unfortunate ending stage of many financially pressed consumers' experience with a car purchase. The case in this chapter involves a class action against an automobile manufacturer's finance company for failing to give the newly enacted part of a post-repossession notice required by a state motor vehicle retail installment sales act.[56] The state law states that the failure to provide the full notice results in the creditor's loss of any deficiency claim. The amended complaint, § 4.1, *infra*, seeks restitution

for the class of made on by them on the defendants' deficiency claims, declaratory and injunctive relief, and attorney fees. The claims were brought pursuant to the state motor vehicle retail installment sales act[57] and the unfair and deceptive acts and practices statute.[58]

In addition, this chapter contains plaintiff's first request for production of documents to defendant motor credit company (§ 4.2), plaintiff's first set of requests for admission (§ 4.3), plaintiff's responses to defendant creditor's third set of special interrogatories (§ 4.4), plaintiff's memorandum of points and authorities in support of motion for summary adjudication of declaratory relief cause of action (§ 4.5), plaintiff's memorandum of points and authorities in opposition to defendant's motion for summary judgment, or in the alternative, summary adjudication (§ 4.6), and plaintiff's reply memorandum in support of motion for summary adjudication of declaratory relief cause of action (§ 4.7).

Summary judgment was entered for the consumer in a case raising similar claims.[59]

Chapter 5 Claims Against Health Maintenance Organizations for Delay in Authorizing and Paying for Cancer Treatment

This chapter contains in § 5.1 a complaint against a Health Maintenance Organization (HMO) and several health care providers for the delaying the authorization of the treatment of an insured for cancer that rapidly became terminal. When the patient desperately sought urgently needed treatment without waiting for a painfully slow authorization process to wind its course, the HMO refused to pay for the expensive treatment and subsequent treatment. The complaint alleges that the capitation and/or risk sharing agreement between the HMO and the primary care provider created a conflict of interest between the physician and patient resulting in the fatal delay in providing the patient's cancer treatment. The complaint alleges breach of the duty of good faith and fair dealing, breach of contract, negligent interference with a contractual relationship, intentional interference with a contractual relationship, intentional infliction of emotional distress, negligent infliction of emotional distress, wrongful death due to medical malpractice, and wrongful death due to breach of the duty of good faith and fair dealing.

Sections 5.2 and 5.3 are interrogatories and a motion to produce.

---

56 *See* National Consumer Law Center, *Repossessions and Foreclosures* § 6.5.2 (4th ed. 1999).

57 *See generally*, National Consumer Law Center, *The Cost of Credit* (2d ed. 2000 and Supp.).

58 *See generally*, National Consumer Law Center, *Unfair and Deceptive Acts and Practices* (5th ed. 2001).

59 Mortera v. Ford Motor Credit Co., No. CV779239 (Santa Clara Superior Court March 10, 2000), reported in LRP Publications, Consumer Financial Services Law Report 3 (April 14, 2000).

Section 5.4 contains a memorandum in opposition to the defendant's post trial motions after a jury verdict of $ 747,655 in compensatory damages and $ 116 million in punitive damages. The memorandum argues that the punitive damages were justified by the defendant's misconduct, the amount of the defendant's liability insurance coverage and its gross income, and should not be reduced. The memo also addresses a number of evidentiary rulings and other issues that arose in the case.

Litigation against HMOs is a complicated, dynamic area of the law requiring careful research because of the limited remedies provided by Employee Retirement Income Security Act (ERISA)[60] and ERISA's potential preemption of many state claims against HMO's. Recently in Pegram v. Herdrich,[61] the Supreme Court held that an HMO may not be sued under ERISA for breach of fiduciary duty based on rationing healthcare, although a malpractice claim against the physician would presumably be available. The Supreme Court called on Congress to deal with the difficult issue of HMO's accountability, including decisions of how to ration its provision of health care and on accountability for mistaken diagnosis in that process. This decision does not affect a state's right to permit malpractice claims against an HMO based on the quality of care received.[62]

Chapter 6 Credit Overcharges

The first case involves a class action complaint against a finance company for imposing an origination fee in a loan which refinanced its own home loan with the consumer and also charged a $50 annual fee in addition to maximum finance charge. The complaint in § 6.1 alleges that each of those charges violate the state usury as exceeding the maximum permissible interest and violating the unfair and deceptive acts and practices (UDAP) law. See generally National Consumer Law Center, The Cost of Credit § (2000 and Supp.); National Consumer Law Center, Unfair and Deceptive Acts and Practices § 5.1 (5th ed. 2001). Section 6.2 is a brief arguing that the claims involving the origination fee and UDAP should not be dismissed.

The second case involves a claim against a car dealer and the dealer's service contract provider for charging the consumer an excessive price for a service contract where the dealer retained a portion of the price the consumer paid for the service contract. A service contract provides for specified repairs of the automobile under certain conditions. The complaint alleged that the consumer was charged $1180.00 plus interest at 12% per year for the service contract, but that the seller paid the service contract issuer less than that amount and retained the difference. The complaint in § 6.3

avers that this practice violated the motor vehicle sales finance act,[63] the state UDAP statute,[64] the dealer's fiduciary duty to the consumer,[65] and resulted in unjust enrichment.

Chapter 7 Defeating the Sovereign Immunity Defense in Bankruptcy Litigation

Debtors are increasingly being faced with the sovereign immunity defense in bankruptcy litigation. Where the debtor is attempting to force a state actor to comply with federal bankruptcy law, one approach to counter a possible immunity defense involves bringing the action against a state official seeking prospective declaratory and injunctive relief under the *Ex Parte Young* doctrine.[66] In the first case, the debtor claimed that certain automobile insurance surcharges had been discharged in her bankruptcy case. In the complaint at 7.1.1, the debtor filed the action against the director of the state motor vehicle agency and other state officials seeking a prospective injunction preventing future collection of the insurance surcharge debts and requiring the state officials to obey federal law. Although the case was resolved favorably for the debtor without the need for further briefing, the debtor's counsel submits at 7.1.2 a memorandum that provides an overview of the sovereign immunity issues.

The second case takes another tact by addressing the prerequisite issue of whether the agency even has the right to claim immunity. To be a "sovereign" for Eleventh Amendment immunity purposes, the agency must prove that it is an "arm of the state," and most Circuit Courts apply a multi-prong test to make this determination. Many of the factors address the degree to which the agency is financially and structurally independent from the state.

Since the guaranty agency raised the immunity defense for the first time on appeal in this student loan dischargeability action, debtor's counsel was unable to engage in formal discovery concerning the agency's status. Nevertheless, by reviewing the agency's enabling statute and conducting some informal discovery (primarily through the agency's website), debtor's counsel was able to present in the brief at 7.2.1 arguments based on each of the "arm of the state" factors. While the brief focuses primarily on sovereign immunity issues, it also discusses the lower court's application of the student loan hardship discharge tests (*e.g.*, the *Brunner* and "totality of circumstances" tests) to the facts of the case. Debtor's counsel reports that the guaranty agency in this case withdrew its appeal after the "arm of the state" issue had been briefed.

---

60 29 U.S.C. §1001 et seq.

61 530 U. S. ___ (June 12, 2000).

62 *See* Corporate Health Insurance, Inc. v. Texas Department of Insurance, 2000 U.S. App. LEXIS 14215 (5th Cir. 2000).

63 *See* National Consumer Law Center, The Cost of Credit (2d ed. 2000 and Supp.).

64 *See* National Consumer Law Center, Unfair and Deceptive Acts and Practices (5th ed. 2001).

65 *See* National Consumer Law Center, The Cost of Credit (2d ed. 2000 and Supp.).

66 *See* National Consumer Law Center, Consumer Bankruptcy Law and Practice § 13.3.2.2 (6th ed. 2000 and Supp.).

Chapter 8 Defending Hospital Collection Cases

A well person is at risk in a hospital, for the possibilities of overdiagnosis and needless treatment there are formidable. Patients should avoid hospitals whenever possible.
—Thomas Preston, M.D.[67]

This chapter is unusual for this book as it is written by Mr. Alop as a practice guide designed to acquaint legal services attorneys with defenses and strategies available to defendants who have been sued by hospitals for unpaid bills. Avenues of defense are discussed, pleadings and discovery materials are provided, and ideas for the trial of these cases are included. These materials are updated and expanded from the materials in Consumer Law Pleadings Number 2 Ch. 15.

Chapter 9 Automobile Sales Fraud Complaint

The complaint that follows is an example of aggressive advocacy by an Attorney General's consumer protection division against automobile sales fraud. The complaint is notable for its detailed factual allegations regarding the internal workings of the dealership, including its sales techniques, its methods of training its sales staff, and the roles of the various owners and the lenders with whom the dealership worked.

The complaint (§ 9.1) alleges that the original owners of the dealership hired a consultant who advertised that he could increase the dealership's profits by training its sales staff and changing its advertising. He had the dealership advertise fictitious cars at low monthly payments. The sales staff's job was to get the consumer to commit to a monthly payment without revealing the price of the car; indeed, the dealership stopped letting the sales staff know the prices. A deskman would then negotiate the consumer to a higher payment which left room to pack in service contracts, credit insurance, and an undisclosed yield spread premium.

The dealership also frequently failed to pay the balance due on consumers' trade-in vehicles, and kept the money consumers paid for taxes, insurance, and service contracts. It sold used vehicles without the Buyer's Guide required by the FTC, and attempted to disclaim implied warranties in violation of West Virginia law.

The complaint sets forth a variety of causes of action under the state's Unfair and Deceptive Acts and Practices (UDAP) statute. It includes claims based on the seller's retention of consumers' tax, insurance, and service contract payments, which the complaint characterizes as excess charges that violated the state consumer credit laws. It also includes detailed allegations about why the failure to disclose the yield spread premium is an unfair and deceptive act

or practice. While the complaint was filed by the Attorney General's office, the causes of action it presents are equally available to private litigants.

Also included in this chapter is a motion for leave to file the amended complaint (§ 9.2).

Used car financing and fraud issues are discussed in National Consumer Law Center, *The Cost of Credit: Regulation and Legal Challenges* § 11.2.2 (2d ed. 2000) and *Unfair and Deceptive Acts and Practices* § 5.4 (5th 2001). Odometer fraud, lemon laundering, and concealment of salvage or other adverse history are treated in National Consumer Law Center, *Automobile Fraud* (1998 and Supp.).

Chapter 10 Unauthorized Release of Credit Report After Imposter Applied for Credit

This chapter presents the complaint and briefs in a groundbreaking Fair Credit Reporting Act case. An imposter had applied for credit using plaintiff's first initial, last name, and Social Security number, but without any of the plaintiff's other identifying information (address, birthdate, etc.) Due to its lax procedures, the credit reporting agency treated the imposter's credit application as if it had come from the plaintiff, and released the plaintiff's confidential credit information to the potential creditors.

A credit reporting agency is allowed to release a report only if it has reason to believe that the creditor intends to use the information in connection with a credit transaction "involving the consumer." 15 U.S.C. § 1681b(3)(A). The complaint (§ 10.1) alleges that the credit reporting agency did not maintain reasonable procedures (such as matching more than first initial, last name, and Social Security number) to determine whether a person applying for credit was really the person whose report was released. The complaint also alleges that the credit reporting procedure violated 15 U.S.C. § 1681e(b) by failing to follow reasonable procedures to assure maximum possible accuracy of the information concerning the plaintiff, that it failed to comply with its reinvestigation duties, and that its acts and omissions also violated the state Unfair and Deceptive Acts and Practices (UDAP) statute.

The creditor moved for summary judgment on liability and on a statute of limitations defense. The plaintiff's brief in opposition to summary judgment (§ 10.2) is notable for its clear and meticulous explanation of the way the credit reporting agency's computer system facilitates improper disclosure of credit reports.

The trial court granted summary judgment against the consumer, but its decision was reversed by the Ninth Circuit. *Andrews v. TRW, Inc.*, 2000 U.S. App. Lexis 16486 (July 17, 2000). The Ninth Circuit broke ranks with the Third, Fifth, Seventh, Tenth and Eleventh Circuits and applied the discovery rule to the FCRA, holding that the two-year statute

---

67   Charles B. Inlander, *Take This Book to the Hospital With You*, at 2 (1985).

of limitations commences when the plaintiff discovers, or should have discovered, the FCRA violation. The court also held that a victim of identity theft can recover for a privacy violation—wrongful release of the credit report—not just an accuracy violation. Moreover, the court reinstated the plaintiff's claim for punitive damages for this privacy violation. The plaintiff's reply brief in the Court of Appeals is included as § 10.3.

The Court of Appeals decision is also significant for recognizing the admissibility of expert opinions regarding the prevalence of identity theft, which would make it unreasonable for the credit reporting agency to rely on superficial matches to release a consumer's record. Expert testimony on automated procedures the defendant could have used to reduce inaccuracies was also admissible, but the court found this error to be harmless in the unique circumstances of the case.

All of these issues are discussed in National Consumer Law Center, Fair Credit Reporting Act (4th ed. 1998), which also includes sample complaints and discovery involving inaccurate investigative reports and inaccurate consumer reports. Other FCRA complaints and discovery can be found at National Consumer Law Center, Consumer Law Pleadings Number Two Ch. 10 (claims regarding inaccurate information against credit reporting agencies and furnishers); Consumer Law Pleadings Number Three Ch. 5 (victim's claim regarding release of report to imposter, which enabled imposter to steal victim's identity, and regarding inaccuracy); and Consumer Law Pleadings Number Five Ch. 1 (identity theft victim's claim regarding inaccuracy of data, and failure to correct it).

Chapter 11 Gray Market Vehicle Sales

The complaint that follows deals with the sale of a "gray market" vehicle, in this case a motorcycle. Gray market products are items that were manufactured for a foreign market but are sold in the United States. Gray market vehicles often do not meet U.S. safety and emission requirements. Some lack equipment necessary for operation in U.S. climates. The manufacturer's warranty may be void in the U.S.

The complaint (§ 11.1) is not only useful for gray market vehicle cases, but also for warranty cases in general, as it pleads a variety of warranty, UDAP, and state law claims. When the complaint was filed, it was clear that the motorcycle, which was sold as new, had not been manufactured for U.S. use. It was not clear, however, whether the dealer had imported the motorcycle or had purchased it from a prior owner who had brought it into the U.S. from Germany. In the latter case, the dealer's misrepresentation of the motorcycle as new would be actionable, but proof that the dealer knew that the motorcycle was a gray market vehicle would be more difficult. The complaint pleads the facts without great detail in order to preserve both of these claims.

The discovery requests (§§ 11.2–11.5) hone in on the origins of the motorcycle. Section 11.2 is a Request for Production of Documents to the manufacturer and the financing entity. It seeks the basic documents regarding the motorcycle, including any that relate to its importation from another country. § 11.3 is a set of interrogatories to the manufacturer that focus particularly on gray market issues. §§ 11.4 and 11.5 are sets of interrogatories to the dealer that probe the factual basis for the dealer's affirmative defenses and the question whether the dealer committed other similar acts.[68]

Gray market vehicle issues are discussed in National Consumer Law Center, Consumer Warranty Law (2d ed. 2001).

Chapter 12 Brief on Collecting Illegal Charges and the Bona Fide Error Defense under the Fair Debt Collection Practices Act

This chapter contains a Fair Debt Collection Practices Act brief dealing with a collector adding four illegal $100 charges onto a claim on four small bounced checks, and the collector's defense that the collection of the illegal charge could be forgiven as a bona fide error.[69] The brief goes through several of the steps that the debt collector failed to take to make out a bona fide error defense under 15 U.S.C. § 1692k(c)[70] and should be helpful whenever that defense is raised. The first part of the brief deals with violations of the Minnesota pre-judgment garnishment statute that provided the basis for the FDCPA claim that the collector misrepresented that it was entitled to a $100 penalty on each check when Minnesota law clearly provided *up to* $100 per check. Because the amount of the penalty was discretionary, the collector also misrepresented that it was entitled to pre-judgment garnishment which was not available unless the amount of the claim was liquidated.

Chapter 13 Delay in Repossession Discharges Obligation of Cosigner on Car Sale

A person who cosigns an obligation may be released from liability by the inaction of the creditor. In this case a consumer cosigned a retail installment sales contract for the

---

68 Evidence of other bad acts is relevant for a number of purposes, including proof of intent or motive, which is critical in fraud cases but also necessary in some states to win multiple UDAP damages; knowledge; absence of mistake; and entitlement to punitive damages. *See* National Consumer Law Center, Automobile Fraud § 9.7.1.1 (1998 and Supp.).

69 *See* Picht v. Hawks, 77 F. Supp. 2d 1041 (D. Minn. 1999), appeal docketed, No. 00-1270 (8th Cir. 2000).

70 *See* National Consumer Law Center, Fair Debt Collection § 7.4 (4th Ed. 2000).

husband of her daughter's friend. The borrower the failed to pay most of the installments owed and some years later brought suit against the purchaser and the cosigner. The cosigner defended on several basis including that she was a surety and that her obligation was discharged by the failure of the creditor to repossess in a timely fashion the car which was collateral for the sale. See § 13.1. She also alleged that the failure to repossess the car was a commercially unreasonable practice violating U.C.C. 9-504 entitling her to damages under U.C.C. 9-507, and that the claim was barred by laches or the statute of limitations, and by equitable estoppel. Section 13.2 is a memorandum of law supporting the claims.

Chapter 14 Bank's Debt Collection Suits in Distant Forum are Abuse of Process and Unfair Trade Practice

The materials in this chapter are from a class action by California credit card holders against the card issuer bank that had brought collection suits against them in a Virginia court. The practice of filing suit in a distant forum for the purpose of obtaining unfair advantage and hindering a consumer's defense is known as "distant forum abuse."[71] The named plaintiffs, who had never lived or worked in Virginia, accepted a "pre-approved" credit card offered and sent to them through the mail by the Virginia bank. When they became unable to continue their payments, the bank sued them in a municipal court in Virginia, obtained a default judgment against them, and a wage garnishment order issued by the Virginia court. The bank then served the order on a Virginia branch office of the consumer's California employer, with instructions that it be forwarded to California, and seized almost $4,000 of the consumer's wages over the course of six months, without ever domesticating the Virginia judgment in the courts of this state.

The consumers were victims of what the bank called it's "Long Arm Program," a debt collection practice they engaged in for several years in which they sued consumers living in states throughout the country, including California, in municipal courts in Virginia for allegedly unpaid credit card debts. This action alleges that defendants deliberately engaged in this unlawful and abusive debt collection practice in order to obtain default judgments against California consumers, seized the wages of those consumers who happened to be employed by a company subject to service in Virginia, and to otherwise intimidate, threaten and coerce consumers as a collection tactic. The action was filed on behalf of a consumer couple and a proposed class of at least 8,800 California consumers who were subjected to the practice.

This chapter contains the class action complaint against the bank in § 14.1. The trial court's entry of summary judgment for the bank was reversed by the court of appeals and review was denied by the California and the United States Supreme Courts.[72] The remainder of the chapter are the consumer's four appellate briefs dealing with the bank's various arguments that it's misconduct could not be attacked collaterally in the California courts.

Section 14.2 is the consumers' opening brief in the court of appeals. It argues:

- The trial court's finding that the Virginia court had personal jurisdiction to enter default judgment against the consumers in the bank's "long arm" action was clearly erroneous.

- The trial court was required to make an independent determination as to whether the bank's "long arm" judgment was entered in the absence of jurisdiction.

- The Virginia judgment was not res judicata on the issue of jurisdiction.

- The consumers' claims in this action were not barred by the federal "Rooker-Feldman" doctrine.

- The trial court erred in holding that the only forum for plaintiffs to challenge defendants' "long arm" practices was the appellate court in Virginia.

- The trial court's finding that defendants' violations of California domestication and wage garnishment statutes were "irrelevant" was clearly erroneous.

- Defendants may be held liable for their unlawful and abusive practices under the causes of action alleged in plaintiffs' second amended complaint.

These arguments are recast in the Reply brief in § 14.3, in the Answer to Petition to Review in § 14.4, and in the Opposition to Petition for Writ of Certiorari in § 14.5 as the bank unsuccessfully reformulate its argument that the Virginia court's default judgments could not be attacked in the California courts.

Chapter 15 Real Estate Settlement Procedures Act Claim Alleged Against Broker for Sharing in Title Insurance Fees

Section 15.1 is a state class action complaint by real estate sellers against a company engaged in real estate brokerage and settlements and the title company which it used sharing the proceeds of the title insurance fees without disclosing effectively that the companies had common principals and without disclosing clearly how the broker profited from engaging the related title company. The broker was also alleged to have misrepresented that the title insurance company's rates were regulated by the state when the state

---

71 *See* National Consumer Law Center, Fair Debt Collection § 5.9, 10.6.3, 11.2.4.3 (4th Ed. 2000); National Consumer Law Center, Unfair and Deceptive Acts and Practices (5th ed. 2001) .

72 Consumer v. Signet Bank/Virginia, 69 Cal. App. 4th 1377; 1999 Cal. App. LEXIS 124; 82 Cal.(1999), *review denied*, 1999 Cal. LEXIS 3644, cert. denied, 145 L. Ed. 2d 312, 120 S. Ct. 400, 1999 U.S. LEXIS 7098, 68 U.S.L.W. 3289 (U.S. 1999).

exercised almost no oversight over those rates. The complaint sought treble the title insurance premium, attorney fees, and costs for its claims under the Real Estate Settlement Procedures Act (RESPA).[73] Section 15.2 is combined discovery requesting documents and containing interrogatories in the action and Section 15.3 is the memorandum of law in support of certifying the class.

Section 15.4 is a state class action complaint by real estate sellers against a company engaged in real estate brokerage and a company providing settlements and title insurance which the broker required buyers to use and in exchange received a discount on the settlement charges billed to the seller. This arrangement was alleged to stymie competition in the title insurance business. The claims were brought under both RESPA and a state consumer protection statute. Section 15.5 is a memorandum of law in opposition to a motion to dismiss. Section 15.6 is the memorandum of law in support of certifying the class. Section 15.7 is reply memorandum on class certification.

Chapter 16 Enforcement of the Bankruptcy Discharge Injunction

During the 1990's, many creditors engaged in illegal practices related to bankruptcy reaffirmations. Perhaps the most common practice was to obtain reaffirmation agreements from consumers without filing them with the court, making the agreements unenforceable under § 524(c). Creditors' collection efforts on those unenforceable agreements have therefore been found to violate the injunction on collection of debts associated with the bankruptcy discharge.[74]

Most of the early class action cases brought on these theories resulted in successful settlements. Retailers including Sears, Federated Department Stores, and the May Companies agreed to refund money to the affected debtors with interest.[75]

More recently, though, some courts have denied relief in class action cases based on illegal reaffirmation practices.[76] These courts have held that the only remedy for collection of a discharged debt is an individual proceeding for contempt in the bankruptcy court that entered the discharge, that there is no private right of action under 11 U.S.C. § 524 or § 105 to enforce the discharge, and that the discharge injunction preempts state or federal equitable remedies such as restitution and legal claims such as UDAP.

The appellate briefs contained in this chapter are from the First Circuit appeal in Cox v. Avco Financial Services, Inc. The opening brief of the plaintiff/debtor class found at 16.1 and the reply brief at 16.2 thoroughly address the arguments in favor of finding a private enforcement mechanism within the Bankruptcy Code for violations of the discharge injunction. These briefs also seek reversal of the lower court's dismissal of a RICO cause of action. The *amicus curiae* brief at 16.3 filed by the National Association of Consumer Bankruptcy Attorneys provides some additional arguments based on the inherent equitable authority of federal district courts to order restitution. It also contains a discussion of the preemption issue.

Chapter 17 Damages, Cancellation, and FCRA Violations in Home Improvement Scam

The pleadings that follow arise from a home improvement contract in which the contractor not only started but completed the work before entering into a contract with or giving any disclosures to one of the two borrowers. As part of its strategy for obtaining her signature on the contract, the contractor accessed that borrower's credit report without her permission. Then it misrepresented that she had to sign the contract since the work was already done. This was the third contract that the contractor presented, having already obtained the husband's signature on two earlier versions.

The complaint (§ 17.1), filed against both the contractor and the assignee, seeks cancellation under both the Truth in Lending Act and the state Home Solicitation Sales Act. It also asserts a fraud claim for actual and punitive damages and a state UDAP claim for actual damages and attorney fees. On the Fair Credit Reporting Act violation, the complaint includes punitive damages allegations consistent with *Yohay v. City of Alexandria Employees Credit Union*, 827 F.2d 967 (4th Cir. 1987). *See* National Consumer Law Center, *Fair Credit Reporting Act*, § 13.4 (4th ed. 1998 and Supp.) for a discussion of punitive damages under the FCRA. Additional sample FCRA complaints are found in Appx. H of that book and National Consumer Law Center, *Consumer Law Pleadings Number Two,* Chapter 10 (1995), *Consumer Law Pleadings Number 3,* Chapter 5 (1997), and *Consumer Law Pleadings Number 4,* Chapter 7 (1998).

Also included in this chapter are a number of discovery requests. First are requests to the contractor (§ 17.2) and assignee (§ 17.3) for the basic documents in the transaction. Next the chapter includes interrogatories to the contractor (§ 17.4) and the assignee (§ 17.5) seeking information about their contacts with each other, their actions with respect to the transaction, the identity of documents and witnesses, their employees' training and criminal records, and the existence of insurance. The final items are requests for admissions, one set directed to the contractor (§ 17.6) and

---

73 See 12 U.S.C. § 2601, et seq. See generally, National Consumer Law Center, Inc., The Cost of Credit (2d ed. 2000 and Supp.)

74 *E.g.,* In re Vazquez, 221 B.R. 222 (Bankr. N.D. Ill. 1998); *In re* Latanowich, 207 B.R. 326 (Bankr. D. Mass. 1997).

75 *See, e.g.,* Conley v. Sears Roebuck & Co., 222 B.R. 181 (D. Mass. 1998).

76 *E.g.,* Cox v. Zale Delaware, Inc., 242 B.R. 444 (N.D. Ill. 1999); Cox v. Avco Financial Services, Inc., 240 B.R. 147 (D.R.I. 1999) *appeal pending* C.N. 2291 (1st Cir.)

one to the assignee (§ 17.7). They seek to establish the authenticity of documents, the contractor's coverage by the Truth in Lending Act and the Home Solicitation Sales Act, the timing of the transaction in relation to the work on the home, the contractor's receipt of and failure to respond to the cancellation letters, and the contractor's violation of the Truth in Lending Act and Fair Credit Reporting Act.

Truth in Lending law is explored in detail in National Consumer Law Center, *Truth in Lending* (4th ed. 2000). Cases interpreting state home solicitation sales acts are analyzed in National Consumer Law Center, Unfair and Deceptive Acts and Practices § 5.8.2 (5th ed. 2001).

Consumer Law Pleadings With Disk, Number Seven (2001)

Chapter 1 Equal Credit Opportunity Act (ECOA)

The pleadings in this chapter were filed in the case of *[Plaintiffs] v. Nissan Motor Acceptance Corporation*, pending in the United States District Court for the Middle District of Tennessee, Nashville Division (Judge Todd Campbell presiding) in the summer and fall of 2000. The Plaintiffs in the lawsuit, originally filed in 1998, are African-American consumers who contend that Nissan Motor Acceptance Corporation's ("NMAC") credit pricing policy is racially discriminatory.

The case involves the Equal Credit Opportunity Act (ECOA), 15 U.S.C. §§ 1691 *et seq*, which prohibits discrimination in the pricing of credit. Plaintiffs claim that NMAC authorizes dealers to markup finance charges, which increases the cost of credit. Plaintiffs further claim that NMAC's Markup Policy has a discriminatory effect upon African-American consumers. Plaintiffs have filed statistical analyses of NMAC data showing that African-Americans in Tennessee, and across the country, pay materially more for credit than white consumers with comparable credit ratings. Plaintiffs contend that the markup charges are split by NMAC and the dealer and that the consumer is totally unaware that the cost of credit is being marked up. NMAC has countered that any discrimination is being caused by the dealers and not by the finance company, which, it claims, cannot be held responsible under the circumstances for the purported violations of ECOA.

Based, in part, upon the Memorandum in Support of Plaintiffs' Renewed Motion for Class Certification filed on April 10, 2000 (§ 1.1) and Plaintiffs' Reply to NMAC's Memorandum in Opposition to Class Certification filed on June 10, 2000 (§ 1.2), the District Court conditionally certified the case as a hybrid F.R.C.P. Rule 23(b)(2)/(b)(3) national class action in August 2000. Subsequently, the Plaintiffs submitted a Brief in Support of Class Notice

Proposal on October 9, 2000 (§ 1.3). Before the class notice issues were resolved, however, NMAC petitioned the Sixth Circuit Court of Appeals pursuant to F.R.C.P. Rule 23(f) to review the certification decision. The Court of Appeals accepted the request and the interlocutory appeal currently is awaiting oral argument prior to the issuance of a decision.

Chapter 2 Suit Against Long Distance Telephone Carrier for Charging in Excess of Agreed Rates Provided in its Tariff

Section 2.1 is a complaint by consumer against a long distance telephone company alleging that it charged her more than the agreed rate per minute for her long distance calls. It alleges a national class claim under the federal Communications Act, 47 U.S.C. § 203. Section 2.2 is memorandum of law in opposition to a motion to dismiss. It argues that the filed rate doctrine does not prevent this suit since this claim relies on a filed rate, that primary jurisdiction does not require referral of the case to the Federal Communications Commission because it does not ordinarily hear consumer claims, and that the named plaintiff is a member of the alleged class. The motion to dismiss was denied in the case on which these materials were based.[77]

Chapter 3 Claim for Harassment and Unauthorized Practice of Law under the Fair Debt Collection Practices Act

Section 3.1 is a complaint under the Fair Debt Collection Practices Act alleging numerous types of debt collection activities violating that Act. Among the violations of the Act alleged were: phoning third parties; threatening arrest; threatening garnishment; creating a false sense of urgency that payment was required; not turning payments over to the creditor; engaging in the unauthorized practice by the collection agency by hiring an attorney to use court process in the name of the creditor without the creditor's authorization; and directing a racial slur at the consumer.

The pleadings in this chapter are based on a case where a collection agency continued to collect on a debt after its collection contract with the creditor had expired and where it did not forward $650 of the $750 collected. The court held that the collection agency and its owner-operator violated the FDCPA by engaging a lawyer to bring suit in the creditor's name after the authority from the creditor to collect the debt expired resulting in misrepresentation of its authority to sue since the suit filed violated the state law on unauthorized practice of law.[78] The court held that the

---

77 1 *Lipton v. MCI Worldcom, Inc.* 135 F. Supp. 182 (D.D.C. 2001).
78 *Id. See also*, NCLC, Fair Debt Collection §§ (4th ed. 2000 and Supp.)

collection was unauthorized and the consumer was entitled to recover the $650 paid and not forwarded as actual damages.[79]

The court also awarded $1000 statutory damages against each defendant based in part on prior violations of the FDCPA and $17,766 in attorney fees.

Section 3.2 are interrogatories and a request for production of documents. Section 3.3 is a request for admissions. Section 3.4 is a motion for partial summary judgment seeking judgment on two claims and statutory damages. Section 3.5 is a motion for the award of attorney fees. Section 3.6 is the affidavit of the consumer's attorney in support of the request for attorney fees. Section 3.7 is the rebuttal memorandum of law in support of the award of attorney fees.

Chapter 4 Fair Debt Collection Practices Act Demand Letter and Motion to Strike

Section 4.1 is a demand letter alleging several violations of the Fair Debt Collection Practices Act, 15 U.S.C. § 1692, in a dunning letter and offering to settle the consumer's FDCPA claim. Section 4.2 is a motion to strike defenses of the type commonly interposed in a FDCPA case. Section 4.3 is a draft order to strike defenses. The motion was partially successful.

Chapter 5 Automobile Fraud: Spot Delivery

The materials in this Chapter are from several spot delivery cases. A spot delivery is a practice in the used car industry where the consumer takes delivery of a used car on the spot and before title transfer and financing is finalized.[80] There are a number of variations on how the practice may develop from there. A common variation is for the seller to phone the consumer with the news that the financing for the car is more expensive than originally believed and requires signatures from the consumer on new, more expensive contract documents.

Section 5.1 is a complaint based on the seller never having or intending to deliver title, but requiring the consumer to return the car purchased previously on the spot without returning the consumer's downpayment (until the consumer enlisted the help of an attorney to obtain the downpayment). The complaint includes federal claims for violation of the Truth in Lending Act (including a processing

fee in the amount financed instead of the finance charge),[81] charging interest before extending credit,[82] failing to provide written disclosures[83] and not labeling estimates as such[84]), and violation of the Federal Odometer Act (failing to provide the odometer reading on the official title).[85] The state claims are conversion (of the consumer's trade-in, downpayment, and the title to the car purchased), deception violating the UDAP statute (misrepresenting credit was approved, misrepresenting that title was transferred to the consumer, misrepresenting that the seller held the title of the car it sold, failing to make state required odometer disclosures, requiring the consumer to use the seller to transfer title, charging an excessive title fee, not itemizing the charges on the buyer's order form, refusing to return the consumer's downpayment, advertising goods with the intent not to sell them), breach of express warranty of title, fraud, violating UCC § 507 (by using the false threat of arrest to seize the car from the consumer when there was no default), and conspiracy of the defendants to engage in all of the violations.

Section 5.2 is a spot delivery complaint where the seller demanded the return of the car sold and delivered unless the consumer provided a cosigner. The consumer had gone to the seller seeking an advertised new car for $8999 and ended up leaving with a used car with a cash price of $13,000. When the consumer returned to the seller to get new temporary license tags, she and her young son were surrounded and trapped by the seller's employees demanding that she leave the car with them. The complaint alleges negligence (not transferring title and making fear for her safety when she returned for temporary plates); conversion (later seizing the car sold in the middle of the night); deception and fraud (by not selling the advertised car to the consumer, by refusing to transfer title to the consumer, and by seizing the car, charging a processing fee for work it did not do); violation UCC § 9-504 by not providing notice of disposition of the seized car. Actual, statutory, and punitive damages and an award of attorney fees were sought in both complaints.

Section 5.3 contains discovery requests including requests for admissions, interrogatories, and requests for documents. Section 5.4 is a memorandum of law arguing that releases and confidentiality agreements that the seller had required the consumers to sign to get back part of their downpayments was illegal and void under state law. The memorandum also argues that the federal Odometer Act claim is sufficiently pled where it alleges that the required

79 Jones v. Vest, 2000 U.S. Dist. LEXIS 18413 at n.2 (E.D. Va. 2000).

80 *See* National Consumer Law Center, Unfair and Deceptive Acts and Practices (5th ed. 2001); National Consumer Law Center, Automobile Fraud 1.3.4 (1998); National Consumer Law Center, Truth in Lending § 4.4.1 (4th ed. 1999).

81 *See* National Consumer Law Center, Truth in Lending § 3.6 (4th ed. 1999).

82 *See Id.* § 4.6.4.

83 *See Id.* § 4.2.

84 *See Id.* § 4.4.2.

85 *See* National Consumer Law Center, Automobile Fraud § 3.6.5 (1998).

disclosure was made in the wrong place with the intent to defraud the buyer.

Chapter 6 Consumer Borrowers' Objections to High Rate Mortgage Lender's Chapter 11 Bankruptcy Plan

Chapter 6 is the objection of borrowers to the chapter 11 reorganization plan of a bankrupt high-rate lender. The objection argues first that the lender is a predatory lender that is subject to a variety claims from its borrowers. It then argues that the borrowers should be treated as secured creditors of the lender and that the reorganization plan is not fair and equitable. In the alternative, the objections argue that, if the borrowers' claims are treated as unsecured, the plan may not be approved because it provides less for the consumer borrowers than they would receive if the lender was liquidated. Finally, the attempt of the reorganization plan to cut off consumer borrowers' claims and defenses violates the Bankruptcy Code and consumer protection laws.

Chapter 7 Fair Debt Collection Practice Act Claim of a Confusing Debt Validation Notice

Section 7.1 is a class action complaint seeking statutory damages for California consumers for violations of the Fair Debt Collection Practice Act (FDCPA), declaratory relief pursuant to 28 U.S.C. §§ 2201 and 2202, and, on behalf of the People of the State of California, to enjoin the abusive collection practices and restitution and disgorgement of profits under California Business & Professions Code § 17200. The consumer won summary judgment on the claim that the 30-day validation notice required by the FDCPA was confusing regarding the person the consumer was required to contact to obtain verification of the debt,[86] and the case was subsequently settled. Section 7.2 contains interrogatories and section 7.3 a request for the production of documents. Section 7.4 is the consumer's motion for class certification and section 7.5 is the memorandum in support of the motion for class certification. Certification of two classes is sought base on the different statute of limitations for the federal claim (one year) and the state claim (four years). Section 7.6 is the consumer's memorandum opposing the debt collector's motion for summary judgment. Section 7.7 is the consumer's motion for partial summary judgment and section 7.8 is the memorandum in support of that motion.

Chapter 8 Fair Debt Collection Materials

Section 8.1 involves the collection of a claim for a medical bill paid by Medicaid. Section 8.1.1 is a motion for summary judgment. Section 8.1.2 is the consumer's statement of uncontested facts. Section 8.1.3 is a memo of law in support of summary judgment. It argues that a provider of health services is prohibited by federal law from billing a Medicaid patient for those services. Reporting such a debt as disputed to a credit reporting agency is alleged to violate the Fair Debt Collection Practices Act, the Fair Credit Reporting Act, and the state consumer protection statue. Damages were sought under the FDCPA and an injunction under the state claim.

Section 8.2 involves Fair Debt Collection Practices Act claims for seeking payment from an unobligated spouse, suing in a distant court, unauthorized practice of law as a result of a collection agency retaining, directing, and paying a lawyer, and communicating with a represented consumer. Section 8.2.1 is a motion for summary judgment. Section 8.2.2 is the consumer's statement of uncontested facts. Section 8.2.3 is a memo of law in support of summary judgment. The memo argues that suing the spouse and attaching her bank account in a county other than where she lived, by claiming she was liable for her husband's dental work when she never assumed that responsibility and reasonable value of the work had been paid by dental insurance, violated the FDCPA. The memo also argues that the collection agency engaged in the unauthorized practice of law interposing itself between the creditor and the attorney by retaining, directing, and paying a lawyer.

Section 8.3 is a memo of law on whether the court may exercise long arm jurisdiction over a debt collector even if it involves only a single purposeful contact to collect a debt. The memo of law points out that, where the issue of personal jurisdiction is raised by a motion to dismiss, the decision is based on the pleadings, which are construed broadly in favor of jurisdiction and that evidentiary support of jurisdiction is not required at that point. The memo then points out that the court have found only a single purposeful contact to collect a debt is sufficient to create personal jurisdiction over an out of state collector where the contact is tortious.

Section 8.4 argues on a number of basis that an award of court costs against an unsuccessful consumer in a FDCPA suit should be reduced or denied altogether. The memo argues that court costs cannot be awarded against an unsuccessful consumer under the FDCPA without proof that the suit was brought in bad faith and for the purpose of harassment. Alternatively the memo argues that the court may exercise its discretion to reduce the costs due from the plaintiff because of the disparity in the parties' resources and the extravagance of the defendant's defense. The memo argues that the plaintiff was permitted to proceed in forma pauperis and that costs should not be assessed for that reason. The memo argues that only necessary costs should be taxed to the other party. The memo argues for the reduction of specific items on various basis, for example,

---

86 *See* National Consumer Law Center, Fair Debt Collection § 5.7.2.3 (4th ed. 2000).

that a witness's airfare should be reduced to exclude a side trip.

Chapter 9 Fair Debt Collection Practices Act Briefs

Section 9.1 is an appellate brief from a case in which a debt collector sold two consumer accounts to another collector after the first collector's suits on the accounts had been dismissed with prejudice. The second collector settled the consumer's FDCPA claim against it, and the district court dismissed the FDCPA complaint against the first collector stating that the "sale of accounts by" the first collector "does not constitute a violation of the Fair Debt Collection Practices Act." The brief argues that the complaint states a FDCPA claim by alleging that the first collector was attempting to collect a debt that was not owed by selling to the second collector.

Section 9.2 is an appellate brief from *Picht v. Hawks*,[87] a FDCPA case in which the consumer prevailed on the claim that the check collection agency's prejudgment garnishment of the consumer's checking account was a threat of unlawful collection action violating 15 U.S.C. § 1692e(5) because it claimed the maximum civil penalty before there was any judicial determination that it was entitled to any penalty. The brief also successfully argued that the FDCPA bona fide error defense was not available; it was waived. The bone fide error defense was not available for mistakes of law and the defendant failed to introduce evidence supporting the defense. Finally, the brief discusses the strict liability approach of most FDCPA provisions and the corresponding lack of an intent requirement to establish liability.

Section 9.3 and 9.4 are the consumer's memorandum of law opposing a debt collection agency's motion for summary judgment. The collection agency argued that it was exempt from the FDCPA because it was collecting on dishonored checks for the district attorney and fell within the exemption for government agencies and officials in 15 U.S.C. § 1692a(6)(C). The collector also argued that the protections of the FDCPA and a similar state statute should not extend to bad check writers who could be involved in fraudulent activities. These are not meritorious arguments.[88] This type of collection conduct was recently described in NCLC REPORTS.[89]

Chapter 10 National Bank Not Entitled to Preempt State Second Mortgage Laws Where the Bank's Assignor Lacked Preemption Rights

Section 10.1 is an amicus brief arguing that a national bank cannot assert federal preemption of a state second mortgage statute because the preemption was not available to the originator of the mortgage. The National Bank Act and other federal laws authorize certain lenders to lend at rates in excess of those permitted by state law.[90] This brief argues that the preemption insulation from state usury laws applies when a federally protected lender originates the mortgage but not when the lender purchases the mortgage from a originating lender which was subject to state usury laws.

Chapter 11 Suit for Damages From Mortgage Servicer's Practices

Section 11.1 is an amended complaint against a mortgage originator and the purchasers of its mortgages and successors to its mortgage originating and servicing business. The claims asserted in the Amended Complaint are based on five alleged practices:

First, the homeowners allege that the mortgage originator and owners improperly charged loan advances to the homeowners' outstanding balances where the accounts were not actually in arrears. According to the homeowners, the mortgages assessed periodic bill charges that were too low to cover homeowners' property taxes, insurance, water or sewage charges. They then added loan advances to homeowners' outstanding balances to cover the shortfall, without notice.

Second, the homeowners allege that the mortgage holders improperly placed into escrow periodic bill payments belonging to mortgagors whose mortgages required use of the capitalization method for applying the periodic bill payments. According to the homeowners, the homeowners were entitled to the capitalization method applying periodic bill payments, under which they receive the effect of lowering the interest which accrued annually on the unpaid balance.

Third, the homeowners allege that the mortgage holders improperly charged interest on loan advances from the first of each month for loan advances made later in the month.

Fourth, the homeowners allege that the mortgage holders improperly delayed payment until March of 1996 on escrow interest that accrued during 1995 that they were entitled to receive by year end 1995.

Fifth, the homeowners allege that the mortgage holders improperly sent annual statements on or after April 8, 1987

---

87   236 F.3d 446 (8th Cir. 2001).

88   *See* National Consumer Law Center, Fair Debt Collection §§ 4.3.3, 4.4.2.1, H.1.2.2.4 (4th ed. 2000).

89   *See* "Consumer Challenges Collection Agency's Operation of Bad Check Diversion Program," 19 NCLC REPORTS, Debt Collection and Repossessions Ed. 5 (Sept/Oct. 2000).

90   *See* National Consumer Law Center, The Cost of Credit Ch. 3 (2d ed. 2000).

that implied that a prior mortgage owner was the current mortgage owner. The homeowners allege that the new mortgage owner's acquisition of mortgages was deceptively concealed from homeowners.

The practices were alleged to involve breach of contract, unfair and deceptive acts and practices, tortious interference with contract, and breach of fiduciary duty.

One of the very interesting opinions issued by the court in the case on which the pleadings in this chapter are based was an opinion denying defendants' motion to dismiss and sustaining the homeowners' claims that a document *under seal* was subject to a 20 year statute of limitations in Pennsylvania. This case, although it only included 144 homeowners, was the subject of very, very extensive litigation.

Section 11.2 is the homeowners' interrogatories to the mortgage servicer about its practices and employees involved and section 11.3 are interrogatories designed to obtain information needed for certification of the class action. Sections 11.4 and 11.5 are motions to produce documents directed to the mortgage servicer and the mortgage owner.

Section 11.6 is the homeowner's memorandum of law opposing the motion to dismiss filed by the mortgage servicer. The memorandum argues that the complaint states a claim, that the claims were not released in a prior class action against the servicer, and that the claims are not time barred because they were subject to state 20 year limitation period for documents under seal. The motion to dismiss was denied. [91]

Section 11.7 is the homeowner's memorandum of law opposing the motion to dismiss filed by the transferee of the ownership of the mortgage. The memorandum argues that the transferee was not a government instrumentality entitled to governmental immunity, had engaged in unfair and deceptive acts and practices violating state law, and had violated its obligations as a trustee under the mortgage. This motion to dismiss was granted.[92]

Finally, the parties' joint settlement motion (§11.8) with attached settlement agreement (§11.9), class notice (§11.10), and proposed order (11.11) are included in the materials. The proposed settlement established a settlement fund of $235,000 and provided that it would be distributed pro rata to the class members after deducting attorney fees of 30%, costs up to $7000, costs of distribution, and a $2500 incentive payment to the named plaintiffs. The settlement was pending before the court at press time.

Chapter 12 Arbitration Clauses in Car Contracts Attacked

Section 12.1 is an appellate brief seeking reversal of a trial court decision compelling arbitration in automobile sale case where the dealer claimed that the initial financing sought was not available and tried to switch the consumer to a more expensive lease of the car that had been taken by the consumer.[93] The core arguments in the brief are that the arbitration clauses were in contract forms that did not become binding or were invalid and that, if the contracts did become enforceable, that the arbitration clauses were unconscionable.[94] The brief argues that the validity of the arbitration clause should be determined by the courts. The brief argues that the original financing in the case was rescinded by the seller and that the subsequent agreement to lease which was offered by the seller was nullity by its own terms when it was signed.

Section 12.2 is a reply brief in the same case. The brief makes three basic arguments. First, it argues that the arbitration clause was not in a binding contract. Second, it argues that the arbitration clause was void as a nullity as the lease contract form in which it was contained was not supported by consideration. Third, the brief argues that arbitration clause was substantively and procedurally unconscionable.

Chapter 13 Obtaining Damages for Bank's Wrongful Set-off of Its Customer's Social Security Deposits

Section 13.1 is a complaint by a depositor against her bank which used its banker's self-help right of set-off to take social security and federal civil service retirement benefits from a depositor's account to pay a balance owed on a loan to the bank. The complaint alleges that taking social security and federal civil service retirement benefits violates those laws which prohibit creditors from attaching or using legal process to seize those types of funds.[95] The complaint also alleges that the seizure of the exempt funds also violates the state unfair and deceptive acts and practices (UDAP) statute entitling the consumer to treble damages and attorney fees

---

91 *See [Plaintiff] v. Standard Mortgage Corp.*, 1999 U.S. Dist. LEXIS 15787 (W.D. Pa. 1999).

92 *See [Plaintiff] v. Standard Mortgage Corp.*, 129 F. Supp. 2d 793 (W.D. Pa. 2000) (Defendant Freddie Mac dismissed as not liable for acts of its mortgage servicers).

93 *See* National Consumer Law Center, Unfair and Deceptive Acts and Practices (5th ed. 2001).

94 *See* National Consumer Law Center, Unfair and Deceptive Acts and Practices § 7.7 (5th ed. 2001).

95 42 U.S.C. § 407(a) ("[N]one of the moneys paid or payable or rights existing under this subchapter shall be subject to execution, levy, attachment, garnishment, or other legal process. . . ."); 5 U.S.C. § 8346(a) ("The money mentioned in this subchapter is not . . . subject to execution, levy, attachment, garnishment, or other legal process, except as otherwise may be provided by Federal laws."). *See* NCLC, Fair Debt Collection § 12.6.7 (4th ed. 2000)

as well as return of the funds seized.[96]

Section 13.2 is the motion for summary judgment, section 13.3 is the memorandum in support of summary judgment and section 13.4 is the response to the bank's argument that its self-help remedy of a banker's set-off or banker's lien is not legal process barred to creditors by the two federal exemption statutes. Section 13.5 is the appellate reply brief covering the same arguments more comprehensively.

Chapter 14 An Offer of Judgment to Named Plaintiff May Not Be Used to Moot Fair Debt Collection Practices Act Class Action

This chapter contains a memorandum opposing a debt collector's motion for summary judgment. The memorandum argues that a Rule 68 offer of judgment made to the named plaintiff does not moot the class action.

Chapter 15 Brief Requesting Review of the Adequacy of the Capitalization of Restructured Insurer of Environmental Hazards

The brief in this case is an amicus brief seeking court review of the adequacy of the capitalization of the restructuring of the corporations insuring of environmental hazards. The insurer created a new insurance company that was to assume the liabilities under a group of insurance policies and engage in no new other insurance business. Amicus asserted that the state insurance departments that approved this restructuring did not address the adequacy of the capitalization of the new insurer, that the capitalization was substantial but finite and inadequate, and sought court determination of the continuing liability of the original insurer. The insurer argued that the state agencies' approval of the restructuring was approval of its future immunity from claims and that the insureds had no claim under the state consumer protection statue without alleging an injury (that would not occur until the new insurer proved to be insolvent). The brief also addresses the importance of insurance company solvency, the unfairness standard under the California consumer protection act, and standing issues.

Chapter 16 Suppression of Credit Life Insurance Coverage from Heirs of Insured

Section 16.1 is a complaint by the estate of a car purchaser who had purchased credit disability and life insurance which would pay off the balance on the retail installment purchase of a car if he became disabled or died. Rather than canceling the debt when notified that the consumer was sick and, later, when he died, the financer represented that they would repossess the car if the balance was not paid and the car was repossessed. The complaint alleges violations of the UCC, conversion, breach of obligation of good faith, UDAP claims, and constructive fraud. It seeks UCC damages, actual and punitive damages. Section 16.2 are interrogatories and requests for production of documents.

Consumer Law Pleadings Number Eight (2002)

Chapter 1 Long Distance Telephone Company's Arbitration Clause is Unconscionable

This chapter contains pleadings and briefs from a class action suit against a long distance telephone company for attempting to supplant its customers' class action remedies with a mandatory arbitration clause that would effectively immunize the phone company from liability for most types of wrongs that it might commit, such as charging rates in excess of its agreement or slamming.[97] The complaint alleges that the arbitration clause was a stuffer in a monthly bill with little to call attention to its waiver of fundamental remedies. The complaint (§1.1), which alleges that the arbitration clause was unconscionable and violated the California Consumer Legal Remedies Act and Unfair Competition Law, was the basis for the favorable trial decision in *[Plaintiff] v. AT&T.*[98] That decision found AT&T's arbitration clause to be unconscionable and violative of the California consumer protection statutes. The court found that the notice was mailed and presented in a manner calculated to minimize attention to it. It found that long distance consumers did not have a significant choice of long distance carriers offering services without mandatory arbitration clauses. The clause also prohibited the seeking of class relief in arbitration which effectively eliminated most relief for potential consumer claims since the costs of arbitration was so high and few consumers had large claims unless they were aggregated in a class action. AT&T's adhesion contract also imposed a two-year statute of limitations on claim against it violating the policy of the consumer protection statutes of

---

96 In the case on which this complaint is based, the trial court granted the consumer summary judgment on the violation of the two federal exemption statutes as well as the breach of contract claim but denied the state UDAP claim. The bank appealed, and the trial court's decision on the federal claims was upheld but the decision on the contract claim was reversed as the claim had not been pursued by the consumer in her motion for summary judgment. See *[Plaintiff] v. First American Credit Union*, 151 F.3d 1289 (10th Cir. 1998).

97 See National Consumer Law Center, Access to Utility Services § 2.6 (2d ed. 2001).
98 182 F. Supp. 2d 902; 2002 U.S. Dist. LEXIS 749 (N.D. Cal. 2002).

allowing claims for three years. AT&T's adhesion contract also imposed a confidentiality obligation regarding the arbitration proceeding which was found to be unconscionable. AT&T's attempt to avoid any liability for punitive, reliance, consequential, and special damages was illegal as such a clause was prohibited by a general California statute prohibiting such clauses in contracts.[99]

Section 1.2 contains Plaintiffs' Memorandum of Points and Authorities in Support of Motion for Preliminary Injunction and section 1.2.1 is Plaintiffs' Reply Brief in Support of Motion for Preliminary Injunction.

Section 1.3 is Plaintiffs' Amended Trial Brief which argues that the long distance carrier's adhesion contract violates consumer protection laws and was unconscionable. It also argues that those laws were not preempted by the Federal Communication Act or the Federal Arbitration Act.

Section 1.4 is the Plaintiffs' Post-Trial Brief covering a variety of issues including the validity of AT&T choice of N.Y. law in the adhesion contract in dispute, FCC barring of state suits against long distance carriers, the inadequacy of FCC relief for aggrieved consumers, and the validity of the Plaintiffs' expert's consumer survey. Section 1.4.1 is the affidavit of Plaintiffs' counsel in support of the Post-Trial Brief, providing testimony supporting the validity of the survey and showing the inadequacy of FCC proceedings for consumers. Section 1.4.2 is Plaintiffs' Post-Trial Brief Reply which includes arguments that the Federal Communications Act does not preempt state consumer protection laws.

Section 1.5 is a [Proposed] Final Judgment declaring certain clauses of the adhesion contract illegal and void, enjoining the enforcement of those provisions, and awarding costs and attorney fees. Section 1.5.1 is Plaintiffs' Brief in Response to Defedant's Proposed Form of Permanent Injunction which argues that notice of the trial court's injunction should be given to the defendant's 7 million California customers so that their rights are restored and that the defendant will not suffer irreparable harm if that notice is sent pending appellate court review.

Chapter 2 Seizure of Exempt Funds in Bank Account

This Chapter includes materials from a case where a bank took all of the exempt funds of a Supplemental Security Income (SSI)[100] recipient as well as her daughter's SSI to satisfy the bank's claim of set off. The majority of courts hold that a banker's right of setoff is "other legal process" to which the social security and SSI exemptions apply so that those funds may not be frozen or setoff.[101] The bank's claim arose from a forged check that the consumer cashed at the bank for the forger without knowing about the forgery. Included in this chapter are the demand letter, § 2.1, sent by the consumer's

attorney in the case, the complaint, § 2.2, and memorandum of law in support of summary judgment, §2.3.

Chapter 3 Electric Company Overcharges in a Deregulated Market

This chapter contains a class action complaint and settlement documents that arose out of excessive charges for residential electricity service.[102] The complaint in section 3.1 alleges that the defendant electric companies charged higher rates of customers who moved residences within the service area of the electric utility company than the "standard offer rate" to which the companies agreed when the companies were "deregulated" in 1997. The complaint alleges that the utilities' misconduct was a breach of contract, unjust enrichment, and unfair and deceptive practices. The complaint sought damages, restitution, a declaratory judgment, injunctive relief, and attorney fees.

This Chapter also includes Paintiff's Assented to Motion for Preliminary Approval of Settlement Agreement (§ 3.2), Plaintiff's Memorandum In Support of Motion for Preliminary Approval of Settlement Agreement (§3.3), Stipulation and Agreement of Compromise and Settlement (§ 3.4), Order and Final Judgment (§ 3.5), Affidavit of Counsel in Support of Motion for Preliminary Approval of Settlement Agreement (§3.6), Order Certifying Class for Settlement (§ 3.7), and Notice of Proposed Class Action Settlement (§ 3.8).

Chapter 4 Defending Hospital Collection Cases

This chapter is unusual for this book as it is written by Mr. Alop as a practice guide designed to acquaint legal services attorneys with defenses and strategies available to defendants who have been sued in Illinois by hospitals for unpaid bills. Avenues of defense are discussed, pleadings and discovery materials are provided, and ideas for the trial of these cases are included. These materials are updated and expanded from the materials in Consumer Law Pleadings Number 2 Chapter 15 and Consumer Law Pleadings Number 6 Chapter 8.

Chapter 5 Failure to Disclose that a Trade-in was Given in a Car Lease

Section 5.1 is a complaint alleging violations of the federal Truth in Leasing Act,[103] the Tennessee Consumer Protection Act (UDAP), misrepresentation, and unconscio-

---

99 Cal. Civ . Code § 1668.

100 *See* National Consumer Law Center, Surviving Debt 23 (2002).

101 *See* NCLC, Fair Debt Collection § 12.6.7 (4th ed. 2000).

102 *See* generally National Consumer Law Center, Access to Utility Service § 1.4 (2d ed. 2001).

103 *See* National Consumer Law Center, Truth In Lending Ch. 9 (4th ed. 1999).

nability.[104] The complaint alleges that instead of identifying the trade-in and disclosing its value the defendant car dealer filled in the applicable box as "NA," usually used to indicate "not applicable" and that this violated the requirements of the Truth in Leasing Act[105] as well as being deceptive, unconscionable and misrepresenting what transpired. The complaint also alleges that the consumer was told that the selling price of the leased car was less than that used to calculate the lease and that the defendant failed to disclose the consumer's cash paid at signing the lease.

Section 5.2 is the consumer's Statement of Undisputed Material Facts In Support of Summary Judgment, Section 5.2.1 is the consumer's Memorandum of Law in Support of Summary Judgment, and Section 5.2.2 is the consumer's Memorandum of Law in Opposition to Defendant's Motion for Summary Judgment.

Chapter 6 Suit for the Combustion of a Recalled Car

This chapter contains a complaint (§ 6.1) and interrogatories (§6.2) from a case filed where the consumer's car burned because of a defect which had been the subject of a recall, although the consumer did not become aware of the recall until after the fire. The Mazda RX-7 automobile had a defective fuel line that leaked gasoline onto the hot engine block causing fires. The consumer alleged numerous causes of action including violation of the Tennessee UDAP statute,[106] negligence,[107] breach of warranty,[108] and strict liability in tort.[109]

Chapter 7 New Car Lemon Suit

This chapter contains items from a suit involving a new car that was alleged to be a lemon. Section 7.1 is a complaint against the manufacturer alleging that the doors were misaligned on the new car and alleging claims under the Tennessee Lemon Law for failing to remedy the defect despite numerous attempts.[110] Section 7.2 is a Request for Production of Documents and section 7.3 are Interrogatories.

Chapter 8 Attack on Contract Clause Choo Distant Forum and Arguing Tru Lending Statute of Limitations 1 by Soldiers' and Sailors' Relief Act

Section 8.1 is a Memorandum of Law in Opposition to a Motion to Dismiss. The Memorandum of Law argues that the consumer's Truth in Lending claim was not time barred because the Consumer was engaged in active military duty tolling the Truth in Lending statute of limitations.[111] It further argues that the choice of law clause in the car sales contract was not valid as if it was an unfair trade practice for it to select a distant forum for litigation related to the sale.[112] The memorandum goes on to argue that the Truth in Lending claim should not be dismissed because it was not a compulsory counterclaim to a collection action filed by the car financer in the distant forum.[113] Finally the memorandum's Law argues that the abstention doctrine does not apply. Section 8.2 is a Supplemental Memorandum of Law arguing that a U.S. Supreme Court case upholding a sales contract clause selecting distant forum[114] was not controlling. Section 8.3 is a Memorandum of Law In Support of Motion to Dismiss a similar but different collection case that was filed in a distant forum by the car financer pursuant to the forum selection clause in the sales contract.

Chapter 9 No Federal Court Jurisdiction Over Car Dealer's Counterclaims in Consumer's Truth in Lending Suit

Section 9.1 is a motion to dismiss the creditor's counterclaims and section 9.2 is a memorandum of law in support of the motion. The consumer filed a Truth in Lending action against a car dealer, and the car dealer responded with three state law counterclaims, for example alleging the consumer misrepresented the consumer's trade in as a six cylinder engine when it was only four. The consumer moved to dismiss the counterclaims arguing that the court lacked supplemental jurisdiction over the counterclaims because they did not involve the same facts, evidence, law or logical relationship.[115]

---

104 *See* generally, National Consumer Law Center, Unfair and Deceptive Acts and Practices (5th ed. 2001).

105 *See* National Consumer Law Center, Truth In Lending § 9.3.6.2 (4th ed. 1999).

106 *See* National Consumer Law Center, Unfair and Deceptive Acts and Practices § 5.4.7.10 (5th ed. 2001).

107 *See* National Consumer Law Center, Consumer Warranty Law § 12.4. (2d ed. 2001).

108 *See* National Consumer Law Center, Consumer Warranty Law Ch. 3.4 (2d ed. 2001)

109 *See* National Consumer Law Center, Consumer Warranty Law § 12.1 (2d ed. 2001).

110 *See* National Consumer Law Center, Consumer Warranty Law § 13.2 (2d ed. 2001).

111 *See* National Consumer Law Center, Fair Debt Collection § 9.10 (4th ed. 2000)

112 *See* National Consumer Law Center, Unfair and Deceptive Acts and Practices § 5.1.4 (5th ed. 2001); National Consumer Law Center, Fair Debt Collection §§ 5.9, 10.6.3, 11.2.4.3 (4th ed. 2000)

113 *See* National Consumer Law Center. Truth In Lending § 7.5.3.2 (4th ed. 1999).

114 Carnival Cruise Lines, Inc. v. Shute, 499 U.S. 585 (1991).

115 *See* National Consumer Law Center. Truth In Lending § 7.5.3.2 (4th ed. 1999).

Chapter 10　Expert Witness Testimony on Fair Debt Collection Practices Act Damages

Section 10.1 is Mr. Newburger's Expert Report regarding the intentionality of the violations of the Fair Debt Collection Practices Act alleged in a FDCPA suit. Intentionality is one of the criteria for determining FDCPA statutory damages.[116] Section 10.2 lists the expert's qualifications. Section 10.3 is Plaintiff's Memorandum Of Law Contra Defendant's Motion In Limine To Preclude Expert Report. Section 10.4 Plaintiff's Answer to Defendant's Motion In Limine To Preclude Expert Report and Opinions. Section 10.5 is a daft order denying the motion to preclude the consumer's expert's testimony. The motion to preclude was denied in the case in which these documents were submitted.[117]

Chapter 11　Truth in Lending Rescission for HOEPA Violations Argued to be Not Subject to Arbitration.

Section 11.1 is a complaint seeking to enforce two consumers' exercise of their Truth in Lending (TIL) rescission rights.[118] The complaint alleges that the creditor failed to provide the required number of rescission notices and HOEPA notices. The compliant seeks a declaration that the transaction was rescinded, an injunction against foreclosure, damages and attorney fees.

Section 11.2 is Plaintiff's Objections to Magistrate's Report and Recommendations. The Magistrate recommended that the Defendant's motion to compel arbitration and dismiss the action be granted. The consumer argued that the TIL rescission had voided the arbitration clause and the complaint should not be dismissed. It should be noted that the courts are split on this issue.[119]

Chapter 12　Suit for Continuing to Dun and Harass Consumer After the Creditor's Claims Had Been Litigated and Settled

This chapter contains an Answer and Counterclaim (§12.1) and a Complaint (§ 12.2) which arose out of the failure of a bank and its collection law firm to stop collecting on a claim after their claim had been formally settled with an elderly consumer. The consumer had sought to buy an inexpensive pickup truck and instead was leased the truck at more than $10,000 more than it should have cost. The consumer sued the bank and car dealer, and the bank counterclaimed for the debt. That case was settled with payment to the consumer and dismissal of the claims with prejudice. Subsequently, the bank and it collection law firm continued to dun the consumer and, despite their attention being repeatedly called to the settlement, the bank filed a second collection suit against the consumer. In § 12.1 the consumer raised the defense of res judicata, among others, and counterclaimed alleging breach of the settlement agreement, negligence for furnishing inaccurate information to credit reporting agencies,[120] defamation,[121] invasion of privacy,[122] emotional distress,[123] and violation of the Fair Credit Reporting Act by obtaining credit reports without a legitimate business need.[124] Section 12.2 is a federal court complaint against the collection lawyers that alleges that they violated the Fair Debt Collection Practices Act (by not ceasing collections after request[125] and suing without a legal basis[126]), the Ohio Sales Practices Act,[127] Ohio Civil Procedure Rule 11, intentional infliction of emotional distress,[128] and invasion of privacy.[129]

Chapter 13　Abusive Debt Collection Complaint

This chapter contains a complaint against a finance company for waging a vicious campaign of harassment against the daughter of the borrower. The complaint alleges claims for violations of the California Fair Debt Collection Practices Act,[130] intentional and negligent infliction of emotional distress,[131] state credit reporting act violations,[132] and vio-

---

116　*See* National Consumer Law Center, Fair Debt Collection § 6.4.3 (4th ed. 2000).
117　Tenuto v. Transworld Systems, Inc., 2000 U.S. Dist. LEXIS 17566 (E.D. Pa. 2000).
118　*See* National Consumer Law Center, Truth In Lending Ch. 6 (4th ed. 1999).
119　*See* Livingston v. Associates Fin., Inc., 2001 U.S. Dist. Lexis 8678 (N.D. Ill. 2001); National Consumer Law Center, Consumer Arbitration Agreements § 4.5.3 (2001).
120　*See* National Consumer Law Center, Fair Credit Reporting Act Ch. 2a (2001 Supp).
121　*See* National Consumer Law Center, Fair Debt Collection § 10.5 (4th ed. 2000).
122　*See* National Consumer Law Center, Fair Debt Collection § 10.3.2 (4th ed. 2000).
123　*See* National Consumer Law Center, Fair Debt Collection § 10.2 (4th ed. 2000).
124　*See* National Consumer Law Center, Fair Credit Reporting Act Ch. 4 (2001 Supp).
125　*See* National Consumer Law Center, Fair Debt Collection § 5.3.8 (4th ed. 2000).
126　*See* National Consumer Law Center, Fair Debt Collection § 5.5.3 (4th ed. 2000).
127　*See* National Consumer Law Center, Unfair and Deceptive Acts and Practices (5th ed. 2001).
128　*See* National Consumer Law Center, Fair Debt Collection § 10.2 (4th ed. 2000).
129　*See* National Consumer Law Center, Fair Debt Collection § 10.3.2 (4th ed. 2000).
130　*See* National Consumer Law Center, Fair Debt Collection § 11.2 (4th ed. 2000).
131　*See* National Consumer Law Center, Fair Debt Collection § 10.2 (4th ed. 2000).
132　*See* National Consumer Law Center, Fair Credit Reporting Act § 12.4 (4th ed. 1998).

lations of California's consumer protection statutes.[133]

Chapter 14 Motion to Compel Discovery in Face of Unsupported Claims of Confidentiality of Proprietary Information

Section 14.1 is a motion to compel defendant's response to interrogatories and requests to produce. Section 14.2 is a memorandum of law in support of the motion to compel that argues that the consumer is entitled to all discovery that will lead to relevant evidence, that it is the defendant's burden to persuade the court that the information sought is outside the scope of permissible discovery, that the consumer is entitled to know the amount paid by the collector for the consumer's debt, that the defendant's operating manuals are of a type routinely provided in discovery, and that the defendant's agreements with credit reporting agencies may establish misrepresentation by the defendant. Section 14.3 argues that the price paid for the debt is part of an inquiry of whether the purchase of the consumer's debt was a sham, that the price of distressed debts are published regularly on the internet and cannot be considered confidential, operating manuals should not be considered confidential or a trade secret. The motion to compel was granted in the case in which these documents were submitted.[134]

Chapter 15 Fair Debt Collection Practices Act Pleadings for Collection of Debt Which Expired by the Passage of Time

This chapter contains a variety of pleadings in a case seeking to enjoin and collect damages against the practice of attempting to collect a timed barred debt where the applicable Wisconsin law adopts the minority states' rule that the expiration of the statute of limitations eliminated the debt, rather than the majority rule simply barring the remedy of suit of debts where the statute of limitations has run and considering the debt still owed. Therefore, the collector's dunning letter asserting the debt was owed was deceptive.[135] Section 15.1 is a complaint for class damages, declaratory and injunctive relief and attorney fees. Section 15.2 is a supplemental complaint based on the collector sending the consumer an additional dunning letter after the initial com-

plaint was filed. The supplemental brief alleges the same violations as the original complaint as well as the FDCPA violation of contacting a consumer known to be represented by counsel.[136]

Section 15.3 is a notice of deposition. Section 15.4 is a memorandum in support of a motion to compel Rule 26(a) Disclosures. The memorandum of law in support of certifying a Wisconsin class of consumers for damages, injunctive and declaratory relief is in § 15.5. Sections 15.6 and 15.7 are memorandum of law in support of summary judgment for the consumer. Section 15.8 is a memorandum of law in support of the consumer's motion for a permanent injunction. Section 15.9 is the consumer's memorandum in support of attorney fees.

Chapter 16 Car Dealers' Truth in Lending Disclosures Must Be Given to the Consumer Before the Contract is Signed

This chapter contains an appellate brief arguing that the car dealer did not provide Truth in Lending disclosures until the consumer signed the contract and was bound whereas the Truth in Lending Act requires disclosures to be made prior to consummation. The dealer argued that the contract was not consummated until a creditor to finance the contract accepted the contract. The court in which the brief was submitted affirmed the lower court holding that the contract by its plain terms was binding on the consumer and therefore consummated when it was signed by the consumer.[137]

Chapter 17 Banker's Setoff of Social Security Funds in Checking Accounts Violates Exemption in Social Security Act

The Ninth Circuit recently held that a bank's taking of social security funds to pay for an overdraft and overdraft charges pursuant to a right of setoff provision in the deposit account agreement violated the 42 U.S.C. § 407(b) prohibition of taking social security funds pursuant to "legal process." The bank has requested the Ninth Circuit to reconsider the decision. NCLC and AARP filed an amicus brief supporting the decision and opposing rehearing which is included in this chapter.[138]

---

133 *See* National Consumer Law Center, Unfair and Deceptive Acts and Practices § 5.1.1 (5th ed. 2001).

134 [Plaintiff] v. Risk Management Alternatives, Inc., 2002 U.S. Dist. Lexis 8821 (D. Ct. 2002).

135 *See* National Consumer Law Center, Fair Debt Collection § 5.5.1.8.3, 5.6.2, 10.6.3 (4th ed. 2000) (In the majority rule states, the threat of suit on a time barred debt is deceptive, but many courts have held that the representation that the debt is owed is not deceptive.).

---

136 *Id.* at § 5.3.3,

137 [Plaintiff-Appellee] v.Palm SpringsMotors, Inc, 2001 U.S. Dist. LEXIS 13756 (C.D. Cal. 2001), *aff'd.* 11046 (9th Cir. 2002).

138 *See* also National Consumer Law Center, Consumer Law Pleadings on CD-Rom Ch. 2 (2002) (pleadings involving the same issue in a different case); National Consumer Law Center, Truth In Lending § 5.14 (4th ed. 1999) (bank may not offset deposit account to pay credit card).

The bank made a number of arguments that were rejected on appeal. It argued that the self help remedy of banker's setoff was not "legal process" and was outside the protections of the exemption. The court followed a number of decisions which had rejected this narrow approach to the exemption and looked to its purpose of protecting the funds from all creditors for the purchase of necessities. The court refused to infer consumer consent to the setoff from the boilerplate the consumer signed when opening the account.

The court also found that one of the consumers' three state law claims based on the illegal offset was preempted by banking regulations. And, a concurring opinion expressed the concern that the check overdraft protection may be lost by social security recipients as a result of the enforcement of the exemption-a dubious perceived tradeoff.

The amicus brief in this chapter makes a number of arguments. The bank's overdraft accounts were exorbitantly expensive with devastating consequences for Social Security recipients. The bank's seizure of the full amount of the overdraft was exactly the type of process Congress intended to prohibit in 42 U.S.C. § 407(a). The brief of the United States adopts a position not contained in any Social Security regulation or policy document and was entitled to no deference. The position of the Office of Thrift Supervision was contrary to their previous pronouncements and therefore was entitled to no deference.

Chapter 18 Importance of Cy Pres Distribution to Obtaining Class Action Relief

Chapter 18 contains an amicus curiae brief of the National Consumer Law Center explaining how a giving the undistributed residual of a class action recovery to a local legal services program may be the use of those funds which best accomplishes the purposes of the consumer protection law being enforced.

Chapter 19 FDCPA, UDAP, and Tort Claims for a Collection Agency's Seeking Attorney Fees and Engaging in Unauthorized Practice of Law

Section 19.1 is a class complaint against a collection agency alleging both federal and state claims based on the collection agency filing collection complaints in state court and obtaining judgment which included an award of collection attorney fees when no attorney was significantly involved in filing the complaint or obtaining the judgment. The complaint alleges that these acts were the unauthorized practice of law under state law[139] and misrepresented the

involvement of an attorney.[140] The complaint alleges that the conduct violated the FDCPA and the state consumer protection (UDAP) statute,[141] and stated claims for infliction of mental distress,[142] fraud,[143] and abuse of process.[144]

Section 19.2 is a motion for certification of the class action accompanied by an exhibit indicating the large number of attorney fee awards obtained by the collection agency and the affidavit of the named plaintiffs.

Chapter 20 Suit for Outrageous Debt Collection Practices

Section 20.1 is an individual complaint for debt collection harassment grounded in the torts of invasion of privacy[145] and intentional infliction of mental distress.[146] It seeks punitive, as well as actual, damages. Section 20.2 contains additional claims that may apply in particular debtor harassment cases. Those claims include negligent supervision (may be necessary for punitive damages against the employer); extortion by using threats of criminal prosecution; theft, trover and conversion, and forgery for the unauthorized use of the consumer's bank account; defamation and libel. Section 20.3 and 20.4 are interrogatories and a motion to produce directed to the debt collector.

Chapter 21 FTC Holder Rule Preserves Consumer Claims That Are Less Than Rescission

This chapter contains a state court brief arguing that the Federal Trade Commission's Trade Regulation Rule Concerning Preservation of Consumers' Claims and Defenses authorizes consumers with limited damages from seller misconduct to enforce their rights under the FTC's rule in lawsuits filed against the holders of their credit contracts.[147] The holder of the note argued that only consumers whose damages warrant rescission may file lawsuits to assert their rights under the FTC rule; consumers with limited damages

---

139 *See* National Consumer Law Center, Fair Debt Collection §§ 5.5.7.3, 5.6.2, 11.4, 11.6 (4thed. 2000).

140 *See* National Consumer Law Center, Fair Debt Collection § 5.5.5 (4th ed. 2000).

141 *See* National Consumer Law Center, Fair Debt Collection § 11.3 (4th ed. 2000), National Consumer Law Center, Unfair and Deceptive Acts and Practices §§ 2.2.2, 5.1.1 (5th ed. 2001).

142 National Consumer Law Center, Fair Debt Collection § 10.2 (4th ed. 2000).

143 National Consumer Law Center, Unfair and Deceptive Acts and Practices §§ 4.2.3.1, 9.6.3 (5th ed. 2001).

144 National Consumer Law Center, Fair Debt Collection § 10.6 (4th ed. 2000).

145 National Consumer Law Center, Fair Debt Collection § 10.3 (4th ed. 2000).

146 National Consumer Law Center, Fair Debt Collection § 10.2 (4th ed. 2000).

147 *See* National Consumer Law Center, Unfair and Deceptive Acts and Practices § 6.6 (5th ed. 2001).

cannot assert their rights unless sued by the holders of their credit contracts. The brief argues that such a drastic limit on affirmative actions contravenes the FTC official commentary in which the FTC refused to limit consumers to a defensive position.

Chapter 22 Foreclosure Defense

Section 22.1 is an Answer, Counterclaim, and Third Party Complaint filed in response to a foreclosure action on a high rate first mortgage against a residential homeowner. The homeowner asserted that she was entitled to rescind the mortgage and obtain actual and punitive damages as a result of Truth in Lending,[148] Home Owner and Equity Protection Act,[149] consumer fraud,[150] and Real Estate Settlement Procedures Act[151] violations, breach of fiduciary duty,[152] and unclean hands. Among other allegations the complaint states that the consumer was given two different Truth in Lending disclosure statements on the same day, both marked "final." The complaint also alleged that the mortgage broker agreement provided that the broker fee was owed even if the consumer decided not to go ahead with the loan, contradicting and misrepresenting her Truth in Lending rescission right.[153]

Section 22.2 is the consumer's memorandum of law arguing that the court should deny the mortgage servicer's motion to to dismiss her counterclaim and affirmative defenses. Section 22.3 is the consumer's motion to dismiss the complaint because the mortgage servicer who brought the complaint was not the assignee or purchaser of the mortgage and therefore was not the real party in interest. Section 22.4 is the consumer's Motion For Entry of Document Preservation Order, and section 22.5 is a proposed Document Preservation Order.

Chapter 23 Class Action for Deceptive Labeling of Calcium Supplement

This Chapter includes materials from a national class action law suit against a company that deceptively marketed its 300 mg. and 600 mg. softgel calcium dietary supplements as Calcium '900' and Calcium 1200. The complaint (§ 23.1) alleges that the company's labeling was unconscionable and deceptive in violation of the New Jersey consumer protection statute and the UDAP statutes of the other states because it misrepresents the potency and the cost of the supplement. The complaint also alleged that the mislabeling was a breach of express warranty and violated federal and state laws on misbranding food and drugs.

Section 23.2 is the consumer's first set of interrogatories, and section 23.3 is the first request for production of documents.

Section 23.4 is the consumer's memorandum in support of her motion to certify the class action, section 23.5 is the consumer's reply memorandum in support of her motion to certify the class action, and Section 23.6 is Plaintiff's Reply To Defendant's Sur-Reply In Opposition To Plaintiff's Motion For Class Certification.

Section 23.7 is the consumer's memorandum in support of her motion for summary judgment and section 23.8 is the consumer's reply brief in support of summary judgment.

Section 23.9 is the consumer's Brief In Opposition To Defendant's Motion For Decertification arguing that the class of purchasers of mislabeled calcium supplements was properly certified even though the members of the class must be self identified as they could do that by affidavit and there could be fluid recovery for those that do not come forward. It further argues that individual proof of reliance is not required.

Section 23.10 is the consumer's Brief In Opposition To Defendant's Motions In Limine. It outlines the evidence to introduced by the consumer. It argues that the consumer complaints received by the defendant about its mislabeling of the calcium supplements are admissible evidence. It argues that statements of the Defendant's founder in a book on dietary supplements are admissible. It argues that its expert's years of experience in monitoring the marketing of dietary supplements qualified him to testify to the capacity of the supplements labels at issue to mislead despite no formal training in marketing or consumer cognition.

Section 23.11 is Plaintiff's Supplemental Submission in Opposition to Defendants' Motion to Bar the Testimony of Plaintiff's Expert which argues that the jury will benefit from the expert's explanation of history of the Federal Drug Administration's nutritional supplements labeling rules. It also argues that the expert will not be offering just a bare conclusion but will base his opinion on facts.

Section 23.12 are jury instructions tendered by the consumer and 23.13 and 23.14 are jury instructions tendered by the defendant and modified by the consumer. Section 23.15 are questions to the jury.

Section 23.16 is Plaintiff's Memorandum Of Law In Opposition To Defendant's Motion For Jnov And New Trial. It argues that the jury's use of the per item retail price to calculate damages was within the methods reasonable available to the court to manage the damages question.

---

148 *See* National Consumer Law Center, Truth In Lending Ch. 4 (4th ed. 1999).

149 *See* National Consumer Law Center, Truth In Lending Ch. 10 (4th ed. 1999).

150 *See* National Consumer Law Center, Unfair and Deceptive Acts and Practices § 11.2.1.4.1 (5th ed. 2001).

151 *See* National Consumer Law Center, The Cost of Credit §11.3 (2d ed. 2000).

152 *See* National Consumer Law Center, The Cost of Credit §11.9 (2d ed. 2000).

153 *See* National Consumer Law Center, Truth In Lending Ch. 6 (4th ed. 1999).

Consumer Law Pleadings Number Nine (2003)

Chapter 1   Predatory Mortgage Lending Jury Trial and Summary Judgment Materials

Section 1.1.1 is the Joint Pretrial Statement for a jury trial in a predatory mortgage loan case brought by six homeowners against the loan broker, the lender and an assignee of one of the loans. The consumers asserted UDAP,[154] Truth in Lending,[155] and Home Ownership and Equity Protection Act (HOEPA)[156] claims. The core claim was that the homeowners were called and given a false promise that they would be better off with the loan that the broker would procure. This section includes voluminous jury instructions as well as a description of the witnesses, objections, and other plans for trial. Section 1.1.2 contains the consumer's special jury verdict questions. Section 1.1.3 contains the broker's special jury questions. Section 1.2 contains exhibits prepared by Mr. Leymaster as an expert to show how the predatory mortgage loans did not improve the borrowers' financial condition as promised by the loan broker and the lender.[157]

Section 1.3.1 is the homeowners memorandum of law in support of summary judgment, and § 1.3.2 is a statement of undisputed material facts. The memorandum of law addresses HOEPA claims. Section 1.4.1 is one of the homeowners opposition to the loan assignee's motion for judgment on the TIL rescission claim, and § 1.4.2 supplements that memorandum. Section 1.5.1 is a draft order and 1.5.2 is a memorandum in support of a motion in limine to preclude testimony by the loan assignee that it exercised due diligence in reviewing the mortgage for HOEPA violations when that defense had not been pled and contradicted the Rule 30(b)(6) deposition.

Chapter 2   Automobile Sales and Finance Fraud Suit

Section 2.1 is a complaint against a car dealer and car financer where the salesperson represented that they were providing single digit financing for a visually impaired consumer when the rate was actually provided was 12.5%. Claims are made for fraud and violations of the Michigan Motor Vehicle Installment Sales Act, the Truth in Lending

Act, the Michigan titling statute, and the Michigan Consumer Protection Act. The complaint alleges the salesperson obtained the consumer's signature on the contract when it contained blank spaces violating the Michigan Motor Vehicle Installment Sales Act.[158] It alleges the failure to provide a copy the TIL disclosures for the consumer a before consummation.[159] It claims that the seller imposed an interest rate in the transaction in excess of the rate that the finance company was willing to extend credit. This hidden charge is referred to as a yield spread premium or dealer finance charge markup. The dealer would generally receive some or the entire markup as additional profit.[160] A series of additional discovery requests are also included in this chapter. Section 2.2 is a memorandum of law on each of the claims.

Chapter 3   Fair Debt Collection Claims for Using a Fictitious Collection Agency Name and Other Violations

Section 3.1 is multi plaintiff complaint alleging fair debt collection violations by a debt collection agency which was collecting posing as a collection department of the creditor, a time share resort seller. This was one of several suits involving deception and this time share resort. The claim was that the collector misrepresented its name and its relationship to the creditor as well as engaging in other deceptive practices[161] violating the federal Fair Debt Collection Practices Act, the Wisconsin Consumer Act, and the North Carolina Debt Collection statute. It was alleged that the North Carolina statute applied because that is the location of the collection agency and the creditor, and the place from which the misrepresentations were sent. While the use of North Carolina law was rejected under Wisconsin's choice of law rules,[162] other states choice of law could allow its application.

---

154   *See* National Consumer Law Center, Unfair and Deceptive Acts and Practices §§ 5.1.8–5.1.11 (5th ed. 2001).

155   *See* National Consumer Law Center, Truth In Lending (4th ed. 1999).

156   *See Id.* Ch. 10.

157   One file is in Microsoft PowerPoint format, which can be read on a free viewer that can be downloaded by going to http://office.microsoft.com/downloads/9798/Ppview97.aspx.

158   *See* National Consumer Law Center, Unfair and Deceptive Acts and Practices § 5.4.4.6 (5th ed. 2001).

159   *See* National Consumer Law Center, Truth In Lending § 4.3.5 (4th ed. 1999 & 2002 Supp.).

160   *See* National Consumer Law Center, Cost of Credit § 11.2.2.6 (2nd ed. 2000 and 2002 Supp); National Consumer Law Center, Credit Discrimination § 8.4 (3d ed. 2002).

161   Courts are not entirely consistent on how specific a claim must be stated in federal court. *See* National Consumer Law Center, Fair Debt Collection § 2.3.2 (4th ed. 2000). In the case in which this pleading was filed the court granted summary judgment for several additional FDCPA claims based on the generalized pleading. *See* Hartman v. Meridian Fin. Servs., Inc., 191 F. Supp. 2d 1031 (W.D. Wis. 2002) (Complaint that listed sections of the FDCPA that the collector was alleged to have violated but failed to list other sections did not waive the right to claim violations of the unlisted sections and instead stated a claim for generally violating the FDCPA under federal notice pleading requirements.).

162   *See* Hartman v. Meridian Financial Services, 2001 WL 1823617 (W.D.Wis. Aug. 28, 2001) (Dismissed claim of violation of N.C. debt collection statute as not the choice of law that Wisconsin

Section 3.2 contains discovery requests in the case.

Section 3.3.1 contains the consumers' memorandum of law in support of summary judgment. The memorandum successfully[163] argued that in addition to violating the prohibitions against using a fictitious name, the collector violated the FDCPA by contacting consumer despite knowing that they were represented by counsel, failed to provide validation notices within the first five days of the initial communication with the consumers, made numerous misrepresentations about its collections, and failed to indicate that the debts were disputed in its reports to a credit reporting agency.[164] It also argues that the collector violated the Wisconsin Consumer Act in numerous ways. The brief rebuts the collection agency's arguments that it was not a debt collector because it was a part of the creditor and that there was no debt collection because the collector began collections when the accounts were only eleven days delinquent.[165]

Section 3.3.2 is consumers' reply brief in support of summary judgment. The brief argues that notice pleading does not require the complaint to state every section of the FDCPA and state debt collection statute violated. The brief argues that the collection agency was not an in-house debt collector so closely supervised by the creditor that it was

entitled to FDCPA exemption. The brief argues that the collector did not prove each element that was required to establish a bona fide error defense.[166]

Chapter 4 Attorney Fee Award in Time Share Resort Litigation

Chapter 4 contains a memorandum of law in support of an award of attorney fee under the Wisconsin unfair practices law, the Wisconsin Timeshare Act, and the Wisconsin Consumer Act. The memorandum stresses that the settlement in the case resulted only after the consumer had sought to avoid litigation by canceling the transaction and the consumer's subsequent suit was vigorously contested by the defendant before it finally settled with nearly complete relief for the consumer and an agreement to pay the consumer's attorney fees and costs. The brief then analyzes the fees sought using the criteria from Johnson v. adopted by Wisconsin court for awarding statutory attorney fees.

Chapter 5 Federal Motor Vehicle Information and Cost Savings Act Claims for Suppressing the Identity of Vehicle's Prior Owner and Nature of Its Use

Car dealers like to sell cars driven on the paved streets of an uncongested, small town by a mature, conservative driver. Where that is not the situation, some dealers may suppress the truth about the prior owner or use of the car to enhance the price and saleability of the car. Where a dealer concealed the title of a truck so that the purchaser would rely on the seller's misrepresentation that the truck was from the city streets of Phoenix rather than from rough roads of the adjacent Navajo reservation as would have been revealed by prior owner's address on the truck's certificate of title, the dealer was found to have violated the federal Motor Vehicle Information and Cost Savings Act. See *Yazzie v. Amigo Chevrolet, Inc.*[167] That Act requires a disclosure of a used vehicle's odometer reading on the vehicle's certificate of title, which would have stated the prior owners name and address. The failure to disclose the reading on the certificate was a violation of that Act and fraudulent where the violation of the Act was to cover up the vehicle's prior owner and use.[168] The memorandum of law from *Yazzie* is in § 5.4.

---

courts would make where consumer claimed violations of that law as well as the FDCPA and the Wisconsin Consumer Act's debt collection provisions).

163 *See* Hartman v. Meridian Fin. Servs., Inc., 191 F. Supp. 2d 1031 (W.D. Wis. 2002).

164 Hartman v. Meridian Fin. Servs., Inc., 191 F. Supp. 2d 1031 (W.D. Wis. 2002) (Once notified of the consumers' representation by an attorney, the debt collector's direct communications with the consumers violated the FDCPA The third party debt collector's communication with consumers in the name of the creditor was a false representation in violation of 1692e. Collector's threat to report to a credit bureau any debt left unpaid more than 45 days from the "date of placement," without any explanation of when the account was so "placed," was a confusing and misleading misrepresentation in violation of § 1692e. The third party debt collector's initial communications with consumers in the name of the creditor failed to contain the validation notice, thus violating § 1692g.).

165 The collector lost both arguments. *See* Hartman v. Meridian Fin. Servs., Inc., 191 F. Supp. 2d 1031 (W.D. Wis. 2002) (A third-party debt collector collecting in the name of the creditor was not subject to the § 1692a(6) (A) exemption since the person so collecting was not an "officer or employee of the creditor." A collector acting on behalf of a creditor, where both "are related by common ownership or affiliated by corporate control," was not within the § 1692a(6) (B) exemption where the collector's principal business was the collection of debts and where it collected on behalf of unrelated entities as well. A third party who obtained accounts only once a payment was overdue (i.e. beyond the contractual due date) was not exempt from the definition of a debt collector as a pre-collection billing service. Although the creditor claimed that it considered accounts in default only after they were at least 30 days late, the debt collector still was not subject to the § 1692a(6) (F) (iii) exception when it obtained the debts once the payments were overdue but for less than 30 days, since the underlying contracts defined default as not making payment by the due date.

166 *See* Hartman v. Meridian Fin. Servs., Inc., 191 F. Supp. 2d 1031 (W.D. Wis. 2002) (Debt collector's purported misunderstanding of its legal obligations under the FDCPA did not qualify as an error for the bona fide error defense. Debt collector could not avail itself of the bona fide error defense since it did not have in place any relevant preventative procedures.).

167 189 F. Supp.2d 1245 (D.N.M. 2001).

168 *See* National Consumer Law Center, Automobile Fraud §§ 3.6.5.2, 4.3.2 (1998 & 2002 Supp.).

Sections 5.1–5.3 are complaints where a car dealer suppressed information about a used car that would be revealed by the certificate of title, and the dealer failed to provide the federal odometer disclosure on the certificate as required. The complaint in § 5.1 alleges that the car dealer suppressed that the car sold had been in a wreck and had been owned by a well known car rental company. It alleges the consumer would not have bought the car if she had known those facts. It alleges violation of the Motor Vehicle Information and Cost Savings Act, the New Mexico Unfair Practices Act, and the New Mexico Motor Vehicle Dealers Franchising Act and fraud and misrepresentation. It seeks actual and statutory damages and attorney fees.

Section 5.2 is a complaint alleging that the concealed certificate of title was stamped "SALVAGE" in three places but the sale was arranged so that the consumer did not see the title until she had owned the car for six months. It alleges the consumer would not have bought the car if she had known those facts. It alleges violation of the Motor Vehicle Information and Cost Savings Act, the New Mexico Unfair Practices Act, the federal Truth in Lending Act, and the New Mexico Motor Vehicle Dealers Franchising Act and fraud and misrepresentation. It seeks actual and statutory damages and attorney fees.

Section 5.3 is a complaint that alleges that the concealed certificate of title would have disclosed that the prior owner was a well known car rental agency and that the consumer would not have purchased the car if he had known. The dealer also concealed that it failed to provide a safety inspection certificate required by state law and made errors on the application for license tags for the vehicle leading to the state's seizure of the vehicle's tags, and the immobilization of the car for more than eight months. It alleges violation of the Motor Vehicle Information and Cost Savings Act, the Magnuson-Moss Warranty Act, a state credit statute by charging $160 for state fees that cost only $40, and the Maryland Consumer Protection Act, failed to identify the correct vehicle identification number on the sales and financing agreements as required by state law, breach of implied warranty of merchantability, conversion and deceit.

Chapter 6 Mortgage Servicer's Failure to Timely Credit Payments, Junk Charges, and Foreclosure Threat

This chapter contains a class action complaint about the illegal practices of a subprime mortgage servicing company (§ 6.1). The company would fail to timely credit homeowners' timely payments and then add specious charges to the account asserting that the payment had been late. In the following months the same thing would happen and payments would be applied first to the specious charges resulting in increasing assertions of delinquency, demands for payments of $2000 to $4000, and threats of foreclosure if the larger payments were not made. The complaint asserts claims for breach of duty of good faith and fair dealing,[169] breach of fiduciary duty of trustee,[170] illegal pursuit of forfeiture, unauthorized charges, and illegal debt collection. The complaint seeks declaratory and injunctive relief, actual and punitive damages, civil penalties, and attorney fees.

Section 6.2 is a motion for temporary injunction seeking to enjoin the servicing company from foreclosing on homes, adding illegal fees to accounts, and failing to promptly credit payments upon receipt.

Chapter 7 Answers, Counterclaims, and Third Party Complaints in Predatory Mortgage Loan Foreclosure Cases

Section 7.1.1 is a combined answer, counterclaim and third party complaint alleging numerous claims as a result of a predatory loan foreclosure. The pleading alleges the young homeowners were solicited by a loan broker posing a bank loan officer to refinance their home so that they could save $50,000 to $75,000 by lowering their interest rate. It was not until long after the loan papers were signed in their home that they learned that the loan financed a large broker fee and involved a higher interest rate than their prior loan, an unaffordable monthly payment, and a balloon payment in excess of the amount borrowed after fifteen years. When they called to cancel the loan, they were told not to cancel and that they would get a better loan in a few months without charge. When they complained to the bank, the bank employees laughed at their gullibility. The homeowners became depressed and had increasing difficulty making their payments. The answer raises as defenses the homeowners' ability to cure any defaults under state law and the broker and lender's unlawful and unconscionable acts and omissions.

Section 7.1.2 is a motion to compel discovery and extend the time for discovery, and section 7.1.3 is an order granting that relief. Section 7.1.4 is a motion for sanctions for failing to produce documents, and §7.1.5 is a supporting memorandum. Section 7.1.6 is the homeowners' opposition to the mortgagee's motion for summary judgment, and § 7.1.7 is the homeowner's affidavit supporting the opposition to summary judgment.

Section 7.2 is another combined answer, counterclaim and third party complaint alleging numerous claims as a result of a predatory loan. The answer raises as defenses the homeowners' ability to cure any defaults under state law, the failure of the plaintiff to show its interest in the mortgage, and the lender's unlawful and unconscionable acts and omissions. The pleading alleges that the new homeowners were unsophisticated. One of them was disabled, unable to communicate verbally and has visual and hearing impair-

---

169 *See* National Consumer Law Center, Cost of Credit § 11.8 (2nd ed. 2000).

170 *See generally, Id.* § 11.9.

ments. The other spouse was employed as a laborer. The very small home they bought had rotten floors and roofs and was sold a few years before for $3000. The homeowners were lead to believe that they would save a lot of money by refinancing their home. The broker obtained a fraudulent appraisal of $105,000 on the housing so that it could inflate the predatory loan with fees and charges. The payments were unaffordable and the cost of the loan was greatly in excess of their prior mortgage.

The counterclaims in both cases allege violations of the Ohio Mortgage Broker Act, breach of fiduciary duty, undue influence, breach of contract, violation of the Ohio Home Solicitation Sales Act, violation of the Ohio Consumer Sales Practices Act, fraud, intentional infliction of emotional distress, civil conspiracy, violation of the federal Real Estate Settlement Procedures Act (hereafter RESPA), and violation of the federal Truth in Lending Act. It seeks actual, statutory, and punitive damages as well as cancellation and rescission of the broker and loan agreements. Statutory attorney fees would also be available in many instances for many of these violations.

Chapter 8 Jury Verdict Form for Automobile Lemon Case

This chapter contains a jury verdict form for an automobile lemon case. Jury questions are asked on claims involving the UCC, Magnuson-Moss Warranty Act, Michigan Lemon Law, Motor Vehicle Service and Repair Act, misrepresentation, and UDAP.

Chapter 9 Claims Arising From Credit Reports

Sectrion 9.1 addresses the failure to correct inaccurate credit reports that result from mixing credit data of different people in an individual's credit reports. Sections 9.1.1, 9.1.2 and 9.1.3 are complaints against credit reporting agencies (and a creditor in § 9.1.3) for failing to correct inaccurate data in credit files after being notified that they were mismerged files[171] mixing credit information pertaining to other people in the consumer's credit file. Sections 9.1.1 and 9.1.3 are individual claims and § 9.1.2 is a national class complaint. The complaints assert claims under the Fair Credit Report Act for failing to correct inaccurate information.[172] The complaints seek injunctive relief, actual and punitive damages and attorney fees.[173]

Section 9.2 addresses the failure to correct inaccurate credit reports after learning of an identity theft. Section 9.2.1 is a complaint against a credit reporting agency, a credit card

issuer, and debt collection agencies in a case arising out of identity theft, where a thief posed as the consumer applied for credit and obtained the credit in the consumer's name.[174] The complaint alleges claims for negligence, defamation, invasion of privacy, and Fair Credit Reporting Act violations. It seeks actual and punitive damages, attorney fees and costs, and an order correcting the consumer's credit report.

Section 9.3 addresses the continuous reporting of inaccurate information to a credit reporting agency after being notified of the error. Section 9.3.1 is a complaint against bank for repeatedly billing for forced placed car insurance after a car loan had been paid in full and where the consumer had fully insured the car. The bank also reported its erroneous claim as a delinquency on the consumer's credit report. The complaint alleges claims under the Fair Credit Reporting Act, for fraud, breach of contract, defamation, negligence, UDAP, and misrepresentation. A claim for violation of the Fair Credit Billing Act was included even though the claim was not open end credit.[175] Section 9.3.2 is a complaint against an automobile finance company for reporting inaccurate credit information to credit reporting agencies after requests from the consumer to correct its reports. The complaint alleges claims for negligence, defamation, invasion of privacy, intentional infliction of mental distress, and UDAP. Section 9.3.3 is a memorandum of law opposing dismissal of a Fair Credit Reporting Act claim in a related case. Section 9.3.4 is a memorandum of law in a related case opposing compelling arbitration on the basis that the agreement to arbitrate was unrelated to the consumer claim that the credit card issuer was reporting derogatory credit information about another person as information about the consumer. Section 9.3.5 is a motion for production of documents in a related case.

Section 9.4 addresses the denial of low-cost car insurance premium on the basis of a credit report without telling the consumer. Section 9.4.1 contains a statewide class complaint against a car insurance company alleging that it denied the consumer its lowest premium car insurance based on the consumer's credit report and failed to notify the consumer that it had taken an adverse action as required by the Fair Credit Reporting Act.[176] The complaint seeks statutory and punitive damages and attorney fees. Section 9.4.2 is a motion and draft order for the filing of the amended complaint.

Section 9.5 contains discovery materials from credit reporting cases. Sections 9.5.1 and 9.5.2 are interrogatories to creditors, and § 9.5.3 are interrogatories to a credit reporting agency. Section 9.5.4 is a request for admissions to a credit reporting agency. Sections 9.5.5 and 9.5.6 are requests to creditors for production of documents, and § 9.5.7 is a request to a credit reporting agency for production of docu-

---

171 *See* National Consumer Law Center, Fair Credit Reporting Act § 7.2.4 (5th ed. 2002).
172 *See Id.* § 7.8.
173 *See Id.* Ch. 10.

174 *Id.* § 13.5.5.
175 *See* National Consumer Law Center, Truth In Lending § 5.8.1 (4th ed. 1999) (Fair Credit Billing Act likely to be construed to apply only to open end credit).
176 *See Id.* § 6.4.

ments. Sections 9.5.8, 9.5.9, and 9.5.10 are subpoenas commanding the production of documents. Section 9.5.11 is a notice of deposition. Sections 9.5.12 and 9.5.13 are motions to compel discovery with supporting memoranda of law.

Section 9.6 contains motions and memoranda of law from credit reporting cases. Section 9.6.1 is a motion to strike portions of the answer and a supporting memorandum which includes arguments on preemption. Section 9.6.2 is the consumer's opposition to the credit reporting agency's motion to join the identity thief as a defendant. Section 9.6.3 is the consumer's motion and supporting memorandum of law opposing dismissal or summary judgment in a case of unauthorized access of an ex-spouse to the consumer's credit report.[177] Sections 9.6.4, 9.6.5, and 9.6.6 are oppositions to motions to dismiss including discussions of preemption,[178] private right of actions under 15 U.S.C. § 1681s-2(b),[179] the application of the Texas UDAP statute to credit reporting claims,[180] invasion of privacy,[181] and intentional infliction of mental distress.[182] Section 9.6.7 is an opposition to defendant credit reporting agency's motion for summary judgment which includes arguments regarding disputed fact and the running of the statute of limitations. Section 9.6.8 is the plaintiff's statement of material facts in opposition to the defendant's motion for summary judgment. Section 9.6.9 is a consumer's motion for summary judgment in a merged report case under the FCRA accuracy requirement. Section 9.6.10 is reply to the credit reporting agency's opposition to the consumer's motion for summary judgment focusing on the issues raised in the credit reporting agency's employee's affidavit. Section 9.6.11 is the consumer's proposal for the joint pre-trial order.

Chapter 10 Fair Debt Collection Practices Act Covers the Sale of a Paid Debt to a Debt Collector

Chapter 10 contains the consumer's briefs filed in *Magrin v. Unifund CCR Partners, Inc.*,[183] an unpublished decision holding that the consumer stated a valid claim under the Fair Debt Collection Practices Act (FDCPA) when he alleged that a debt collector had made false representations as to the legal status of the debt in connection with the sale, transfer, or assignment of the debt to another debt collector, with the knowledge that purchaser, transferee, or assignee intended to initiate or continue attempts to collect the debt. Magrin brought a FDCPA suit alleging that after Unifund's two

collection suits against Magrin on two accounts were dismissed with prejudice, Unifund sold the account for collection to another debt collector, also a defendant in the FDCPA suit. Magrin alleged the sale of uncollectible debt was abusive, deceptive, and unfair. The briefs focus on the purpose of the FDCPA to prevent collection of debts that have been paid or were not owed in the first place.[184]

Chapter 11 Tax Collection Agency's Illegal Overcharges

A report by private tax collection agencies claimed in 2002 that 42 states were "outsourcing" some of their tax collection work.[185] This chapter contain briefs from two cases arguing that private tax collection agencies were adding excessive and illegal charges to the tax claims. Section 11.1 and 11.2 are the taxpayers' brief and reply brief in the Pennsylvania Supreme Court in Pentlong Corp. v. GLS Capital, Inc.[186] The brief argues that charges imposed by the collection agency that purchased more than $45 million[187] of property tax claims from Allegheny County, Pennsylvania were illegal. The brief argues that the tax collection agency was limited to 10% per annum interest rather than the 12% it imposed, that it could not impose prejudgment attorney fees at all, and that it could not impose a myriad of collection feed not actual incurred. The Pennsylvania Supreme Court rejected the interest claim, upheld the prohibition of collection attorney fees prejudgment, and remanded the issue of the collection of the fees.[188] The brief and the opinion also address the authority of the County to assign tax claims, and the authority of the tax collection agency to collect them.

The briefs in §§ 11.3 and 11.4 involve another case about the private collection of taxes as well as water and sewer charges. The brief in § 11.3 argues that the suit for the restitution of interest paid on taxes was not prevented by the defense of voluntary payment made by mistake of law as the payment was coerced by the threat of seizing the taxpayer's residence for back taxes, as the restitution sought was for illegal interest, as the voluntary payment doctrine does not apply to payments to the government, and the state adoption of a policy of honest tax collection. The brief argues that it would be inequitable to allow the private collector to retain illegal interest because of the equitable defenses of laches or estoppel. The brief argues that the compounding of interest was not permitted.

177　*See Id.* § 5.3.
178　*See Id.* §§ 10.4.3, 10.4.4.
179　*See Id.* Ch. 3.
180　*Id.* § 10.4.2.
181　*See Id.* § 16.3.
182　*See generally*, National Consumer Law Center, Fair Debt Collection § 10.2 (4th ed. 2000).
183　2002 WL 31804268 (9th Cir. Dec. 10, 2002) (not for publication).
184　*See generally*, National Consumer Law Center, Fair Debt Collection § 3.2 (4th ed. 2000).
185　Advisory Committee Report, "IRS Outsourcing of Delinquent Tax Receivables" (Nov. 13, 2002), available at www.collectionindustry.com/downloads/IRS_Outsourcing.pdf
186　_____ A.2d _____, 2003 WL 1337984 (Pa. March 19, 2003).
187　The tax collection agency agreed to pay 97% of the face value of many of the claims. *Id.*
188　*Id.*

The brief in § 11.4 argues two questions certified to the appellate court. It argues that where a local ordinance authorized the collection of interest in excess of that permitted by state statute that no interest should be retained by the collector, rather than allowing retention of the lawful amount. It also argues that Truth in Lending disclosures should have been made for the tax payment plans offered by the private collectors, an argument previously rejected by the court.[189]

Chapter 12 Rule 68 Offer of Judgment Does Not Moot Class Action

Chapter 12 is the appellate brief from *Colbert v. Dyamacol*[190] which upheld the decision in the district court that a defendant in a Fair Debt Collection Practices Act class action may not defeat the class action by mooting the case by picking off individual class representatives with a F. R. Civ. P. 68 offer of judgment offering relief only to the named plaintiff. The brief argues that the offer of judgment was not full relief as it did not offer class relief that was sought in the complaint nor did the offer even provide for the named plaintiff's actual damages.[191]

Chapter 13 Opposition to Inadequate Consumer Class Action Settlement Regarding Defective Post-Repossession Notices

Chapter 13 contains a counsel's affidavit in support of an intervening consumer's opposition to a class action settlement (§13.1.1) and memorandum of law (§13.1.2). The memorandum and affidavit argue that the proposed class settlement should be rejected because the named plaintiff was not a member of the class settlement as it excluded persons like her against whom the defendant had obtained a deficiency judgment, the class action had not been vigorously litigated, the named plaintiff had a conflict of interest and violated a duty to report related suits to the courts involved, the agreed relief provided much less relief to consumers than similar class settlements, and the agreed attorney fee was excessive in a case where no discovery was conducted nor motions filed. Also included is the affidavit of an expert on class actions asserting that the settlement did not provide sufficient relief to absent class members (§3.2).

Chapter 14 Motion for Statutory Attorney Fee Award Exceeding the Consumer's Damages

This chapter contains a motion for the award of attorney fees under the Fair Debt Collection Practices Act.[192] The brief first argues that where an offer of settlement is silent about the consumer's attorney fees in a suit under a statute providing for fee shifting to a successful consumer, the court should determine and award the consumer's reasonable attorney fee.[193] The brief then argues that awarding attorney fees much larger than the consumer's damages is necessary to provide for the private enforcement of the Act intended by Congress.

Chapter 15 State Courts Are Not Bound by U.S. Supreme Court's Limitation in Buckhannon on Federal Class Actions

Chapter 15 contains a memorandum of law arguing that state statutes based on federal law should be construed with deference to federal interpretations at the time of enactment but not postenactment interpretations. So the U.S. Supreme Court's decision in *Buckhannon Board & Care Home, Inc., v. West Virginia Dep't of Health & Human Resources*,[194] overruling years of federal cases awarding statutory attorney fees where counsel's effort were the "catalyst" for a substantial benefit to the class, should not be applied to interpret the state consumer protection act.[195]

Chapter 16 Appeal of Denial of Class Certification

This chapter contains a Petition to Appeal the Denial of a Class Action and the Brief in Support of Petition to Appeal the Denial of a Class Action[196] in a case where the district court refused to compel necessary discovery on the numerosity[197] of the class and denied class action certification for lack of numerosity. The case involved the refusal of a student loan debt collector to provide pregarnishment hearings to student borrowers as required by state and federal law. The consumer asserted that the district court abused its discretion by denying certification based on its determination of the disputed factual issue of numerosity, without providing the consumer either adequate discovery or an evidentiary hearing, despite repeated requests. The con-

189 Pollice v. National Tax funding, L.P., 225 F.3d 379 (3rd Cir. 2000). The brief reurges the argument base on Pentlong Corp. v. GLS Capital, Inc. 780 A.2d 734 (Pa. Commw. 2001) which was reversed in relevant part at _____ A.2d _____, 2003 WL 1337984 (Pa. March 19, 2003).

190 Colbert v. Dymacol, Inc., _____ F.3d ____ (3rd Cir. March 10, 2003), *aff'g*, 2001 WL 34083813 (E.D. Pa. Oct. 2, 2001).

191 *See* National Consumer Law Center, Fair Debt Collection § 2.3.7 (4th ed. 2000).

192 *See* National Consumer Law Center, Fair Debt Collection § 6.8 (4th ed. 2000).

193 *See* National Consumer Law Center, Fair Debt Collection § 2.3.7 (4th ed. 2000).

194 121 S. Ct. 1835 (2001).

195 *See* National Consumer Law Center, Consumer Class Actions § 15.1.3 (5th ed. 2002).

196 *See* National Consumer Law Center, Consumer Class Actions § 9.10 (5th ed. 2002).

197 *See Id.* § 9.2.

sumer asserted that the lower court erred by ruling that claims for non-Florida residents, which were raised by an amended pleading, did not relate back to the time when he initially filed the Complaint based on Florida debt collection law. Finally the consumer argued the court erred as a matter of law by refusing to use the class definition urged by the consumer or to craft its own.

Chapter 17 Per se Massachusetts UDAP Claims

Section 17.1.1 is demand letter against a car rental company for including illegal limitations on its coverage of claims under collision damage waivers sold to its customer. The demand is made under a Massachusetts statute regulating the exclusions in car rental agencies' collision damage waivers and Mass. Gen. Laws ch. 93A, the Massachusetts UDAP statute. The demand letter is required as a condition of filing a ch. 93A suit. Section 17.1.2 is a class action complaint in the same case. The complaint seeks declaratory and injunctive relief as well as damages, treble damages under 93A, and attorney fees. It states additional claims for breach of the covenant of good faith and fair dealing and unjust enrichment. Sections 17.1.3 and 17.1.4 are memorandum of law in support of partial summary judgment in the case. Section 17.1.4 focuses its attack on the defendant's argument that it did not enforce the illegal exclusions in its rental contract.

Section 17.2.1 is a demand letter against a credit card issuer for repeatedly obtaining credit reports of the consumer's without a permissible purpose and despite the consumer's protest of the company's conduct. The letter states that after the consumer complained several time the card issuer stated it had been seeking the credit reports of the consumer's father, who had the same name. However, the card issuer repeated its mistake after explaining it. Claims were made under the federal and state Fair Credit Reporting Acts as well as the statute privacy statute and Mass. Gen. Laws ch. 93A, the UDAP statute. Section 17.2.2 is the complaint in that case seeking actual, punitive and treble damages, declaratory and injunctive relief, and attorney fees and costs.

Chapter 18 Closing Jury Arguments in a Satellite Dish Door-to-Door Scam

This chapter is the consumers' closing argument from a case in which the jury awarded $581 million in damages for fraudulently selling satellite dishes door to door. The closing argument emphasized the fraud perpetrated by the defendants: telling their door to door victims that they would only have to make payments for three years when the documents provided for payments for four years and four months. It was pointed out that the documents provided for payments totaling $1800 when the satellite dish was only worth $199.

The argument emphasized that in addition to the plaintiffs, there were hundreds of other victims in the state-the defendant testified that they received thousands of complaints at their national headquarters each week. It emphasized that a significant award was necessary to send a message to the board of the defendant and the other companies selling door-to-door in the state.

Chapter 19 Predatory Mortgage Lending Claims in Bankruptcy Arising from an Illegal Yield Spread Premium: TIL Rescission and Damages, RESPA and UDAP

Section 19.1 is a letter giving the creditor notice of rescission of the mortgage pursuant to the Truth in Lending Act.[198] The individual complaint in section 19.2 alleges claims for TIL Rescission and Damages, and RESPA[199] and UDAP[200] claims for illegal payment of a yield spread premium of over $3,000 to a loan broker by the lender. The complaint seeks rescission, TIL damages in recoupment, RESPA and UDAP treble damages, and attorney fees.

Section 19.3.1 is a request for production of documents to the loan broker, and Section 19.3.2 is a request for production of documents to the lender. Section 19.3.3 are interrogatories to the lender. Sections 19.3.4 and 19.3.5 are notices of depositions. Section 19.4.1 is a notice of and motion for partial summary judgment. Section 19.4.2 is a draft order granting summary judgment. Section 19.5 is the memorandum of law in support of summary judgment on liability for TIL rescission and for the claims that the yield spread premium was illegal.

Consumer Law Pleadings Number Ten (2004)

Chapter 1 Fair Credit Reporting Act Furnisher Liability Briefs

Section 1.1 is the consumer's successful brief in *Johnson v. MBNA America Bank, NA* in the Fourth Circuit of the U.S. Court of Appeals.[201] Johnson argued that MBNA failed to investigate her statement that she had taken no steps to assume any liability on a credit card issued to and used solely by her ex-husband and which MBNA reported on her

198 *See* National Consumer Law Center, Truth in Lending 6.4.2, Appx. E (4th ed. 1999).
199 *See* National Consumer Law Center, Cost of Credit § 11.3.1.5.1 (2nd Ed. 2000 and 2002 Supp.).
200 *See* National Consumer Law Center, Unfair and Deceptive Acts and Practices § 5.1.11.3 (5th ed. 2001).
201 *See* in Johnson v. MBNA America Bank, NA, 357 F.3d 426 (4th Cir. 2004).

credit report as having a delinquent balance of $18,000, which her ex-husband had discharged in bankruptcy. MBNA was required by the Fair Credit Reporting Act to "investigate" "disputed information."[202] It asserted that it need only keep verifying the erroneous information in its computer database and did not need to check the credit application or correspondence related to the credit card. The court held:

> The key term at issue here, "investigation," is defined as "[a] detailed inquiry or systematic examination." *Am. Heritage Dictionary* 920 (4th ed.2000); see *Webster's Third New Int'l Dictionary* 1189 (1981) (defining "investigation" as "a searching inquiry"). Thus, the plain meaning of "investigation" clearly requires some degree of careful inquiry by creditors. Further, § 1681s-2(b)(1)(A) uses the term "investigation" in the context of articulating a creditor's duties in the consumer dispute process outlined by the FCRA. It would make little sense to conclude that, in creating a system intended to give consumers a means to dispute—and, ultimately, correct—inaccurate information on their credit reports, Congress used the term "investigation" to include superficial, un reasonable inquiries by creditors. Cf. *Cahlin v. Gen. Motors Acceptance Corp.*, 936 F.2d 1151, 1160 (11th Cir.1991) (interpreting analogous statute governing reinvestigations of consumer disputes by credit reporting agencies to require reasonable investigations); *Pinner v. Schmidt*, 805 F.2d 1258, 1262 (5th Cir.1986) (same). We therefore hold that § 1681s-2(b)(1) requires creditors, after receiving notice of a consumer dispute from a credit reporting agency, to conduct a reasonable investigation of their records to determine whether the disputed information can be verified.[203]

Sections 1.2 and 1.3 are the consumer's brief and reply brief in another appeal under the Fair Credit Reporting Act. In that case the bank misapplied a payment by the consumer but argued that consumer's FCRA claim was time barred because the statute of limitations ran from the time the consumer first pointed the error out to the bank rather than from the date the consumer requested the credit reporting agency and the bank to reinvestigate the bank's error. While the bank admitted the error, the error had not been corrected even after suit. The Ninth Circuit in an unpublished opinion held that the claim was not time barred.[204]

Chapter 2   Automobile Claims: Lemon RV Laundering, Rebuilt Wrecks, Padded Repair Bills, FTC Used Car Rule

Section 2.1.1 is a complaint against the manufacturer, seller and financer of a resold lemon recreational vehicle ("RV") without the disclosure of 47 of the 49 prior defects in the RV.[205] Claims are made under the Ohio Lemon Law, the Federal Warranty Act, the Ohio Consumer Act, the Ohio Motor Vehicle Sales Rule, the Truth in Lending Act, and for fraud. The complaint seeks actual, punitive and statutory damages, attorney fees, declaratory relief, and replacement or a buyback of the RV. Section 2.1.2 are combined interrogatories, requests for admissions, and document requests to the dealer. Section 2.1.3 and 2.1.4 are similar discovery requests to the manufacturer and the financer respectively. Sections 2.1.5 and 2.1.6 are follow-up discovery requests to the dealer and financer. Section 2.1.7 is a letter to the client explaining the attorney's settlement strategy. Section 2.1.8 is a settlement offer by the consumers seeking a take back of the RV, damages, attorney fees, cy pres payments to public interest organizations and the state consumer protection office, and a consent decree. Section 2.1.9 is a graphically based presentation by the consumers prepared for a mediation conference. Section 2.1.10 is a chart of the repair history of the vehicle.

Section 2.2 is a complaint against a car dealer and the financer for selling a rebuilt wrecked rental car as a "one-owner," "garage kept" car that "had never been in rain, sleet, or snow."[206] The dealer offered guaranteed financing and a warranty. The complaint alleges misrepresentations, unfair and unconscionable conduct in violation of the Ohio Consumer Sales Practices Act, the Ohio Motor Vehicle Sales Rule, the FTC Used Car Rule, the privacy protections of the Gramm-Leach-Bliley Financial Institutions Act, breach of contract, breach of contract, Magnuson Moss Warranty Act, and Fraud. The complaint seeks actual, statutory, and punitive damages, and attorney fees.

Section 2.3 is a class action complaint against a car dealer for padding repair bills with deceptive surcharges, such as "Misc," "EPA/Shop Supplies," and "Cinergy Surcharge."[207] The complaint alleges that these surcharges resulted in $185,000 of deceptive overcharges each year that should be returned to the class with statutory damages, and attorney fees. Section 2.4 is a class complaint against a car dealer and the supplier of a used car window sticker that violated the FTC Used Car Buyers' Guide Window Sticker requirements.[208] The complaint alleged that the violation of the FTC rule violated the Ohio Consumer Sales Practices

---

202   *See* National Consumer Law Center, Fair Credit Reporting Act § 7.3.4 (5th Ed. 2002 and Supp.).

203   Johnson v. MBNA America Bank, NA, 357 F.3d 426, 430–431 (4th Cir. 2004).

204   Bishop v. U.S. Bancorp, 91 Fed. Appx. 583, 2004 WL 557299 (9th Cir. 2004).

205   *See* National Consumer Law Center, Automobile Fraud §§ 1.4.6, 2.1.5, 2.4.5.5, 6.3 (2d ed. 2003 and Supp.).

206   *Id.* § 2.1.4.

207   *See generally* National Consumer Law Center, Consumer Warranty Law § 17.8 (2d ed. 2001 and Supp.).

208   *Id.* § 14.7.

Description of Pleadings

Act and sought $200 minimum damages for each member of the class, injunctive relief and attorney fees.

Chapter 3 Debt Collection Depositions and Memoranda

Section 3.1 is a deposition of a collection lawyer involved in collecting the plaintiff consumer's account and § 3.2 is the deposition of the collection lawyer who is the owner of the collection firm that employed the first lawyer deposed. The depositions illustrate some of the difficulties of determining basic facts in a debt collectors' depositions.

Section 3.3 is a memorandum in support of a motion for partial summary judgment in another FDCPA case. It argues that the check collector violated the Fair Debt Collection Practices Act and the Connecticut debt collection statutes by alleging illegally excessive charges were due,[209] by falsely threatening criminal and civil proceedings,[210] and by threatening to obtain personal information from the state department of motor vehicles from the consumer's social security number. Section 3.4 is a reply memorandum in support of summary judgment on the same issues and alleging additional violations: failure to disclose a second alleged creditor involved in the alleged debts and seeking "restitution" when the amount of the collector's claim included illegal collection charges. The reply memorandum also states that the consumer's claims for deception satisfy the state law requirement of ascertainable loss and argue for punitive damages under state law.

A memorandum of law in support of summary judgment in another suit involving different alleged debts is in § 3.5. It alleges violations of the Fair Debt Collection Practices Act and state debt collection statutes by collecting without a state debt collection license, contacting a consumer known to be represented by counsel, demanding excessive amounts, and threatening to sue on a time barred debt. The argument that unlicensed collection violates the FDCPA is an uphill battle.[211]

Chapter 4 Debt Collection Harassment of Identity Theft Victim

Section 4.1 is a complaint in which the consumer alleges that the debt collector could not provide written verification[212] of a thirteen-year-old debt allegedly taken out by an imposter in her name and social security number. The debt collector persistently misrepresented that the consumer was responsible for this debt and must fill out an affidavit to

support her claim of identity theft and fraud. The complaint is based on the Fair Debt Collection Practices Act and the tort of invasion of privacy.[213]

Section 4.2 is a combined discovery request including interrogatories, admissions, and production of documents. Section 4.3 is the consumer's request to inspect the debt collector's premises. Section 4.4 is a form for consumers to use to keep notes of collection contacts. Section 4.5 is the deposition of a consumer class representative in a FDCPA class action where the defense attorney seeks to question her adequacy as a class representative.

Chapter 5 Repeated Debt Collection Calls as an Invasion of Privacy

Section 5.1 is a state court complaint against a collection law firm and some of its debt collectors alleging that they tortiously invaded the consumers' privacy[214] by calling repeatedly at their home and workplaces, and discussing the consumers' debt with third parties. Those acts were also alleged to constitute the tort of intentional infliction of mental distress.[215] The complaint sought $74,500 in compensatory damages and punitive damages. Section 5.2 adds a debt collector defendant. Section 5.3 is the Second Amended Complaint adding numerous claims under the Fair Debt Collection Practices Act and adding attorney fees to the relief sought and increasing the damages sought to $2 million.[216]

Section 5.4 are the first set of interrogatories, section 5.5 are the first request for admissions, section 5.6 is the first request for the production of documents, and section 5.7 is a notice of taking deposition, all serviced with the first state court complaint. Subsequent discovery and proceedings were conducted in federal court. Section 5.8 is a second request for the production of documents repeating requests for employee compensation information from the collection law firm and for documents relating to consumer suits against the debt collector. Section 5.9 is the third request for production of documents seeking debt collector employee's personnel and complaint files, telephone bills and logs, contracts between the collector and the creditor, and other documents. Section 5.10 is the fourth request for production of documents regarding documents mentioned in the following depositions of the debt collectors. Section 5.11 is the deposition of an experienced debt collector who had been assigned the consumers' account for collection. Section 5.12 is the deposition of the debt collector owner who was active in the business after she had reviewed the consumers' tape recordings of two harassing telephone calls.

Section 5.13 is a memorandum of law opposing the debt collectors' motion for summary judgment. It argues that the

209 *See* National Consumer Law Center, Fair Debt Collection Practices § 5.5.3.2 (5th Ed. 2004)
210 *Id.* §§ 5.5.7, 5.5.9.
211 *Id.* § 5.5.8.5.
212 *Id.* § 5.7.
213 *Id.* § 10.3.
214 *Id.*
215 *Id.* § 10.2.
216 *Id.* at Ch. 5.

evidence established a campaign of intentional harassment and false threats of arrest, garnishment, and suit, and insults that resulted in severe physical and emotional distress, invaded the consumers' privacy, and that the employer had failed to exercise due diligence and ordinary care in supervising its employees despite numerous prior complaints. The memorandum of law further argues that the defendants' argument that their liability for attorney fees under the FDCPA should terminate with their admission of FDCPA liability is erroneous because the consumers are entitled to a trial on the FDCPA actual damages including mental anguish. Section 5.14 is a consent judgment for the consumers in the amount of $90,000.00.

Chapter 6 Contempt Action Against Check Collector for Violating Injunction

Section 6.1 is an application in federal court for an order of contempt against a check collection agency that failed to abide by an injunction issued under a state law claim made supplementally with a Fair Debt Collection Practices Act claim.[217] The defendant failed to include the face amount of its check in its collection letters, demanded treble damages under state law when it was not entitled to them, and made false threats.[218] Section 6.2 is a memorandum of law in support of the contempt application. Section 6.3 is a reply memorandum of law to the check collector's arguments that its violations were not significant and that the collector's chief operating officer should be held in contempt. Section 6.4 is a draft order holding the debt collector in contempt.[219]

Chapter 7 Complaint Against Mortgage Servicer for Responding to Billing Errors with Foreclosure

This chapter contains a complaint against a mortgage servicing company for failing to respond the qualified written requests pointing out its repeated billing errors. The Real Estate Settlement Procedures Act (RESPA), 12 U.S.C. § 2605(e)(2) requires a mortgagors and their servicers to investigate and respond to qualified written requests for correction of errors.[220] The mortgage servicing company erroneously demanded the homeowners maintain homeowners insurance on their second home when the mortgage was on the first home. The homeowners pointed out the mistake and provided proof of insurance on the mortgaged home. Rather than correcting the error the mortgage servicing company forced placed insurance on the second home which

was the billing address but not collateral for the mortgage and added over $1000 each year for two years for forced placed insurance to the mortgage account. The homeowners repeatedly wrote protesting the error as did several attorneys on their behalf, to little avail. The complaint also alleges that the reporting of their account as delinquent was defamatory, that asserting erroneous charges on the account was a conversion, and that the servicer negligently serviced the loan in breach of its duty to maintain accurate records.

Chapter 8 Fair Debt Collection Practices Act Class Action: Deposition and Class Certification Memo

Section 8.1 is memorandum in support of certifying a Fair Debt Collection Practices Act class action seeking statutory damages.[221] The collection letters were allegedly sent by an unlicensed collector,[222] were confusing about their source, and included false threats. Section 8.2 is the deposition of the corporate representative for the collection agency.

Chapter 9 Complaint against Payday Lender Disguising Its Loans as Sales of Internet Access

Section 9.1 is a class action complaint against a payday lender who was disguising its payday loans to avoid complying with consumer protection laws. Payday lending involves very expensive short term consumer loans that are payable at the consumer's payday but often renewed at great cost.[223] The payday lender allegedly disguised its loans as sales of internet access and of career training video tapes. The complaint alleges that the disguised loans violate the Florida usury laws, the Florida civil criminal practices act, the Truth in Lending Act,[224] the Electronic Funds Transfer Act,[225] the Forida collection practices act,[226] and Florida UDAP.[227] The compliant seeks declaratory and injunctive relief, actual damage, and attorney fees.

---

217 *Id.* § 6.9 (5th Ed. 2004).
218 *See* Irwin v. Mascott, 112 F. Supp.2d 937 (N.D. Ca. 2000).
219 *See* Irwin v. Mascott, 2004 WL 1233984 (9th Cir. 2004).
220 National Consumer Law Center, Repossessions and Foreclosures § 19.2 (5th Ed. 2002 and Supp.).
221 *See* National Consumer Law Center, Consumer Class Actions Ch. 9 (5th Ed. 2002 and Supp.).
222 *But see* National Consumer Law Center, Fair Debt Collection Practices § 5.5.8.4 (5th Ed. 2004).
223 *See* National Consumer Law Center, Cost of Credit § 7.5.5 (2d Ed. 2000 and Supp.). *See also* National Consumer Law Center, Consumer Law Pleadings Number 3 § 4.1.
224 *See* National Consumer Law Center, Truth in Lending § 2.2.4.3.5 (5th Ed. 2003 and Supp.).
225 *See* National Consumer Law Center, Consumer Banking and Payments Law § 4.4. (2d Ed. 2002 and Supp.).
226 *See* National Consumer Law Center, Fair Debt Collection Practices § 11.2 (5th Ed. 2004).
227 *See* National Consumer Law Center, Unfair and Deceptive Acts and Practices § 3.2 (6th Ed. 2004).

Chapter 10 Deposition of Trans Union Employee Regarding Changes in Information in the Credit Reporting Agency File

Section 10.1 is the deposition of a supervising employee in the customer relations division of Trans Union, a credit reporting agency. The deposition describes the procedures for responding to consumer disputes of credit information.

Chapter 11 Deposition of Equifax Employee About Correcting Errors in a Credit File

Section 11.1 is the deposition of a supervising employee in the customer service department of Equifax, a credit reporting agency. The deposition describes the procedures for responding to consumer disputes of credit information.

Chapter 12 Banking Expert's Opinion Analysis on Credit Issues

Section 12.1 is expert opinion analysis of the direct damages to a consumer as a result of a foreclosure being recorded against their house pointing out that the public record of a foreclosure is kept forever, not just for the seven years that credit reporting information may be retained. It points out that a foreclosure will make business credit unavailable for the borrower and that a mortgage loan in the subprime market is likely to cost an extra $115,000 on an existing home and $175,000 on a new home. It quantifies similar penalties on car loans and student loans.

Section 12.2 is expert opinion analysis of a secured "credit card" that is so expensive that its benefit to the consumer was illusory. It analyzes the misrepresentations made in the telemarketing of the "credit card." It concludes that the lender did not deal with the consumer in good faith and fairly as required by banking standards. Section 12.3 is an expert opinion analysis of a car dealer's and bank's incentives to inflate the interest rate on a nonrecourse credit sale of an automobile to a consumer. It describes how the the bank closely controls the terms of the credit transaction. Section 12.4 is an expert opinion analysis of Truth in Lending and HOEPA (Home Ownership and Equity Protection Act) applicability to a predatory mortgage loan concluding that the loan violated both laws.

Chapter 13 Expert Witness Report and Analysis Regarding Credit Reporting

Section 13.1 is Hendricks' expert witness report in a Fair Credit Reporting Act case involving the mixing of files of two consumers with the same name, and the failure of the credit reporting agency to use the consumers' social security numbers to properly separate the two consumers' credit files with the result that the erroneous mixed information was repeatedly remixed after one of the consumers complained of the error. The report continues with an analysis of the consumer's damages as a result of the repeated mixed credit files, the consumer's youth, and the harm to his good reputation. Section 13.2 is an excerpt from Chapter 20, "Damage and Damages," from Hendricks' new book, *Credit Scores & Credit Reports* (Privacy Times 2004). It analyzes how consumers are damaged by often repetitive inaccuracies in their credit reports and describes a paradigm for calculating the resulting damages.

Chapter 14 Fraudulent Spanish Language Representations of Mortgage Refinancing Terms

Section 14.1 is a complaint against a mortgage lender for actual, statutory and punitive damages for fraudulently misrepresenting in the consumers' native language of Spanish the annual percentage rate and that the monthly payment included escrows for taxes and insurance in a refinancing of the consumer's mortgage. Section 14.2 is a request for production of the lender's documents regarding the loan and its lending policies. Section 14.3 is the consumers' memorandum of law arguing that arbitration should not be compelled as the lender's arbitration clause was unconscionable. Section 14.4 is the consumer's affidavit in opposing arbitration stating that the consumer did not read English, that the lender's Spanish speaking did not inform them of the arbitration clause, and it would take six months to save the $1000 necessary to initiate arbitration.

Section 14.5 is the consumers' supplemental trial brief arguing that even if it is shown that the consumer misrepresented information on the credit application given to the lender that the defense of in *pari delicto* does not necessarily apply. It argues that Truth in Lending (TIL) damages are available for the lender's failure to rescind the transaction. It argues that an unclean hands defense does not apply to a TIL claim. It argues that the preponderance of evidence standard applies to a TIL claim.

Section 14.6 is the consumers' proposed jury instructions.

Section 14.7 is the consumers' response to the lender's post-trial motions. The consumers argued that the court properly directed a verdict against the lender's defenses, that the jury could not infer that the consumers understood their tax returns when the consumers did not understand English, that the expert could not establish whether the lender relied on the consumers' tax returns in deciding to extend credit, and that $500,000 in .punitive damages was not excessive where actual damages awarded were $45,000 given the potential harm that they avoided by quick action.

Chapter 15 Depositions of Auto Dealer Mangagers Concerning Yo-Yo and Other Sales Techniques

Section 15.1 is the deposition of an F & I (finance and insurance) Director at a franchised automobile dealer regarding his standard operating procedures for preparing the paperwork, financing, additional charges, and disclosures involved in the "yo-yo" or spot delivery[228] sale of an automobile. It mentions the Beacon credit scoring system used by Equifax and finance companies.[229] Section 15.2 is the deposition of a general sales manager at a franchised automobile dealer. It discusses closing car sales and determining whether to engage in "yo-yo" or spot delivery sales to marginal credit risks and also financer conditions on approval of financing.

Chapter 16 Retainer Agreement with Contingent Fee in a Consumer Case

This chapter contains a contingent fee retainer agreement for a consumer client. State standards for client retainer forms vary from state to state and require the careful consideration of counsel before adapting a retainer form for a particular case.[230]

Chapter 17 Challenge to Municipal Water Shutoff of Tenants Where Only Notice Went to Landlord

Section 17.1 is a proposed second amended class complaint by tenants against water authorities for shutting off the water service to their apartment.[231] The tenants argue that termination of their water service with notice only to the landlord violated due process,[232] equal protection, and the federal Equal Credit Opportunity Act. The complaint seeks

injunctive and declaratory relief and also actual and punitive damages and attorney fees. Section 17.2 is an appellate brief and 17.3 is a reply appellate brief in support of the claims.

Chapter 18 Depositions in Cases Alleging the Resale of Rebuilt Wrecked Cars

Section 18.1 is the deposition, with editorial comments, of a used car manager at a franchised automobile dealer alleged to have sold a rebuilt wreck to the consumer without disclosure that the car had been rebuilt and representing it was like new when a routine inspection by a sales person or mechanic would have revealed that the car had been wrecked.[233] The used car manager describes the process for purchasing used cars from automobile auctions, refurbishing used cars, and reselling them. The used car manager admitted that he had almost no personal recollection of the purchase of the car or its resale so that he could not dispute the consumer's description of events.

Section 18.2 is the deposition of the former used car manager at a car dealer who had no recollection of the sale of a rebuilt wreck to one of the dealer's car salesmen. It discusses what the dealer's file shows about the car and the dealer's asserted general practices of inspecting used cars before sale and disclosing all known defects. Sections 18.3a and 18.3b are the deposition of the business manager for a franchised automobile dealer about a car sale for which he arranged the financing. The deponent had no recollection of the transaction at all at the beginning of the deposition or even of meeting with the dealer's attorney about the suit six months before the deposition. The deposition details the dealer's normal steps in arranging high rate car financing.

Chapter 19 Jury Instructions in an Abusive Debt Collection and Repossession Case

This chapter contains jury instructions for abusive debt collection and repossession of a car. The instructions include instructions on claims under the Fair Debt Collection Practices Act, trespass, unfair and deceptive acts and practices, fraud, actual, statutory, and punitive damages. Also included are special verdict forms and interrogatories to the jury.

---

228 *See* National Consumer Law Center, Automobile Fraud § 1.3.4 (2d Ed. 2003 and Supp.).

229 *See* National Consumer Law Center, Fair Credit Reporting (5th ed. 2002 and Supp.).

230 *See* National Consumer Law Center, Practice of Consumer Law § 4.6 (2003).

231 *See* National Consumer Law Center, Access to Utility Service § 11.5.3 (3d Ed. 2004).

232 *Id.* § 12.2.

---

233 *See* Bird v. John Chezik Homerun, Inc., 152 F.3d 1014 (8th Cir. 1998).

Pleadings by Contributor

This listing provides summary biographical information on those contributing to the National Consumer Law Center's *Consumer Law Pleadings on CD-Rom*, Numbers One through Ten (1994–2004). This listing does *not* include those who have contributed pleadings to other manuals.

This listing provides basic information about contributors and is recommended for readers who want the background of an attorney drafting a particular pleading. Other listings (for example, "Contributors by State" and "Contributors by Title") allow the reader to locate contributors of interest by state and by title of pleading.

Irv Ackelsberg is a consumer specialist with Community Legal Services, Inc., in Philadelphia, where he has practiced for 26 years, now serving as a Managing Attorney. He has extensive experience in the areas of foreclosure defense, bankruptcy, real estate, student loans and consumer fraud. In recent years he has concentrated most of his work on the predatory lending practices of the subprime mortgage industry. He successfully litigated the first reported case decided under the Home Ownership and Equity Protection Act (HOEPA), *Newton v. United Companies Financial Corp.*, 24 F. Supp. 2d 444 (E.D. Pa. 1998). He served on the Official Creditors Committee in the United Companies Financial chapter 11 case and was actively involved in the legislative campaign to enact anti-predatory legislation before the Philadelphia City Council.

Mr. Ackelsberg has authored a number of articles and is a contributor to the Pennsylvania Consumer Law treatise. He is a frequent lecturer at training events for lawyers, for Legal Services clients, and for the larger community. He was the 2001 recipient of the Philadelphia Bar Association's Andrew Hamilton Award for exemplary service in the public interest and the 1997 recipient of the Striving Towards Excellence Award presented by Pennsylvania Legal Services. Mr. Ackelsberg received his B.A. from Haverford College in 1972 and his J.D. from the Rutgers-Camden Law School in 1976. Community Legal Services, Inc., 3638 N. Broad Street, Philadelphia, PA 19140, (215) 227-2400, fax: (215) 227-2435, e-mail: Iackelsberg@clsphila.org.

CLP2 Chapter 13; CLP4 Chapter 2; CLP5 Chapter 9

Alan A. Alop is Deputy Director of the Legal Assistance Foundation of Metropolitan Chicago, 111 West Jackson, Chicago, Illinois, phone: (312) 347-8310, fax: (312) 341-1041. Mr. Alop has over twenty-five years experience in litigating consumer cases, including consumer fraud, RICO, collection abuse, consumer credit matters, and defense of collection matters. He is the author of *Defending Hospital Collection Cases: A Practical Guide* and was lead attorney in *Rosario v. Livaditis*, 963 F.2d 1013 (7th Cir. 1992), a successful fraud class action against a vocational school.

Mr. Alop is a 1971 graduate of the University of Chicago Law School. He worked for six years with the Duval County Legal Aid Association in Jacksonville, Florida from 1971-1977, as a staff attorney and later Director of Litigation. Since 1977 he has been employed as a supervisory attorney with the Legal Assistance Foundation of Chicago (LAFC), where he specialized in consumer fraud and consumer credit cases. In 1997 he was named Deputy Director of LAFC. In 1998 the National Consumer Law Center named Alop the Ninth Annual Vern Countryman Award winner. Mr. Alop has litigated over a hundred class action cases and lectured on consumer-law-related topics.

CLP2 Chapters 8, 12, 15; CLP6 Chapter 8; CLP8 Chapter 4

Paul Arons operates a law office with Sharon Grace at 685 Spring Street, #104, Friday Harbor, Washington, (360) 378-6496, Fax: (360) 378-6498, lopa@rockisland.com. He began his legal career representing plaintiffs in labor and employment law disputes. In the early 1990's he began focusing his efforts on class actions under the FDCPA, suing debt collectors who collect on dishonored checks. He has participated as class counsel in a number of large class actions in California including *Newman v. Checkrite*, 912 F.Supp. 1354, *Irwin v. Mascott*, 112 F. Supp. 2d 937, 959 (N.D. Cal. 2000) and *Ballard v. Equifax Check Services, Inc.* 158 F. Supp. 2d 1163 (E.D. Cal. 2001).

CLP10 Chapter 6

Alden L. Atkins is a private attorney with Vinson & Elkins L.L.P, 1455 Pennsylvania Avenue, N.W., Suite 700, Washington, D.C., 20004, (202) 639-6500, fax: (202) 639-6604. Mr Atkins has thirteen years of experience litigating commercial and pro bono cases. He specializes in commercial and criminal litigation, and his clients include one of the high-profile entities involved in the Whitewater investigation. Among his other pro bono work, he has prepared numerous briefs in *Martin v. Wilks*. Mr. Atkins is a member of the New York and District of Columbia bar associations.

CLP3 Chapter 1

Charles M. Baird practices law in Atlanta, Ga. (235 Peachtree Street, Suite 400, Atlanta, Georgia 30303-1400, phone: (404) 287-2383, fax: (404) 522-9486, e-mail: charlesmbaird@att.net. He specializes in consumer representation (individual and class actions), primarily focused on predatory mortgage lending. He does a good bit of co-counseling with legal services attorneys. Much of his current litigation involves mortgage closing costs. Mr. Baird has approximately twenty years of experience specializing in Truth in Lending and other consumer law topics as a legal services attorney with Georgia Legal Services and Legal Services of Greater Miami and a staff attorney with the National Consumer Law Center. He has written extensively and lectured on these subjects. Mr. Baird was counsel for the borrower in *Rodash v. AIB Mortgage Co.*, 16 F.3d 1142 (11th Cir. 1994), one of the most notable recent Truth in Lending cases.

CLP1 Chapter 11; CLP8 Chapter 11

Charles H. Barr of Croen & Barr, LLP, 250 East Wisconsin Avenue, Ste. 1020, Milwaukee, WI 53202, (414) 225-2080, (414) 226-2070, received his bachelor's degree from Cornell University in 1973 and his law degree from Harvard Law School in 1977. He has been engaged in the private practice of law since graduation from law school. He is a partner in the Milwaukee, Wisconsin, firm of Croen & Barr L.L.P., which he and Frederick R. Croen founded in 1993. Croen & Barr is a three-attorney firm that concentrates its practice in the area of business, real estate, employment, and civil trials and appeals.

CLP6 Chapter 15

Mr. Barr is the former co-chair of the Milwaukee Bar Association's Bench/Bar Court of Appeals Committee, which initiated a comprehensive review and currently proposed revision of the rules governing Wisconsin appellate courts. He presently serves on the MBA's Courts Committee and Bench/Bar Circuit Court Civil Division Committees. He is a member of the Litigation and Appellate Sections of the State Bar of Wisconsin and the Wisconsin Employment Lawyers Association. He has served as a Moot Court Judge in Marquette Law School and regional competitions. He has taught in continuing legal education courses on discovery, witness preparation, civil procedure and written advocacy, and has participated in numerous bar-sponsored volunteer activities to bring information about the legal system to the general public. In May 2000, Mr. Barr was appointed as the Municipal Judge in Bayside, Wisconsin.

Nancy Barron is a partner in the firm of Kemnitzer, Anderson, Barron & Ogilvie, LLP, 445 Bush Street, 6th Fl., San Francisco, CA 94108. The firm has represented consumers in automotive affairs including lemon law, fraud, products liability, and leasing for more than ten years. She is the California State Bar approved CLE provider for seminars on lemon law litigation, and author of numerous articles on lemon law issues. She is a member of the Litigation Section of the California Bar Association, Consumer Attorneys

CLP2 Chapters 5, 6

of California, the Marin County Bar Association, and a life member of the Fulbright Alumni Association.

Peter F. Barry is a licensed attorney admitted to practice in the State of Minnesota and the owner of The Barry Law Office, Ltd. 342 County Road D East St. Paul, MN 55117-1275, (651) 714-8800 ext. 135, Fax: (651) 501-8800, pbarry@lawpoint.com. His practice is dedicated exclusively to protecting consumers against illegal debt collection activity. He was recently named by his peers as a Super Lawyer® for 2003 by *Minnesota Law & Politics Magazine*. In 1996, Barry graduated from William Mitchell College of Law in St. Paul, Minnesota where he competed nationally on the school's trial advocacy team and won top honors for his appellate work. Barry did extensive clinical work with several organizations including the Ramsey County Public Defenders Office, Legal Assistance to Minnesota Prisoners, and the St. Paul Tenants Union. He opened his law practice directly out of law school and has been enjoying his private plaintiff's practice ever since.

CLP10 Chapter 4

Barry volunteers annually with Habitat for Humanity and the Minnesota State Bar Association's High School Mock Trial Program as a judge. He also devotes volunteer time to various William Mitchell clinical programs and maintains an ongoing pro-bono legal services commitment in the area of consumer rights. In 2003, Barry was named an adjunct Professor of Law at William Mitchell College of Law where he now teaches Consumer Rights Law. In addition to being admitted to practice in Minnesota and Wisconsin state and federal courts, Barry was also recently admitted in the Northern District of Texas and the 8th Circuit Court of Appeals. He was born in San Jose, California in 1964 and lives in St. Paul, Minnesota.

Daniel L. Berger is a partner in the New York law firm of Bernstein Litowitz Berger & Grossmann LLP. Mr. Berger served as an Assistant Attorney General of the State of New York, Civil Rights Division, and is principally responsible for his firm's discrimination and securities practice groups. Mr. Berger currently is a member of the faculty of the Practicing Law Institute and a member of the National Employment Lawyers' Association. Bernstein Litowitz Berger & Grossmann, L.L.P., 1285 Avenue of the Americas, New York, NY 10019; (212) 554-1400; fax: (212) 554-1444; e-mail: dan@BLBGLAW.com.

CLP7 Chapter 1

Marlowe J. Blake, attorney at law, 520 W. Hallandale Beach Blvd., Hallandale, FL 33009, phone: (305) 670-3379. He concentrates on Fair Credit Reporting Act violations and general civil litigation in state and federal courts, including fourteen suits involving credit reporting agencies. Mr. Blake has an AV rating by Martindale-Hubble and is admitted to the Florida, Eleventh Circuit Court of Appeals, and the United States District Court (Southern and Middle Districts) bars.

CLP2 Chapter 10

Paul F Bland is a staff attorney for Trial Lawyers for Public Justice, and directs TLPJ's Mandatory Arbitration Abuse Prevention Project. He works on socially significant precedent-setting complex civil litigation, particularly on the appellate level. Successful arguments include *Riemer v. Columbia Medical Plan*, 358 Md. 222, 747 A.2d 677 (Md. 2000) (unanimously holding that Maryland HMO's may not pursue members for subrogation of recoveries members receive from third parties); *United States v. United States ex. rel. Thornton*, 207 F.3d 769 (5th Cir. 2000) (holding that realtors under *qui tam* provisions of the False Claims Act are entitled to receive a statutory share of the value of certain non-cash proceeds of a settlement between the government and the defendants); *Chisolm v. TranSouth Financial Corp.*, 184 F.R.D. 556 (E.D. Va. 1999) (certifying class in revolving repossessions car churning case).

CLP8 Chapter 1

LaBarron N. Boone practices consumer law with the firm of Beasley, Allen, Crow, Methvin, Portis & Miles, P.C., P.O. Box 4160, Montgomery, Alabama 36103-4160, (334) 269-2343, Fax: (334) 954-7555, email: labarron.boone@beasleyallen.com. His areas of

CLP9 Chapter 18

Pleadings by Contributor

practice include consumer fraud, insurance litigation, personal injury law, products liability law, and product liability. He is a graduate of the University of Alabama Law School: (J.D., 1995) and Auburn University (B.I.E., 1990).

LaBarron concentrates his practice in product liability, consumer fraud, and personal and injury. He is the recipient of the "Chairman's Award of Excellence" presented by MCDC Young Democrats on September 28, 2000. He is a lecturer for The Association of Trial Lawyers of America. He was president of Kappa Alpha Psi Fraternity. He was featured in the April 2001 edition of the Kappa Alpha Psi Journal discussing the law and how it related to consumer issues. LaBarron was also featured in the December 1999 issue of Jet Magazine that focused on victories for consumers and on the two cases he tried which resulted in verdicts of $581 and $116 million—respectively, *Merriweather v. Whirlpool* and *Aultman v. Terex Telelect*. A cover story was done on LaBarron in the Urban Metro June 2000 issue titled, "Lawyer Makes Big Strides in Alabama's America's Community." He was the 2000-2001 President of the Capital City Bar Association and also serves as president of the Alabama Lawyers Association.

Rand Bragg is a private attorney whose offices are at Horwitz, Horwitz & Associates, 25 East Washington Street, Suite 900, Chicago, IL 60602, (312) 372-8822, Fax: (312) 372-1673, rand@horwitzLaw.com. He specializes in consumers' rights litigation, particularly debt collection abuse, automobile leases, misuses of credit reports, and truth in lending. Previously, Mr. Bragg was a litigation coordinator with the UAW Legal Services Plans, and practiced with Legal Services Corporation-funded programs in Pennsylvania. He graduated from West Virginia University College of Law in 1973 and has practiced law in West Virginia, Pennsylvania, Delaware, and Illinois as well as many federal courts. Since 1989 Mr. Bragg has co-authored National Consumer Law Center's *Fair Debt Collection* and annual supplements. For several years he has wrote a chapter entitled "Fair Debt Collection Practices Act," for *Ohio Consumer Law*. Mr. Bragg has lectured and conducted trainings on the Fair Debt Collection Practices Act for various groups including: Kansas City Metropolitan Bar Association (1996); National Association of Consumer Advocates (1991-1995); Commercial Law League (1992); and UAW Legal Services Plans (1985-1992).

CLP2 Chapter 14; CLP3 Chapter 9; CLP7 Chapter 7; CLP10 Chapter 6

Brian Bromberg is in private practice at 40 Exchange Place, Suite 2010, New York, NY 10005, (212) 248-7906, Fax: (212) 248-7908, brian@brianbromberg.com, and has been a NACA member since 2001.

CLP10 Chapter 19

Paul A. Brooks is an attorney, working for the past nine years with Community Legal Services, Inc., 1424 Chestnut St., Fifth Floor, Philadelphia, Pennsylvania 19102, (215) 981-3826, fax: (215) 981-0434. He specializes in consumer and bankruptcy law. Mr. Brooks is a member of the Pennsylvania state and federal bars.

CLP2 Chapter 4

Bernard Brown has been in private practice in Kansas City since 1980, and is presently at the Brown Law Firm, 3100 Broadway, Suite 223, Kansas City, MO 64111, (816) 960-4777, Fax: (816) 960-6777, brlawofc@swbell.ne. Between 1984 and 1996 his office was devoted entirely to representing consumer plaintiffs who were victims of car fraud — such as the fraudulent sales of rebuilt wrecks and cars with odometer rollbacks. More recently he has also worked on consumer class actions relating to vehicle sales and financing, and on "home equity" fraud cases. A sizable number of his cases have resulted in published court decisions of significance in these areas of the law.

Mr. Brown began doing public interest work when he was in college, starting with volunteer work at the headquarters of Common Cause in Washington, D.C. He has worked regularly with National Consumer Law Center staff for many years on various materials, and has written or contributed to many articles relating to consumer law. He is a founding member and one of the two original Co-chairs of the National Association of Consumer Advocates ("NACA"). He has worked closely on a number of issues with other leading

CLP2 Chapter 6; CLP10 Chapter 18

consumer groups (such as Consumers Union, Consumer Federation of America, Public Citizen, U.S. PIRG, Center for Auto Safety, and Consumers for Auto Reliability and Safety), and has drafted legislation and testified for these groups in the U.S. and state legislatures. He is often consulted by media and business entities regarding car industry-related consumer issues. He is extensively involved in networking and idea-sharing efforts of consumer advocate attorneys across the country, and regularly provides lectures for other attorneys and consumer advocates on various consumer law issues. He also serves as an adjunct law school professor teaching consumer protection law.

Karen Brown is a staff attorney with Atlanta Legal Aid Society, Inc. Home Defense Program, 340 West Ponce de Leon Avenue, Decatur, GA 30030, (404) 377-0701, FAX (404) 377-2349. Her work includes representation of low-income and elderly homeowners in cases involving home improvement and predatory mortgage lending scams. Ms. Brown previously served as a staff attorney in Atlanta Legal Aid Society's Senior Citizens Law Project. She has been involved in a number of major litigation cases in the consumer area including pending lawsuits against Ford Consumer Finance Co. regarding alleged violations of RESPA mortgage broker kickback provisions. Ms. Brown is a founding member and Vice Chair of the Consumer Law Center of the South and a participant in the Housing Action Team of Atlantans Building Leadership through Empowerment.

CLP3 Chapter 6

Edward D. Buckley, III, is a partner in the firm Greene, Buckley, et al, #1400, Marquis, 285 Peachtree Ave., Atlanta, GA 30303, (404) 781-1100, fax: (404) 781-1101. Mr. Buckley specializes in civil rights and employment discrimination. He is President of the Georgia Division of the National Employment Laywers Association. He was the chairman of the State Bar of Georgia Seminar, "Trial of a Race Discrimination Case," and the Atlanta Bar Association Seminar, "Trial of a Sexual Harassment Case." Mr. Buckley is a regular speaker for the Council on Education in Management, for Personnel Law update Seminars, and for the State Bar of Georgia and the Atlanta Bar Association on employment discrimination issues. He is author of *Litigating Negligence in Employment: A Plaintiff's Tactics in Negligence in Employment Law, Felieu & Johnson (BNA 2002)*. Mr. Buckley has an AV rating by Martindale-Hubbell and is admitted to practice in all state courts, appellate courts, federal district courts in the state of Georgia, in the Eleventh Circuit Court of Appeals and the United States Supreme Court.

CLP3 Chapter 9

Ronald L. Burdge is an attorney with the Burdge Law Office Co., LPA, 2299 Miamisburg Centerville Rd., Dayton, OH 45459, Telephone: (937) 432-9500, Fax: (520) 432-9503, e-mail: Ron@OhioLemonLaw.com, websites: www.OhioLemonLaw.com, www.RvLemonLaw.com, www.KentuckyLemonLaw.com, www.OhioConsumerLaw.com and others. Co-counseling and coaching website: www.TheLawCoach.com. Ronald L. Burdge is in the private practice of law in Dayton, Ohio, and is known throughout Ohio as a leading Consumer Law attorney who has represented literally thousands of consumers in "lemon" car lawsuits over the last twenty years, and actively co-counsels and coaches other consumer law attorneys. He has authored articles and lectured on the Ohio Lemon Law, Assistive Device Lemon Laws, Recreation Vehicle Lemon Laws. Although the majority of his court cases have involved defective motor vehicle litigation, he has also represented consumers in Udap, product defect, odometer tampering, contract breach, fraud, and commercial litigation in both state and federal courts throughout Ohio, in Indiana and Kentucky. With extensive trial and appellate experience related to motor vehicles and dealership business practices, he has also successfully argued cases in various courts of appeals and the Ohio Supreme Court. He was admitted to the Ohio Bar in 1978. His bar admissions include all Ohio state courts, several United States District Courts (Ohio and Indiana), 6th Circuit Court of Appeals, and the United States Supreme Court. He is a member of numerous bar associations, has obtained several multi million dollar verdicts, and handled numerous ground breaking Consumer Law and Lemon Law cases.

CLP4 Chapter 15; CLP6 Chapter 2; CLP8 Chapter 12; CLP10 Chapter 2

CLP4 Chapter 13

The Law Offices of **Sheldon V. Burman**, P.C., 110 East 59th Street, 23rd Floor, New York, NY 10022, (212) 935-1600, fax:(212) 223-4911, has a national reputation, with a concentration in the consumer class action field, having been involved in landmark litigation in that area. Sheldon V. Burman is a graduate of New York University School of Law and has an extensive background as a lecturer and author of numerous articles on consumer class actions and consumer law. Reported cases in which the firm has been a lead counsel in consumer class actions include *Branch v. Crabtree*, 197 A.D.2d 557, 603 N.Y.S.2d 490 (2d Dept. 1994); *Weinberg v. Hertz Corp.*, 69 N.Y.2 979, 516 N.Y.S.2d 652 (1987), *aff'g*, 116 A.D.2d 1, 499 N.Y.S.2d 693 (1st Dept. 1986); *Weinberg v. Sprint*, 165 F.R.D. 431 (D.N.J. 1996); *Eisen v. Carlisle & Jacquelin*, 417 U.S. 156 (1974) (amicus curiae brief on behalf of N.Y.S. Trial Lawyers Association) Karlin v. IVF America, Inc., 93 N.Y.2d 282, 690 N.Y.S.2d 495 (Ct. App. 1999); Hayes v. County Bank, 286 A.D.2d 371, 728 N.Y.S.2d 709 (A.D. 2d Dept. 2001), aff'd. 185 Misc.2d 414, 713 N.Y.S.2d 267 (Sup. Queens 2000); Selby v Principal Mutual, 197 F.R.D. 48 (S.D.N.Y. 2000); Colbert v. Rank America, Inc., 273 A.D.2 209, 709 N.Y.S.2d (A.D.2 Dept. 2000). Mr. Burman's lectures include: "Current Class Action Litigation," Class Action Committee, N.Y.S. Bar Association, Jan. 1998; "Class Action Update," Consumer Affairs Committee, N.Y. County Lawyer's Association, Oct. 1996; "Legal Safari Through the Class Action Jungle," National Consumer Law Center Conference, Chicago, Illinois, Oct. 1993; "Arbitration and Class Actions," National Association of Consumer Agency Administrators, Chicago, Illinois, June 2000; "Consumer Class Actions," Consumer Affairs Committee, Association of the Bar of the City of New York, February 2000. Mr. Burman has contributed a variety of publications: National Consumer Law Center, Consumer Class Actions: A Practical Litigation Guide (3d ed. 1995); N.Y.S.B.A. Journal, Dec. 1987 "Class Actions on behalf of Bank Customers"; Book Review: *Newberg on Class Actions* (2d ed.) New York Law Journal, June 6, 1986, p. 2; *Class Actions in New York: A Terminal Case Gets Statutory Relief*, 4 Class Action Reports (May–June, 1975). He is a founding member of the National Association of Consumer Advocates, a former member of the editorial board of *Class Action Reports*, a member of the Consumer Affairs Committee, N.Y. County Lawyers Assoc., and various consumer and class action Bar Association committees.

CLP6 Chapter 1

Linda J. Cahn is in private practice in New York City, where she is developing a consumer protection and healthcare litigation practice. She graduated cum laude from Princeton University in 1976 and graduated with honors from Hofstra Law School in 1979. She was admitted to the Bar of the state of New York in 1980 and thereafter to the Eastern and Southern Districts of New York. She clerked for a year in the Eastern District and practiced law with several firms in the interim.

CLP4 Chapter 3

Eric M. Carlson is an attorney in the Los Angeles office of the National Senior Citizens Law Center, 3435 Wilshire Blvd., Suite 2860, Los Angeles, CA 90010. Mr. Carlson specializes in the law governing long-term care facilities, including nursing homes and assisted living facilities. He counsels attorneys from across the country in issues relating to long-term care, and also participates in litigation on residents' behalf. He was co-counsel in *Podolsky v. First Healthcare Corp.*, 50 Cal. App. 4th 632, 58 Cal. Rptr. 2d 89 (1996), which established that the guarantee agreements that had been used routinely by nursing facilities were illegal and unenforceable.

Mr. Carlson is the author of numerous publications and articles, including "Long Term Care Advocacy," the leading legal treatise on long-term care issues. He is the principal author of NSCLC's Nursing Home Law Letter, a comprehensive bimonthly summary of developments in long-term care. He speaks regularly, across the country, on issues relating to long-term care. He has spoken at numerous national conferences and at several programs organized by state government agencies.

Mr. Carlson received his B.A. degree from the University of Minnesota in 1982 and his J.D. degree from the Boalt Hall School of Law at the University of California at Berkeley in 1988. National Senior Citizens Law Center, 3435 Wilshire Boulevard, Los Angeles, CA 90010, (213) 639-0930

Steve R. Conley practices consumer law in Metairie, Lousiana (3350 Ridgelake Drive, Suite 200 Metairie, Louisiana 70002, (504) 734-9804, fax:(504) 733-1744). He has been a member of the National Association of Consumer Advocates since 1998. Since 1992, he has had a solo practice concentrating in consumer protection litigation under a variety of federal and state law including Fair Debt Collection Practices Act, Truth-in-Lending Act, Fair Credit Reporting Act, and Equal Credit Opportunity Act. In 2000-2001 he was Chair, Public Access and Consumer Protection Committee, Louisiana State Bar Association.. He graduated from the Tulane University School of Law with a J.D. in 1991 and served on the Tulane Law Review. His publications include "Lejune v. Rayne Branch Hospital: Allowing Bystander Mental Anguish Claims in Louisiana," 65 Tul. L. Rev. 918 (1991).

CLP10 Chapter 16

Eric L. Crandall is an attorney practicing at 275 South Third Street, Suite 101, Stillwater, Minnesota 55082, phone: number: 651-430-8187, fax: 651-439-1034, e-mail: ericleighton@mcleodusa.net. His practice is focused on representing consumers in the areas of unfair debt collection practices, privacy rights, mortgage fraud, and credit insurance abuse. Mr. Crandall is a member of the bars of, and licensed to practice in, Minnesota and Wisconsin. Mr. Crandall is a 1988 graduate of William Mitchell College of Law, Saint Paul, Minnesota.

CLP8 Chapter 15

Mark A. Chavez practices with the firm of Chavez & Gertler LLP, 42 Miller Avenue, Mill Valley, CA 94941, phone: (415) 381-5599, fax: (415) 381-5572, e-mail: mark@chavezgertler.com

CLP1 Chapter 2; CLP6 Chapter 4; CLP7 Chapter 15; CLP9 Chapter 13

Mark Chavez received his Juris Doctorate degree from Stanford Law School in 1979. During law school he was a Judicial Extern for the Honorable Mathew O. Tobriner, then Senior Associate Justice of the California Supreme Court, a co-founder and the first Managing Editor of the Stanford Environmental Law Annual and a founding member of the Stanford Public Interest Law Foundation.

Mr. Chavez was selected through the Attorney General's Honors Program and joined the Civil Division of the United States Department of Justice in Washington, D.C. after graduating from law school. In 1983, he entered private practice working first at Pillsbury, Madison & Sutro in San Francisco, California and subsequently at Farrow, Bramson, Chavez & Baskin in Walnut Creek, California. In 1994, Mr. Chavez and Jonathan E. Gertler founded the law firm of Chavez & Gertler LLP. Both Mr. Chavez and Mr. Gertler are AV-rated by Martindale-Hubbell.

In the course of his career, Mr. Chavez has represented consumers in a wide variety of class actions and private attorney general cases involving financial services, lending practices and insurance charges. His significant class action experience includes arguing *Linder v. Thrifty Oil*, 23 Cal.4th 429 (2000) before the California Supreme Court and acting as co-counsel for the plaintiff class in *Briseno v. Washington Mutual*, 24 Cal.4th 906 (2001). Mr. Chavez has served or is currently serving as lead or co-lead counsel in over eighty class actions filed in federal and state courts in Arizona, California, Colorado, Florida, Idaho, Missouri, New Jersey, Ohio, Tennessee, and Washington. These class actions have resulted in some of the largest recoveries ever achieved in consumer cases in California. *See, e.g., Moultrie v. Nissan Motor Acceptance Corp.* (San Francisco Superior Court No. 302601) ($68 million); *Clark, et al. v. Ford Motor Credit Company* (Alameda Superior Court No. 6745257) ($58 million).

Mr. Chavez was one of the founders and is the former Co-Chair of the National Association of Consumer Advocates and serves on the board of the Stanford Public Interest Law Foundation. In recent years, Mr. Chavez has been the Co-Chair of the Practising Law Institute's Consumer Financial Services Litigation program in New York and San Francisco. He also has spoken at the annual conventions of the American Bar Association, the California State Bar, and the Consumer Attorneys of California. In 1994 he delivered the opening address at the National Consumer Law Center's Consumer Rights Litigation Conference.

Mr. Chavez is admitted to practice in California and before the United States Supreme Court, the United States Court of Appeals for the District of Columbia Circuit, the Ninth Circuit and the Eleventh Circuit, as well as the United States District Courts for the Central, Eastern, Northern and Southern Districts of California. He is a member of the Editorial Boards of Class Action Reports, Consumer Financial Services Law Report and Forum.

Andrew Cogdell is an attorney and co-director of Catawba Valley Legal Services, 211 East Union Street, Morganton, NC, 28655-3449, (828) 437-8280, fax: (828) 437-9397. He specializes in federally subsidized housing and private landlord/tenant law. Mr. Cogdell briefed and argued *Stanley v. Moore* before the Supreme Court of North Carolina, 454 S.E.2d 225 (1995). He is a member of the North Carolina state bar and, while he still considers himself a novice at consumer law, has applied consumer law remedies to housing cases in a number of contexts.

CLP2 Chapters 1, 4, 9

Cathleen M. Combs is a named partner in the Chicago law firm of Edelman, Combs and Latturner which practices in the area of consumer class actions. She formerly supervised the Northwest office of the Legal Assistance Foundation of Chicago, where she was lead or co-counsel in class actions in the areas of unemployment compensation, prison law, social security law, and consumer law. Decisions in which she has argued include:

Bessette v. Avco Financial Services, 230 F. 3d 439 (1st Cir. 2000) (held bankruptcy debtor induced to pay a discharged debt by means of an invalid reaffirmation agreement may sue to recover the payment)

Emery v. American General, 71 F.3d 1343 (7th Cir. 1995) (practice of "loan flipping," in which consumers are solicited for new loans and are then refinanced, with "short" credits for unearned finance charges and insurance premiums being given through use of the "Rule of 78s." found to state a claim for violation of mail fraud statute)

Miller v. McCalla Raymer, 214 F. 3d 872 (7th Cir.) (held demand letter by mortgage foreclosure attorneys which failed to inform the debtor the exact amount due under a mortgage in default violated the FDCPA).

CLP8 Chapter 22

Jean Constantine-Davis has been an attorney with AARP and AARP Foundation, 601 E Street NW, Washington, D.C. 20049, (202) 434-2158 (202) 434-6424 (FAX), since 1985. She is currently working in the Foundation's litigation group on issues involving fraudulent and predatory mortgage lending practices targeted at elderly homeowners. Prior to joining the litigation group, Ms. Constantine-Davis worked for AARP's Legal Counsel for the Elderly representing low-income elderly residents of the District of Columbia who were threatened with eviction and foreclosure on their homes. In 1995, she was awarded the Jerrold Scoutt Prize for her work on behalf of the low-income and vulnerable elderly population of D.C. Ms. Constantine-Davis has been a consumer fellow of the American Bar Association's Consumer Financial Services Committee since 1995. She also served as a member of HUD's Negotiated Rulemaking Committee on the Mortgage Broker Rule and as a consumer representative in the Mortgage Reform Working Group's deliberations on reform of Truth in Lending and RESPA. Ms. Constantine-Davis graduated *magna cum laude, Phi Beta Kappa* in 1973 from the University of Maryland. She received her law degree from Catholic University of America in 1978.

CLP9 Chapter 1

Frank N. Darras is a partner with the law firm of Shernoff Bidart & Darras LLP and heads the firm's Health and Disability Department. As one of the nation's top civil litigators specializing in bad faith insurance claims, Mr. Darras has made a career out of holding insurance companies accountable for their short-term, long-term, and individual disability policies.

Having evaluated over 6,000 disability cases since the start of his career, Mr. Darras is widely recognized as one of the nation's foremost authorities on litigating disability

CLP6 Chapter 5

claims. Mr. Darras also represents policyholders in bad faith disputes concerning denials of cutting-edge medical procedures and skilled nursing care, restricted access to specialists, and pre-existing condition exclusions.

Mr. Darras is a frequent lecturer and media commentator on insurance bad faith, including disability coverage issues, bad faith, HMO liability, and ERISA preemption. Mr. Darras has been featured in the Wall Street Journal, Medical Economics, and Lawyers Weekly USA, and is a regular contributor to Mealey Publications and Bottom Line Personal. Among his numerous articles, Mr. Darras has authored "Disabling the Disability Carrier: The Insurers' Top 10 Defenses and How To Defeat Them," "Insureds' Health v. Insurers' Wealth: Bad Faith in the Healthcare Industry," and "The Iceberg is Melting: ERISA Preemption and How To Avoid It." Mr. Darras has been a featured speaker for various conferences, including the Association of Trial Lawyers of America, the American Bar Association, the American Conference Institute, National Consumer Law Center, and Consumer Attorneys of California.

Mr. Darras has received the highest rating, "AV," from by Martindale-Hubbell, an internationally recognized independent attorney rating organization, which signifies that Mr. Darras is an attorney recognized for the highest levels of skill and integrity. Mr. Darras is also listed in The National Registry of Who's Who. Mr. Darras serves as President of the Board of Directors of the Western State University College of Law Foundation.

Mr. Darras received his J.D. from Western State University in 1986, and attended Emory University as an undergraduate. Before joining the firm in 1988, Mr. Darras trained with the Los Angeles County District Attorney's Office Trial Attorney Project. Mr. Darras is a member of the Los Angeles County, San Bernardino County, and American Bar Associations, the Association of Trial Lawyers of America, Trial Lawyers for Public Justice, Consumer Attorneys of California, and Consumer Attorneys Association of Los Angeles. He has sat on the American Trial Lawyers Executive Board on Insurance Litigation and is a faculty member at the National College of Advocacy of the Association of Trial Lawyers of America and currently co-chairs the Bad Faith Litigation Group of the Association. Frank N. Darras may be reached at Shernoff Bidart & Darras, 600 S. Indian Hill Blvd., Claremont, CA 91711 (909) 621-4935, e-mail: fdarras@shernoff.com.

Susan L. DeJarnatt is a staff attorney with Community Legal Services, Inc., Law Center Northeast, 3207 Kensington Avenue, Philadelphia, PA 19134-1917, (215) 427-4850, fax: (215) 427-4895. Her practice concentrates in the areas of consumer protection and bankruptcy law. She also is an adjunct instructor at Rutgers-Camden School of Law and a member of the Pennsylvania Bar Association, the National Lawyers Guild, and the Eastern District of Pennsylvania Bankruptcy Conference.

CLP2 Chapter 12

Dan Deneen of Deneen & Deneen, 202 S. Eldorado Road, Bloomington, IL 61704, (309) 663-0555, fax: (309) 663-0556, is a general practice attorney in Bloomington, Illinois, concentrating in commercial law, probate and estate planning. He has been invoked in cases relating to automobile manufacturers, dealers, and other retailers. His published works include "Automobile Finance, Warranty, and Insurance Extras: What the Consumer Should Know and How an Attorney Can Attack the Deceptive Practices," 6 Loyola Consumer Law Reporter 5 (1993), and "900-Number Services: Abuses, Regulation and Relief," 80 Ill. Bar J. 406 (1992). Dan is not as actively involved in the consumer law area since Illinois effectively exempted automobile dealers from its provisions in the mid-90's.

CLP5 Chapter 4

Thomas A. Dickerson is a Judge on the Westchester County Court, State of New York; Chairman of the Class Action Committee, New York State Bar Association, 1985–present; Member, Westchester County Bar Association; Member, Consumer Affairs Committee, 1986–1989, 1997–1999, 2000–2002; Association of the Bar of the City of New York; Member of the Editorial Boards of *Class Action Reports* and International Travel Law Journal.

CLP4 Chapter 5

Judge Dickerson has an M.B.A. from the Johnson Graduate School of Management, Cornell University, 1973 and a J.D. from Cornell Law School, 1973. Thomas A. Dickerson practiced law in New York City from 1975 through 1993 at which time he became a Judge. During his years as a practicing attorney he specialized in litigation, consumer law, travel law and class actions. Thomas A. Dickerson has written over two hundred legal articles, most frequently on class actions and travel law. Thomas A. Dickerson is the author of *Travel Law* (Law Journal Press, New York 1981–2002), and *Class Actions: The Law of 50 States* (Law Journal Press, 1988–2002) His web pages at http://members.aol.com/judgetad/index.html and http:www.classactionlitigation.com/articles_of_interest.htm provide additional information about his publications and decisions.

Tom Domonoske of the Law Offices of Dale Pittman, 461 Lee Avenue, Harrisonburg, VA 22802, (540) 442-8616, fax: (540) 442-7706, began practicing law in California in 1990 before moving to North Carolina where he taught classes at the University of North Carolina Law School. He then practiced as a legal aid lawyer with the Virginia Legal Aid Society at its Farmville office from 1993 to 1996. From July 1996 through August 2000, he was a Senior Lecturing Fellow at Duke Law School. While at Duke, he maintained a small consumer law practice in Virginia through an Of Counsel relationship with the Law Office of Dale W. Pittman. He is now back in full-time practice of law in Virginia. His primary emphasis is on auto fraud and mobile home fraud issues, the reason being that both involve Certificates of Titles that require prescribed forms and both involve dealer-arranged financing. He has published articles about the titling laws and about illegal lease termination provisions in NACA's *The Consumer Law Advocate*, as well an article on processing fees in car sales in the Virginia Trial Lawyers Association's *The Journal*. Additionally, he has contributed to drafting new subsections of NCLC's manual, *Truth in Lending*. In the past four years, he has given over twenty consumer law trainings at various conferences around the country.

CLP6 Chapter 17; CLP7 Chapter 5

Michael D. Donovan, a founding member of the Philadelphia law firm Donovan Miller, LLC, is admitted to practice before the Supreme Court of the United States, the United States Courts of Appeals for the Second, Third, Eighth, Ninth and Tenth Circuits, the United States District Court for the Eastern District of Pennsylvania, the United States District Courts for the Southern and Eastern Districts of New York as well as the state courts of Pennsylvania and New York and the courts of Washington, D.C. He is a graduate of Vermont Law School (J.D. cum laude 1984) and Syracuse University (A.B. 1981). He was the Head Notes Editor and a staff member of the Vermont Law Review from 1982 through 1984. While on the Law Review, he authored Note, Zoning Variance Administration in Vermont, 8 Vt. L. Rev. 370 (1984). Following graduation from law school, Mr. Donovan was an attorney with the Securities and Exchange Commission in Washington, D.C., where he prosecuted numerous securities cases and enforcement matters, including injunctive and disciplinary actions against public companies, broker/dealers and accounting firms. Mr. Donovan has co-authored Preserving Judicial Recourse for Consumers: How to Combat Overreaching Arbitration Clauses, 10 Loyola Consumer L. Rev. 269 (1998); "The Overlooked Victims of the Thrift Crisis," Miami Review, Feb. 13, 1990 and "Conspiracy of Silence: Why S&L Regulators Can't Always Be Trusted," Legal Times, Feb. 5, 1990.

CLP4 Chapter 1; CLP9 Chapter 12

Mr. Donovan has served as co-lead counsel in the following securities class actions: *Lines v. Marble Financial Corp.*, Nos. 90-23 and 90-100 (D. Vt. 1991) (settled for $2 million together with substantial changes to the company's loan loss reserve procedures); *Jones v. Amdura Corp.*, No. 90-F-167 (D. Colo. 1991) (action against directors settled for $4,962,500 and against company after bankruptcy for $1.2 million); *In re Columbia Shareholders Litigation* (Del. Ch. 1991) (merger case settled for $2 per share increase in amount paid to shareholders); *Rosen v. Fidelity Investments*, [Current] Fed. Sec. L. Rep. ¶ 98,949 (E.D. Pa. Nov. 28, 1995) (opinion certifying class of mutual fund purchasers). In addition, Mr. Donovan has had a substantial role in the prosecution of the following cases, among others: *In re Trustcorp Securities Litigation*, No. 3:89-CV-7139 (N.D. Ohio 1990) (settled for $5,600,000); *Moskowitz v. Lopp*, 128 F.R.D. 624 (E.D. Pa. 1989) (opinion certifying class of stock and option purchasers in fraud on the market and insider trading case); In re Hercules Corporation Securities Litigation, No. 90-442 (D. Del. 1992) (settled for $17.25 million).

In the area of consumer justice, Mr. Donovan has argued before the Supreme Court of the United States in *Smiley v. Citibank* (South Dakota), N.A., No. 95-860, 116 S. Ct. 806 (argued Apr. 24, 1996) and obtained favorable appellate rulings from the New Jersey Supreme Court in *Sherman v. Citibank* (South Dakota), N.A., 668 A.2d 1036 (N.J. 1995) and *Hunter v. Greenwood Trust Co.*, 668 A.2d 1067 (N.J. 1995) and from the Pennsylvania Superior Court in *In re Citibank Credit Card Litigation*, 653 A.2d 39 (Pa. Super. 1995) and *Gadon v. Chase Manhattan Bank, N.A.*, 653 A.2d 43 (Pa. Super. 1995). Each of the cases challenged the authority of out-of-state banks to impose default charges on residents of states where such charges are prohibited. Mr. Donovan has also filed numerous friend of the court briefs concerning federal preemption of state consumer protection statutes. In this regard, Mr. Donovan has appeared as a panel speaker at the Pennsylvania Bar Institute's Banking Law Update, the Practicing Law Institute's Financial Services Litigation Forum, the Consumer Credit Regulation Forum of the New Jersey Bar Association, and the National Consumer Rights Litigation Conference sponsored by the National Consumer Law Center. More recently, Mr. Donovan has served as class counsel in several class actions challenging negative option billing practices by cable companies as well as cases challenging the miscalculation of interest charged or paid by banks. In April 1996 and July 1997, he obtained favorable appellate decisions from the Appellate Division of the New Jersey Superior Court and the New Jersey Supreme Court in *Lemelledo v. Beneficial Finance Co.*, 674 A.2d 582 (N.J. App. Div. 1996), aff'd, 150 N.J. 255, 696 A.2d 546 (N.J. 1997), concerning loan and insurance packing. Mr. Donovan is a member of the American Bar Association (Litigation and Business Law Sections), the Pennsylvania Bar Association, the New York Bar Association, and the District of Columbia Bar Association. He is the Chair of the Consumer Law Subcommittee of the ABA Litigation Section's Class Actions and Derivative Suits Committee. He is also the Vice Chair of the National Association of Consumer Advocates and an active member of Trial Lawyers for Public Justice and Public Citizen.

Lynn Drysdale has been a staff attorney with Jacksonville Area Legal Aid, Inc. for 16 years, at 126 West Adams Street, Suite 502, Jacksonville, FL 32202, (904) 356-8371, Fax: (904) 224-7050, lynn.drysdale@jaxlegalaid.org. Her focus is in the area of consumer finance and bankruptcy with an emphasis on asset preservation and community economic development , unfair and deceptive consumer practices, debt collection and other consumer concerns raised by low-income individuals. She is involved in litigation, legislative advocacy and community education. Ms. Drysdale is a 1985 graduate of the University of Florida College of Law. She is also a licensed mediator.

Daniel A. Edelman is a principal in Edelman, Combs & Lattumer, LLC, 120 South LaSalle Street, 18th Floor, Chicago, IL 60603, web site: www.edcombs.com, e-mail: edcombs@aol.com. He is 1976 graduate of the University of Chicago Law School. From 1976 to 1981 he was an associate at the Chicago office of Kirkland & Ellis with heavy involvement in the defense of consumer class action litigation (such as the General Motors Engine Interchange cases). In 1981, he became an associate at Reuben & Proctor, a medium-sized firm formed by some former Kirkland & Ellis lawyers, and was made a partner there in 1982. Since the end of 1985, he has been in private practice in downtown Chicago. Virtually all of his practice involves litigation on behalf of consumers.

Mr. Edelman is the author or coauthor of numerous publications on class actions and consumer protection law, including *Predatory Lending Litigation in Illinois* (2001); *Consumer Class Action* (2d-5th editions), National Consumer Law Center 1990—2002; *Payday Loans: Big Interest Rates and Little Regulation*, 11 Loy. Consumer L. Rptr. 14

(1999); *Fair Debt Collection Practices Act Update 1999*, Chicago Bar Ass'n 1999; *An Overview of The Fair Debt Collection Practices Act*, in Financial Services Litigation, Practicing Law Institute (1999); *Consumer Fraud and Insurance Claims, in Bad Faith and Extracontractual Damage Claims in Insurance Litigation*, Chicago Bar Ass'n 1992; Chapter 8, "Fair Debt Collection Practices Act," Ohio Consumer Law (1995 ed.); *Fair Debt Collection: The Need for Private Enforcement*, 7 Loy. Consumer L. Rptr. 89 (1995); *The Fair Debt Collection Practices Act: Recent Developments*, 8 Loy. Consumer L. Rptr. 303 (1996); *Residential Mortgage Litigation*, in Financial Services Litigation, Practicing Law Institute (1996); *Automobile Leasing: Problems and Solutions*, 7 Loy. Consumer L. Rptr. 14 (1994); *Current Trends in Residential Mortgage Litigation*, 12 Rev. of Banking & Financial Services 71 (1996); *Applicability of Illinois Consumer Fraud Act in Favor of Out-of-State Consumers*, 8 Loy. Consumer L. Rptr. 27 (1996); *Illinois Consumer Law* (Chicago Bar Ass'n 1996).

Veronika Fabian of DNA-People's Legal Services, 1907 N. San Francisco, Flagstaff, AZ 86001, (520) 213-4815, fax: (928) 774-9452, is the project director of DNA-People's Legal Services' Consumer Law Project and currently works in Flagstaff, Arizona. As project director, Ms. Fabian coordinates the consumer litigation and education efforts of all of DNA's nine offices on and near the Navajo Nation. For the past four years, Ms. Fabian has represented low-income consumers in tribal, state, and federal court. Ms. Fabian has handled a wide variety of claims, primarily related to the purchase of automobiles, raising claims under the Truth in Lending Act, Odometer Act, Magnuson-Moss Warranty Act, the Fair Debt Collection Practices Act, the Fair Credit Reporting Act, the New Mexico and Arizona unfair practices acts, the Uniform Commercial Code, and the Navajo Nation law governing repossessions. Before becoming project director, Ms. Fabian served as a DNA staff attorney for two years in Window Rock, Arizona, the capital of the Navajo Nation. Ms. Fabian is a graduate of Michigan Law School and is a member of the Arizona, New Mexico, Oregon, Washington, and Navajo Nation bars.

CLP7 Chapters 13, 16

Joanne S. Faulkner is in solo practice in New Haven, Connecticut, restricted to consumer matters, preferably for persons who cannot afford to pay a lawyer. Her office is at 123 Avon Street New Haven, CT 06511-2422. She is a past chair of the Consumer Law section of the Connecticut Bar Association and currently editor of its newsletter. She was a member of the Federal Reserve Board's Consumer Advisory Counsel, and has served on advisory committees to the Connecticut Law Revision Commission. She was on the Board of Directors of the National Consumer Law Center and is presently a trustee thereof.

Ms. Faulkner frequently lectures for the Connecticut Bar Association on consumer laws, and has assisted NCLC in updating various manuals, including its Fair Debt Collection, Odometer Law Manual, Equal Credit Opportunity Manual, Fair Credit Reporting Act Manual and supplements. Her successes include Connecticut v. Doehr, 111 S.Ct. 2105 (1991) (due process, prejudgment attachments) and Clomon v. Jackson, 988 F.2d 1314 (2d Cir. 1993) (FDCPA violated by attorney who allows collection agency to use his name.). Ms. Faulkner is a graduate of Cornell Law School (LL.B. 1963), admitted to practice in New York in 1963, and in Connecticut in 1967.

CLP1 Chapter 9; CLP2 Chapter 11; CLP4 Chapter 4; CLP5 Chapter 8; CLP7 Chapter 8; CLP8 Chapter 14; CLP10 Chapter 3

Richard N. Feferman of the Law Offices of Richard Feferman, 300 Central Avenue, SW, # 2000E, Albuquerque, NM 87102, (505) 243-7773, fax: (505) 243-6663, is a 1971 graduate of the University of Michigan Law School. Mr. Feferman spent thirteen years in Legal Services before entering private practice.

The firm handles a wide variety of individual and class action consumer cases throughout New Mexico, Arizona and Colorado. Most of the firm's cases are federal suits against car dealers, debt collectors and lenders. In 1999 the firm was nominated for trial lawyers of the year by the Trial Lawyers for Public Justice, for their $669,000 jury verdict against a New Mexico car dealer for odometer fraud and tortious debt collection practices. Recent favorable published decisions include: *Yazzie v. Ray Vicker's Special Cars, Inc.*, 12 F. Supp. 2d 1230

CLP5 Chapter 3; CLP9 Chapter 5

(D.N.M. 1998) (pawn "storage fee" was undisclosed finance charge under TILA) and 180 F.R.D. 411 (granting class certification); *Lee v. Gallup Auto Sales, Inc.*, 135 F.3d 1359 (10th Cir. 1998) (striking illegal regulation exempting older vehicles from federal odometer act); *Bitah v. Global Collection Services, Inc., et al*, 968 F. Supp. 1997) (lawyer liability under FDCPA); *Halwood v. Cowboy Auto Sales, Inc.*, 124 N.M. 77, 946 P.2d 1088 (Ct. App. 1997) (upholding punitive damages for on-reservation tort by non-Indian).

Lynn D. Feiger is partner in the firm of Feiger & Collison, P.C., 1543 Champa Street, Ste. 400, Denver, CO 80202, (303) 571-0777. Ms. Feiger received her J.D. at the University of Southern California in 1971, and her M.S. in Law and Society from the University of Denver in 1974. She is one of the leading litigation attorneys in Colorado in the area of civil rights, including sex discrimination, sexual harassment, age and race discrimination, and employment law in general. In 1978, Ms. Feiger was the first attorney in the United States to try a Title VII sexual harassment case. She is also responsible for numerous landmark court decisions in the employment area, helping establish the enforceability of personnel policy handbooks in the seminal Colorado case of *Continental Airlines, Inc. v. Keenan*, and for developing public policy wrongful discharge law in Colorado. Ms. Feiger is listed in *Best Lawyers in America* and has received the top rating available in the Martindale Hubbell Law Directory as rated by her peers.

Ms. Feiger has tried many employment cases in the last two decades, obtaining numerous seven-figure verdicts and settlements. At her firm, Ms. Feiger spends considerable time developing the skills of the attorneys who work with her and has trained numerous plaintiffs' attorneys in Colorado.

Ms. Feiger's professional affiliations in the past five years include Elected Fellow, ABA College of Labor and Employment Law; Co-Chair, Labor Law Committee, Colorado Bar Association Colorado Board of Bar Examiners; and Board Member, Colorado Chapter of Plaintiff's Employment Lawyers Association. Ms. Feiger's publications in the last ten years include numerous articles and chapters on employment litigation.

CLP4 Chapter 3

Dmitry Feofanov graduated from the Chicago-Kent College of Law in 1994. After serving as a law clerk for the Iowa Supreme Court and Illinois Appellate Court, he did municipal law and, in 2002, established ChicagoLemonLaw.com. He may be reached at Feofanov@ChicagoLemonLaw.com.

CLP10 Chapter 19

Michael Ferry is executive director of Gateway Legal Services, Inc., 4232 Forest Park Ave., Suite 1800 St. Louis, Missouri 63108, phone: (314) 534-0404, fax: (314) 652-8308, e-mail: mferry@gatewaylegal.org. He is a Consumer Fellow of the ABA's Uniform Commercial Code Committee, a Fellow of the American College of Consumer Financial Services Lawyers, Uniform Law Commissioner for the State of Missouri, adjunct professor at Washington University School of Law, and chair of the Consumer Law Committee of the Bar Association of Metropolitan St. Louis. He is a former member of the Consumer Advisory Council of the Board of Governors of the Federal Reserve System and a former Fellow of the ABA's Consumer Financial Services Committee. He has contributed to several NCLC publications, including Repossessions and Foreclosures (1999) and Consumer Warranty Law (2001), sits on NCLC's Board of Directors, and was the 1994 recipient of the Vern Countryman Consumer Law Award.

CLP2 Chapter 4

James B. Fishman is a partner in the law offices of 305 Broadway, Suite 900, New York, NY 10007, phone: (212) 897-5840, fax: (212) 897-5841. Mr. Fishman's practice involves all areas of consumer law on behalf of consumers, including automobile Lemon Law, automobile fraud cases, consumer credit, deceptive business practices cases, credit reporting matters and illegal debt collection claims. Mr. Fishman is a graduate of Bard College (1976) and New York Law School (1979). He is admitted to the Bar of the State of New York as well as the bars of the United States Supreme Court, the United States Court of Appeals for the Second Circuit and the Southern and Eastern District of New

CLP2 Chapters 7, 10, 12; CLP4 Chapter 8; CLP5 Chapter 1

York. He is a charter member of the National Association of Consumer Advocates. Mr. Fishman served as an Assistant Attorney General in the Bureau of Consumer Frauds and Protection of the New York State Department of Law and as a Senior Staff Attorney with the Civil Division of The Legal Aid Society. Mr. Fishman's publications include "New York General Practice," Consumer Law Chapter, West Pub. Co., 1992; Lemon Law pleadings from *Walker v. General Motors*, published by Bender's Forms, CPLR Art. 75, 1994 edition; "Applying Consumer Protection Laws in Landlord-Tenant Disputes," New York State Bar Association Continuing Legal Education Committee, October, 1994; *Purchase Of New and Used 'Lemons,'* Caveat Venditor, Julius Blumberg, Inc., New York, New York, 1994; *New York Needs A Private Right Of Action For Debt Collection Abuse*, New York Law Journal, p. 1, June 23, 1983.

Cary Flitter is a partner with Lundy, Flitter, Beldecos & Berger, P.C., 450 N. Narberth Avenue, Narberth, PA 19072, (610) 822-0782, Fax: (610) 667-0552, practicing in suburban Philadelphia and southern New Jersey. He handles both individual cases and class actions. Mr. Flitter serves on the adjunct faculty at Philadelphia College (Commercial Law) and Widener University School of Law (Consumer Law and Litigation). He is a contributing author to the treatise Pennsylvania Consumer Law, a graduate of the National Institute for Trial Advocacy, and a member of NACA.   CLP8 Chapter 10

William J. Flanagan is an attorney with Flanagan, William—Duran & Flanagan, 2307 Fargo Street, Los Angeles, CA 90039. Mr. Flanagan specializes in home equity fraud and consumer litigation. He is a member of the California and Florida bar associations.   CLP3 Chapter 1

Neil J. Fogarty is a senior attorney with Hudson County Legal Services, 574 Summit Avenue, Jersey City, NJ 07306-2797, (201) 792-6363, (201) 386-9721, practicing bankruptcy and consumer law since 1977. He is admitted to practice in New Jersey and New York. He was a member of the Federal Reserve Board's Consumer Advisory Council from 1986 to 1988 and has been the President of the Consumers League of New Jersey since 1985. He was a member of the New Jersey Supreme Court Committee on Special Civil Part for five years and a lecturer at the Institute for Continuing Legal Education on consumer credit regulation for five years. He has contributed to the National Consumer Law Center's publications Consumer Law in a Box; forms for *Consumer Bankruptcy Law and Practice*; *Repossessions and Foreclosures*; and *Truth in Lending*. He has practiced before the Third Circuit Court of Appeal as well as the New Jersey Supreme Court.   CLP6 Chapters 7, 13

Mary Catherine Fons is a sole practitioner operating the Fons Law Office in Stoughton, Wisconsin. Her practice is limited to representing consumers with claims including debt collection harassment, fraud, deceptive sales practices, wrongful repossession, credit reporting errors, tenant rights and other cases involving state and federal consumer protection laws. Ms. Fons is a frequent presenter on consumer protection topics at state and national conferences and seminars. She has taught consumer law at Marquette University Law School in Milwaukee, Wisconsin. Ms. Fons serves on the Consumer Protection Committee and Public Interest Law Board of the State Bar of Wisconsin and on the Advisory Board to the University of Wisconsin Law School Consumer Law Litigation Clinic. She has also served on advisory committees advising on revisions to the Wisconsin Consumer Act and the Revised Uniform Arbitration Act and served in a similar capacity for the Wisconsin Department of Financial Institutions.   CLP9 Chapter 3

James A. Francis is a member of Francis & Mailman, P.C., a law firm located in center city Philadelphia, Pennsylvania that concentrates in consumer litigation, at Land Title Building, 19th Floor, 100 South Broad Street, Philadelphia, PA 19110, (215) 735-8600, Fax: (215) 940-8000, jfrancis@consumerlawfirm.com. The firm was founded in early 1998 with the goal of providing zealous advocacy to consumers subjected to unfair business, industry and trade practices. The firm represents consumers in individual actions,   CLP10 Chapter 10 as well as through class action lawsuits, in the areas of unlawful credit reporting and debt collection practices, unfair trade practices, truth-in-lending and other consumer matters. The firm's attorneys have significant litigation experience both in federal and state trial courts throughout Pennsylvania.

James A. Francis is admitted to practice before the United States Court of Appeals for the Third Circuit, the United States District Court for the Eastern District of Pennsylvania, the United States District Court for the District of New Jersey, as well as the state courts of Pennsylvania and New Jersey. He is a 1992 graduate of Muhlenberg College (B.A., cum laude) and a 1995 graduate of the Temple University Beasley School of Law. While at Temple Law School, he won the 1995 Wapner, Newman & Wigrizer, P.C. award for excellence in civil trial advocacy and was awarded outstanding oral advocacy. Additionally, he served as President of the Student Bar Association from 1994-1995. Following law school, Mr. Francis worked with Kolsby, Gordon, Robin, Shore & Rothweiler in Philadelphia, where his practice was concentrated in catastrophic injury litigation and medical malpractice. Since the formation of Francis & Mailman, P.C. in 1998, he has focused his practice in consumer litigation, with particular concentration in fair credit reporting, fair debt collection practices and consumer class actions. He has tried and successfully litigated cases on behalf of many consumers throughout Pennsylvania. He has been certified to serve as class counsel by state and federal courts in both contested and settlement class actions. These cases include *Petrolito v. Arrow Financial Services, LLC*, __ F.R.D. __, 2004 WL 515761 (D. Conn. 2004); *Orloff v. Syndicated Office Systems, Inc.*, 2004 WL 870691 (E.D. Pa 2004); *Bonett v. Education Debt Services, Inc.*, 2003 WL 21658267 (E.D. Pa. 2003).

In 2004, Mr. Francis was voted and named one of Pennsylvania's Top 100 Super Lawyers in a recent study by Law and Politics published by *Philadelphia Magazine* and *Pennsylvania Super Lawyers 2004*. Mr. Francis has lectured before judges, lawyers and professional associations on the topics of consumer rights litigation. In June 2002 and May of 2004, he was a speaker at the National Associates of Consumer Advocates Fair Credit Reporting Act Conferences. He has appeared on the NBC Philadelphia affiliate News 10's Consumer Alert and ABC Channel 6's Action News programs to discuss credit reporting issues. Mr. Francis regularly serves as a certified arbitration panelist chair with the Court of Common Pleas of Philadelphia County-Trial Division Program. He is a member of the Pennsylvania Trial Lawyers Association, Philadelphia Trial Lawyers Association, Philadelphia Bar Association and National Association of Consumer Advocates.

Eric L. Frank is an attorney with the law firm of Miller, Frank & Miller in Philadelphia, Pennsylvania, where he concentrates in personal and commercial bankruptcy and consumer protection law. Previously, he was a supervising attorney at Community Legal Services, Inc. in Philadelphia. Mr. Frank is a member of the federal Judicial Conference Advisory Committee on Bankruptcy Rules, on which he has served since his appointment by the Chief Justice in 1998. He is the Contributing Author to Chapter 523 of the treatise, *Collier on Bankruptcy*. Mr. Frank is a member of the Eastern District of Pennsylvania Bankruptcy Conference, for which he has served as Chair of the Steering Committee, Co-Chair of its Education Committee, and a Member of the Local Bankruptcy Rules Advisory Committee. Mr. Frank is a past President and current Member of the Board of Directors of the Consumer Bankruptcy Assistance Project in Philadelphia, which provides pro bono representation in bankruptcy cases to low- income persons. He lectures and writes regularly for continuing legal education organizations on bankruptcy and consumer protection related topics. He served as a law clerk to the late Justice Samuel J. Roberts of the Pennsylvania Supreme Court and to U.S. Bankruptcy Judge Bruce Fox. He received his J.D. from the University of Pennsylvania Law School in 1976 and his B.A. from S.U.N.Y. at Binghamton in 1973.

CLP9 Chapter 19

Jamie S. Franklin is a 1997 graduate of the University of Chicago Law School. She is an associate at Edelman & Combs, a Chicago consumer law firm. She was formerly an intern in consumer law at the Legal Assistance Foundation of Chicago.

CLP4 Chapter 6

Pleadings by Contributor

Thomas Frohman is a senior attorney with Indiana Legal Services in Bloomington, Indiana. He has been with legal services since 1985 and specializes in family law, unemployment and housing issues.

CLP8 Chapter 2

Charli Fulton is a senior assistant attorney general in the West Virginia Attorney General's Consumer Protection Division, P.O. Box 1789, Charleston, WV 26326-1789, (304) 558-8986. In addition to her interest in automobile sales and financing practices, Ms. Fulton has litigated in the areas of sweepstakes and title pawning. A favorable appellate ruling in a title pawning case in which she was involved, *State ex rel. McGraw v. Pawn America*, 205 W. Va. 431, 518 S.E.2d 859 (1998), has precluded this industry from doing business in West Virginia. The West Virginia Court of Appeals' ruling in *State ex rel. McGraw v. Imperial Marketing*, 203 W. Va. 203, 506 S.E.2d 799 (1998), another case in which she was counsel, affirmed a permanent injunction that was granted as a summary judgment. The Supreme Court held that the question of whether sweepstakes solicitations violated the West Virginia Prizes and Gifts Act and the West Virginia Consumer Credit and Protection Act depended on the language of the solicitations and did not require the presentation of extrinsic evidence. (In response to the Court's ruling that the state could only obtain a single $5000 civil penalty for repeated and willful violations, the West Virginia legislature amended the Act to provide for a civil penalty of up to $5000 for each violation). The Consumer Protection Division has also been active in the areas of payday loans, spurious open-end credit offers, loan packing, and student loan scams.

CLP6 Chapter 9

Stephen Gardner is an attorney in private practice since 1992 specializing in consumer litigation. His office is at 6060 North Central Expy., Ste. 560, Dallas, Texas 75206, (214) 800-2830, Fax: 214/800-2834, steve@consumerhelper.com. He focuses on consumer class actions and on representing individuals and such organizations as the Center for Auto Safety and the Center for Science in the Public Interest. He received his B.A. in 1972 and J.D. in 1975 from the University of Texas. From 1992–1995, Gardner was the Assistant Dean of Clinical Education and visiting assistant professor of law at Southern Methodist University. He was an assistant attorney general in Texas and New York, from 1982 until 1991, and was involved in major consumer protection initiatives against such companies as AAMCO, Mobil Oil, Kellogg Company, and TCZ Cable. In 1991, Mr. Gardner coordinated efforts of numerous attorneys general and the Federal Trade Commission to investigate and bring law enforcement actions against TRW and other major consumer reporting agencies for violations of the Fair Credit Reporting Act. He became of counsel, National Consumer Law Center, in 2002.

CLP4 Chapters 12, 16; CLP9 Chapter 16; CLP10 Chapter 8

His publications include How Green Were My Values: Regulation of Environmental Marketing Claims, *Toledo Law Review (1991); See Dick and Jane Sue: A Primer on State Consumer Protection Laws*, American Law Institute 1992; *Caveat Vendor* (editor), State Bar of Texas 1980–1982. He is coauthor of National Consumer Law Center, *Practice of Consumer Law* and a contributing author of National Consumer Law Center's *Consumer Class Actions* and *Unfair and Deceptive Acts and Practices*, and H. Newberg & A. Conte, *Newberg On Class Actions* (4th ed. 2002).

Mr. Gardner is a member of the Board of Directors, Consumers Union of the United States, 1997– 2002 and was a member of the Consumer Advisory Council, Federal Reserve Board, 1986–1989, and was a Consumer Law Fellow, National Consumer Law Center, 1980. The Center for Science in the Public Interest inducted Mr. Gardner into their Nutrition Action Hall of Fame in 1991. He was named to Adweek Magazine's Top Ten Enemies of Advertising in 1991 and received the National Association of Attorneys General's Marvan Award in 1988.

Wyman O. Gilmore, Jr. is licensed to practice in Tennessee and Alabama. Mr. Gilmore's practice primarily involves personal injury, consumer fraud, and class actions. Mr. Gilmore has been practicing law since 1983. He has served as Special Deputy Attorney General for the State of Alabama and has served on the executive committee of the

CLP7 Chapter 1

Alabama Trial Lawyer's Association. Gilmore Law Office, 116 Court Street P.O. Box 729 Grove Hill, Alabama; (251) 275-3115; fax: (251) 275-3847; e-mail: wogilmore@tds.net.

Mitchell D. Gliner is a sole practitioner at 3017 West Charleston Boulevard, Ste. 95, Temple Plaza, Las Vegas, NV 89102, (702) 870-8700, (702) 870-0034. He practices in the area of consumer rights litigation under the Fair Credit Reporting Act, routinely initiating actions against credit reporting agencies and furnishers and users of information. Mr. Gliner has contributed information regarding the prosecution of civil actions addressing the unauthorized accessing of consumer credit reports. Mr. Gliner is a member of the Connecticut, Nevada, and New York Bar Associations and was a Captain in the United States Marine Corps.

CLP4 Chapter 7

Phil Goldsmith has practiced consumer law in Portland, Oregon, for nearly 25 years, representing plaintiffs in class actions and individuals with financial institution problems including predatory lending cases, at Law Office of Phil Goldsmith, 222 SW Columbia Street, Suite 1600, Portland, OR 97201, (503) 224-2301, Fax: (503) 222-7288, phil@lopglaw.com. Since 1987, he has been the principal in a one- or two-lawyer firm. He is a 1978 graduate of the Yale Law School. He served as co-lead counsel in *Vasquez-Lopez v. Beneficial Oregon, Inc.*, a predatory lending case which resulted in a jury verdict in January, 2004 that included $500,000 in punitive damages. The punitives have subsequently been reduced on post-trial motions and the case is currently on appeal. Other recent significant cases include: *Bruce v. EarthLink*, a class action for degraded Internet service which resulted in a $2,000,000 settlement; *Hutson v. US Bank, National Association*, a wage and hour class action which settled on terms favorable to the plaintiff class; and *Rosted v. First USA Bank*, a nationwide class action challenging a credit card bait and switch scheme, which settled with non-monetary class relief valued by the court as being in excess of $86 million. He was a panelist at the 2004 NCLC predatory lending mini-conference session on trying predatory lending cases. He previously has spoken at NCLC and NACA conferences on credit card litigation and attorney fees in class actions. He is currently a member of NACA's legislative committee.

CLP10 Chapter 14

Samuel D. Gollis is a solo practitioner. His office is at 3939C San Pedro Drive N.E., Suite 5, Albuquerque, NM 87110, (505) 883-4696, fax: (505) 884-4331. Mr. Gollis was previously an associate with Williams, Janov & Cooney in Albuquerque. Prior to that, he worked on the Navajo and Hopi Indian Reservations as a staff attorney for DNA-People's Legal Services, Inc.

CLP7 Chapter 13

Tara L. Goodwin of Edelman, Combs & Latturner, 120 S. LaSalle, 12th Floor, Chicago, IL 60603, has a J.D. with High Honors from IIT Chicago-Kent College of Law and a B.A. from the University of Chicago. She is currently a partner at Edelman, Combs & Latturner, in Chicago, Illinois, where she has practiced for nine years. She specializes in consumer class actions, with concentrations in mortgage and bankruptcy issues.

CLP6 Chapter 16

Robert S. Green of Green Fauth & Jigarjan, LLP, 235 Pine Street, 15th Floor, San Francisco, CA 94104, has extensive experience representing consumers in telecommunication, telemarketing, credit card and insurance cases. Mr. Green is Co-Lead Counsel in the Providian Credit Card Cases, which settled in December 2000 for $105 million. Mr. Green and his firm are also pursuing claims against Direct Merchants Bank, First National Bank of Marin, First Union and the American Fair Credit Association (AFCA), among others. The firm has obtained substantial settlements in actions against First USA Bank and Advanta Bank. Mr. Green recently obtained a Ninth Circuit opinion expanding the rights of credit card holders under TILA. *Demando v. Morris (Capital One)*, 206 F.3d 1300 (9th Cir. 2000). Mr. Green also serves on the Editorial Board of Consumer Financial Services Law Report.

CLP7 Chapter 2

The firm is also actively pursuing consumer claims against insurance companies. For example, the Orange County California Superior Court recently certified a class of claimants against Mercury Casualty Company in connection with allegations of illegal elimination of the "Good Driver Discount." Daniel C. Girard of Girard & Green is Co-Lead Counsel in the MCI Non-Subscriber Telephone Rates Litigation and obtained one of the largest settlements on record for "slamming" in a case against Business Discount Plan, Inc. (BDP). The firm is presently pursing telecom claims against NOS, Quantumlink, Affinity, Inc., MCI/Worldcom, and others.

Mark E. Griffin since 1988 has been a partner in Griffin & McCandish, located at 111 SW Naito Parkway, Portland , Oregon, 97204-3500, (503) 224-2348, FAX (503) 224-3634. His firm emphasizes complex civil litigation in personal injury and products liability; franchise, consumer, and investment fraud; employment discrimination and wage claims; professional malpractice with an emphasis on legal malpractice; and class actions. He is a 1976 graduate of the Northwestern School of Law, Lewis & Clark College. He served as co-lead counsel in *Vasquez-Lopez v. Beneficial Oregon, Inc.*, a predatory lending case which resulted in a jury verdict in January, 2004 that included $500,000 in punitive damages. The punitives have subsequently been reduced on post-trial motions and the case is currently on appeal. He has previously received other substantial punitive damage awards including *Gleaves v. MacTools*, a franchise fraud case with a $2.4 million verdict including $2.2 million in punitive damages; *Mc Nicholas v. Maring, Capital Resource Finance Corp*, a breach of fiduciary suit by a minority shareholder which resulted in a substantial verdict for compensatory and punitive damages; and *Hobbs v. Care Ambulance*, a sexual discrimination case with a jury verdict of over $200,000 for lost wages and punitive damages. He is a member of the Oregon Trial Lawyers Association, the Association of Trial Lawyers of America and Trial Lawyers for Public Justice. He has published articles on federal criminal procedure, state civil procedure, and privacy rights and is a frequent lecturer at Continuing Legal Education seminars.

CLP10 Chapter 14

Leah Guggenheimer is an associate in the New York law firm of Bernstein Litowitz Berger & Grossmann LLP Ms. Guggenheimer is a member of the National Employment Lawyers Association and the Women's Bar Association. She also serves on the Women's Rights Committee of the New York County Lawyers Association. Ms. Guggenheimer served as law clerk to Hon. Stephen Eilperin, D.C. Superior Court. Bernstein Litowitz Berger & Grossmann, L.L.P., 1285 Avenue of the Americas, New York, NY 10019; (212) 554-1400; fax: (212) 554-1444; e-mail: leah@BLBGLAW.com.

CLP7 Chapter 1

W. Howard Gunn is a private attorney in Aberdeen, Mississippi, whose practice includes consumer litigation. He can be reached at W. Howard Gunn & Associates, 113 1/2 W. Commerce St., PO Box 157, Aberdeen, MS 39730, (662) 369-8533, fax: (662) 369-9844.

CLP8 Chapter 19

Daniel L. Haller has worked as an attorney for more than twenty years with Neigborhood Legal Services, 926 Penn Ave., Pittsburg, PA 15222. He has concentrated on consumer and bankruptcy law for over twenty years. He is a member of the Debtors' Bar, Bankruptcy Judge Merit Selection Committee and Western District of Pennsylvania. He is the author of the mortgage foreclosure chapter in *Pennsylvania Consumer Law* and co-author of "Debtor's Power to Avoid" in *Consumer Bankruptcy* (Penn. Bar Inst). He is a member of the Allegheny County Bar.

CLP2 Chapter 3

Penny Hays is a partner with Alabama Injury Lawyers, P.C. Penny received her B.A. from Samford University and her J.D. from Cumberland School of Law in 1994. Ms. Hays has been representing individuals in their claims for workers' compensation, wrongful termination, and social security disability since joining the firm in 1995. For the past five years, her practice has focused on representing consumers in their claims under the FCRA, FDCPA, and Alabama state law claims. Alabama Injury Lawyers, P.C., is a small firm

CLP10 Chapter 5

located at 401 Office Park Drive, Birmingham, AL 35223, (205) 870-9848, Fax: (205) 871-8882.

Daniel F. Hedges is director of Mountain State Justice, 922 Quarrier St., Ste. 525, Charleston, WV 25301, (304) 344-3144, fax: (304) 344-3145 and is also in private practice at 8 Hale Street, Charleston, WV 25301, (304) 346-0361, fax: (304) 346-1054. He has been a consumer law specialist in West Virginia since 1969.

CLP5 Chapter 12, CLP9 Chapter 6

Andrew R. Henderson is a partner in the Los Angeles law firm of Hall & Henderson, L.L.P., 10951 W. Pico Boulevard, 3rd Floor, Los Angeles, CA 90064, (310) 441-8300, fax: (310) 474-7083. He graduated with honors in 1990 from the University of North Carolina School of Law, where he was a member of the North Carolina Law Review. From 1990 to 1994, he was an associate at O'Melveny & Myers in Los Angeles. Before law school, he was active in both real estate development and parkland preservation on the southern coast of North Carolina. He also received a Master of Business Taxation degree from the University of Southern California in 1981.

CLP6 Chapter 10

Mr. Henderson left corporate practice in 1994 to practice public interest litigation with his current partner, Carlyle W. Hall, Jr., one of the original founders of Center for Law in the Public Interest. Mr. Henderson has a broad-based litigation practice with emphasis on land-use environmental issues and consumer rights. Specifically concerning the latter, he co-counseled throughout the successful trial of the then-record-setting *Wenger v. Trans Union Corporation* case in 1996. He has since litigated two other impact cases against credit reporting agencies. Most recently, he argued the case, *Andrews v. TRW Inc.*, before the Ninth Circuit Court of Appeals, resulting in ground-breaking appellate precedent concerning both the applicability of the discovery rule to the Fair Credit Reporting Act and the obligations of credit reporting agencies to protect the privacy of consumers' credit histories in light of the epidemic of identity theft. He has also been active in *pro bono publico* matters and was the principal draftsperson of the City of Los Angeles' 1995 Ordinance for the Protection of Medical Facilities. He also recently served the City of Los Angeles as an appointed commissioner helping to revise the City's seventy-four-year-old charter.

Evan Hendricks, since 1981, has served as Editor/Publisher of the *Privacy Times*, a biweekly newsletter in Washington that reports on privacy and freedom of information law. He has served as an expert witness in several cases involving the Fair Credit Reporting Act. He may be contacted at evan@privacytimes.com, Privacy Times, PO Box 302, Cabin John MD 20818, (301) 229 7002, fax: (301) 229 8011. Hendricks is author of the books, *Credit Scores & Credit Reports* (2004), *Your Right To Privacy* (1990 So.Ill.Univ.Press), and *Former Secrets*, a 1982 compilation of 500 examples of significant disclosures to the public under the FOIA. From 1977-80, he was Editor of Access Reports and a newsletter on FOIA/Privacy. A graduate of Columbia University, Hendricks regularly lectures on information policy issues in the United States, Canada and Europe. Some of his recent lectures and expert presentations include Harvard University's Kennedy School of Government, Brookings Institution, the 16th Annual Conference on Data Protection in The Hague, The Netherlands, and Reed College Lecture Series on Privacy and Censorship.

CLP10 Chapter 13

He has been interviewed on various FOIA and privacy issues by the *Oprah Winfrey Show, Geraldo, ABC Nightline* and *World News Tonight, NBC Nightly News, CBS Evening News, CNN News Watch, The Washington Post, New York Times, Wall Street Journal*, and radio talk shows such as KABC (Ray Briem, LA), KFI (Tom Likus-LA) WLS (Both Tom Johnson and Bob Wade), Scams Across America (Business Radio Network, Richard Cooper) WOR (New York) and KFYI, (Phoenix). He has done contract research for the Office of the Canadian Privacy Commissioner and the Australian Human Rights & Equal Opportunity Commission, as they needed a survey of American experiences in the course of formulating their national policies. In 1991, Hendricks became Chairman of the U.S. Privacy Council, a new organization and the first dedicated to the protection of privacy and improving our nation's law and policy. Hendricks is a native of Portland, Oregon.

Edward A. Icove is a principal in the firm of Smith and Condeni LLP, Ohio Savings Plaza, Suite 900, 1801 East 9th Street, Cleveland, OH 44114, (216) 771-1760, Fax: (216) 771-3387, Edward@smith-condeni.com. Mr. Icove was a VISTA attorney and legal services attorney with the Cincinnati Legal Aid Society and Southeastern Ohio Legal Services. He is as a Board Member (and former and Vice-President) of the Cleveland Legal Aid Society. He has handled numerous individual and class consumer cases in both state and federal courts. See, e.g., *Barney v. Holzer Clinic, Inc.*, 110 F.3d 1207 (6th Cir. 1997) (ECOA); *Smith v. Transworld Systems, Inc.*, 952 F.2d 1025 (6th Cir. 1992) (FDCPA, adopting the "least sophisticated" consumer standard in the Sixth Circuit); *Shorts v. Palmer*, 155 F.R.D. 172 (S.D. Ohio 1994) (FDCPA); *Lewis v. Marlin*, Clearinghouse No. 53021 (S.D. Ohio 1999) (FDCPA); *Pyles v. Johnson,* 143 Ohio App.3d 720 (4th Dist. 2001) (CSPA, RISA, and fraud); and *Edwards v. McCormick*, 136 F.Supp.2d 795 (S.D. Ohio 2001) (FDCPA and CSPA). A Cleveland collection attorney complained that Ed was a "champion of the poor."

CLP6 Chapter 3; CLP10 Chapter 17

Raymond G. Ingalsbe (Ch. 15) received a B.A. from the University of Cincinnati in 1973, and his J.D. from the University of Miami in 1976. Mr. Ingalsbe has been a board certified civil trial lawyer since 1985. He is a member of the Academy of Florida Trial Lawyers and is involved in attempting to draft changes to Florida's Deceptive and Unfair Trade Practices Act as a member of the Consumer Protection Committee of the Florida Bar and the AFTL. Mr. Ingalsbe was the chairman of the Palm Beach County Bar Association Consumer Law Committee for four years. He is a frequent lecturer on sales fraud and deceptive and unfair trade practices, and has received two pro bono awards from the Palm Beach County Bar Association for his work in consumer law, and received an award for his work on the Academy of Florida Trial Lawyers journal. Mr. Ingalsbe is a charter member of the National Association of Consumer Advocates. His office is at 4400 PGA Boulevard, Ste 800, Palm Beach Garden, FL 33410, (561) 775-3505, Fax: (561) 624-3533, rgingalsbe@aol.com. His practice is limited to consumer claims.

CLP10 Chapter 15

David B. Irvin is a Senior Assistant Attorney General and Chief of the Antitrust and Consumer Litigation Section of the Office of the Virginia Attorney General, 900 East Main Street, Richmond, VA 23219, (804) 786-2116, fax: (804) 786-0122. He specializes in consumer protection law and, in recent years, has been lead counsel in cases alleging advance fee loan fraud, usury (payday and title pawn loans), charitable solicitation fraud, credit repair fraud and deceptive advertising. Mr. Irvin is a member of the Virginia state and federal bar associations.

CLP3 Chapter 4

Danita Ivory is an associate in the law firm of Edelman, Combs and Latturner. She is a 2000 graduate of DePaul College of Law. She has been working at Edelman, Combs, & Latturner since. The cases she has litigated include:

Chandler v. American General Finance Company, 329 Ill. App.3d 729, 768 N.E.2d 60 (1st Dist. 2002) (held that compliance with the Truth in Lending Act did not preclude liability under the Illinois Consumer Fraud Act and the Illinois Consumer Installment Loan Act where the fraud alleged occurred outside of the loan documents).

Mallen v. MyInjuryClaim.Com Corporation, 2002 WL 598400 (1st Dist. 2002) (held that Illinois recognizes a private right of action for the unauthorized practice of law).

Phillips v. Associates Home Equity Services, Inc., 179 F. Supp. 2d 840 (N.D. Ill. 2001) (denying a motion to compel arbitration where the plaintiff would have to pay prohibitively high costs to arbitrate her claims).

CLP8 Chapter 22

Edward Josephson is the Director of the Housing Law Unit, Brooklyn Legal Services, Corp B, 105, Court St., Brooklyn NY, (718) 237-5500, fax: (718) 855-0733. His main areas of practice are landlord/tenant and federally assisted housing law. Mr. Josephson is a member of the New York bar.

CLP2 Chapter 1

De Vonna Joy is a solo practitioner with the Consumer Justice Law Center in Muskego, Wisconsin. She has a statewide practice in Wisconsin. Ms. Joy limits her practice to consumer protection cases, representing consumers with claims involving unfair and deceptive trade practices, debt collection harassment, autofraud, warranty disputes, credit report errors, and other cases involving state and federal consumer protection laws. Ms. Joy is the consumer law group moderator for badgerlaw.net, a public interest advocacy group network sponsored by Legal Action of Wisconsin, Inc. Ms. Joy is the 2003 recipient of the Association For Women Lawyer's Pro Bono Award and the 2002 recipient of the Volunteer Lawyers Project Outstanding Pro Bono Attorney Award presented by the Waukesha County Bar Association and the Legal Action of Wisconsin Volunteer Lawyers Project.

CLP9 Chapter 3, 4

Suzanne Keys is a private attorney with Byrd & Associates, P.O. Box 19, Jackson, MS 39205, (601) 354-1210, fax: (601) 354-1250. Ms. Keys is a member of the Mississippi and Wisconsin bar associations.

CLP3 Chapter 9

Gary Klein is an attorney with the Boston law firm of Grant & Roddy. He specializes in consumer bankruptcy and foreclosure law. Mr. Klein graduated from Yale University and Rutgers Law School. He is a past director of the National Association of Consumer Bankruptcy Attorneys and is currently a director of the American Bankruptcy Institute. He formerly served as a Senior Attorney at the National Consumer Law Center in Boston and directed its Massachusetts Shelter Preservation Clinic project. Mr. Klein also was formerly a managing attorney with the New Hampshire Legal Assistance, Inc., a supervising attorney at Community Legal Services, Inc., of Philadelphia, Pennsylvania, and a clerk for Judge Bruce Fox of the Bankruptcy Court of the Eastern District of Pennsylvania.

CLP1 Chapter 7; CLP7 Chapter 1; CLP8 Chapter 3

Mr. Klein is a nationally recognized expert on consumer law and consumer education. His practice focuses upon unfair business practice cases, consumer protections for predatory lending, creation of sustainable homeownership opportunities, and bankruptcy. Mr. Klein also designed and tested two leading adult education programs to teach financial literacy to American consumers. Mr. Klein is editor and has been co-author of NCLC's book for attorneys, Consumer Bankruptcy Law and Practice. He is also co-author of NCLC's books on foreclosure, Truth in Lending, and NCLC's popular book for consumers: Surviving Debt (3d ed. 1999).

Mr. Klein has testified frequently before both houses of Congress on consumer credit issues and the Bankruptcy Code. He has been involved in hundreds of cases involving consumer protection issues and is a frequent expert witness in litigation across the country. He has also conducted numerous national trainings on consumer bankruptcy, consumer credit and foreclosure prevention. Grant & Roddy, 44 School Street, Boston, MA 02108; (617) 248-8700; fax: (617) 248- 0720; e-mail: klein@grantroddy.com.

Henry Korman is currently assistant general counsel at The Community Builders, Inc., 95 Berkeley Street, #500, Boston, MA 02116, a non-profit developer of affordable housing. He worked as a legal services advocate from 1977 until 2001, a paralegal and staff attorney at Western Massachusetts Legal Services, a housing specialist at the Massachusetts Law Reform Institute, and as Chief Counsel and office manager at Cambridge and Somerville Legal Services. The pleadings submitted in this volume were developed with the support and assistance of the National Consumer Law Center. He may be reached at The Community Builders, Inc., 95 Berkeley Street, Suite 500, Boston, MA 02116, (617) 695-9595 fax:: (617) 695-9483, e-mail: henryk@tcbinc.org.

CLP4 Chapter 14

Robert Lax is a partner in the firm of Robert I. Lax & associates, 535 5th Avenue, Floor 21, New York, NY 10176, phone: (212) 818-9150, fax: (212) 682-9040, a firm that practises exclusively in the area of complex commercial litigation, placing particular emphasis on representing plaintiffs in class action and derivative suits in the state and federal courts. In a relatively short period of time, Robert I. Lax & Associates has become

CLP7 Chapter 14

vn for its academic approach to the practice of law as well as its dedicated sense advocacy.

I. Lax & Associates is actively involved in cases representing clients in actions involving issues of securities fraud and corporate governance, consumer finance, advertising fraud, and royalty and intellectual property disputes. Robert I. Lax & Associates 's ability and expertise in handling these matters has been recognized by both the judiciary as well as members of the bar, with the result that Robert I. Lax & Associates has been appointed class counsel and invited to serve on the litigation committees of several of the nation's most prominent class action litigations.

David A. Leen is a principal in the firm of David Leen & Associates, PLLC, 520 E. Denny Way, Seattle, WA 98122, phone: (206) 325-6022, fax: (206) 325-1424. He specializes in real estate litigation and consumer class actions. He is a member of the Washington bar and of the Seventh, Eighth, and Ninth Circuit Courts.

CLP2 Chapter 3

Seth R. Lesser is a partner in the New York law firm of Bernstein Litowitz Berger & Grossmann LLP. Mr. Lesser is principally responsible for his firm's consumer fraud and environmental practices. Mr. Lesser currently is the chairman of the ABA's Environmental Litigation Subcommittee of the Business & Corporate Litigation Committee of the Business Law Section. He also is a member of the ABA's Consumer and Personal rights Committee and the New York City Bar Association's Federal Courts Committee. Bernstein Litowitz Berger & Grossmann, L.L.P., 1285 Avenue of the Americas, New York, NY 10019; (212) 554-1400; fax: (212) 554-1444; e-mail: seth@BLBGLAW.com.

CLP7 Chapter 1

Michael Lewis formerly practiced law with his wife and law partner, Pauline S. Lewis, in Clarksdale, Mississippi. Mr. Lewis has been a member of the Mississippi Bar since 1977. His firm specializes in personal injury with an emphasis on medical malpractice, product liability, insurance, and consumer issues. Mr. Lewis authored the "medicaid tobacco recovery theory," which casts the state as victim and entitles it to recover damages caused by tobacco-related illnesses. Mr. and Mrs. Lewis represented the State of Mississippi in *Moore v. Phillip Morris, et al,* and recovered a settlement of $4 billion on behalf of the state of Mississippi. Mr. Lewis is admitted to practice in all state and federal courts in Mississippi as well as the U.S. District Court of Tennessee (Western Division), the U.S. District Court of Texas (Southern Division), and the U.S. Supreme Court. The identity theft case in Chapter One of *Consumer Law Pleadings*, Number Five, is one of several in which Mr. Lewis was involved.

CLP5 Chapter 1

Mark Leymaster, who designed and presented the exhibits in section 1.2 of Chapter 1, consults on expert legal systems, electronic document assembly, and consumer finance and also develops custom computer software as the Managing Partner at Renaissance Software in Silver Spring, Maryland, (301) 495-4877. He was previously an administrative law judge, insurance regulator, and rate-maker with the Commonwealth of Massachusetts. As an Assistant Attorney General for the Commonwealth of Massachusetts, he did adversary administrative litigation and other public protection law enforcement. Mark specialized in consumer credit mathematics, Truth in Lending, repossessions, and payment system law when he worked at the National Consumer Law Center in Boston. He is the author of National Consumer Law Center's *Consumer Usury and Credit Overcharges* (1982). He also contributed an analysis on APR mathematics for National Consumer Law Center's *Truth in Lending* (1986) and wrote articles on electronic banking and the poor before the electronic benefit transfers were mandated.

CLP9 Chapter 1

Dani K. Liblang, of the Birmingham, Michigan law firm of Liblang & Associates, P.C., 165 N. Old Woodward Avenue, Birmingham, MI 48009, (248) 540-9270, (248) 433-1989, has successfully handled thousands of consumer warranty claims. She is the author of the Breach of Warranty chapter in ICLE's *Michigan Causes of Action Formbook*. She has

CLP5 Chapter 6; CLP6 Chapter 11; CLP9 Chapters 2, 8

spoken on warranty litigation at the Consumer Rights Litigation Conference and ATLA's annual convention. She is a member of the National Association of Consumer Advocates and a past Vice President of the Michigan Trial Lawyers Association-Oakland Chapter. Ms. Liblang graduated from the University of Detroit Mercy School of Law, *cum laude*, in 1982. In addition to warranty law, Ms. Liblang specializes in personal injury, no-fault insurance and employment law.

Charles Lorant, the founding partner of Alabama Injury Lawyers, P.C., has been representing plaintiffs and consumers in Alabama for over 20 years. Charlie received his B.A. from the University of North Carolina Chapel Hill and his J.D. from the University of Alabama School of Law. While Charlie continues to represent injured individuals in their claims for personal injuries, fraud, and discrimination, for the past five years, his practice has become focused on representing consumers in their claims under the FCRA, FDCPA, and Alabama state law claims. While their firm is small, the lawyers have done battle with numerous giants across the country, including Equifax, Experian, Trans Union, First USA, Wachovia, Bank of America, American Express, Direct Merchants/Metris, Capital One, National Financial Systems, Risk Management Alternatives, Arrow, NCO, and countless others. Alabama Injury Lawyers, P.C., is a small firm located at 401 Office Park Drive, Birmingham, AL 35223, (205) 870-9848, Fax: (205) 871-8882, charlie@lorantlaw.com.

CLP8 Chapter 20; CLP10 Chapter 5

Michael P. Malakoff has been a member since 1971 of Malakoff Doyle & Finberg, P.C. (or its predecessors), where he specializes in class action litigation. He is a founding member of the National Association of Consumer Advocates ("NACA") and served on its Board. He was Chairman of the NACA Issues Committee from 1994 to 2002.

Over the last thirty years, he has participated in over 200 class actions, beginning as a former Regional Smith Fellow working at Neighborhood Legal Services Association ("NLSA") (in Pittsburgh) in 1970-71. He and members of his law firm have continued to work on class actions with NLSA attorneys, Community Justice Project and National Consumer Law Center ("NCLC") attorneys. He has also worked with multiple other nonprofit organizations, including Public Citizens (Washington, D.C.) and Trial Lawyers for Public Justice (Washington, D.C.), as well as private law firms. An example of a class action in which he has recently participated with Community Justice attorneys is the protracted tax lien litigation in *Pollice v. National Tax Funding, L.P.*, 59 F. Supp. 2d 474 (W.D. Pa. 1999), which was affirmed in part at 225 F.3d 379 (3d Cir.).

Throughout his years of legal practice, he has also participated in a number of NLSA and NCLC seminars and legal workshops. His post-1998 activities include contributing author in NCLC "Consumer Class Actions" (1999) (4th Ed.). His consumer law pleadings have been featured in a number of NCLC's Consumer Law Pleadings Treatises, including No. 1 (1994), No. 4 (1998), No. 5 (1999), No. 6 (2000) and No. 7 (2001).

He also assisted in drafting the NACA's class action guidelines entitled "Standards and Guidelines for Litigation and Settling Consumer Class Actions" published in 176 F.R.D. 375-404 (October 8, 1997) ("NACA Guidelines"). He has served as a consultant and was honored when selected by the United States Court of Appeals for the Third Circuit as one of five private attorneys, along with five District Judges, to participate in the Court Awarded Attorneys Fees Report by the Third Circuit Task Force, the report for which was republished at 108 F.R.D. 237 (October 8, 1985) (Reporter, Arthur R. Miller).

He has been on the Editorial Board of Class Action Reports since 1985 and has been a consumer advisor for the Consumer Financial Services since 1998. He can be reached at 412.281.8400; facsimile: 412.281.3262 or e-mail: malakoff@mdfpc.com.

CLP1 Chapter 6; CLP4 Chapter 9; CLP5 Chapter 5; CLP6 Chapter 6; CLP7 Chapter 11; CLP8 Chapter 21; CLP9 Chapter 11

Marsha M. Mansfield is a partner with Lawton & Cates, S.C., 10 East Doty Street, Ste. 400, P.O. Box 2965, Madison, WI 53701, (608) 282-6200, fax: (608) 282-6252, a law firm that specializes in complex litigation matters. Ms. Mansfield has participated in multi-plaintiff consumer litigation in Wisconsin, including successful prosecution of a consumer action against a manufacturer of prefabricated housing, *Leverance et al., v. Tri State*

CLP5 Chapter 7

Homes, Inc. She has also managed lemon law cases against Ford and General Motors and is currently working on several projects with the Consumer Law Litigation Clinic at the University of Wisconsin Law School. Other members of the firm serve on the Board of the Center for Public Representation, a nonprofit organization that provides legal assistance and referrals in areas including consumer advocacy.

James A. Mayhew is the managing attorney with St. Ambrose Legal Services, 321 East 25th Street, Baltimore, MD, 21218, (410) 366-8550, fax: (410) 235-7180. He specializes in consumer protection law. Mr. Mayhew was formerly a staff attorney with the Legal Aid Bureau in Baltimore where he specialized in public benefits and housing law. He is a member of the Maryland state bar association and is admitted to practice in the U.S. District Court for Maryland and the U.S. Fourth Circuit Court of Appeals.

CLP3 Chapter 10

Cyrus Mehri is a founding partner of the law firm Mehri & Skalet, PLLC. In 2001, he was named by *Regardie's Power* magazine as one of "Washington's Ten Most Feared Lawyers." Mr. Mehri served as Class Counsel in the two largest race discrimination class actions in history. *Roberts v. Texaco Inc.* settled in 1997 for $176 million and *Ingram v. The Coca-Cola Company* settled in 2001 for $192.5 million. Both settlements include historic programmatic relief, featuring independent Task Forces with sweeping powers to reform key human resources practices such as pay, promotions and evaluations. In 1997, for his work on the *Texaco* case, Mr. Mehri was named a finalist for "Trial Lawyer of the Year" by Trial Lawyers for Public Justice. In 2001, he was nominated again as co-lead counsel in the *Coca-Cola* case. In other class actions in the past, Mr. Mehri has represented defrauded investors, pensioners and consumers, as well as small businesses subjected to price-fixing. For example, in 1993, *Florin v. NationsBank* restored $16 million to a pension plan that was bilked by company insiders at Simmons Mattress Company. In 1991, *In re Bolar Pharmaceutical Co.* returned over $25 million to defrauded shareholders. Currently, Mr. Mehri serves as co-lead counsel in numerous consumer class actions.

CLP9 Chapter 15

He was appointed to, and currently serves, on the Settlement Committee in the multidistrict litigation related to the Firestone Tire recall. Mr. Mehri has fought on taxpayers' behalf in cases such as one terminating an illegal telephone tax in Los Angeles based on the Commerce Clause. Now he represents individuals "blowing the whistle" on corporate entities under the False Claims Act and has cases on file against some of the largest healthcare companies in the country that are accused of defrauding the government. Another whistleblower suit currently on file seeks to recover for U.S. taxpayers the illegal fees charged on labor costs at the Department of Energy's nuclear facility in Hanford, Washington.

Mr. Mehri has been active in many pro bono cases, as well. In *Roosevelt v. E. I. Dupont de Nemours and Co.*, he worked to hasten an end to the production of chlorofluorocarbons, which cause ozone depletion and global-warming. Mr. Mehri represented an African-American college basketball player who was the victim of a racially motivated attack in a small town near his Maryland college. In July 2001, Mr. Mehri's law firm and Johnnie L. Cochran, Jr., commissioned and released a report evaluating the appellate success rates of employment discrimination litigants in federal courts. The report, entitled "Double Standard on Appeal," received national press coverage for shedding light on the judiciary's bias against employment discrimination plaintiffs.

Mr. Mehri graduated magna cum laude in 1983 from Hartwick College in Oneonta, New York, and received the "Most Outstanding Young Alumnus" award from Hartwick in 1998. After graduating from college, he was a consumer advocate at Public Citizen in Washington, D.C., where he worked to reauthorize the federal Superfund bill and to reduce telephone charges for residential customers. Mr. Mehri graduated in 1988 from Cornell Law School, where he served as Articles Editor for the *Cornell International Law Journal*. After law school, he clerked for the Honorable John T. Nixon, U.S. District Judge for the Middle District of Tennessee. From 1989 to 1997, Mr. Mehri was an associate at Cohen, Milstein, Hausfeld & Toll, PLLC, a preeminent class action firm in Washington, D.C. Recently appointed to the Cornell Law School Advisory Council, Mr. Mehri now sponsors an annual public interest lecture series at Cornell. He lives in Washington with his wife and their two children.

Tom Methvin began his legal career with Beasley, Allen in 1988 representing people who have been victimized by consumer fraud. He pioneered many legal theories that are still in use today throughout the country. Some of these theories include lender liability causes of action known as "loan flipping," "insurance packing," and "yield spread premiums." He also became a national spokesman for the rights of consumers and for the law which applies to such rights. He was the lead attorney in a landmark case involving a door-to-door sales and finance scam which resulted in a settlement of $581 million dollars. As a result of this litigation, the finance company in question ceased to be involved in such activities in the state of Alabama.

CLP1 Chapter 5; CLP9 Chapter 18

Since 1998, Mr. Methvin has been the managing shareholder of Beaseley, Allen. As a result of his reorganization of the firm, each lawyer has been allowed to focus on certain types of cases and to be on the cutting edge in their fields of expertise. He has helped Beasley, Allen, to become a national powerhouse in representing victims of wrongdoing.

Tom was recently named by the Montgomery Advertiser newspaper as one of the "Top 40 under 40." This is a list of the top 40 business people in Central Alabama under the age of 40.

Tom has authored numerous papers including "The Law of Unfair Competition—A Plaintiffs Perspective," "Business Torts from a Plaintiffs Perspective," "Preparing Yourself to Take an Experts Deposition," "Consumer Fraud Class Action: A Plaintiff's Perspective," "Damages, Theories & Trial Strategies," "The Workup of a Debit Insurance Fraud Case," "Mortgage Fraud", "Winning and Collecting Big Verdicts Against Fringe Market Sellers," "The Workup of a Consumer Credit Fraud Case," "Alabama's Poverty Industry," "Fraud in Alabama," "Binding Arbitration and Its Effect on Consumer Finance Cases," "When Business Needs a Trial Lawyer," "Negotiations and Settlements of a Civil Action from a Plaintiffs Perspective," and "Alabama—The Arbitration State."

Tom is on the Board of Alabama Trial Lawyers for Children and the Cystic Fibrosis Advisory Panel. He also serves on the Board of the Let God Arise Ministries. Tom is married to the former Amy Agee of Birmingham and they have two sons. He attends church at Christ Community Church in Montgomery. He can be reached at Beasley, Allen, Crow, Methvin, Portis, & Miles, P.C., P.O. Box 4160, Montgomery, AL 36130, (334) 269 2343, fax: (334) 954 7555.

Elizabeth Miller is a 1982 graduate of Brown University and a 1990 graduate of Yale Law School. Ms. Miller is currently working with the National Consumer Law Center on fair debt collection issues. From 1994 until 2000, she practiced consumer law at Grant & Roddy in Boston, primarily bringing class and individual actions for violations of the Truth in Lending Act, Fair Debt Collection Practices Act, Fair Credit Billing Act, Fair Credit Reporting Act, Consumer Leasing Act, Massachusetts consumer protection law and for predatory "equity skimming" foreclosures. Before joining Grant & Roddy, Ms. Miller worked as a litigator at the New York law firm of Anderson, Kill, Olick & Oshinsky and at Edwards & Angell of Boston, and then as a staff attorney at Greater Boston Legal Services representing homeowners in the Roxbury and Dorchester neighborhoods of Boston faced with foreclosure. She may be contacted at andresliz@attbi.com.

CLP1 Chapter 8

Donna Siegel Moffa is a member of Rodriguez & Richards, 3 Kings Highway East, Haddonfield, NJ 8033 (856) 795-9002, e-mail: donna@rr-law.com. She is admitted to practice before the United States Courts for the Districts of New Jersey and the District of Columbia as well as the Supreme Court of New Jersey and the District of Columbia Court of Appeals. She is a 1982 graduate (with honors) of Georgetown University Law Center. She received her undergraduate degree, also with honors, from Mount Holyoke College in Massachusetts in 1979.

CLP8 Chapter 23

Prior to entering private practice, Ms. Moffa was a staff attorney at both the Federal Energy Regulatory Commission (FERC), where she worked in the Divisions of Administrative Law and Hydroelectric Licensing, and the Federal Trade Commission (FTC). At the FTC, as a member of the Bureau of Consumer Protection, she litigated cases involving allegations of deceptive and unsubstantiated advertising against R.J. Reynolds and General Nutrition Company. In addition, both at FERC and the FTC, Ms. Moffa was involved in a wide range of administrative and regulatory issues including labeling and marketing claims, compliance, FOIA and disclosure obligations, employment matters, and licensing. She has also participated in a number of rulemaking proceedings and contributed to the Final Report to the Federal Trade Commission on the Children's Advertising Rulemaking Proceeding.

In private practice, Ms. Moffa has continued to focus on consumer protection litigation and has substantial experience in consumer class actions. On behalf of individuals and classes, she has prosecuted claims in cases involving consumer financing, automobile sale practices, force-placed insurance, senior-citizen housing, deceptive labeling practices, and anti-competitive conduct arising under the state and federal laws. Prior to joining the Firm, Ms. Moffa worked with Ms. Rodriguez as co-lead counsel in successfully challenging the practices of certain companies in the rent-to-own industry in New Jersey. As a result of that case, a significant monetary recovery was obtained for consumers and changes were made in the contracts these companies use to provide more information to consumers.

Ms. Moffa is currently involved in class actions against lenders, dietary supplement manufacturers, car dealers, and drug manufacturers. Additionally, Ms. Moffa's practice continues to include representation of individuals and businesses in commercial, contractual and tort litigation. She has successfully represented such clients in invasion of privacy actions, wage and hour proceedings, and contractual disputes. She has also addressed consumer protection and litigation issues in presentations to consumer groups, unions, and organizations, as well as to professional associates. In addition, she has contributed to professional publications for consumer advocates.

Manuel H. Newburger is the vice-president of Barron & Newburger, P.C., 811 Barton Springs Road, Suite 250, Austin, Texas 78704, (512) 476-9103, Fax: (512) 476-9253. He has been with this firm since prior to the time he was licensed and through its evolution from Barbara M. Barron & Associates to Barron, Newburger & Rowe, P.C., to Barron, Newburger & Associates, P.C., to its present form of Barron & Newburger, P.C. In addition to his employment with Barron & Newburger, P.C., he is also an adjunct faculty member of the University of Texas School of Law, where he teaches consumer protection law. *CLP8 Chapter 10*

He has practiced consumer law for almost eighteen years. He is a past Chairman of the Consumer Law Section of the State Bar of Texas and current Chairman of the Texas State Bar's Advisory Commission on board certification in consumer law. He is also a member of the Commercial Law League of America and serves as Advisor to the Fair Debt Collection Practices Act Committee of that organization, which committee he chaired for four years. In 1997, he served on the Texas Supreme Court's Home Equity Foreclosure Rules Task Force. More information on Mr. Newburger may be found in Chapter 10 (section 10.2) of *Consumer Law Pleadings*, Number Eight, "Qualifications of Expert."

Jerome Noll was a partner in the firm of Lax & Noll, a New York firm that practised exclusively in the area of complex commercial litigation, placing particular emphasis on representing plaintiffs in class action and derivative suits in the state and federal courts. In a relatively short period of time, the firm became well known for its academic approach to the practice of law as well as its dedicated sense of client advocacy. *CLP7 Chapter 14*

Stephen Norman is a staff attorney with Vermont Legal Aid, Inc., P.O. Box 1367, Burlington VT 05401, (802) 863-5620, fax: (802) 863-7152. He has twenty-four years experience in individual and class representation on housing, consumer, and public benefit issues, including antitrust, bankruptcy, and mobile home park law. *CLP2 Chapter 2*

Stephen H. Olden is a senior attorney at the Legal Aid Society, 215 East Ninth Street, #200, Cincinnati, OH 45202, e-mail: solden@lascinti.org. He has practiced in the consumer and housing fields for over twenty years. He currently heads the office's consumer/homeowner practice team, which includes a student loan and trade school project initiated in 1996. He has represented defrauded students in class action litigation as well as in proceedings with the U.S. Department of Education. He has also been a trainer at numerous consumer and student-loan discharge training events. Mr. Olden is a member of the Massachusetts, Ohio, and federal bars.

CLP5 Chapter 9

David J. Philipps is a partner in the firm of Gomolinski & Philipps, Ltd., 8855 S.Roberts Road, Hickory Hills, Illinois, 60457, (708) 974-2900, fax: (708) 974-2907, e-mail: davephilipps@aol.com. The firm concentrates its practice in consumer class actions, including those involving the Fair Debt Collection Practices Act, consumer fraud, and securities. He is a member of the state and federal bars of Illinois and is a founding member of the National Association of Consumer Advocates. He is a member of the Chicago Bar Association's Class Litigation Committee and has served as the committee's recent developments coordinator and legislative liaison from 1992–1995. He has spoken about the FDCPA and class action lawsuits at various seminars and to several bar groups.

CLP3 Chapter 3

James M. Pietz, Malakoff Doyle & Finberg, P.C., Suite 200, The Frick Building, Pittsburgh, Pennsylvania 15219, (412) 289-8400, fax: (412) 281-3262. The firm specializes in class action litigation and consumer and insurance issues. The firm has served as class counsel in seven class actions, which to date have recovered over $10 million for consumers purchasing interests in campgrounds. James M. Pietz has extensive experience in consumer class action litigation, particularly involving financial institutions' liability for campground fraud and life insurer sales practices.

CLP1 Chapter 6

Dale Pittman maintains a consumer protection litigation practice based at 112-A West Tabb Street, The Eliza Spotswood House, Petersburg, VA 23803-3212, (804) 861-6000. In addition to an emphasis on representing consumer debtors under the Fair Debt Collections Practices Act, he represents consumers in credit reporting abuse, predatory lending, automobile fraud, mobile home fraud, and "home improvement fraud" matters. Opinions from some of his FDCPA cases appear at *Creighton v. Emporia Credit Service, Inc.*, 981 F. Supp. 411 (E.D. Va. 1997); *Withers v. Eveland*, 988 F. Supp. 942 (E.D. Va. 1997); *Morgan v. Credit Adjustment Board*, 999 F. Supp. 803 (E.D.Va. 1998); and *Talbott v. GC Services Limited Partnership*, 53 F. Supp. 2d 846 (W.D. Va. 1999). Courts in North Carolina and Virginia have certified class actions against collection agencies in cases in which Mr. Pittman represented classes of consumers, including *Woodard v. Online Information Servs.*, 191 F.R.D. 502 (E.D.N.C., Jan. 19, 2000); and *Talbott v. GC Services Limited Partnership*, 191 F.R.D. 99 (W.D. Va. 2000).

CLP2 Chapters 1, 4, 6; CLP5 Chapter 4; CLP6 Chapter 17; CLP7 Chapter 3; CLP10 Chapter 7

Bren J. Pomponio is an attorney who, in 2000, joined Mountain State Justice, Inc., 922 Quarrier St., Suite 525, Charleston, WV 25301, 304.344.5565, 304.344.3145 (fax), bren@msjlaw.org. Prior to that, he was a law clerk for West Virginia United States District Judges Charles H. Haden II and Joseph R. Goodwin.

CLP9 Chapter 6

Kieron F. Quinn is a member of the bars of Maryland, New York, the District of Columbia, a number of U.S. Circuits and the Supreme Court. He is a graduate of Georgetown University and the George Washington University School of Law, where he was a Trustee Scholar who graduated first in his class, served on the Law Review, and was elected to the Order of the Coif. He thereafter served as a Trial Attorney in the United States Department of Justice. His practice concentrates in representing plaintiffs in class actions. He served as Damages and Discovery Chair for the Environmental Plaintiffs in both the class and non-class Exxon Valdez litigation in state court in Alaska and was lead class counsel for plaintiffs in *Escamilla v. Asarco, Inc.* in Denver, CO, a toxic tort action

CLP3 Chapter 9

Pleadings by Contributor

in which the jury awarded the class in excess of $30 million. He was lead counsel in *Chisolm v. Charlie Falk's Auto Wholesalers and TranSouth Financial Services, Inc.*, a RICO and consumer protection action which was taken to the Fourth Circuit four times and which ultimately resulted in a recovery of approximately $15 million for the class, for which he was awarded the Public Justice Award by the Trial Lawyers for Public Justice. More recently, Mr. Quinn litigated a class action against Blue Cross/Blue Shield—in which a class of Maryland subscribers recovered $2.3 million as a consequence of being required to pay excess co-payments to health care providers—and several successful class actions against automobile dealers arising from phoney charges. Mr. Quinn teaches at the University of Maryland School of Law and has also lectured at a number of law schools. He has written several articles and delivered a number of papers at CLE symposia. He is an editor of Class Actions Reports and two other legal periodicals. Mr. Quinn has been selected for inclusion in the publication, The Best Lawyers in America, each year since it began publishing in the mid 1980's, was selected by Baltimore Magazine in March, 1995 as one of the best lawyers in Baltimore, and was the co-recipient in 1993 of the TLPJ Trial Lawyer of the Year Award.

Kieron Quinn is located at Quinn, Gordon & Wolf Chtd. 40 West Chesapeake Ave. Suite 408 Baltimore, MD 21204, phone: (410) 825-2300, fax: (410) 825-0066, e-mail: kquinn@quinnlaw.com.

Michael J. Quirk is the NAPIL Consumer Rights Fellow with Trial Lawyers for Public Justice in Washington, D.C., where he engages in socially significant and precedent-setting consumer litigation and works extensively on TLPJ's Mandatory Arbitration Abuse Prevention Project. He was co-counsel in *[Plaintiff] v. AT&T*, 182 F. Supp. 2d 902 (N.D. Cal. 2002) (holding AT&T's consumer arbitration clause illegal under California's Consumer Legal Remedies Act) and in *Wells v. Chevy Chase Bank*, 768 A.2d 620 (Md. 2001) (holding that credit card lender's contractual arbitration clause was not binding on consumers and that Federal Arbitration Act does not preempt state law allowing appeal of trial court's arbitration order). He co-authored the manual *Consumer Arbitration Agreements: Enforceability and Other Topics* (Boston: National Consumer Law Center and The TLPJ Foundation, 2001), part of NCLC's Consumer Credit and Sales Legal Practice Series, and has written several articles. Mr. Quinn graduated cum laude in 1999 from the University of Michigan Law School.

CLP8 Chapter 1

David Ramp was a senior litigator practicing consumer law with Mid-Minnesota Legal Assistance in Minneapolis and is now with the Attorney General's Office, 445 Minnesota St.,1100, St. Paul, MN 55101, (651) 297-5907. Mr. Ramp is nationally recognized for his expertise on the rent-to-own industry, an expertise arising from his class action litigation against the largest firms in an industry that often overcharges low-income consumers and structures its contracts to avoid many consumer protection laws. In 1997, David received the National Consumer Law Center's Vern Countryman award honoring the accomplishments of public interest lawyers contributing significantly to the rights and welfare of low-income consumers. He has testified before Congress and been invited to draft new consumer protections. Recently, he also became a founding member of the Minnesota Consumer Attorneys Association, a growing group of private and public and legal services attorneys specializing in consumer law, modeled after the National Association of Consumer Attorney. In addition, Mr. Ramp has been especially active in tenant screening litigation. He continues to work with foundation- and Dayton-Hudson-supported efforts to create alternative resources for populations drawn to rent-to-own outlets.

CLP4 Chapter 11

John Rao has been a staff attorney at the National Consumer Law Center since 1996. He specializes in consumer credit and bankruptcy issues. Mr. Rao directs the Center's case consulting services, providing technical assistance and litigation support to attorneys in a wide range of consumer law cases. He is an experienced consumer law attorney who has litigated many cases involving bankruptcy, consumer law, and utility regulation issues.

CLP6 Chapter 7; CLP7 Chapter 17

Prior to coming to the Center, he served as head of the consumer law unit at Rhode Island Legal Services. Mr. Rao is a co-editor of NCLC's Consumer Law Pleadings manual, contributing author to NCLC REPORTS, and co-editor of NCLC's *Consumer Bankruptcy Law and Practice.*

Elizabeth Renuart is a staff attorney with the National Consumer Law Center. She is responsible for writing and supplementing two of the treatises in NCLC's Consumer Credit and Sales Legal Practice series, *Truth In Lending* (3d ed. and 1997 Supp.) and *Cost of Credit* (1995 and 1997 Supp.), and is the author and editor of NCLC's bimonthly newsletter titled NCLC REPORTS, *Consumer Credit and Usury.* She provides direct service to attorneys representing low-income and elderly consumers, including analyzing mortgage loan documents. In addition, she has testified and commented orally and in writing to proposed Congressional and administrative agency action affecting low-income and elderly consumers, particularly in the area of mortgage lending. She has conducted conferences and seminars on mortgage lending and defenses to foreclosure. NCLC hosts an annual conference in which she participates as a facilitator and speaker.

CLP4 Chapter 12; CLP7 Chapter 10

Prior to coming to the National Consumer Law Center, she managed a small legal services program in Baltimore, Maryland from 1991–1996 that specialized in representing homeowners in danger of losing their homes. In this capacity, she handled numerous cases involving mortgage loans, real estate issues, foreclosure, and bankruptcy. Prior to that position, she managed a legal services office in Frederick, Maryland, for twelve years and served as a staff attorney in a legal services office in Augusta, Georgia for a year and a half. In those capacities, she represented low-income clients in a wide variety of cases. She has been practicing law for over twenty years.

She is a member of the Maryland Bar, the Georgia Bar (inactive), and the federal bars of the United States Supreme Court, the Fourth Circuit Court of Appeals, the District of Maryland, and the Southern District of Georgia. She graduated from the Columbus School of Law, the Catholic University of America, Washington, D.C. in 1977. Since coming to the National Consumer Law Center, she has been retained as an expert in several cases pending in state and federal courts, all of which involve mortgage loans.

John Roddy is a partner in the Boston law firm of Grant & Roddy, 44 School Street, Suite 400, Boston MA 02108, (617) 742-4488, fax: (617) 248-0720, and he specializes in consumer credit litigation and class actions. He is a 1980 honors graduate of Boston College Law School. From 1980–1985 he enforced state and federal consumer laws in the Consumer Protection Division of the Massachusetts' Attorney General's Office. These lawsuits remedied unfair and deceptive business practices, which harmed hundreds and sometimes thousands of consumers. From 1986–1987 he was legislative counsel to the Attorney General in the office's Executive Bureau.

CLP1 Chapter 8; CLP3 Chapter 8; CLP5 Chapter 2; CLP8 Chapter 3; CLP9 Chapter 17

Mr. Roddy has written and lectured on the substantive and practical applications of the Massachusetts consumer protection act for Mass. Continuing Legal Education, Inc.; co-authored (with former Massachusetts Attorney General Francis X. Bellotti) part of an ABA Teleconference Seminar on consumer protection laws nationally; written for and lectured to national seminars of the National Association of Housing and Redevelopment Officials on remedying predatory lending practices in the core city; and frequently writes and lectures on consumer law and class action litigation for diverse organizations, including the Practicing Law Institute, the National Consumer Law Center, the Review of Banking and Financial Services, MCLE, and the Florida Bar Association. He is co-chair of the Practicing Law Institute's annual Financial Services Conferences in New York City and San Francisco. He is a board member of the Massachusetts Appleseed Foundation and a sponsor member of the National Association of Consumer Advocates.

Lisa J. Rodriguez is a member of the firm of Trujillo Rodriguez & Richards, L.L.C., 3 Kings Highway East, Haddonfield, NJ 08033, (856) 795-9002, (856) 795-9887, which has offices in Philadelphia, PA, Cherry Hill, NJ, and Mexico City, Mexico. The firm's practice

CLP4 Chapter 11

trated in the area of complex litigation, with an emphasis on antitrust, consumer, , international, and general business litigation as well as white- collar criminal and international transactions. The firm's consumer practice has focused on involving force-placed insurance, insurance packing, rent-to-own transactions, and other financial services issues. Recently, the firm and its co-counsel made headlines by obtaining summary judgment on liability and damages on behalf of a certified class against Thorn Americas, which operates the Rent-A-Center chain. Thorn itself has estimated that the judgment will require it to pay $120 million. Also, the firm and its co-counsel obtained an important decision from the District of New Jersey sanctioning a bank for attempting to coerce a class representative to breach her duties to other class members.

Lisa J. Rodriguez, a member of the firm, is a 1983 graduate (with honors) of the George Washington University Law School. She served as a law clerk to the Honorable Mitchell H. Cohen, Senior Judge of the United States District Court for the District of New Jersey. Ms. Rodriguez has appeared as a panel speaker for the Practicing Law Institute on Securities Regulation and has also appeared as a lecturer for the Philadelphia Bar Education Center on consumer and class action issues. Ms. Rodriguez is co-lead counsel in litigation in New Jersey state court involving the rent-to-own industry in which the court entered summary judgment on liability against three defendants. In addition, Ms. Rodriguez is lead or co-lead counsel in litigation involving force-placed insurance and credit insurance packing.

Ms. Rodriguez is admitted to practice before the United States Court of Appeals for the Third Circuit, the United States District Courts for the Eastern District of Pennsylvania, the District of New Jersey, and the Northern District of California. She is also admitted to the Supreme Court of Pennsylvania, the Supreme Court of New Jersey, and the United States Supreme Court.

Phillip C. Rogers is a private attorney at 40 Pearl Street, N.W., Suite 336, Grand Rapids, MI 49503, (616) 776-1176, Fax: (616) 776-0037. His practice is focused on representing consumers in the areas of fraud in the sale and finance of automobiles, Truth in Lending, and the Fair Debt Collection Practices Act. Mr. Rogers is a member of the Michigan state and federal bars. *(CLP3 Chapter 9)*

Stuart Rossman is an NCLC staff attorney directing the Center's litigation efforts. He is an experienced trial attorney who, after thirteen years of private practice, served as chief of the Trial Division and chief of the Business and Labor Protection Bureau (consisting of the Fair Labor and Business Practices Division, the Insurance Fraud Division, the Medicaid Fraud Control Unit, and the Unemployment Fraud Division) at the Massachusetts Attorney General's Office. He also founded and chaired the Attorney General's Abandoned Housing Task Force, a project created to assist municipalities and community groups in seeking solutions to abandoned properties. *(CLP7 Chapter 1; CLP8 Chapter 18)*

Stuart is the former chairman of the Volunteer Lawyers Project, the oldest and largest pro bono legal services program in Massachusetts, and continue to serve on its Board of Directors. He is a member of the adjunct faculty of the Northeastern University School of Law where he has taught Civil Trial Advocacy since 1993. Stuart is a graduate of the University of Michigan and Harvard Law School.

Richard J. Rubin is a private attorney with an office at 1300 Canyon Road, Santa Fe, NM 87501, (505) 983-4418, Fax: (505) 983-2050, DickRubin@cs.com, whose federal appellate practice is limited to representing consumers in both federal consumer credit protection, including credit reporting and debt collection abuse litigation, and to consulting for other consumer rights specialists around the country. He and his solo practice were the subject of a profile published in the January 1993 ABA Journal. Mr. Rubin has taught consumer law at the University of New Mexico School of Law, is a regular contributor to the Consumer Credit and Sales Legal Practice Series manuals published by NCLC, and presents continuing legal education and attorney-training programs nationally in the areas *(CLP1 Chapter 3; CLP2 Chapter 11; CLP6 Chapter 12; CLP7 Chapter 9; CLP8 Chapter 16; CLP9 Chapter 10; CLP10 Chapter 1)* of consumer credit, warranty law, and debt collection abuse. The United States Court of Appeals for the Seventh Circuit has acknowledged Mr. Rubin as a "nationally known consumer-rights attorney" (*Bass v. Stolper, Koritzinsky, Brewster & Neider, S.C.*, 1997 U.S. App. LEXIS 41397, *5 (June 6, 1997). Mr. Rubin is the past chair of the National Association of Consumer Advocates (NACA) and in 2000 was the recipient of the Vern Countryman Award.

L. Kendall Satterfield is with the firm of Finkelstein, Thompson & Loughran, 1055 Thomas Jefferson Street, N.W., Suite 601, Washington, DC 20007.

CLP7 Chapter 2

Margot Saunders is managing attorney of NCLC's Washington, DC office. Her duties include analysis of water and energy issues as they affect low-income people and representing low-income clients on financial credit issues. She has testified on numerous occasions before Congressional committees on the impact of various proposals on low-income households and has just completed terms on the Federal Reserve Board's Consumer Advisory Council and the American Water Works Association Public Advisory Forum. She is co-author of *Access to Utility Service* (1996), Energy, The Manual on Water Affordability Programs (AWWA, 1998), as well as numerous articles on consumer and utilities laws.

CLP8 Chapter 17

Prior to joining NCLC Margot was the consumer specialist for North Carolina Legal Services where she represented low-income clients before the appellate courts and regulatory agencies. She lobbied the state legislature on consumer issues and for several sessions was voted one of the top twenty most effective lobbyists. She was the recipient of the Vern Countryman Award, a national award recognizing attorneys for outstanding advocacy on behalf of low-income consumers. She is a 1975 graduate of Brandeis University and a 1978 graduate of the University of North Carolina School of Law.

David A. Searles, of Donovan Searles, LLC, 1845 Walnut, Ste. 1100, Philadelphia, PA 19103, (215) 732-6020, is a founding member of the firm and is admitted to practice before the Supreme Court of the United States, the United States Court of Appeals for the Third Circuit, the United States District Court for the Eastern District of Pennsylvania, as well as the state courts of Pennsylvania. He is a 1975 graduate of the American University School of Law, Washington, D.C., where he served on law review. Following graduation from law school, Mr. Searles was an attorney for Community Legal Services of Philadelphia, where he specialized in consumer and bankruptcy law. In 1990, he successfully argued the first consumer reorganization bankruptcy case considered by the U.S. Supreme Court, *Pennsylvania v. Davenport*, 495 U.S. 552 (1990), and has served as lead counsel and presented argument in numerous bankruptcy and consumer law cases before the United States Court of Appeals for the Third Circuit. From 1992 through 1997, Mr. Searles was associated with the Philadelphia law firm of Drinker Biddle & Reath LLP, where his practice focused on Chapter 11 bankruptcy and creditor's rights.

CLP5 Chapter 10; CLP9 Chapters 12, 14

Mr. Searles is the author of "Tips In Handling Individual Bankruptcy Cases," Pennsylvania Bar Association Quarterly, January 1997, and is a contributing author of *Pennsylvania Consumer Law* (1990). Along with Mr. Donovan, he co-authored Preserving Judicial Recourse for Consumers: How to Combat Overreaching Arbitration Clauses, 10 Loyola Consumer L. Rev. 269 (1998). He has taught advanced bankruptcy law at Rutgers University School of Law—Camden, business law at Widener University, and bankruptcy law at Pierce Junior College, Philadelphia. He is a past co-chairperson of the Education Committee of the Eastern District of Pennsylvania Bankruptcy Conference.

Thomas R. Seel is a senior attorney at the Legal Aid Society of Greater Cincinnati. He is branch office managing attorney at 10 Journal Square, Suite 300, Hamilton, Ohio 45011, (513) 241-9400, FAX (513) 894-7669, tseel@lascinti.org. He has thirteen years general legal services experience, including experience in the areas of consumer law and bankruptcy. Mr. Seel now specializes in rental housing and homeowner litigation. He is member of the Ohio, Kentucky, bar and federal bar.

CLP9 Chapter 7

Nina F. Simon has been an attorney with AARP and the AARP Foundation since 1985. Ms. Simon is currently working with the AARP Foundation's Litigation group on issues involving fraudulent and predatory mortgage lending practices targeted at elderly and minority homeowners. Prior to joining the Litigation Group, Ms. Simon worked for AARP's Legal Counsel for the Elderly representing low-income elderly residents of the District of Columbia. In 1995, she was awarded the Jerrold Scoutt Prize for her work on behalf of the low-income and vulnerable elderly population of D.C. She has been a Consumer Fellow of the American Bar Association's Consumer Financial Services Committee since 1995 and currently serves as the Vice chair of the subcommittee on Consumer Litigation. She also served as a member of HUD's Negotiated Rulemaking Committee on the Mortgage Broker Rule and is a frequent speaker on TILA, RESPA and predatory mortgage lending. Ms. Simon was an active consumer representative in the Mortgage Reform Working Group and in HUD's deliberations on reform of Truth in Lending and RESPA. Ms. Simon graduated *magna cum laude, Phi Beta Kappa* from Brandeis University in 1975. She received her law degree *cum laude* in 1978 from New York University Law School, where she was made a member of the *Order of the Coif.*

CLP9 Chapter 1

Kimberly M. Skaggs is the Executive Director of the Equal Justice Foundation, a nonprofit organization located at 88 East Broad Street, Suite 1590, Columbus, OH 83215, (614) 221-9800, that provides civil legal services in the form of class-action litigation to indigent, minority or disabled individuals. Ms. Skaggs is a former Assistant Federal Public Defender and a former law clerk to the Honorable R. Guy Cole, Jr., United States Court of Appeals for the Sixth Circuit and to the Honorable John D. Holschuh, United States District Court for the Southern District of Ohio. She is a past president of the Columbus Chapter of the Federal Bar Association and the 2003-04 recipient of The Ohio State University Moritz College of Law Alumni Society Public Service Award. In addition to her administrative duties, Ms. Skaggs actively litigates consumer class-action cases. *See, e.g., Matthews v. New Century Mortgage*, 185 F. Supp.2d 874 (S.D. Ohio 2002) (predatory lending); *Mick v. Level Propane Gases, Inc.,* 168 F. Supp.2d 804 (S.D. Ohio 2001) (grant of preliminary injunction in consumer class action); *Mick v. Level Propane Gases, Inc.,* 203 F.R.D. 324 (S.D. Ohio 2001) (certification of 23(b) (3) class in consumer class action); *Turner v. City of Chillicothe*, Case No. C2-00-980 (S.D. Ohio 2000) (class-action utilities termination case).

CLP10 Chapter 17

David W. Snyder is an associate with Malakoff, Doyle & Finberg, P.C., Suite 200, The Frick Building, Pittsburgh, PA 15219.

CLP4 Chapter 10

Henry J. Sommer is of counsel to Miller, Frank & Miller and Supervising Attorney at the pro bono Consumer Bankruptcy Assistance Project, 1424 Chesnut Street, Philadelphia, PA 19102. He has litigated many major cases involving bankruptcy, consumer law, civil rights, and other issues. Previously, he was the head of the Consumer Law Project at Community Legal Services in Philadelphia, where he worked for over twenty-one years. Mr. Sommer has also served as a Lecturer-in-Law at the University of Pennsylvania Law School. He received his A.B. degree from Harvard College, *magna cum laude*, and his J.D. degree from Harvard Law School, *cum laude.*

CLP1 Chapter 10; CLP3 Chapter 7

Mr. Sommer is Editor in Chief of Collier on Bankruptcy and the entire Collier line of bankruptcy publications. He is the author of *Collier Consumer Bankruptcy Practice Guide* (Matthew Bender 1997); *Consumer Bankruptcy Law and Practice* (6th Ed. 2000) published by the National Consumer Law Center, Boston, Ma.; *Consumer Bankruptcy: The Complete Guide to Chapter 7 and Chapter 13 Personal Bankruptcy* (John Wiley & Sons 1994); as well as numerous articles on bankruptcy law. He is the co-author of *Collier Family Law and the Bankruptcy Code* (Matthew Bender 1991). He is also a contributing author to the Matthew Bender treatise on Debtor-Creditor Law.

Mr. Sommer is a former member of the Federal Judicial Conference Advisory Committee on Bankruptcy Rules (appointed by the Chief Justice of the Supreme Court) and a member of the National Bankruptcy Conference, for whom he served as Reporter for the Bankruptcy Code Review Project's Working Group on Individual Debtors. He is a Fellow of the American College of Bankruptcy, a member of the American Law Institute, and a former member of the Federal Reserve Board Consumer Advisory Council. He is also Vice President of the National Association of Consumer Bankruptcy Attorneys, a former Chairman of the Eastern District of Pennsylvania Bankruptcy Conference, and Vice President of the Coalition for Consumer Bankruptcy Debtor Education.

He has been asked to testify many times before the House and Senate Judiciary Committees, as well as the National Bankruptcy Review Commission, on bankruptcy and consumer law issues. He has served on the faculty of numerous continuing legal education programs including those presented by the Federal Judicial Center, NYU Law School, the National Conference of Bankruptcy Judges, the Southeastern Bankruptcy Law Institute, the Executive Office of U.S. Trustees, the ABA Family Law Section, ALI-ABA and the Pennsylvania Bar Institute. Mr. Sommer was the first recipient of the National Consumer Law Center's Vern Countryman Consumer Law Award. Henry J. Sommer, Consumer Bankruptcy Assistance, 1424 Chestnut St., Philadelphia, PA 19102, (215) 242-8639, e-mail: hsommer@netaxs.com.

Andrew Spark of the Law Office of Andrew Bennett Spark, 2033 Main Street, Suite 106, Sarasota, FL 34237, e-mail: abspark@msn.com, is a *cum laude* graduate of The Wharton School at the University of Pennsylvania and an honors graduate of the University of Florida College of Law. His practice primarily involves consumer litigation, including class actions, and he served as Vice Chair of the Consumer Protection Law Committee of The Florida Bar in 2001–2002. He is admitted to practice in Florida, New York, and New Jersey, and has served as a lemon law arbitrator under the auspices of the Florida Attorney General.

CLP7 Chapter 4

Mark H. Steinbach is a partner in the Washington, D.C., law firm of O'Toole, Rothwell, Nassau & Steinbach, 1350 Connecticut Avenue Suite 200, N.W. Washington, D.C. 20036, (202) 775-1550(202) , 775-0008 (fax). From 1974–1977, he served as a staff attorney with the Center for Auto Safety, a non-profit consumer advocacy group in Washington, D.C. Since then, he has been in private practice, beginning his concentration in consumer law in 1982. He has represented many individuals and consumer groups (such as the Disgruntled Diesel Owners' Group, the Audi Victims Network, and the Fiero Firefighters) and has been involved in class action litigation against auto dealers and manufacturers. He has been active for many years as a member of the Consumer Affairs Committee of the D.C. Bar. He serves on the Board of Directors of the Maryland Consumer Rights Coalition. In 2002, he joined the Board of Directors of the National Association of Consumer Advocates.

CLP9 Chapter 5

Robert Stempler is an attorney in private practice at 44-100 Monterey Avenue, Ste. 216M, Palm Desert, CA 92260, (760) 345-8883, fax: (760) 345-3344.

CLP7 Chapter 7

Robert S. Stevens is an attorney with Charlottesville Albemale legal Aid, 617 W. Main street #3, Charlottesville, VA 22902. Mr. Stevens has a concentration in consumer protection and debtor relief. He is a member of the Virginia bar association.

CLP3 Chapter 2

Darnley D. Stewart is a partner in the New York law firm of Bernstein Litowitz Berger & Grossmann LLP. Ms. Stewart clerked on the Massachusetts Court of Appeals. Along with Daniel Berger, she is the partner principally responsible for her firm's employment discrimination and employee rights practice group. Ms. Stewart is a member of the Title VII Committee of the National Employment Lawyers Association and the individual Rights and Responsibilities Committee of the New York State Bar Association. In addition, she serves as Plaintiffs' Co-Chair of the Class Action Subcommittee of the ABA's Employment Rights and Responsibilities Committee. Bernstein Litowitz Berger & Gross-

CLP7 Chapter 1

mann, L.L.P., 1285 Avenue of the Americas, New York, NY 10019; (212) 554-1400; fax: (212) 554-1444; e-mail: darnley@BLBGLAW.com.

The Sturdevant Law Firm, 475 Sansome Street, Suite 1750, San Francisco, CA 94111, (415) 477-2410, fax: (415) 477-2420, is a firm of five lawyers that specializes in complex and class litigation on behalf of consumers exposed to unlawful business practices, financial services fraud, misrepresentation and overcharging, employment discrimination, environmental damage, toxic torts, civil rights, vocational school fraud, and insurance packing, among others. Most of the firm's work takes place in the state and federal trial courts in the Bay Area.

CLP5 Chapters 11, 12;
CLP6 Chapters 14, 15;
CLP8 Chapter 1

James C. Sturdevant, the founder of the firm, has been engaged in the practice of law for more than twenty-five years. *Badie v. Bank of America* (1998) 69 Cal. App. 4th 779, 79 Cal. Rptr. 2d 273 (compulsory non-consensual ADR imposed on consumers via bill stuffer found to be invalid attempt to modify existing account agreement) and *Beasley v. Wells Fargo Bank, N.A.* (1991) 235 Cal. App. 3d 1383, 1 Cal. Rptr. 2d 446 (credit card late and overlimit charges constitute illegal and excessive penalties for breach of contract) are two examples of his litigation. Mr. Sturdevant serves on the boards of several trial lawyers' organizations and has received numerous awards for his work on behalf of consumers.

Patricia Sturdevant has focused her practice on consumer protection for more than two decades. She has advocated on behalf of consumers in both the public and private sectors, in two legal services programs in Southern California, and in private practice in San Francisco and Washington D.C. In those capacities, she has recovered more than $160 million in damage awards in class actions and private attorney general cases, directed the work of multidisciplinary teams engaging in media and outreach campaigns and distributing those awards, and been instrumental in the development of the law.

CLP1 Chapters 1, 12

Ms. Sturdevant is a co-founder of the National Association of Consumer Advocates and was its first Executive Director and General Counsel. She is credited with pioneering the modern use of cy pres remedies and has been responsible for providing indirect benefits to class members through awards to consumer advocacy organizations in amounts in excess of $6 million.

She is the only person ever to have received both the Vern Countryman Award and the William F. Willier Award from the National Consumer Law Center, and has been recognized by the State Bar of California, the California Trial Lawyers Association, and the Bar Association of San Francisco for her work protecting consumers. She is a past president of the San Francisco Women Lawyer's Alliance, 1988–89 and Board member from 1984 through 1990; Board member and Officer, San Francisco Trial Lawyers Association, 1989–1997; Board member, San Francisco Neighborhood Legal Assistance Foundation, 1992–1997; and Board Member, Consumer Action, 1995 to present.

David A Szwak is a partner with Bodenheimer, Jones & Szwak at 401 Market Street, Suite 240 American Tower, Sheveport, LA 71101, (318) 424-1400, Fax: (318) 424-1476, bjks1507@aol.com. He specializes in insurance defense, personal injury, consumer credit, and commercial litigation. Mr. Szwak has written many credit-related and other articles, including *Theft of Identity—A Credit Nightmare*, Texas Bar Journal, 1993; *Theft of Identity, Call It Data Rape*, Alaska Bar Association's The Alaska Bar Rag (1994); *Theft of Identity: Roadkill on the Information Highway*, New Hampshire Bar Association's Trial Bar News (1994); *Theft of Identity: Data Rape*, Colorado Bar Association's The Colorado Lawyer (1995); and *Credit Cards in America*, Shreveport Bar Association's The Bar Review (1995). Mr. Szwak received a J.D. from Paul M. Herbert Law Center, Louisiana State University, and holds a B.S. from Louisiana State University in Baton Rouge.

CLP3 Chapter 5; CLP9 Chapter 9; CLP10 Chapter 11

Thomas Tarter is the Managing Director of the Andela Consulting Group, Inc. ("ACG"), 15250 Ventura Boulevard, Suite 610, Sherman Oaks, CA 91403, (818) 380-3102, Fax: (818) 501-5412, ttarter@earthlink.net, a consulting firm whose services

CLP10 Chapter 12

include the providing of research; financial, management and turn around consulting services; board of directorships and expert testimony services on a variety of matters including banking and lending standards and practices involving processing. He has served as a management consultant, business advisor and on the board of directors of public, financially troubled and closely held corporations (large and small) including serving as a reorganization advisor to The Bank of Saipan and for SEC reporting corporations such as First Alliance Mortgage Company. Mr. Tarter was appointed to First Alliance's board of directors subsequent to its filing for bankruptcy protection. First Alliance was active in the subprime lending market. It was accused of predatory lending practices and unfair and deceptive sales tactics involving consumer loans.

Mr. Tarter's experience in the financial institutions industry spans more than 35 years. He started his career at Lloyds Bank California, where he was a Vice President in the Corporate finance and California Divisions; and continued it at the Sanwa Bank of California, as Vice President and the Senior Credit Officer for Southern California; Bank of Los Angeles, as Founding Director, President and Chief Executive Officer; Center Nation Bank, as Director, President and Chief Executive Officer; First Los Angeles Bank, as Executive Vice President; Western States Bankcard Association, as a director and ACG. He was also a director of the Fort Ord Credit Union, advisor to Matadors Community Credit Union and a founder and organizer of Hancock Saving Bank. Mr. Tarter has been appointed to the mediator panel for the Bankruptcy Mediation Program of the United States Bankruptcy Court for the Central District of California and was a member of the Board of the Los Angeles Bankruptcy Forum. He received a Master of Business Administration from Santa Clara University and a Bachelor of Science in business from the University of California at Los Angeles.

Steven Taterka is in private practice in Kingston Springs, Tennessee. His practice is primarily consumer law focusing on automobile cases, including lemon law, odometer fraud, salvage fraud, financing (TILA), leasing (CLA), and sales practice (UDAP) issues. He also litigates title pawn and check cashing (check loan) cases.

CLP8 Chapters 5, 6, 7, 8, 9

Michael Terry is a partner in the Nashville law firm of Terry & Gore. Mr. Terry is a former Deputy Attorney General for the State of Tennessee. Mr. Terry has been involved in federal litigation for more than twenty years, handling cases at all levels, including the United States Supreme Court. Terry & Gore, 209 Tenth Avenue South, Suite 310, Cummins Station, Nashville, TN 37203; (615) 256-5555; fax: (615) 256-5652; e-mail: tglaw@home.com.

CLP7 Chapter 1

Alec Trueblood has a private practice in Los Angeles, California, emphasizing unfair credit reporting, unfair debt collection practices, auto dealer fraud, lemon law, and class actions. He is a graduate of the University of California, Berkeley and the UCLA School of Law. He began his career in the litigation department at Morrison & Foerster and subsequently worked for Chavez & Gertler in Mill Valley, California, where he specialized in class actions and unfair business practices.

CLP8 Chapter 13

Susan M. Warren joined the Law Offices of Richard Feferman, 300 Central Avenue, SW, # 2000E, Albuquerque, NM 87102, (505) 243-7773, fax: (505) 243-6663, in 1996. She graduated from Harvard Law School in 1990 and practiced with DNA-People's Legal Services for six years before joining the Law Offices of Richard Feferman.

CLP5 Chapter 3

The firm handles a wide variety of individual and class action consumer cases throughout New Mexico, Arizona and Colorado. Most of the firm's cases are federal suits against car dealers, debt collectors and lenders. In 1999 the firm was nominated for trial lawyers of the year by the Trial Lawyers for Public Justice, for their $669,000 jury verdict against a New Mexico car dealer for odometer fraud and tortious debt collection practices. Recent favorable published decisions include: *Yazzie v. Ray Vicker's Special Cars, Inc.*, 12 F. Supp. 2d 1230 (D.N.M. 1998) (pawn "storage fee" was undisclosed finance charge

Pleadings by Contributor

under TILA) and 180 F.R.D. 411 (granting class certification); *Lee v. Gallup Auto Sales, Inc.*, 135 F.3d 1359 (10th Cir. 1998) (striking illegal regulation exempting older vehicles from federal odometer act); *Bitah v. Global Collection Services, Inc., et al*, 968 F. Supp. 1997) (lawyer liability under FDCPA); *Halwood v. Cowboy Auto Sales, Inc.*, 124 N.M. 77, 946 P.2d 1088 (Ct. App. 1997) (upholding punitive damages for on-reservation tort by non-Indian).

Clint Watkins is a graduate of Vanderbilt Law School. Mr. Watkins is licensed in Tennessee as an attorney and certified public accountant (inactive). Mr. Watkin's practice is primarily federal litigation. Law Office of Clint W. Watkins, 5214 Maryland Way, Suite 402, Brentwood, TN 37027; (615) 376-7000; fax: (615) 376-2628; e-mail: cwatkins@nashvillelaw.com.

CLP7 Chapter 1

Mary Welford is a partner in the law firm Witten, Woolmington, Bongartz, Campbell, Boepple & Welford, P.C. in Manchester Center, Vermont, phone: (802) 362-2560. Her main areas of practice are civil litigation, including consumer protection and landlord/tenant, family, Social Security disability, and elder law. Prior to joining her firm. Ms. Welford had a solo practice in Manchester for six years and spent the previous seven years as a staff attorney with Vermont Legal Aid and the Vermont Senior Citizens Law Project. She is a member of the state and federal Vermont bars.

CLP2 Chapter 1

Alan M. White is an attorney with Community Legal Services, Inc., 3638 North Broad Street, Philadelphia, Pennsylvania 19140, (215) 227-2400, fax: (215) 227-2435. He has also been a fellow and consultant with the National Consumer Law Center in Boston. His practice includes representation of low-income consumers in mortgage foreclosures, bankruptcies, student loan disputes, real estate matters, and consumer fraud class actions. He has served on the Education Committee of the Eastern District of Pennsylvania Bankruptcy Conference and has been a course planner or faculty member for numerous continuing legal education programs on consumer and bankruptcy law, including National Association of Consumer Advocates, Pennsylvania Bar Institute, Philadelphia Bar Education Center, and Pennsylvania Legal Services. He has published a number of research papers and articles on consumer law issues and has testified at hearings held by the Federal Reserve Board and the U.S. Department of Housing and Urban Development on predatory mortgage lending. Mr. White received his B.S. from the Massachusetts Institute of Technology in 1979 and his J.D. from the New York University School of Law in 1983.

CLP2 Chapter 13; CLP7 Chapter 6

Peter S. Wright is a partner with Franklin Pierce Law Center, Two White Street, Concord, NH 03301. Mr. Wright specializes in cases involving usurious or illegal lending practices, debt collection abuses, and illegal home foreclosure. He was formerly a staff attorney with New Hampshire Legal Assistance and with Bucks County Legal Aid Society in Pennsylvania. Mr. Wright is a member of the New Hampshire Bar Association, American Bar Association, and the National Association of Consumer Advocates.

CLP2 Chapter 3

Contributors by State

This listing facilitates the search for pleadings and/or consumer law experts from a particular state. The listing is organized by state, indicating where the contributor is from (not where the pleading was created), the name of the contributor, and the pleadings which the contributor submitted to NCLC's ten *Consumer Law Pleadings* volumes.

More information about contributors can be found in the alphabetical listing of contributors. More information about the pleadings submitted can be found at "Pleadings by Title" and "Description of Pleadings."

Alabama	Charles Lorant	CLP10 Chapter 5
Alabama	Gil Gilmore	CLP7 Chapter 1
Alabama	Jerry O. Lorant	CLP8 Chapter 20
Alabama	LaBarron N. Boone	CLP9 Chapter 18
Alabama	Penny Hays	CLP10 Chapter 5
Alabama	Thomas Methvin	CLP1 Chapter 5
Alabama	Thomas Methvin	CLP9 Chapter 18
Arizona	Veronika Fabian	CLP7 Chapter 13
Arizona	Veronika Fabian	CLP7 Chapter 16
California	Alec Trueblood	CLP8 Chapter 13
California	Andrew Henderson	CLP6 Chapter 10
California	Eric Carlson	CLP4 Chapter 3
California	Frank N. Darras	CLP6 Chapter 5
California	James C. Sturdevant	CLP8 Chapter 1
California	James Sturdevant	CLP5 Chapter 11
California	James Sturdevant	CLP5 Chapter 12
California	James Sturdevant	CLP6 Chapter 14
California	James Sturdevant	CLP6 Chapter 15
California	Mark Chavez	CLP9 Chapter 13
California	Mark Chavez	CLP1 Chapter 2
California	Mark Chavez	CLP6 Chapter 4
California	Mark Chavez	CLP7 Chapter 15
California	Nancy Barron	CLP2 Chapter 5
California	Nancy Barron	CLP2 Chapter 6
California	Patricia Sturdevant	CLP1 Chapter 1
California	Patricia Sturdevant	CLP1 Chapter 12
California	Robert Green	CLP7 Chapter 2
California	Robert Stempler	CLP7 Chapter 7
California	Thomas Tarter	CLP10 Chapter 12
California	William Flanagan	CLP3 Chapter 1
Colorado	Lynn Feiger	CLP4 Chapter 3
Connecticut	Joanne Faulkner	CLP1 Chapter 9
Connecticut	Joanne Faulkner	CLP2 Chapter 11

Connecticut	Joanne Faulkner	CLP4 Chapter 4
Connecticut	Joanne Faulkner	CLP5 Chapter 8
Connecticut	Joanne Faulkner	CLP7 Chapter 8
Connecticut	Joanne Faulkner	CLP10 Chapter 3
Connecticut	Joanne Faulkner	CLP8 Chapter 14
District of Columbia	Alden Atkins	CLP3 Chapter 1
District of Columbia	Cyrus Mehri	CLP9 Chapter 15
District of Columbia	Jean Constantine-Davis	CLP9 Chapter 1
District of Columbia	L. Kendall Satterfield	CLP7 Chapter 2
District of Columbia	Margot Saunders	CLP8 Chapter 17
District of Columbia	Mark H. Steinbach	CLP9 Chapter 5
District of Columbia	Michael J. Quirk	CLP8 Chapter 1
District of Columbia	Nina F. Simon	CLP9 Chapter 1
District of Columbia	Paul F. Bland	CLP8 Chapter 1
District of Columiba	Evan Hendricks	CLP10 Chapter 13
District of Columiba	Paul Arons	CLP10 Chapter 6
Florida	Andrew Spark	CLP7 Chapter 4
Florida	Charles Baird	CLP1 Chapter 11
Florida	Lynn Drysdale	CLP10 Chapter 9
Florida	Lynn Drysdale	CLP3 Chapter 4
Florida	Lynn Drysdale	CLP4 Chapter 2
Florida	Lynn Drysdale	CLP7 Chapter 12
Florida	Marlowe Blake	CLP2 Chapter 10
Florida	Raymond G. Ingalsbe	CLP10 Chapter 15
Georgia	Charles M. Baird	CLP8 Chapter 11
Georgia	Edward D. Buckley III	CLP3 Chapter 9
Georgia	Karen Brown	CLP3 Chapter 6
Illinois	Alan A. Alop	CLP2 Chapter 12
Illinois	Alan A. Alop	CLP2 Chapter 15
Illinois	Alan A. Alop	CLP2 Chapter 8
Illinois	Alan A. Alop	CLP6 Chapter 8
Illinois	Alan A. Alop	CLP8 Chapter 4
Illinois	Cathleen M. Combs	CLP8 Chapter 22
Illinois	Dan Deneen	CLP5 Chapter 4
Illinois	Daniel Edelman	CLP1 Chapter 4
Illinois	Daniel Edelman	CLP1 Chapter 9
Illinois	David J. Philipps	CLP3 Chapter 3
Illinois	Dmitry Feofanov	CLP10 Chapter 19
Illinois	Jamie Franklin	CLP4 Chapter 6
Illinois	O. Randolph Bragg	CLP2 Chapter 14
Illinois	O. Randolph Bragg	CLP3 Chapter 9
Illinois	O. Randolph Bragg	CLP7 Chapter 7
Illinois	O. Randolph Bragg	CLP10 Chapter 6
Illinois	Tara Goodwin	CLP6 Chapter 16
Indiana	Thomas Frohman	CLP8 Chapter 2
Kansas	Bernard E. Brown	CLP2 Chapter 6
Louisiana	David A. Szwak	CLP10 Chapter 11
Louisiana	David A. Szwak	CLP3 Chapter 5
Louisiana	David A. Szwak	CLP9 Chapter 9
Louisiana	Steve R. Conley	CLP10 Chapter 16

Maryland	James A. Mayhew	CLP3 Chapter 10
Maryland	Kieron F. Quinn	CLP3 Chapter 9
Maryland	Mark Leymaster	CLP9 Chapter 1
Massachusetts	Elizabeth Miller	CLP1 Chapter 8
Massachusetts	Elizabeth Renuart	CLP4 Chapter 12
Massachusetts	Elizabeth Renuart	CLP7 Chapter 10
Massachusetts	Gary Klein	CLP1 Chapter 7
Massachusetts	Gary Klein	CLP7 Chapter 1
Massachusetts	Gary Klein	CLP8 Chapter 3
Massachusetts	Henry Korman	CLP4 Chapter 14
Massachusetts	John Rao	CLP6 Chapter 7
Massachusetts	John Rao	CLP7 Chapter 17
Massachusetts	John Roddy	CLP1 Chapter 8
Massachusetts	John Roddy	CLP3 Chapter 8
Massachusetts	John Roddy	CLP5 Chapter 2
Massachusetts	John Roddy	CLP8 Chapter 3
Massachusetts	John Roddy	CLP9 Chapter 17
Massachusetts	Stuart Rossman	CLP7 Chapter 1
Massachusetts	Stuart Rossman	CLP8 Chapter 18
Michigan	Dani K. Liblang	CLP9 Chapter 2
Michigan	Dani K. Liblang	CLP9 Chapter 8
Michigan	Dani Liblang	CLP5 Chapter 6
Michigan	Dani Liblang	CLP6 Chapter 11
Michigan	Philip Rogers	CLP3 Chapter 9
Minnesota	David Ramp	CLP4 Chapter 11
Minnesota	Eric L. Crandall	CLP8 Chapter 15
Minnesota	Peter F. Barry	CLP10 Chapter 4
Mississippi	Michael Lewis	CLP5 Chapter 1
Mississippi	Suzanne Keys	CLP3 Chapter 9
Mississippi	W. Howard Gunn	CLP8 Chapter 19
Missouri	Bernard Brown	CLP10 Chapter 18
Missouri	Michael Ferry	CLP2 Chapter 4
Nevada	Mitchell D. Gliner	CLP4 Chapter 7
New Hampshire	Peter Wright	CLP2 Chapter 3
New Jersey	Donna Siegel Moffa	CLP8 Chapter 23
New Jersey	Lisa Rodriguez	CLP4 Chapter 11
New Jersey	Neil J. Fogarty	CLP6 Chapter 13
New Jersey	Neil J. Fogarty	CLP6 Chapter 7
New Mexico	Richard J. Rubin	CLP10 Chapter 1
New Mexico	Richard J. Rubin	CLP8 Chapter 16
New Mexico	Richard J. Rubin	CLP9 Chapter 10
New Mexico	Richard N. Feferman	CLP5 Chapter 3
New Mexico	Richard N. Feferman	CLP9 Chapter 5
New Mexico	Richard Rubin	CLP1 Chapter 3
New Mexico	Richard Rubin	CLP2 Chapter 11
New Mexico	Richard Rubin	CLP6 Chapter 12
New Mexico	Richard Rubin	CLP7 Chapter 9
New Mexico	Samuel D. Gollis	CLP7 Chapter 13
New Mexico	Susan Warren	CLP5 Chapter 3
New York	Brian Bromberg	CLP10 Chapter 19

New York	Daniel Berger	CLP7 Chapter 1
New York	Darnley D. Stewart	CLP7 Chapter 1
New York	Edward Josephson	CLP2 Chapter 1
New York	James B. Fishman	CLP2 Chapter 10
New York	James B. Fishman	CLP2 Chapter 12
New York	James B. Fishman	CLP2 Chapter 7
New York	James B. Fishman	CLP4 Chapter 8
New York	James B. Fishman	CLP5 Chapter 1
New York	Jerome Noll	CLP7 Chapter 14
New York	Leah Guggenheimer	CLP7 Chapter 1
New York	Linda J. Cahn	CLP6 Chapter 1
New York	Robert Lax	CLP7 Chapter 14
New York	Seth Lesser	CLP7 Chapter 1
New York	Sheldon Burman	CLP4 Chapter 13
New York	Thomas A. Dickerson	CLP4 Chapter 5
North Carolina	Andrew Cogdell	CLP2 Chapter 1
North Carolina	Andrew Cogdell	CLP2 Chapter 4
North Carolina	Andrew Cogdell	CLP2 Chapter 9
Ohio	Edward A. Icove	CLP10 Chapter 17
Ohio	Edward Icove	CLP6 Chapter 3
Ohio	Kimberly M. Skaggs	CLP10 Chapter 17
Ohio	Ronald L. Burdge	CLP10 Chapter 2
Ohio	Ronald L. Burdge	CLP4 Chapter 15
Ohio	Ronald L. Burdge	CLP6 Chapter 2
Ohio	Ronald L. Burdge	CLP8 Chapter 12
Ohio	Stephen H. Olden	CLP5 Chapter 9
Ohio	Thomas R. Seel	CLP9 Chapter 7
Oregon	Mark Griffin	CLP10 Chapter 14
Oregon	Phil Goldsmith	CLP10 Chapter 14
Pennsylvania	Alan White	CLP2 Chapter 13
Pennsylvania	Alan White	CLP7 Chapter 6
Pennsylvania	Cary Flitter	CLP8 Chapter 10
Pennsylvania	Daniel Haller	CLP2 Chapter 3
Pennsylvania	David A. Searles	CLP5 Chapter 10
Pennsylvania	David A. Searles	CLP9 Chapter 12
Pennsylvania	David A. Searles	CLP9 Chapter 14
Pennsylvania	David W. Snyder	CLP4 Chapter 10
Pennsylvania	Eric L. Frank	CLP9 Chapter 19
Pennsylvania	Henry J. Sommer	CLP1 Chapter 10
Pennsylvania	Henry J. Sommer	CLP3 Chapter 7
Pennsylvania	Irv Ackelsberg	CLP2 Chapter 13
Pennsylvania	Irv Ackelsberg	CLP4 Chapter 2
Pennsylvania	Irv Ackelsberg	CLP5 Chapter 9
Pennsylvania	James A. Francis	CLP10 Chapter 10
Pennsylvania	James Pietz	CLP1 Chapter 6
Pennsylvania	Michael D. Donovan	CLP4 Chapter 1
Pennsylvania	Michael D. Donovan	CLP9 Chapter 12
Pennsylvania	Michael P. Malakoff	CLP1 Chapter 6
Pennsylvania	Michael P. Malakoff	CLP4 Chapter 9
Pennsylvania	Michael P. Malakoff	CLP5 Chapter 5

Pennsylvania	Michael P. Malakoff	CLP6 Chapter 6
Pennsylvania	Michael P. Malakoff	CLP7 Chapter 11
Pennsylvania	Michael P. Malakoff	CLP8 Chapter 21
Pennsylvania	Michael P. Malakoff	CLP9 Chapter 11
Pennsylvania	Paul Brooks	CLP2 Chapter 4
Pennsylvania	Susan L. DeJarnatt	CLP2 Chapter 12
Tennessee	Clint Watkins	CLP7 Chapter 1
Tennessee	Michael Terry	CLP7 Chapter 1
Tennessee	Steven Taterka	CLP8 Chapter 5
Tennessee	Steven Taterka	CLP8 Chapter 6
Tennessee	Steven Taterka	CLP8 Chapter 7
Tennessee	Steven Taterka	CLP8 Chapter 8
Tennessee	Steven Taterka	CLP8 Chapter 9
Texas	Manuel H. Newburger	CLP8 Chapter 10
Texas	Stephen Gardner	CLP10 Chapter 8
Texas	Stephen Gardner	CLP4 Chapter 12
Texas	Stephen Gardner	CLP4 Chapter 16
Texas	Stephen Gardner	CLP9 Chapter 16
Vermont	Mary Welford	CLP2 Chapter 1
Vermont	Stephen Norman	CLP2 Chapter 2
Virginia	Dale Pittman	CLP10 Chapter 7
Virginia	Dale W. Pittman	CLP2 Chapter 1
Virginia	Dale W. Pittman	CLP2 Chapter 4
Virginia	Dale W. Pittman	CLP2 Chapter 6
Virginia	Dale W. Pittman	CLP5 Chapter 4
Virginia	Dale W. Pittman	CLP6 Chapter 17
Virginia	Dale W. Pittman	CLP7 Chapter 3
Virginia	David Irvin	CLP3 Chapter 4
Virginia	Robert S. Stevens	CLP3 Chapter 2
Virginia	Thomas Domonoske	CLP6 Chapter 17
Virginia	Thomas Domonoske	CLP7 Chapter 5
Washington	David Leen	CLP2 Chapter 3
West Virginia	Bren J. Pomponio	CLP9 Chapter 6
West Virginia	Charli Fulton	CLP6 Chapter 9
West Virginia	Daniel F. Hedges	CLP5 Chapter 12
West Virginia	Daniel F. Hedges	CLP9 Chapter 6
Wisconsin	Charles Barr	CLP6 Chapter 15
Wisconsin	De Vonna Joy	CLP9 Chapter 3
Wisconsin	De Vonna Joy	CLP9 Chapter 4
Wisconsin	Marsha M. Mansfield	CLP5 Chapter 7
Wisconsin	Mary Catherine Fons	CLP9 Chapter 3

Contributors by State

Contributors by Title

This listing identifies contributors of specific pleadings and the state in which they practice law. The listing identifies by chapter each of NCLC's ten *Consumer Law Pleadings* volumes and lists the names of the contributors and the states they practice in.

More information about contributors can be found in the alphabetical listing of contributors. More information about the pleadings submitted can be found at "Pleadings by Title" and "Description of Pleadings."

CLP1 Chapter 1	Patricia Sturdevant	California
CLP1 Chapter 2	Mark Chavez	California
CLP1 Chapter 3	Richard Rubin	New Mexico
CLP1 Chapter 4	Daniel Edelman	Illinois
CLP1 Chapter 5	Thomas Methvin	Alabama
CLP1 Chapter 6	James Pietz	Pennsylvania
CLP1 Chapter 6	Michael P. Malakoff	Pennsylvania
CLP1 Chapter 7	Gary Klein	Massachusetts
CLP1 Chapter 8	Elizabeth Miller	Massachusetts
CLP1 Chapter 8	John Roddy	Massachusetts
CLP1 Chapter 9	Daniel Edelman	Illinois
CLP1 Chapter 9	Joanne Faulkner	Connecticut
CLP1 Chapter 10	Henry J. Sommer	Pennsylvania
CLP1 Chapter 11	Charles Baird	Florida
CLP1 Chapter 12	Patricia Sturdevant	California
CLP2 Chapter 1	Andrew Cogdell	North Carolina
CLP2 Chapter 1	Dale W. Pittman	Virginia
CLP2 Chapter 1	Edward Josephson	New York
CLP2 Chapter 1	Mary Welford	Vermont
CLP2 Chapter 2	Stephen Norman	Vermont
CLP2 Chapter 3	Daniel Haller	Pennsylvania
CLP2 Chapter 3	David Leen	Washington
CLP2 Chapter 3	Peter Wright	New Hampshire
CLP2 Chapter 4	Andrew Cogdell	North Carolina
CLP2 Chapter 4	Dale W. Pittman	Virginia
CLP2 Chapter 4	Michael Ferry	Missouri
CLP2 Chapter 4	Paul Brooks	Pennsylvania
CLP2 Chapter 5	Nancy Barron	California
CLP2 Chapter 6	Bernard E. Brown	Kansas
CLP2 Chapter 6	Dale W. Pittman	Virginia
CLP2 Chapter 6	Nancy Barron	California
CLP2 Chapter 7	James B. Fishman	New York
CLP2 Chapter 8	Alan A. Alop	Illinois
CLP2 Chapter 9	Andrew Cogdell	North Carolina

CLP2 Chapter 10	James B. Fishman	New York
CLP2 Chapter 10	Marlowe Blake	Florida
CLP2 Chapter 11	Joanne Faulkner	Connecticut
CLP2 Chapter 11	Richard Rubin	New Mexico
CLP2 Chapter 12	Alan A. Alop	Illinois
CLP2 Chapter 12	James B. Fishman	New York
CLP2 Chapter 12	Susan L. DeJarnatt	Pennsylvania
CLP2 Chapter 13	Alan White	Pennsylvania
CLP2 Chapter 13	Irv Ackelsberg	Pennsylvania
CLP2 Chapter 14	O. Randolph Bragg	Illinois
CLP2 Chapter 15	Alan A. Alop	Illinois
CLP3 Chapter 1	Alden Atkins	District of Columbia
CLP3 Chapter 1	William Flanagan	California
CLP3 Chapter 2	Robert S. Stevens	Virginia
CLP3 Chapter 3	David J. Philipps	Illinois
CLP3 Chapter 4	David Irvin	Virginia
CLP3 Chapter 4	Lynn Drysdale	Florida
CLP3 Chapter 5	David A. Azwak	Louisiana
CLP3 Chapter 6	Karen Brown	Georgia
CLP3 Chapter 7	Henry J. Sommer	Pennsylvania
CLP3 Chapter 8	John Roddy	Massachusetts
CLP3 Chapter 9	Edward D. Buckley III	Georgia
CLP3 Chapter 9	Kieron F. Quinn	Maryland
CLP3 Chapter 9	O. Randolph Bragg	Illinois
CLP3 Chapter 9	Philip Rogers	Michigan
CLP3 Chapter 9	Suzanne Keys	Mississippi
CLP3 Chapter 10	James A. Mayhew	Maryland
CLP4 Chapter 1	Michael D. Donovan	Pennsylvania
CLP4 Chapter 2	Irv Ackelsberg	Pennsylvania
CLP4 Chapter 2	Lynn Drysdale	Florida
CLP4 Chapter 3	Eric Carlson	California
CLP4 Chapter 3	Lynn Feiger	Colorado
CLP4 Chapter 4	Joanne Faulkner	Connecticut
CLP4 Chapter 5	Thomas A. Dickerson	New York
CLP4 Chapter 6	Jamie Franklin	Illinois
CLP4 Chapter 7	Mitchell D. Gliner	Nevada
CLP4 Chapter 8	James B. Fishman	New York
CLP4 Chapter 9	Michael P. Malakoff	Pennsylvania
CLP4 Chapter 10	David W. Snyder	Pennsylvania
CLP4 Chapter 11	David Ramp	Minnesota
CLP4 Chapter 11	Lisa Rodriguez	New Jersey
CLP4 Chapter 12	Elizabeth Renuart	Massachusetts
CLP4 Chapter 12	Stephen Gardner	Texas
CLP4 Chapter 13	Sheldon Burman	New York
CLP4 Chapter 14	Henry Korman	Massachusetts
CLP4 Chapter 15	Ronald L. Burdge	Ohio
CLP4 Chapter 16	Stephen Gardner	Texas
CLP5 Chapter 1	James B. Fishman	New York
CLP5 Chapter 1	Michael Lewis	Mississippi
CLP5 Chapter 2	John Roddy	Massachusetts

CLP5 Chapter 3	Richard N. Feferman	New Mexico
CLP5 Chapter 3	Susan Warren	New Mexico
CLP5 Chapter 4	Dale W. Pittman	Virginia
CLP5 Chapter 4	Dan Deneen	Illinois
CLP5 Chapter 5	Michael P. Malakoff	Pennsylvania
CLP5 Chapter 6	Dani Liblang	Michigan
CLP5 Chapter 7	Marsha M. Mansfield	Wisconsin
CLP5 Chapter 8	Joanne Faulkner	Connecticut
CLP5 Chapter 9	Irv Ackelsberg	Pennsylvania
CLP5 Chapter 9	Stephen H. Olden	Ohio
CLP5 Chapter 10	David A. Searles	Pennsylvania
CLP5 Chapter 11	James Sturdevant	California
CLP5 Chapter 12	Daniel F. Hedges	West Virginia
CLP5 Chapter 12	James Sturdevant	California
CLP6 Chapter 1	Linda J. Cahn	New York
CLP6 Chapter 2	Ronald L. Burdge	Ohio
CLP6 Chapter 3	Edward Icove	Ohio
CLP6 Chapter 4	Mark Chavez	California
CLP6 Chapter 5	Frank N. Darras	California
CLP6 Chapter 6	Michael P. Malakoff	Pennsylvania
CLP6 Chapter 7	John Rao	Massachusetts
CLP6 Chapter 7	Neil J. Fogarty	New Jersey
CLP6 Chapter 8	Alan A. Alop	Illinois
CLP6 Chapter 9	Charli Fulton	West Virginia
CLP6 Chapter 10	Andrew Henderson	California
CLP6 Chapter 11	Dani Liblang	Michigan
CLP6 Chapter 12	Richard Rubin	New Mexico
CLP6 Chapter 13	Neil J. Fogarty	New Jersey
CLP6 Chapter 14	James Sturdevant	California
CLP6 Chapter 15	Charles Barr	Wisconsin
CLP6 Chapter 15	James Sturdevant	California
CLP6 Chapter 16	Tara Goodwin	Illinois
CLP6 Chapter 17	Dale W. Pittman	Virginia
CLP6 Chapter 17	Thomas Domonoske	Virginia
CLP7 Chapter 1	Clint Watkins	Tennessee
CLP7 Chapter 1	Daniel Berger	New York
CLP7 Chapter 1	Darnley D. Stewart	New York
CLP7 Chapter 1	Gary Klein	Massachusetts
CLP7 Chapter 1	Gil Gilmore	Alabama
CLP7 Chapter 1	Leah Guggenheimer	New York
CLP7 Chapter 1	Michael Terry	Tennessee
CLP7 Chapter 1	Seth Lesser	New York
CLP7 Chapter 1	Stuart Rossman	Massachusetts
CLP7 Chapter 2	L. Kendall Satterfield	District of Columbia
CLP7 Chapter 2	Robert Green	California
CLP7 Chapter 3	Dale W. Pittman	Virginia
CLP7 Chapter 4	Andrew Spark	Florida
CLP7 Chapter 5	Thomas Domonoske	Virginia
CLP7 Chapter 6	Alan White	Pennsylvania
CLP7 Chapter 7	O. Randolph Bragg	Illinois

CLP7 Chapter 7	Robert Stempler	California
CLP7 Chapter 8	Joanne Faulkner	Connecticut
CLP7 Chapter 9	Richard Rubin	New Mexico
CLP7 Chapter 10	Elizabeth Renuart	Massachusetts
CLP7 Chapter 11	Michael P. Malakoff	Pennsylvania
CLP7 Chapter 12	Lynn Drysdale	Florida
CLP7 Chapter 13	Samuel D. Gollis	New Mexico
CLP7 Chapter 13	Veronika Fabian	Arizona
CLP7 Chapter 14	Jerome Noll	New York
CLP7 Chapter 14	Robert Lax	New York
CLP7 Chapter 15	Mark Chavez	California
CLP7 Chapter 16	Veronika Fabian	Arizona
CLP7 Chapter 17	John Rao	Massachusetts
CLP8 Chapter 1	James C. Sturdevant	California
CLP8 Chapter 1	Michael J. Quirk	District of Columbia
CLP8 Chapter 1	Paul F. Bland	District of Columbia
CLP8 Chapter 2	Thomas Frohman	Indiana
CLP8 Chapter 3	Gary Klein	Massachusetts
CLP8 Chapter 3	John Roddy	Massachusetts
CLP8 Chapter 4	Alan A. Alop	Illinois
CLP8 Chapter 5	Steven Taterka	Tennessee
CLP8 Chapter 6	Steven Taterka	Tennessee
CLP8 Chapter 7	Steven Taterka	Tennessee
CLP8 Chapter 8	Steven Taterka	Tennessee
CLP8 Chapter 9	Steven Taterka	Tennessee
CLP8 Chapter 10	Cary Flitter	Pennsylvania
CLP8 Chapter 10	Manuel H. Newburger	Texas
CLP8 Chapter 11	Charles M. Baird	Georgia
CLP8 Chapter 12	Ronald L. Burdge	Ohio
CLP8 Chapter 13	Alec Trueblood	California
CLP8 Chapter 14	Joanne S. Faulkner	Connecticut
CLP8 Chapter 15	Eric L. Crandall	Minnesota
CLP8 Chapter 16	Richard J. Rubin	New Mexico
CLP8 Chapter 17	Margot Saunders	District of Columbia
CLP8 Chapter 18	Stuart Rossman	Massachusetts
CLP8 Chapter 19	W. Howard Gunn	Mississippi
CLP8 Chapter 20	Jerry O. Lorant	Alabama
CLP8 Chapter 21	Michael P. Malakoff	Pennsylvania
CLP8 Chapter 22	Cathleen M. Combs	Illinois
CLP8 Chapter 23	Donna Siegel Moffa	New Jersey
CLP9 Chapter 1	Jean Constantine-Davis	District of Columbia
CLP9 Chapter 1	Mark Leymaster	Maryland
CLP9 Chapter 1	Nina F. Simon	District of Columbia
CLP9 Chapter 2	Dani K. Liblang	Michigan
CLP9 Chapter 3	De Vonna Joy	Wisconsin
CLP9 Chapter 3	Mary Catherine Fons	Wisconsin
CLP9 Chapter 4	De Vonna Joy	Wisconsin
CLP9 Chapter 5	Mark H. Steinbach	District of Columbia
CLP9 Chapter 5	Richard N. Feferman	New Mexico
CLP9 Chapter 6	Bren J. Pomponio	West Virginia

CLP9 Chapter 6	Daniel F. Hedges	West Virginia
CLP9 Chapter 7	Thomas R. Seel	Ohio
CLP9 Chapter 8	Dani K. Liblang	Michigan
CLP9 Chapter 9	David A. Szwak	Louisiana
CLP9 Chapter 10	Richard J. Rubin	New Mexico
CLP9 Chapter 11	Michael P. Malakoff	Pennsylvania
CLP9 Chapter 12	David A. Searles	Pennsylvania
CLP9 Chapter 12	Michael D. Donovan	Pennsylvania
CLP9 Chapter 13	Mark A. Chavez	California
CLP9 Chapter 14	David A. Searles	Pennsylvania
CLP9 Chapter 15	Cyrus Mehri	District of Columbia
CLP9 Chapter 16	Stephen Gardner	Texas
CLP9 Chapter 17	John Roddy	Massachusetts
CLP9 Chapter 18	LaBarron N. Boone	Alabama
CLP9 Chapter 18	Thomas Methvin	Alabama
CLP9 Chapter 19	Eric L. Frank	Pennsylvania
CLP10 Chapter 1	Richard J. Rubin	New Mexico
CLP10 Chapter 2	Ronald L. Burdge	Ohio
CLP10 Chapter 3	Joanne S. Faulkner	Connecticut
CLP10 Chapter 4	Peter F. Barry	Minnesota
CLP10 Chapter 5	Charles Lorant	Alabama
CLP10 Chapter 5	Penny Hays	Alabama
CLP10 Chapter 6	Paul Arons	District of Columiba
CLP10 Chapter 6	Rand Bragg	Illinois
CLP10 Chapter 7	Dale Pittman	Virginia
CLP10 Chapter 8	Stephen Gardner	Texas
CLP10 Chapter 9	Lynn Drysdale	Florida
CLP10 Chapter 10	James A. Francis	Pennsylvania
CLP10 Chapter 11	David A Szwak	Louisiana
CLP10 Chapter 12	Thomas Tarter	California
CLP10 Chapter 13	Evan Hendricks	District of Columiba
CLP10 Chapter 14	Phil Goldsmith	Oregon
CLP10 Chapter 14	Mark Griffin	Oregon
CLP10 Chapter 15	Raymond G. Ingalsbe	Florida
CLP10 Chapter 16	Steve R. Conley	Louisiana
CLP10 Chapter 17	Edward A. Icove	Ohio
CLP10 Chapter 17	Kimberly M. Skaggs	Ohio
CLP10 Chapter 18	Bernard Brown	Missouri
CLP10 Chapter 19	Brian Bromberg	New York
CLP10 Chapter 19	Dmitry Feofanov	Illinois

Quick Reference to the Consumer Credit and Sales Legal Practice Series

References are to sections in *all* manuals in NCLC's Consumer Credit and Sales Legal Practice Series. References followed by "S" appear only in a supplement.

Readers should also consider another search option available at ***www.consumerlaw.org/keyword***. There, users can search all sixteen NCLC manuals for a case name, party name, statutory or regulatory citation, or *any* other word, phrase, or combination of terms. The search engine provides the title and page number of every occurrence of that word or phrase within each of the NCLC manuals. Further search instructions and tips are provided on the web site.

The Quick Reference to the Consumer Credit and Sales Legal Practice Series pinpoints where to find specific topics analyzed in the NCLC manuals. References are to individual manual or supplement sections. For more information on these volumes, see *What Your Library Should Contain* at the beginning of this volume, or go to www.consumerlaw.org.

This Quick Reference is a speedy means to locate key terms in the appropriate NCLC manual. More detailed indexes are found at the end of the individual NCLC volumes. Both the detailed contents pages and the detailed indexes for each manual are also available at NCLC's web site, www.consumerlaw.org.

NCLC *strongly recommends,* when searching for **PLEADINGS** on a particular subject, that users refer to the *Index Guide* accompanying *Consumer Law Pleadings on CD-Rom*, and not to this *Quick Reference.* Another option is to search for pleadings directly on the *Consumer Law Pleadings* CD-Rom or on the *Consumer Law in a Box* CD-Rom, using the finding tools that are provided on the CD-Roms themselves.

The finding tools found on *Consumer Law in a Box* are also an effective means to find statutes, regulations, agency interpretations, legislative history, and other primary source material found on NCLC's CD-Roms. Other search options are detailed at page vii, *supra.*

Abbreviations

AUS	=	Access to Utility Service (3d ed. 2004)
Auto	=	Automobile Fraud (2d ed. 2003 and 2004 Supp.)
Arbit	=	Consumer Arbitration Agreements (4th ed. 2004)
CBPL	=	Consumer Banking and Payments Law (2d ed. 2002 and 2004 Supp.)
Bankr	=	Consumer Bankruptcy Law and Practice (7th ed. 2004)
CCA	=	Consumer Class Actions: A Practical Litigation Guide (5th ed. 2002 and 2004 Supp.)
CLP	=	Consumer Law Pleadings, Numbers One Through Ten (2004)
COC	=	The Cost of Credit (2d ed. 2000 and 2004 Supp.)
CD	=	Credit Discrimination (3d ed. 2002 and 2004 Supp.)
FCR	=	Fair Credit Reporting (5th ed. 2002 and 2004 Supp.)
FDC	=	Fair Debt Collection (5th ed. 2004)
Repo	=	Repossessions and Foreclosures (5th ed. 2002 and 2004 Supp.)
Stud	=	Student Loan Law (2d ed. 2002 and 2004 Supp.)
TIL	=	Truth in Lending (5th ed. 2003 and 2004 Supp.)
UDAP	=	Unfair and Deceptive Acts and Practices (6th ed. 2004)
Warr	=	Consumer Warranty Law (2d ed. 2001 and 2004 Supp.)

References are to sections in *all* manuals in NCLC's Consumer Credit and Sales Legal Practice Series

References are to sections in *all* manuals in NCLC's Consumer Credit and Sales Legal Practice Series

References are to sections in *all* manuals in NCLC's Consumer Credit and Sales Legal Practice Series

References are to sections in *all* manuals in NCLC's Consumer Credit and Sales Legal Practice Series

References are to sections in *all* manuals in NCLC's Consumer Credit and Sales Legal Practice Series

293

References are to sections in *all* manuals in NCLC's Consumer Credit and Sales Legal Practice Series

References are to sections in *all* manuals in NCLC's Consumer Credit and Sales Legal Practice Series

NOTES

NOTES

NOTES

NOTES

NOTES

About the Companion CD-Rom

CD-Rom Supersedes All Prior CD-Roms

This CD-Rom supersedes all prior *Consumer Law Pleadings* CD-Roms and disks, including *Consumer Law Pleadings on CD-Rom with Index Guide* (2001–2003), *Consumer Law Pleadings on CD-Rom* (2000), and *Consumer Law Pleadings Numbers One through Five* (1994–1999). Discard all CD-Roms and disks accompanying prior versions of *Consumer Law Pleadings*. This 2004 CD-Rom contains everything found on the earlier CD-Roms and disks, and contains much additional material.

What Is on the CD-Rom

This CD-Rom contains *all* pleadings found on *all* NCLC manuals, including:

- *Consumer Law Pleadings* Number Ten (2004);
- *Consumer Law Pleadings* Numbers One through Nine (1994–2003);
- Over 150 bankruptcy pleadings;
- Numerous class action pleadings; and
- The pleadings found in all the individual NCLC manuals.

The CD-Rom contains almost every type of consumer law pleading, including:

- Demand letters, notices, retainers;
- Complaints, answers, counterclaims;
- Interrogatories and document requests, requests for admissions, deposition preparation, and discovery motions;
- Numerous types of pre-trial and trial motions;
- Briefs, memoranda;
- Post-trial motions and orders;
- Attorney fee documents;
- Numerous class action pleadings, including authorization to represent, complaints, discovery, protective orders, certification pleadings, class notices, briefs, memoranda, pre-trial motions, trial practice, settlements, objections to settlement, and *cy pres* awards; and
- Over 150 bankruptcy pleadings, including initial forms, automatic stay, turnover of property, utilities, steps after filing, claims, exemptions and lien avoidance, litigation generally, discharge and reaffirmation, plan conversion, modification, dismissal, farm reorganization, and consumers as creditors.

How to Use the CD-Rom

The CD's pop-up menu quickly allows you to use the CD—just place the CD into its drive and click on the "Start NCLC CD" button that will pop up in the middle of the screen. You can also access the CD by clicking on a desktop icon that you can create using the pop-up menu.[1] For detailed installation instructions, see *One-Time Installation* below.

All the CD-Rom's information is available in PDF (Acrobat) format, making the information:

- Highly readable (identical to the printed pages in the book);
- Easily navigated (with bookmarks, "buttons," and Internet-style forward and backward searches);
- Easy to locate with keyword searches and other quick-search techniques across the whole CD-Rom; and
- Easy to paste into a word processor.

While much of the material is also found on the CD-Rom in word processing format, we strongly recommend you use the material in PDF format—not only because it is easiest to use, contains the most features, and includes more material, but also because you can easily switch back to a word processing format when you prefer.

Acrobat Reader 5 and 6.0.1 come free of charge with the CD-Rom. **We strongly recommend that new Acrobat users read the Acrobat tutorial on the Home Page. It takes two minutes and will really pay off.**

How to Find Documents in Word Processing Format

Most pleadings and other practice aids are also available in Microsoft Word format to make them more easily adaptable for individual use. (Current versions of WordPerfect are

---

1 Alternatively, click on the D:\Start.pdf file on "My Computer" or open that file in Acrobat—always assuming "D:" is the CD-Rom drive on your computer.

able to convert the Word documents upon opening them.) The CD-Rom offers several ways to find those word processing documents. One option is simply to browse to the folder on the CD-Rom containing all the word processing files and open the desired document from your standard word processing program, such as Word or WordPerfect. All word processing documents are in the D:\WP_Files folder, if "D:" is the CD-Rom drive,[2] and are further organized by book title. Documents that appear in the book are named after the corresponding appendix; other documents have descriptive file names.

Another option is to navigate the CD in PDF format, and, when a particular document is on the screen, click on the corresponding bookmark for the "Word version of . . ." This will automatically run Word, WordPerfect for Windows, or *any other word processor* that is associated with the ".DOC" extension, and then open the word processing file that corresponds to the Acrobat document.[3]

Important Information Before Opening the CD-Rom Package

Before opening the CD-Rom package, please read this information. Opening the package constitutes acceptance of the following described terms. In addition, the *book* is not returnable once the seal to the *CD-Rom* has been broken.

The CD-Rom is copyrighted and all rights are reserved by the National Consumer Law Center, Inc. No copyright is claimed to the text of statutes, regulations, excerpts from court opinions, or any part of an original work prepared by a United States Government employee.

You may not commercially distribute the CD-Rom or otherwise reproduce, publish, distribute or use the disk in any manner that may infringe on any copyright or other proprietary right of the National Consumer Law Center. Nor may you otherwise transfer the CD-Rom or this agreement to any other party unless that party agrees to accept the terms and conditions of this agreement. You may use the CD-Rom on only one computer and by one user at a time.

The CD-Rom is warranted to be free of defects in materials and faulty workmanship under normal use for a period of ninety days after purchase. If a defect is discovered in the CD-Rom during this warranty period, a replacement disk can be obtained at no charge by sending the defective disk,

postage prepaid, with information identifying the purchaser, to National Consumer Law Center, Publications Department, 77 Summer Street, 10th Floor, Boston, MA 02110. After the ninety-day period, a replacement will be available on the same terms, but will also require a $20 prepayment.

The National Consumer Law Center makes no other warranty or representation, either express or implied, with respect to this disk, its quality, performance, merchantability, or fitness for a particular purpose. In no event will the National Consumer Law Center be liable for direct, indirect, special, incidental, or consequential damages arising out of the use or inability to use the disk. The exclusion of implied warranties is not effective in some states, and thus this exclusion may not apply to you.

System Requirements

Use of this CD-Rom requires a Windows-based PC with a CD-Rom drive. (Macintosh users report success using NCLC CDs, but the CD has been tested only on Windows-based PCs.) The CD-Rom's features are optimized with Acrobat Reader 5 or later. Acrobat Reader versions 5 and 6.0.1 are included free on this CD-Rom, and either will work with this CD-Rom as long as it is compatible with your version of Windows. Acrobat Reader 5 is compatible with Windows 95/98/Me/NT/2000/XP, while Acrobat Reader 6.0.1 is compatible with Windows 98SE/Me/NT/2000/XP. If you already have Acrobat Reader 6.0, we *highly* recommend you install version 6.0.1 from this CD because a bug in version 6.0 interferes with optimum use of this CD-Rom. The Microsoft Word versions of pleadings and practice aids can be used with any reasonably current word processor (1995 or later).

One-Time Installation

When the CD-Rom is inserted in its drive, a menu will pop up automatically. (Please be patient if you have a slow CD-Rom drive; this will only take a few moments.) If you do not already have Acrobat Reader 5 or 6.0.1, first click the "Install Acrobat Reader" button. Do not reboot, but then click on the "Make Shortcut Icon" button. (You need not make another shortcut icon if you already have done so for another NCLC CD.) Then reboot and follow the *How to Use the CD-Rom* instructions above.

[*Note*: If the pop-up menu fails to appear, go to "My Computer," right-click "D:" if that is the CD-Rom drive, and select "Open." Then double-click on "Read_Me.txt" for alternate installation and use instructions.]

---

2 The CD-Rom drive could be any letter following "D:" depending on your computer's configuration.

3 For instructions on how to associate WordPerfect to the ".DOC" extension, go to the CD-Rom's home page and click on "How to Use/Help," then "Word Files."